Samuel Stillman Greene

A grammar of the English language

Samuel Stillman Greene

A grammar of the English language

ISBN/EAN: 9783337086053

Printed in Europe, USA, Canada, Australia, Japan

Cover: Foto ©Paul-Georg Meister /pixelio.de

More available books at **www.hansebooks.com**

A GRAMMAR

OF THE

ENGLISH LANGUAGE.

BY

SAMUEL S. GREENE, A.M.

AUTHOR OF "INTRODUCTION TO THE STUDY OF GRAMMAR," "ANALYSIS OF SENTENCES," ETC.

*Si volet usus
Quem penes arbitrium est et jus et norma loquendi.*
— HORACE.

PHILADELPHIA:
COWPERTHWAIT & CO.
1870.

Entered, according to Act of Congress, in the year 1867, by
SAMUEL S. GREENE,
in the Clerk's Office of the District Court of Rhode Island.

ELECTROTYPED BY MACKELLAR, SMITHS & JORDAN,
PHILADELPHIA.

PREFACE.

LANGUAGE is a growth, and, like every other growth, is primarily dependent upon an inward vital energy. It has its origin and its development in answer to an instinctive desire of the soul to express its thoughts and feelings. The power of speech is stimulated by the presence of external objects, and takes its actual form by means of an unconscious ability to imitate the vocal symbols which chance to be made the conventional representatives of thought. It matters not to what nation or people the child may belong: be he English, French, German, or Chinese, it is all the same. The speech which he hears in his childhood becomes his vernacular tongue, and all others are foreign.

Place him among the cultivated and refined, and he employs, he knows not why, the pure and polished speech of his guardians and associates. On the contrary, let him fall among the rude and illiterate, and he as readily and as surely accepts for his *native* language, his *mother tongue*, their perverted words and incorrect modes of expression.

Unfortunately for the teacher, the period for direct cultivation does not come till after instinct and habit have given a degree of permanency to these malformations which have grown into a vital union with all that is good in the child's style of speaking. The task of correction has become doubly difficult, requiring the uprooting of old expressions and the planting and nurturing of new. Just what should be done to give to the child a knowledge of a foreign language, must now be done to establish a correct and refined use of his own. It is not abstract principles that he wants, but rather a practical use of good, well-authorized expressions. These he will adopt, not by repeating rules, but by discarding the faulty and using the good. He learns to speak good English by speaking good English. He learns the use of new expressions by using them. Of what consequence, then, is it *how* he obtains them,—whether by rule, or by direct dictation from the teacher? The time for the teacher to commence this process of cultivation is the day the pupil enters school.

How unfortunate is the prevailing impression that the cultivation of language and the study of grammar, as a science, must begin together! There is no period from the time the child begins to speak, through his whole life, during which his language may not be improved. On the contrary, there is a time when the technical and scientific statements of grammar are of little or no use. They become valuable when the child has reached such a degree of development as shall enable him to comprehend their application. Shall all the earlier period of his school life be passed without a systematic effort to cultivate his power to use the language correctly?

For some of the methods of this earlier culture, and especially for the processes of transition to the more technical methods of teaching grammar, the reader is referred to the Introduction to the Study of English Grammar, Part I.

Not a few teachers labor under a mistaken idea of the proper function of grammatical rules. Mere rules cannot correct an inveterate habit; the pupil may repeat them with entire verbal accuracy again and again, and as often violate them in his very next utterances. The rule merely informs him of a given analogy of the language. His habit is stronger than his rule, and can be overcome only by that resolute effort and determined purpose which might have given him success at an earlier period, guided merely by the dictation of the teacher. The difference would be this: then, he would have received his law from the teacher; now, he is a law unto himself. He has the means of correction at his own command. But it is only a persistent obedience to law, in either case, that insures success. The rules of grammar are the criteria by which he can test his own language; but it depends upon himself whether these tests shall be applied and enforced. The advantage which he enjoys over those who are ignorant of the rules of grammar is, that he may always *know* whether he is right or wrong, while they are ever in doubt as to the correctness of their own expressions.

The following work contains a discussion of the *principles* of English Grammar. The fundamental rule by which the subject has been developed is, that no theory of grammar is true or reliable that cannot be abundantly verified by direct appeals to the usage of standard authors. The grammar of a language should be derived from the language itself. It is not the province of the grammarian to legislate in matters of language, but to classify and arrange its forms and principles by a careful study of its analogies as seen in the usage of the best writers. He does not *make* the rules and definitions which express these analogies: they had already existed, and were obeyed,—unconsciously, it is true,—long before he formed them into words and published them. Nor are they authoritative *because* he has uttered them, but simply because they are just and faithful interpretations of the already existing laws which underlie and pervade the language itself. He is a discoverer,—not an inventor, not a dictator,—but is true to his task just so far as he investigates and reinvestigates original sources found in the language itself,—not, of course, rejecting the light which cotemporary or previous labor has shed upon his pathway.

In the following classification of the principles of Grammar, great prominence has been given to *thoughts* and *ideas* in their relation to *forms*. The complete sentence is at first regarded as a *unit*,—an expression of a single *thought*,—and that, too, whatever may be the number of propositions combined in it, or whatever may be the characteristic of the thought, as a statement, a command, an inquiry, or an exclamation. The *thought* determines the sentence. The classification of the sentence depends upon its specific peculiarities. Again, in separating the sentence into its parts, the element is taken as the unit, an expression of a single *idea* of the full thought, and that, too, whether it be a single word or a group of words, or whatever may be its form, structure, rank, or office. Here, again, the *idea* determines the element, while the classification depends upon some peculiarity of the element itself. Again, an element of the sentence may itself contain elements which may all unite to express one of the chief ideas of the whole sentence. These, in like manner, are determined and classified. Finally, each single element is itself a *word*, or may be separated into the *words* which form it. Thus, it will be seen that the sentence is not treated at first as an assemblage of *words* (which is the usual way), but as an assemblage of elements variously expressed; and in the final analysis these elements are reduced to words. It is this peculiarity that brings the learner into sympathy with the thought itself,—the vital power which determines all the forms of the sentence. It gives him an interior view of its structure, and enables him to witness its growth and to sit in judgment with the writer in his choice of forms.

The Grammar of the English Language will be found to contain the same classifications of sentences and elements that are embodied in the Analysis, and in all that pertains to the classification, modification, and construction of words, it is believed, is sufficiently full.

It is intended to follow the Introduction, and to precede the Analysis, which is adapted to advanced pupils.

Although each book may be used independently of the others, the order in which they stand is:—

I. The Introduction.
II. The Grammar of the English Language.
III. The Analysis of Sentences.

A careful perusal of the book, it is believed, will justify the following statement of its peculiarities:—

1. It recognizes the sentence as a growth from the subject and the predicate, and proceeds, step by step, to examine each accumulation around these as a centre. (See Models in Syntax.)

2. It gives the relation and effect of whole expressions; that is, it teaches how to *parse* these, as well as to parse single words,—an advantage lost sight of in most treatises.

3. It teaches how to *parse every kind of word*, in its *rare* as well as in its usual relations.

4. It discriminates clearly between important matter to be studied, and useful matter to be read.

5. The several subjects are developed logically and, it is believed, stated clearly.

6. The author has not evaded, or left without an opinion distinctly stated, those perplexing points which often annoy the teacher.

7. It will be found to contain a great variety of models for parsing and analysis.

8. So far as a text-book can do it, the pupil is made to *use* and *apply* his knowledge as fast as he acquires it, by means of exercises which compel him to *think*, *write*, and *invent* for himself.

9. A copious index will enable the teacher to turn readily to any topic.

10. The mechanical execution, both as it respects printing and binding, is superior.

The author acknowledges his indebtedness to many friends for a great variety of suggestions which he has noted, and embodied in some form or other in these pages. A few changes have been made in the arrangement of the matter, and slight modifications will be found in the matter itself. As a whole, it is hoped, the work will be found both complete and convenient as a text-book of English Grammar.

S. S. GREENE.

PROVIDENCE, July, 1867.

INDEX.

[The Section-numbers are indicated by bold figures.]

A, peculiar use of..................**212**, 2
Abridged expressions..................**109**, 8
  propositions..................**167**
  clauses..................**167**, 2
Absolute tenses..................**99**, 4, 5, 6
  nominative..................**191**, 2
Abstract noun, defined..................**36**, 8
Accent, defined..................**21**, 6
  marks of..................**235**, 12
Active verb..................**82**, 5, *a*
  voice..................**87**, 3, 8
Adjective, defined..................**55**, 1
  limiting..................**56**, 2
  qualifying..................**63**, 1
  pronominal..................**59**
  numeral..................**61**
  comparison of..................**64**
  rule for..................**181**
  participial..................**63**, 3; **205**, 2, *a*
  position of..................**181**, 5
Adverb, defined..................**34**, 6
  classes of..................**134**
  modal..................**134**, 6
  independent..................**134**, 11
  conjunctive..................**135**
  comparison of..................**137**
  rule for..................**180**
  position of..................**180**, 3
Adverbial idea, how expressed..................**132**, 2
  elements..................**154**, 1, 6
  phrases..................**199**, 4
Adversative conjunctions..................**143**, 6
  clauses..................**165**, 1
Affirm, how employed..................**80**, 3, 4
After, peculiar use of..................**212**, 2
Agreement of pronouns..................**177**, 1
  of verbs..................**179**, 1
  of verb and pronoun with coördinate nouns..................**195**
Alexandrine verse..................**241**, 9
All, peculiar use of..................**212**, 2
Allegory, defined..................**217**, 4

Alphabet, the..................**8**, 2
Alternative conjunctions..................**143**, 9
  clauses..................**169**, 1
Amphibrach, the..................**239**, 10
Analysis..................**18**, 5; **147**, 10
  directions for..................**170**
  general exercise in..................**171**
Anapæst..................**239**, 8
Anapæstic verse..................**243**
Antecedent, the..................**68**, 3
  when a collective noun..................**177**, 1, *a*
Antiquated words..................**246**, 3
Antithesis..................**217**, 10
Aphæresis..................**215**, 3
Apocope..................**215**, 5
Apostrophe..................**217**, 14
  mark of..................**235**, 2
Apposition, noun in..................**183**, 1, 4
Arrangement of elements..................**168**, 4
  improper, of words..................**209**, 8
  unusual..................**246**, 3
Article, defined..................**57**
  rules for..................**181**, 1
  omitted, inserted, repeated....**181**, 6, 7
As, use of..................**201**, 6, 7, 8; **212**, 2
Aspirates..................**3**, 6
  classes of..................**5**
Asterisk..................**235**, 4
Attribute, rule for..................**175**, 1
  in abridged propositions..................**175**, 1, *b*
Attributive object..................**187**, 1, 9
Auxiliaries, signification of..................**113**
Auxiliary verb..................**84**, 5
  names of..................**111**
  conjugation of..................**112**
  uses of..................**115**

Ballad, the..................**238**, 9
Be, pure verb..................**80**, 5
  as an auxiliary..................**113**, 2
Between and betwixt..................**197**, 5
Blank verse..................**237**, 10

INDEX.

Both, peculiar use of.................212, 1
Brace, the..............................235, 8
Brackets.................................235, 1
But, as preposition.................199, 3
  peculiar use of................212

Caesural pause........................245, 2
Can..113, 10
Capitals, defined......................9, 2
  rules for use of....................11
Caret.....................................235, 5
Case, of nouns........................50
  possessive, how formed.......50, 5
    how used.....72, 2; 185, 2
Cautions, special.....................209
Classes of adverbs..................134
  of connectives.....................143
Clause used as subject.............173
  as attribute......................175, 1, a
Clauses defined......................150, 6
  substantive.......................162, 1
  classes of..........................165, 1
Climax...................................217, 15
Collective noun defined...........36, 7
  as antecedent..................177, 1, a
  as subject of verb............179, 1, a
Colon, use of..........................227, 1
Common form of verb............109, 5, 6
  metre...............................241, 10
Comparative, when used.........181, 10
Comparison of adjectives........64
  rules for.............................65
  of adverbs.........................137
Complex sentence..................150, 2
  element............................150, 3
  subject, how formed...160, 4; 162, 3
  predicate, how formed, 160, 5; 162, 4
  sentence, how contracted....167, 1
  words................................212, 2
Compound word......................23, 3
  personal pronouns.............70, 6
  relative pronouns..............76, 1
  element............................150, 5
  sentences.........................165
  epithets............................246, 2
Conjugation of auxiliaries........112
  of the verb.......................117
  of Be................................119
  of Love.............................121
Conjunction, defined................34, 8
  copulative.......................143, 4, 5
  adversative......................143, 6
  rule for coördinate............193, 1
Conjunctive adverbs........135, 189, 7

Connectives, classes of............143
  rule for subordinate...........201, 1
Consonants, union of..............15
Construction, rules of..............172
  of pronouns......................177, 10
  coördinate........................195
  errors in...........................208
Contracted sentences..............166
Coördinate connectives...........143, 2
  elements..........................153, 3
  conjunctions, rule for........193, 1
  constructions, rules for.....195
Copula, defined......................80, 5
Copulative conjunctions.........143, 4, 5
Correlatives......143, 5; 193, 6; 201, 4
Couplet..................................240, 5

Dactyl....................................239, 9
Dactylic verse........................244
Dash, when used....................229
Declarative sentences............149, 1
Declension of nouns...............51
  of pronouns......................72, 1
Defective verb, defined..........84, 4
  verbs, list of....................129, 2
Derivation, defined................21, 15
Derivative words...................23, 2
Diæresis, mark of...................235, 12
  figure of..........................215, 9
Didactic poetry......................238, 6
Different kinds of poetry........238, 1
  of verse...........................240, 1
Diphthong.............................14, 1
Direct discourse....................163, 1
  object.............................187, 2
Directions for analysis..........170
Discourse, direct and indirect...163
Do, as an auxiliary................113, 3
Dramatic poem.....................238, 3

Elegy, defined......................238, 5
Elementary sounds................3
  table of............................6
Elements of a sentence.........147, 9
  syntax of.........................152, 1
  principal, subordinate, coördinate, 153
  simple, complex, compound...156
  equivalent.......................168, 1
  arrangement of...............168, 4
  punctuation of......220, 222, 224
Ellipses, improper.................209, 5
Ellipsis, defined...................216, 3
  when it occurs.................216, 4
  marks of.........................235, 7

INDEX.

Emphatic form of verb.....**109**, 7, 8; **122**
Enallage, figure of..........................**216**, 7
Epic poem....................................**238**, 2
Epigram, defined.........................**238**, 11
Epitaph, defined..........................**238**, 12
Epithets, compound......................**240**, 3
Equivalent elements....................**168**, 1
Errors in construction..........................**208**
  corrected by cautions...................**209**
  miscellaneous...............................**210**
Etymology, defined............................**32**, 1
  figures of..**215**
Exclamation, figure of..................**217**, 12
  point of...**233**, 1
Exclamatory sentences..................**149**, 4

False syntax. **208**
Feet, poetic................................**239**, 1, 5
Figures, defined.............................**214**, 1
  of etymology..................................**215**
  of syntax..**216**
  of rhetoric......................................**217**
Final pause..................................**245**, 2
Foot, in poetry..............................**239**, 2
Foreign idioms..............................**246**, 3
Forms of the verb..............................**109**
  for each division of time.....**110**, **126**
  of the elements..............................**155**
Future tense.....................................**105**
  perfect tense...................................**106**

Gender, defined................................**47**, 1
  methods of distinguishing..............**48**

Have, as an auxiliary....................**113**, 4
Heroic verse.................................**241**, 9
Hyperbaton, figure of...................**216**, 8
Hyperbole, figure of....................**217**, 11
Hyphen, use of.............................**235**, 6

Iambic verse......................................**242**
Iambus, defined............................**239**, 6
Idea-words....................................**212**, 1
Idiomatic use of words.................**211**, 2
  phrases.......................................**212**, 2
Idioms..**211**, 3
  foreign **246**, 3
Illative conjunction...................**193**, 4, 5
Imperative mode........................**89**, 8, 15
  sentences...................................**149**, 3
Impersonal verb..................**84**, 6; **130**, 3
Improper ellipses.........................**209**, 4
  arrangement of words..............**209**, 8
Incorrect use of words......................**207**

Independent adverb.......**134**, 11; **189**, 2
  nominative.....................................**191**
  participle..................................**205**, 2, *f*
  expressions, punctuation of.........**226**
Index, mark of............................**235**, 9
Indicative mode......................**89**, 5, 10
Indirect discourse........................**163**, 2
  object...**187**, 2
Infinitive mode................**89**, 9, **16**, 17
  rule for.......................................**203**, 1
  subject of...................................**203**, 3
  uses of..**203**, 4
Inflection, defined.........................**21**, 15
  strong and weak, of verbs........**127**, 1
Interjections...................................**34**, 10
  list of..**127**, 2
Interrogation, figure of..............**217**, 13
  point..**233**, 1
Interrogative pronouns........................**78**
  form of verb....................................**122**
  sentences...................................**149**, 2
  conjugation **122**
Irony, figure of............................**217**, 9
Irregular verbs, defined...................**84**, 3
  list of..**127**, 2
It, uses of......................................**70**, 4
  as subject...................................**175**, 2
Italics, use of..................................**11**, 10

Letter, defined...................................**8**, 1
  used as a subject..............................**173**
  used as an attribute.................**175**, *a*
License, poetic...............................**246**
List of prepositions............................**140**
  of irregular verbs.......................**127**, 2
Logical subject.............................**158**, 2
  predicate....................................**158**, 3
Long metre.................................**241**, 10
Lyric poem..................................**238**, 4

May, used as an auxiliary **113**, 9, 10
Metaphor, the.............................**217**, 2
Metonymy, figure of...................**217**, 6
Metre, different kinds of............**241**, 16
Misapplications to be avoided.........**209**, 4
  miscellaneous, in use of words......**210**
Mixed sentences..........................**149**, 2
Modal adverbs.............................**134**, 6
Mode, defined...............................**89**, 1
Modifier, defined.........................**147**, 8
Must, used as an auxiliary............**113**, 11

Negative conjugation........................**122**
Neuter verb................................**82**, 5, *e*

10 INDEX.

No, peculiar use of................................212
Nominative, the, defined...............50, 3
   independent..............................191
   absolute.....................................191, 2
Noun, defined...................................34, 2
   classes of..36
   persons of.......................................39
   numbers of......................................41
   genders of.......................................47
   cases of...50
   declension of..................................51
   as subject....................................173, 1
   as attribute.................................175, 1
   how restricted............................181, 3
   in apposition..............................183, 1
   in the possessive........................185, 1
   participial...................................205, 3
Now, peculiar use of..............................212
Number of noun..41
   of verb...116

Object of transitive verb...................82, 6
   as subject....................................173, 5
   rule for.......................................187, 1
   attributive................................187, 1, 9
   direct and indirect.....................187, 2
   position of..................................187, 8
   of preposition, rule for.............199, 1
   the infinitive as.........................203, 4
Objective, the, defined.....................50, 11
   rule for.......................................199, 1
   as predicate...............................203, 3
Omitted subject................................173, 3
Orthography...2

Paragoge, figure of...........................215, 7
Paragraph, mark of........................235, 11
Parenthesis, when used..................229, 4
Parenthetic expressions, punctuation
   of..226
Parsing, defined......................................53
Participial adjective...............63, 3; 205, 2
   noun..205, 3
Participle, defined..............................91, 1
   different kinds of...............93, 94, 95
   rules for...........................181, 1; 205, 1
   uses of....................................205, 2, 3, 4
Parts of speech, defined.........................34
Passive verb.......................................82, 5, b
   voice..87, 4, 7
   form...109, 11
Past tense...102
   perfect tense..................................104
Pastoral poem..................................238, 7

Pauses, poetic...................................245
Peculiar use of words.......................211
Period of time.................................99, 3
   use of.......................................231, 1
Person, defined...............................39, 1
   of verb..116
Personal pronouns..........................70, 1
   declension of.............................72, 1
Personification, figure of..............217, 5
   applied to inanimate objects...47, 7
Perversions to be avoided.............209, 2
Phrase, a............139, 3; 155, 2; 160, 1
   used as subject............................173
   used as attribute.........................175
   adverbial..................................199, 4
Phrases, idiomatic..........................212, 2
   antiquated................................246, 3
Pleonasm.......................................216, 5
Plural of nouns...................................42
   how formed.........................43, 44
Poetic feet.....................................239, 1
   pauses...245
   license..246
Poetry, defined..............................237, 4
   different kinds of....................238, 1
Point of time...................................99, 2
Points, punctuation..........................218
Position of subject.........................173, 4
   of the pronoun........................177, 7
   of the adjective.......................181, 5
   of the object...........................187, 8
   of the adverb..........................189, 3
Possessive case, defined................50, 5
   formation of.....................50, 6, 7, 8
Possessives, how used....................72, 2
   in apposition..........................183, 12
   rule for......................................185
   constructions..................185, 8, 9, 10
Potential mode......................89, 6, 11, 12
Power of a letter..............................8, 4
Predicate, defined.........................147, 5
   nominative................................82, 7
   adjective.....................................181
   objective..................................203, 3
   logical........................158, 160, 162
Prefixes, defined...........................21, 12
   rules for applying........................27
Prepositions, defined.....................34, 7
   list of..140
   complex..................................140, 1
   rule for....................................197, 1
   object of..................................199, 1
   when omitted........................199, 1, a
Present tense.....................................101

INDEX. 11

Present perfect tense............................102
Primitive word........................... 23, 1
Principal parts of verb...............117, 4
   elements..................................153, 1
Progressive form of verb......109, 9; 124
Pronoun, defined...............................68
   personal......................................70
   compound personal.....................70, 6
   declension of................................72
   relative...................................74, 75
   interrogative................................78
   construction of....................177, 1, 10
   position of............................177, 7, 8
   agreement with coördinate nouns, 195
Proposition, defined........................150, 2
   different kinds of.......................150, 5
   abridged......................................167
Prosody, defined.............................237, 1
Prosthesis.....................................215, 6
Provincialisms...............................209, 3
Punctuation, defined......................218, 1
   marks of.....................................218, 6
Pyrrhic foot..................................239, 10

Quantity, in prosody......................237, 1
Quotation-marks............................235, 3
Quotations, direct and indirect..........163

Radical, or root..............................21, 11
Rather, peculiar use of........................212
Redundant verb..............................130, 1
Reflexive pronouns..........................70, 8
Regular verb....................................84, 2
   use of words.................................172
Relative tenses......................99, 4, 5, 6
   when restrictive.......................177, 12
   when explanatory.....................177, 12
Relatives, simple.................................75
   compound....................................76, 1
   uses of......................................177, 14
Repetitions, unnecessary..................209, 6
Rhetoric, figures of..............................217
Rhyme, defined..............................237, 6
Root, defined.................................21, 11
Rules of syntax..................................172

Satire, defined...............................238, 8
Save, peculiar use of..........................212
Scanning.......................................240, 4
Section, mark of...........................235, 10
Semicolon, use of...........................227, 1
Sentence, defined..........................147, 2
   kinds of, 149, 150, 158, 165, 166
   transformation of............................168
Sentence-making...............................147

Shall and Will, auxiliaries..............113, 5
   rules for use of....................113, 6, 7, 8
Short metre...................................241, 10
Signification of auxiliaries.................113
Simile, defined..............................217, 3
Simple element..............................156, 1
   sentences....................................158
So, peculiar use of..............................212
Sonnet, defined.............................238, 10
Special cautions.................................209
Spelling, defined................................25
   rules for.............................26, 27, 28
Spondee, the.................................239, 10
Stanza, the...................................240, 6
Subject, defined...............80, 7; 147, 4
   complex or logical......158, 2; 160, 4
   as a clause..................................162
   rule for.......................................173
   when omitted............................173, 3
   position of................................173, 4
   of infinitive..............................203, 3
Subjunctive mode..................89, 7, 13, 14
Subordinate connectives................143, 12
   rule for....................................201, 6
   classes of................................143, 15
   elements..................................153, 2
   clause, how abridged................167, 2
Subsequent, the............................139, 2
Subvocals..3, 5
   classes of...5
Suffix, defined..............................21, 13
   rules for applying.............................28
Superlative, when used................181, 17
Syllabication......................................20
Syllables..18
Synæresis, figure of........................215, 8
Syncope, figure of..........................215, 4
Synecdoche, figure of.....................217, 8
Synopsis..124
Syntax, defined.............................147, 1
   preliminary, development of.........147
   of sentences....................................149
   of elements....................................152
   of words...172
   false..208
   figures of..216
Synthesis, defined................18, 5; 147, 10

Table of poetic feet......................239, 12
Tense, defined................................98, 1
   present..101
   present perfect..............................102
   past...103
   past perfect..................................104

INDEX.

Tense, future.................................105
   future perfect..........................106
Tenses in all the modes.................107
Than, before Whom........................199, 5
   showing comparison.................201, 6
That, uses of....................75, 8; 177, 19;
                           181, 10; 201, 8
There, an expletive..............134, 9; 212, 2
They, erroneous use of....................177, 5
Thou, uses of.......................................70, 5
Time, point of....................................99, 2
   period of......................................99, 3
Tmesis, figure of..............................215, 10
To, when omitted............................203, 1, a
Transformation of sentences............168
Transitive verb, defined....................82, 2
Tribrach, the..................................239, 10
Triphthong.......................................14, 4
Trochaic verse....................................242
Trochee, the....................................239, 7
True rhyme.....................................237, 7

Unbecoming expressions................209, 9
Union of vowels..................................14
   of consonants.................................15
   of vowels and consonants................16
Unnecessary repetitions..................209, 6
   words..209, 7
Unusual arrangement of words......246, 3
Use of words................172, 207, 211
Uses of the infinitive........................203, 4
   of the comma.................................219
   of dash and parenthesis..................229
   of the period..................................231
   of semicolon and colon..................227
   of interrogation and exclamation
      points.......................................233
   of other marks...............................235

Verb, defined....................................80, 1
Verb, attributive................................80, 1
   be...80, 6
   transitive....................................82, 2
   intransitive.................................82, 3
   active, passive, neuter.....................82
   regular and irregular..............84, 2, 3
   defective and auxiliary..........84, 4, 5
   impersonal................84, 6; 130, 2, 3
   forms of.......................................100
   list of irregular...........................127, 2
   list of redundant.......................130, 1
   number and person of....................116
   conjugation of................................117
   principal parts of.......................117, 4
   agreement with subject............179, 1
   agreement with coördinate nouns, 195
Verse, defined....................................237
   different kinds of......240, 241, 242,
                                  243, 244
Versification, defined....................237, 2
Vision, figure of............................217, 7
Vocals, defined..................................3, 4
   classes of..4
   union of..14
Voice..87
Vowel-marks.................................235, 12
Vulgarisms....................................209, 1

What, different uses of......75, 7; 189, 5;
                                       212
Will and Shall..................................113
Words, defined...................................21
   classes of.......................................22
   formation of..................................30
   syntax of.....................................172
   unnecessary...............................209, 1
   complex......................................212
   antiquated...............................246, 3
Worth, peculiar use of....................212, 2

ENGLISH GRAMMAR.

1. Definitions and Divisions.

1. **Grammar** is the science which treats of the general principles of language.

2. **English Grammar** treats of the principles and usages of the English language; it teaches us to speak and write it correctly.

3. It relates,—
   - (*a.*) To the elementary sounds and letters of the language;
   - (*b.*) To the classification and modification of its words;
   - (*c.*) To the structure of its sentences,—and
   - (*d.*) To the laws of its versification. Hence,—

4. **Grammar** is divided into four parts,—**Orthography, Etymology, Syntax,** and **Prosody.**

5. **Orthography** treats of elementary sounds, the letters which represent them, and the combination of letters into syllables and words.

   Orthoepy treats of the proper pronunciation of words.

6. **Etymology** treats of the classification, derivation, and various modifications of words.

7. **Syntax** treats of the construction of sentences.

8. **Prosody** treats of the laws of versification.

ORTHOGRAPHY.

2. Definition.

Orthography treats of elementary sounds, the letters which represent them, and the combination of letters into syllables and words.

ELEMENTARY SOUNDS.

3. Number and Classes.

1. An **elementary** sound is the simplest sound of the language.

Ex.—The sound of *a, e; b* or *k*.

2. The English language contains about forty elementary sounds.

3. These sounds are divided into three classes,—**vocals, subvocals,** and **aspirates.**

4. The **vocals** consist of pure tone only.

They are formed by an interrupted flow of vocalized breath.

EXAMPLES.—The sounds of *a, e, i, o, u, ou;* as, in *a*-le, f-*a*-r, b-*a*-ll, h-*a*-t, m-*e*, m-*e*-t, f-*i*-ne, p-*i*-n, g-*o*-ld, m-*o*-ve, n-*o*-t, m-*u*-te, p-*u*-ll, c-*u*-p, f-*ou*-nd.

REMARK.—The letters are but imperfect guides to these sounds.

5. The **subvocals** consist of tone united with breath.

They are formed by an interrupted flow of breath partially vocalized.

Ex.—The sounds of *b, d, g, j, l, m, n, ng, r, th, v, w, z,* z (zh), *y;* as, in *b*-at, *d*-og, *g*-o, *j*-oy, *l*-ot, *m*-an, *n*-o, so-*ng*, ba-*r*, *th*-is, *v*-at, *w*-in, *z*-one, a-*z*-ure, *y*-es.

6. The **aspirates** consist of pure breath only.

They are formed by an interrupted flow of breath without vocality.

Ex.—The sounds of *f, h, k, p, s, t, th, sh, ch, wh;* as, in *f*-aith, *h*-ome, *ır-k*, *p*-ine, *s*-un, *t*-ake, *th*-ink, *sh*-one, *ch*-ur-*l*, *wh*-en.

ORTHOGRAPHY—ELEMENTARY SOUNDS.   15

REMARK.—When closely examined, it will be found that some of the sounds here represented as elementary, as, for example, *i* in isle (*a* in far and *e* in me), *ou* in found (*a* in all and *oo* in fool), *j* in joy (dzh), *ch* in church (tsh), may be resolved into simpler sounds; yet, for practical purposes, they may be regarded as elementary.

4. Classes of Vocals.

1. Vocals are divided into **long** and **short**.

2. The **long** sound is one that can be protracted at pleasure; as in m*ay*——*ay*, b*ee*——*ee*.

3. The **short** sound is one that is uttered with an explosive effort; as in p*i*n, p*e*n, h*a*t, s*i*t.

REMARK.—The long and short vocals are formed with the same position of the organs. Thus, *a* in *hat* is properly the short sound of *a* in *far*, not *a* in *hate;* while *e* in *met* is the short sound of *a* in *hate*. The *i* in *pin* is the short sound of *ee* in *seen*. The *o* in *not* is the short sound of *o* in *nor*, not *o* in *note*. The *u* in *but* is the short sound of *u* in *fur*, not *u* in *mute*.

5. Classes of Subvocals and Aspirates.

1. The subvocals and aspirates are divided, in a similar manner, into **continuous** and **explosive**.

2. The **continuous** are capable of prolongation.

They are the sounds of (subvocals) *l, m, n, ng, r, th, v, w, y,* z = zh*;* as in ba-*ll*, ca-*m*-e, rai-*n*, so-*ng*, ca-*r*, ba-*th*-e, la-*v*-e, *w*-o, *y*-es, ma-*z*-e, a-*z*-ure; (aspirates), *f, h, s, th, sh, wh,* in lea-*f*, *h*-eat, thi-*s*, hea-*th*, lea-*sh*, *wh*-y.

3. The **explosive** are incapable of prolongation.

They are the sounds of (subvocals) *b, d, g, j;* as in ca-*b*, be-*d*, do-*g*, *j*-ob; (aspirates), *p, t, k, ch,* in ti-*p*, pi-*t*, *k*-in, lur-*ch*.

4. The subvocals, represented by *w* and *y*, are nearly allied to the vocals in *oo*-ze and m-*ee*-t. They may be called *semi-vocals*.

5. The aspirates represented by *wh* and *h* are properly *breathings*.

The sound of *h* is formed with an open position of the organs; that of *wh*, with the lips contracted nearly as in the sound of *w*.

6. Of the remaining subvocals and aspirates, sixteen are called **correlatives** or **cognates**, and may be arranged in eight pairs.

Thus, *b-p, d-t, g-k, j-ch, th-th, v-f, z-s, zh-sh*. Each pair is formed with the same position of the organs.

7. The first four pairs are explosive, the others are continuous.

8. The correlatives are sometimes called **mutes**, because, in their formation, the organs are more or less closed.

9. The subvocals, represented by *l, m, n, ng*, and *r*, have no corresponding aspirates. They are called **liquids,** because they flow readily into other sounds.

REMARK 1.—All the liquids are subvocals, while half of the mutes are aspirates.

The liquids are all continuous,—while half of the mutes are explosive.

Every continuous subvocal mute has a rough, buzzing sound; the liquids have a smooth, flowing sound.

A mute may unite with a mute, but it must be a subvocal with a subvocal, or an aspirate with an aspirate. (See **15,** 2.) A liquid may unite with a liquid, as in a*rm*, ba*rn;* or with a mute either subvocal or aspirate, as in ca*rp,* ca*rd,* ha*rt,* ha*rd*. It must not be understood, however, that *any* liquid will combine with any other liquid, or that any liquid will combine with any mute. Thus, the sounds of *mn* will not coalesce; the sound of *l* seldom unites with that of *m* or *n*. The sound of *m* does not readily unite with that of *k;* nor does the sound of *n* with that of *p*.

REMARK 2.—The mutes and liquids have certain affinities for each other, which arise mainly from a similarity in the position of the organs with which they are produced. Thus, the sound of *m* most readily unites with the sound of *p,* or *s* (= *z*), as in he*mp,* la*mp,* ste*ms,* hu*me;* the sound of *n* unites most readily with *t, d, s, c,* or aspirate *th,* as in se*nt,* e*nd,* te*ns,* fe*nce,* te*nth;* also, *ng* with *th,* as in stre*ngth,* le*ngth;* the sounds of *l* and *r* readily unite with nearly all the mutes, as in e*lf,* me*lt,* we*ld,* be*lch,* o*rb,* hea*rth,* a*rk,* la*rge*. These affinities will explain the euphonic changes which so often take place in derivation. (See **27, 28.**)

6. Table of Elementary Sounds.

Vocals.	Subvocals.	Aspirates.	Correlatives.	
1. *a*-le	1. *b*-at	1. *f*-aith	1. *b*-ow	= *p*-ole
2. f-*a*-r	2. *d*-og	2. *h*-ome	2. *d*-og	= *t*-on
3. b-*a*-ll	3. *g*-o	3. ar-*k*	3. *g*-et	= *k*-ind
4. h-*a*-t	4. *j*-oy	4. *p*-ine	4. *th*-is	= *th*-umb
5. m-*e*	5. *l*-ot	5. *s*-un	5. *j*-ob	= *ch*-in
6. m-*e*-t	6. *m*-an	6. *t*-ake	6. *v*-an	= *f*-an
7. f-*i*-ne	7. *n*-o	7. *th*-ink	7. *z*-one	= *s*-on
8. p-*i*-n	8. so-*ng*	8. *sh*-one	8. a-*z*-ure	= *sh*-ut
9. g-*o*-ld	9. ba-*r*	9. *ch*-url		
10. m-*o*-ve	10. *th*-is	10. *wh*-en	**Liquids.**	
11. n-*o*-t	11. *v*-at		*l*-ong	
12. m-*u*-te	12. *w*-ise		*m*-ane	
13. p-*u*-ll	13. *z*-one		*n*-ame	
14. c-*u*-p	14. a-*z*-ure		so-*ng*	
15. f-*ou*-nd	15. *y*-es		*r*-ate	

7. Exercise.

1. The teacher, uttering the sound of *a* in *name*, says, "How many heard my *voice?*" Let the class give the same. The teacher, again, gives the sound of *f* in *fine* (not the name *Eff*, but the sound alone). "Do you hear a *voice sound*, or a *whispering sound?*" The class utter the sound. Adding a slight vocality to the sound of *f*, with the organs in the same position, he gives the sound of *v*. "How many hear any *voice sound* now?" Returning to the sound of *f*,—"Do you now hear any voice sound? or only a whispering or breath sound?" Giving the sound of *o* in *note*,—"What sound do you hear now?" In the same manner treat the other elementary sounds, till *all* are readily distinguished.

2. *Tell by the sound which letters in the following promiscuous examples represent* VOCALS, *which* SUBVOCALS, *and which* ASPIRATES:—

And, great, made, fame, sad, mete, gave, life, voice, six, zebra, full, bridge, sup, thin, thought, thine, when, whiffle, sent, gone, white, lone, fidget, cup, farm, wine, yes, so, knit, type, book, crow, met, line, pin, hat, harp, jug, king, long, nut, move, lot, queer, rind, street, sing, mute, suit, vine, sire, exist, sift, form, risk, mart, park, plum.

3. *In the preceding examples, tell which of the vocals are* LONG, *and*

which SHORT; *tell which of the subvocals and aspirates are* CONTINUOUS, *and which* EXPLOSIVE. Select three words having two aspirate sounds united; two having two subvocal mutes; five having a liquid and a subvocal mute; five having a liquid and an aspirate; and two having two liquids.

LETTERS.

8. The Alphabet.

1. A **letter** is a character used to represent an elementary sound.

2. The English alphabet contains twenty-six letters: A, a; B, b; C, c; D, d; E, e; F, f; G, g; H, h; I, i; J, j; K, k; L, l; M, m; N, n; O, o; P, p; Q, q; R, r; S, s; T, t; U, u; V, v; W, w; X, x; Y, y; Z, z.

3. The *name* of a letter is the term or appellation by which it is known.

Ex.—*Be, De, Aitch.*

4. The *power* of a letter is the elementary sound which it represents.

Ex.—The sound *a* in h-*a*-il, h-*a*-nd.

REMARK.—*Letters* cannot be too carefully distinguished from *elementary sounds.* The letter is an arbitrary mark addressed to the *eye;* an elementary sound is always addressed to the *ear.*

9. Classes of Letters.

1. Letters are divided,—

(*a.*) In respect to their forms, into *capitals* and *small letters.*

(*b.*) In respect to the sounds they represent, into *vowels* and *consonants.*

Let it be remembered that vowels represent vocals; consonants, both subvocals and aspirates.

(*c.*) In respect to their application to these sounds, into *permanent, variable,* and *silent.*

2. **Capitals** are used for the sake of distinction; small letters constitute the principal part of every composition. (See **11.**)

3. The various **styles** of letters are the Roman, the *Italic,* 𝔒𝔩𝔡 𝔈𝔫𝔤𝔩𝔦𝔰𝔥, and *Script.*

10. Exercise.

1. *Tell which letters are vowels, and which are consonants, in the following words:—*

Name, war, come, peace, tree, fish, good, live, old, sad, young, wine, said, yet, win, new, gay, day.

2. *Tell which of the following letters represent vocals, which subvocals, and which aspirates:—*

a, f, g, m, c, k, d, p, o, w, s, h, y, t, r, v, x, l, e, j.

3. *Analyze the following words by giving, in order, the elementary sounds (not the names of the letters); tell how many sounds and how many letters each has; also, what letters are silent:—*

Mete, laugh, bought, fought, believe, phthisic, balm, rough, piece, beauty, thought, blight.

MODEL.—M—ē—t = mete:—three sounds and four letters. The final e is silent.

4. *In the following examples, tell what words contain equivalents of a in name; of a in ball; of a in fare; of e in mete; of e in end; of i in iron; of i in ink; of o in go; of o in dot; of u in music; of u in pull; of u in gun; of ou in plough, and of oi in toil:—*

Grain, air, awl, see, bread, symbol, floor, what, new, could, son, now, deign, lair, nor, defraud, brought, awed, key, deaf, been, owed, blue, should, rough, boy, feign, bear, sea, women, coat, lieutenant, tough, hay, there, lief, buy, beaux, pay, perceive, guile, bouquet, league, rain, sought, nay, brief, bee, deceive, instead.

5. *Tell what words in the following list contain equivalents to any sounds of c, f, g, x, z, sh, and ch:—*

Kent, phlegm, tacks, chagrin, righteous, phonography, physician, sacrifice, champagne, single, exist, ferocious, partition, nation, phonetics, physics, sit, stand, chamois, quarrel, join, Xenophon, passion, phosphorus, just, oceanic, jump, beaux.

11. Rules for the Use of Capitals and other Letters.

1. RULE I.—The **titles of books,** and the heads of their parts, chapters, sections, and divisions, are usually printed in capitals.

EX.—HISTORY OF PHILOSOPHY; CLASSES OF NOUNS; COMPOUND RELATIVES.

When the titles of books are **quoted**, only their principal words should begin with capitals.

Ex.—Watts on the Mind.

Inscriptions on signs and monuments are subject to the same rule.

2. RULE II.—The **first word** of every entire sentence, and of every independent expression or phrase, should begin with a capital.

Ex.—Evil communications corrupt good manners. The words of the prophet.

3. RULE III.—The first word of any **dependent part** of a sentence should begin with a capital,—

(1.) When, to give prominence, that part is made into a distinct line or paragraph

Ex.—Nouns are divided into,—
 Proper, which denote individuals.
 Common, which denote classes.

(2.) When a direct quotation is introduced so as to form a sentence of itself.

Ex.—He saith unto him, Feed my sheep.

(3.) When the words of a resolution or an enactment follow such words as *resolved, be it enacted.*

Ex.—Resolved, *That* a committee of three, &c. Be it enacted, *That,* &c.

4. RULE IV.—**Proper names,** and adjectives derived from proper names, should begin with a capital.

Ex.—America, American; Boston, Bostonian.

(*a.*) When the proper name of a person, a place, a river, or a mountain, has become a consolidated compound word, only one capital should be used.

Ex.—Northampton, Southbridge, Newcastle.

When the parts remain separate, each should begin with a capital.

Ex.—South Berwick, New York, Old Saybrook. In many compound names usage is not uniform. Thus, Newcastle, used as the name of about thirty different places in England, Ireland, and British America, is consolidated; while in the United States, in about twenty different instances, the parts are separated, thus:—New-Castle. The same may be said of New Haven, New Market, and others.

5. RULE V.—Titles of **honor, office, respect,** and **distinction,** usually begin with a capital.

Ex.—Chief Justice Marshall, His Majesty, General Washington.

(*a.*) When a title is used with a proper name merely for the purpose of explanation, it should begin with a small letter.

Ex.—The apostle Peter; The prophet Daniel.

6. RULE VI.—All **appellations of the Deity** should begin with a capital.

Ex.—God, Jehovah, The Eternal, The Almighty.

(*a.*) The personal pronouns, *he, his, him, thou, thy,* and *thee,* when they refer to the Deity, sometimes—especially when emphatic—begin with a capital. This usage is neither universal nor uniform.

7. RULE VII.—The first word of every **line in poetry** should begin with a capital.

8. RULE VIII.—The words **I** and **O** should be capitals.

9. RULE IX.—Any common noun used to denote an **object personified,** or an object to be made specially emphatic, should begin with a capital.

Ex.—Cheered with the grateful smell, old *Ocean* smiles.—*Milton.*
In the *Creed* the same distinction is properly observed.—*Harrison.*

10. RULE X.—*Italics* are used,—

(1.) To direct attention to an emphatic word, phrase, or clause of a sentence.

Ex.—Where he got all these *nothings* I know not.—*Junius.*
This *tenuity* was the only *hard word* that I heard him use during this interview.—*Boswell's Johnson.*

(2.) To distinguish words borrowed from foreign languages.

Ex.—The *res dura et regni novitas* is the great apology of Cromwell.—*Macaulay.*

REMARK.—In the Bible, the words in italics are those supplied by the translators to explain the sense of the original.

(3.) The names of ships, newspapers, and periodicals, and parenthetical words and phrases, are frequently printed in italics.

Ex.—A full report of his speech will be found in to-day's *Tribune*. Chairman (*at the highest pitch of his voice*), "Order!"

REMARK.—A *special* emphasis is indicated by the use of small capitals; as, "I will rear my structure of better materials than painted cards; in a word, I will write HISTORY."—*Walter Scott*.

NOTE.—In writing, italics are shown by a single line drawn under the word; small capitals, by two lines.

Full-faced type is also used for distinction.

12. Exercise.

1. *Explain by rule the use of each capital in the following examples:—*

Dr. Kane relates many curious facts respecting the Esquimaux. "Lossing's Field-Book of the Revolution" gives an interesting account of the surrender of the British army under General Burgoyne, to General Gates, the American commander. He inquired, "For what purpose is this waste?" and I could make no reply. The eye of the Omniscient is ever our guard, and the hand of the Almighty our support. My beauteous deliverer thus uttered her divine instructions: "My name is Religion." In the agony of the moment he exclaimed, "O, I am lost." The Austrians were defeated in the battle of Magenta. President Woolsey's "International Law." Michael Angelo had nearly reached the years of Dryden when he gave the "Last Judgment" to the world. To an American eye, European life presents strange contrasts.

   In colleges in ancient days,
   There dwelt a sage called Discipline.
   With eyes upraised, as one inspired,
   Pale Melancholy sat retired.—*Collins*.

2. *By the preceding rules, correct the erroneous use of capitals in the following examples, and insert them where they should be used:—*

new york is the largest of all american cities. and i heard, but i understood not; then said i, "o my lord, what shall be the end of these things?" huss, the reformer, was a martyr to the cause which he espoused. have you visited the falls of niagara? the auditor has sent in his report. the english custom differs from ours. They Met on the Twenty-Fifth of november, in paris, to form a New

Map of europe. Hail, holy light, offspring of heaven. I am, My Dear sir, your Obedient Servant, jacob trusty.
the lightnings flash along the sky,
The thunder bursts and rolls on high;
jehovah's voice methinks I hear
amid the storm,
as riding on the clouds of even
he spreads his glory o'er the heaven.
but wisdom is justified of her children.

13. Combination of Letters.

1. When two or more letters unite, to represent a union of elementary sounds, they form a **combination** of letters.

Ex.—*Ou, oi, bl, on, no, not, breath, breadth, thrusts.*

2. Sometimes a combination of elementary sounds is represented by a single letter; as, $i = ae$ (a in *far*, and e in *me*); u in *union* = yu; o in *one* = wu.

3. Sometimes a combination of letters represents a single elementary sound.

Ex.—*Th* in *this;* *ti, ci, si, ce,* in *martial, mission, official, ocean; oo, ee, aa, gg, zz, bb, ff, ll, tt,* in *door, feet, Isaac, egg, buzz, ebb, off, call, butt.*

14. Union of Vowels.

1. A **diphthong** is the union of two vowels in one syllable.

Ex.—*Ou* in *sound, oi* in *voice, oy* in *joy, ay* in *say.*

2. A **proper** diphthong is one in which both vowels are sounded.

Ex.—*Ou* in *thou, oi* in *toil.*

3. An **improper** diphthong is one in which one of the vowels is silent.

Ex.—The *a* in *heat, oi* in *hail, un* in *fruit.*

4. A **triphthong** is the union of three vowels in one syllable.

Ex.—*Eau* in *beauty*, *iew* in *view*, *ieu* in *lieu*.

5. A **proper** triphthong is one in which the three vowels are sounded.

Ex.—*Uoy* in *buoy*.

6. An **improper** triphthong is one in which one or two of the vowels are silent.

Ex.—*Ea* in *beauty*, *ie* in *adieu*.

15. Union of Consonants.

1. Two or more consonants are said to unite when their sounds coalesce.

Ex.—*Bl*-e-*nd*, *thr*-ee.

2. If they represent two *mutes*, these must be similar; that is, both subvocals or both aspirates.

Ex.—A*pt*, a*dze*, ha*ts*. (See **5**, Rem.)

3. If two consonants representing dissimilar mutes come together, the sound of one, usually the latter, is changed to its correlative, though the letter remains the same (**5, 6**).

Ex.—Bag, bag*s*, pad, pad*s*, = bag*z*, pad*z*, placed = plac'*d* = plac*t*. In *oath, bath*, and others, *th* aspirate becomes *th* subvocal in the plural, and *s* follows the rule. Not so with *th* in *truths, youths*.

4. When they represent two *liquids*, they are always similar (**5, 8, 9**), and their sounds, with some exceptions, readily coalesce.

Ex.—A*rm*, e*lm*, ba*rn*, ma*rl*. *N* becomes silent after *m*, as in hym*n*, and after *l*, as in kil*n*.

5. When they represent, the one a mute, and the other a liquid, even though dissimilar, their sounds readily unite.

Ex.—Spe*nd*, spe*nt*, ha*lt*, ha*rt*. (See **5**, Rem.)

6. When two identical letters (double letters) come together, whether standing for mutes or liquids, they seldom represent more than a single sound (**13, 3**).

Ex.—E*gg*, bu*tt*, e*bb*, whi*ff* = eg, but, eb, whif.

16. Union of Vowels and Consonants.

Any consonant sound may unite with a vowel sound.

Ex.—A*n*, *n*o, d*i*d, *c*all, *j*at, va*t*l, r*i*b, *j*ob, *g*ig, *h*am.

17. Exercise.

1. *Point out the vowel combinations in the following words; tell whether the diphthongs are proper, or improper:—*

Fear, pear, voice, sound, pierce, receive, Europe, people, view, adieu, beauty, though, chief, fail, Cæsar, how, sew, gaol, mail, deal.

2. *Point out the consonant combinations in the following, and tell what letters are identical, and what are changed into their correlatives:—*

Birds, blend, apt, capped, clapped, buzz, mats, heads, beads, brought, off, skiff, pass, insist, first, faced, round, word, gird, gold, sold, bulb, verb, worm, last, craft, compact, acts.

SYLLABLES.
18. Formation of Syllables.

1. A **syllable** is a letter or a combination of letters the sound of which is uttered with one impulse of the voice.

Ex.—*Mat, mat-ter, ma-te-ri-al, in-com-pre-hen-si-bil-i-ty.*

2. The **essential** part of a syllable is a vowel.

NOTE.—By *vowel* here is meant a vowel sound, whether represented by a single letter, a diphthong, or a triphthong.

3. A syllable may consist,—

(*a.*) Of a vowel.

Ex.—*A*-cre, *ei*-ther.

(*b.*) Of a vowel with one or more consonants prefixed.

Ex.—*Ba*-sis, *bri*-er, *three*, *phthi*-sis.

(*c.*) Of a vowel with one or more consonants affixed.

Ex.—*In*, *elf*, inter-*ests*, *earths*.

(*d.*) Of a vowel with one or more consonants both prefixed and affixed.

Ex.—*N*-oo-*n*, *tr*-u-*th*, *thr*-u-*sts*.

4. A vowel is said to be *modified* by the consonant which unites with it. Thus, in *model*, *o*, and not *e*, is modified by *d*.

5. The process of combining elementary parts is called **Synthesis**, and that of separating a combination into its elements is called **Analysis**.

NOTE.—In analyzing a syllable, let the learner tell,—(1.) the *essential* part, that is, the vowel or diphthong; (2.) the consonant, or combination (**13**) of consonants, which is *prefixed* to it; (3.) the consonant, or combination of consonants, which is *affixed* to it.

19. Exercise.

MODELS FOR ANALYZING SYLLABLES.

An . . is a syllable consisting of two elements:—
A . . . is the essential element,—it is a vowel. (Give its sound.)
n . . . is a consonant, and represents a subvocal; it is affixed to *a*, which it modifies. (Give its sound.)
Break is a syllable consisting of three parts:—
ea . . . is the essential part,—it is a diphthong (why?), improper (why?); *e* is silent,—*a* only is sounded. (Give its sound.)
Br . . is a union (**13**) of two consonants, both representing subvocals, *b* and *r*, which are prefixed to *ea*. (Give their sounds separately, then together.)
k . . . is a consonant representing an aspirate, and is affixed to *ea*. (Give its sound.)

1. *Analyze the following syllables, and describe each element:—*
Kite, dog, numb, boat, friend, truth, day, wax, bat, view, sound, aid, meet, suit, rude, the, think, sit, leave, three, bursts, threats.

2. *Form syllables by prefixing* ONE *consonant to* a, ay, ey, ou, ieu, y; TWO OR MORE *consonants to* e, oo, oe, i, ou, oi, ee, ea, ay, ey; *by affixing* ONE, TWO, OR THREE *consonants to any five of the above vowels or diphthongs.*

3. *Form ten syllables in which one, two, or more consonants shall be prefixed and affixed to any vowel or union of vowels.*

20. Rules for the Division of Words into Syllables.

1. **Syllabication** is the proper division of words into syllables.

2. RULE I.—Every word has as many syllables as there are distinct vowel sounds heard in a correct pronunciation of it.

(*a*.) When two vowels come together, they unite (**14**) in one syllable, if in the pronunciation only one vowel sound, single or combined (**14**, 2, 3), is heard.

Ex.—*Feast, poorly.*

Otherwise, they separate into two syllables.

Ex.—*Li-*on, pu*-erile, coöperate.*

(*b*.) When the two vowels are the same, the separation is often indicated by a diæresis (¨).

Ex.—*Preëmption, coördinate.*

2. RULE II.—The consonants, singly or combined (**15**), are either prefixed or affixed to the vowels (**18**, 3, *b*, *c*, *d*) which they modify.

(*a*.) PRIMITIVE WORDS.—(1.) A single consonant between two vowels is joined to the latter when the former is long (**4**).

Ex.—*Pa-per, la-dy, ci-pher.*

Otherwise, it should be joined to the former.

Ex.—*Lep-er, ep-ic, ech-o.*

NOTE.—The combinations *th, ch, tch, ph, gh, sh, ng, wh,* should be regarded as single consonants (**13, 3**), since they represent only one elementary sound, and are never separated when thus used.

(2.) Two consonants between two vowels are separated, except when a mute and either of the liquids *l* or *r* follow a long vowel.

Ex.—*Cas-ter, dam-per, ap-ple, am-ber; peo-ple, a-cre, tri-fle.*

(3.) When three consonants come between two vowels, the last consonant—or the last two consonants, when they are a mute, and either of the liquids *l* or *r*—must be joined to the latter vowel.

Ex.—*Emp-ty, am-ple, strug-gle.*

(*b*.) DERIVATIVE WORDS.—The prefix should be separated from the root in all cases, except as in Rule II. (1); and the suffix always when it forms a syllable.

Ex.—*Pre-fix, suf-fix;* but *pref-ace,* not *pre-face; good-ness, tru-ly.*

(*c*.) COMPOUND WORDS.—Compound words are separated into the primitive or derivative words which compose them, and these are divided by the preceding rules.

CAUTION.—In writing, never divide a syllable at the end of a line.

NOTE.—Let the pupil take as an exercise the words of any page in the Reader.

WORDS.

21. Formation and Classification of Words.

1. A word in reference to its **sounds** consists of one or more syllables.

REMARK.—Written words are used to represent both *sounds* and *ideas*. As the representatives of sounds, they are classified according to the number of syllables they contain.

2. A word of one syllable is called a **monosyllable**.
Ex.—*Boy, pen, tree.*

3. A word of two syllables is called a **dissyllable**.
Ex.—*Na-ture, faith-ful.*

4. A word of three syllables is called a **trisyllable**.
Ex.—*Nat-u-ral, faith-ful-ness.*

5. A word of four or more syllables is called a **polysyllable**.
Ex.—*Un-nat-u-ral, un-faith-ful-ness.*

6. **Accent** is a stress of the voice placed upon a particular syllable, to distinguish it from other syllables.

7. Every word of more than one syllable has one of its syllables accented.

8. The accented syllable may be either the first, the last, or a middle syllable.
Ex.—*Du'ty, be-long', pre-par'ing.*

9. Some words have a primary and a secondary accent.
Ex.—*In''defat'igable, in''comprehen'sible.*

Similar to accent is the emphasis on one or more words in a sentence.
Ex.—"I go, but I *return.*"

NOTE.—In analyzing a word according to its syllables, it should be separated by (**21,** 1), the accented syllable pointed out, and then each syllable analyzed as in (**19**).

10. A word in reference to its **significant parts** *must* contain a *root*, and *may* contain a *prefix* or a *suffix*.

11. A **root,** or **radical,** is either a word, or that part of a word which is modified by a prefix or a suffix.

Ex.—*Fair,* un-*fair,* un-*fair*-ness.

12. A **prefix** is that part of a word which is placed before the root to modify its meaning.

Ex.—*Re*-turn, *pre*-pay, *un*-fit.

13. A **suffix** is that part of a word which is placed after a root to modify its meaning.

Ex.—Heart-*less,* child-*hood,* good-*ness.*

NOTE.—In analyzing a word according to its significant parts, point out the root, then the prefix or the suffix, and show how it modifies the root.

14. Words are varied by prefixes, suffixes, or by some change in the root.

Ex.—Bond, bond-*s,* dear, dear-*est, she*-goat, man, men, write, wrote.

15. The variation is called,—

Inflection, when it affects neither the part of speech, nor the essential meaning of the word, but merely exhibits some grammatical property, such as comparison, number, tense, &c.

Ex.—Fair, fair-*est,* church, church-*es,* bond, bound.

Derivation, when it gives rise to a new, though related, meaning, or to a change in the part of speech.

Ex.—Fair, *un*-fair-*ly, un*-fair-*ness.* Here we have the negative of the root, and three different parts of speech.

REMARK.—Words are properly called declinable only as they admit of inflection. Thus, farm-**er**-*s* and *be*-neath are both derivatives, the one declinable, the other indeclinable.

22. Exercise.

MODELS FOR ANALYZING WORDS.

(1.) **In reference to their sounds.**

Faithfulness .. is a trisyllable; repeat (**21, 4.**)
Faith . . . . . is the accented syllable; repeat (**21, 6.**)
ful and *ness* . are unaccented syllables.

Change the accent first to *ful*, then to *ness;* restore it to its true place.

Analyze each syllable (**19**).

1. *Analyze and describe the following words:*—

Beat, said, tree; friendship, social, himself, stately; complaining, interpret, indolence; incessantly, condemnation, interdicting, domesticate; consanguinity, confederation, impenetrable; mispronunciation, incomprehensible, indefatigable; impenetrability; incomprehensibility.

2. *Correct the accent in the following words:*—

Local′, indo′lence, memo′rable, ig′noble, frequent′ly, lament′able, actu′al, indispu′table, immuta′ble, retro′spect, com′pletion, late′ral.

3. *Change the accent in the following words to the second syllable, and give their meaning:*—

Au′gust, con′jure, des′ert, en′trance, min′ute, pres′ent, proj′ect, in′valid.

4. *Write the following words upon your slate, and divide them into syllables, marking the accented syllable:*—

Conscience, detecting, inability, indubitable, commotion, laborious, relate, detestation, infesting, exemplary.

MODEL.—Con′science.

(2.) **In reference to their significant parts.**

Impenitent . has two significant parts.
Penitent . . is the root, and signifies *repenting.*
Im . . . . . is the prefix (*in*, see **5**, Rem. 2), and signifies, *not.*

Hence, **Impenitent,** *not repenting.*

Point out the roots, prefixes, and suffixes in the following words:—

Impenitent, shapeless, learning, goodness, insight, unfair, deface, begging.

23. Primitive, Derivative, and Compound Words.

1. A word in no way derived from a root is a **primitive** word.

Ex.—*Form, harm.*

SPELLING. 31

2. A word formed by joining to a root a prefix or a suffix, to modify its meaning, is a **derivative** word.

Ex.—*Re*-form, harm-*less*.

3. A word formed by uniting two or more entire words is a **compound** word.

Ex.—*Inkstand, schoolhouse.*

4. The parts of those compounds which have been long in use are generally united closely.

Ex.—*Nevertheless, sunrise.*

In others, the hyphen (-) is used to separate the parts.

Ex.—*Labor-saving.*

24. Exercise.

1. *Tell which of the following words are* PRIMITIVE, *which* DERIVATIVE, *and which* COMPOUND, *and point out their parts:*—

Bright, fair, told, meek, some, playful, joyless, income, bookstore, play-mate, cloud-capped, ink, housetop, fearful, reform, dismember, dreary.

2. *Form derivative words from the following primitives, and draw a line under the added syllable or letter:*—

Hope, fear, harm, love, care, know, peer, ape, weed, cloud, form, grade, place, joy, truth, poet, fade, weep, laugh.

MODEL.—HOPE*less*.

3. *Form compound words by joining some appropriate word to each of the following:*—

Air, chest, alms, bank, birth, bill, fire, eye, weed, toll, wood, foot, work, play, land, busy, tree, breeze.

MODEL.—Air-*pump*.

SPELLING.
25. Spelling Defined.

Spelling is the art of representing words by their proper letters.

It may be treated of under the three classes of words, *primitive, derivative,* and *compound.*

PRIMITIVE WORDS.
26. Rules for Primitives.

NOTE.—The spelling of primitive words should be learned mainly from the dictionary or the spelling-book. The following are the most obvious rules:—

1. RULE I.—Monosyllables ending in *f, l,* or *s,* preceded by a single vowel, double the final consonant.

Ex.—*Stuff, bell, miss. If, of, as, gas, was, has, yes, is, his, this, us, thus,* are exceptions.

2. RULE II.—Words ending in any other consonant than *f, l,* or *s,* do not double the final letter.

Ex.—*Put, rap, on, trim, brag, star. Add, odd, ebb, egg, inn, bunn, err, burr, purr, butt, buzz, fuzz,* are exceptions.

DERIVATIVE WORDS—PREFIXES.
27. Rules for applying Prefixes.

NOTE.—In applying prefixes to radicals, certain changes often take place, to render the sound more agreeable. (5, Rem. 2.) These changes are made according to the following rules:—

1. RULE I.—DROPPING THE FINAL LETTER.—The final letter of a prefix is sometimes omitted.

Ex.—*Co*-existent, for *con*-existent; *ant*-arctic, for *anti*-arctic.

2. RULE II.—CHANGING THE FINAL LETTER.—The final letter of a prefix is often changed to one which will harmonize in sound with the initial letter of the root. (5, Rem. 2.)

Ex.—*Im*-pious, for *in*-pious.

(*a.*) The final letter of the prefix generally becomes the same as the first letter of the root.

Ex.—*Ill*-limitable, *ir*-radiate, *ac*-cept, *op*-pose.

(*b.*) The principal prefixes which undergo this change are,—

Ad = ac, af, ag, al, an, ap, ar, as, at;

ORTHOGRAPHY—DERIVATIVES. 33

Con = co, cog, com, col, cor;
En = em;
E = ex, ec, ef;
Dis = dif, di;

Ob = of, oc, op;
Sub = suc, suf, sug, sup, sur, sus;
Syn = sym, syl;
Trans = tran, tra.

DERIVATIVE WORDS—SUFFIXES.
28. Rules for applying Suffixes.

NOTE.—In applying suffixes, the final letter or letters of the radical are often changed. Such changes are made according to the following rules:—

1. RULE I.—DOUBLING THE FINAL LETTER.—On receiving a suffix beginning with a vowel, the final consonant of a monosyllable, or of any word accented on the last syllable, is doubled, if the root ends with a single consonant preceded by a single vowel; otherwise it remains single.

Ex.—Dig-*ing*, *digging;* defer-*ing*, *deferring*.

So *appeal'*, becoming in the derivative *appel'*, gives *appel'lant*. Not so *repair-ing*, *defend-ing*, *differ-ing*. *Acquit*, following the rule, gives *acquitted*, since *qu* = *kw*.

(*a.*) In many words ending in *l*, as *travel*, *libel*, *cancel*, *cavil*, *chisel*, *counsel*, *duel*, *equal*, *gravel*, *marvel*, *model*, *pencil*, *revel*, *rival*, *trammel*, *tunnel*, *argil*, &c., some double the *l* on adding a suffix beginning with a vowel, though the accent is not on the last syllable; others follow the rule. To these words add *worship*, *bias*, *kidnap;* *worship-ping*, *bias-sing*, *kidnap-ping*.

(*b.*) As x final is equivalent to *ks*, it is never doubled.
Ex.—*Mix, mixed, mixing*.

(*c.*) When in the derivative word the accent is changed to a preceding syllable of the root, the final letter is not always doubled.

Ex.—From *prefer'*, we have *pref'erence*, and *pref'erable;* from *refer'*, *ref'erence*, and *ref'erable* or *refer'rible;* *infer'*, *in'ference*, *in'ferable*, *infer'rible;* *transfer'*, *trans'ferable* or *transfer'rible*.

The derivatives of *excel'*, and of some other words, though the accent is changed, still double the final letter.

Ex.—*Excel', ex'cellent, ex'cellence*.

2. RULE II.—DROPPING THE FINAL LETTER.—On receiving a suffix beginning with a vowel, in words ending in *e* silent, the final vowel of the radical is dropped.

C

Ex.—Love-*ing, loving;* love-*ed, loved.*

It is also dropped in some words ending in *y* and *i.*

Ex.—Felicity-*ate, felicitate;* dei-*ism, deism.*

(*a.*) Contrary to the general rule, the final *e* is retained when preceded by *c* or *g*, to preserve the soft sound of these letters.

Ex.—Peace-*able, peaceable;* change-*able, changeable.* So, also, we have *singeing* and *swingeing,* to distinguish them from *singing, swinging.*

(*b.*) The final letters *le,* when followed by *ly,* are dropped.

Ex.—Noble-*ly, nobly.*

So, also, *t* or *te* before *ce* or *cy.*

Ex.—Vagrant-*cy, vagrancy;* prelate-*cy, prelacy.*

(*c.*) Words ending in *ll* usually drop one *l* on taking an additional syllable beginning with a consonant.

Ex.—Skill-*ful, skilful.*

(*d.*) Sometimes when the final *e* is preceded by a vowel, it is dropped before a suffix beginning with a consonant.

Ex.—*True, truly; awe, awful.*

Sometimes it is retained.

Ex.—*Rue, rueful; shoe, shoeless.*

The final *e* preceded by a consonant is dropped before a suffix beginning with a consonant, in the words *whole, wholly; judge, judgment; abridge, abridgment; acknowledge, acknowledgment.*

3. RULE III.—CHANGING THE FINAL LETTER.— The final *y* of a root is generally changed to *i*, if preceded by a consonant; otherwise it usually remains unchanged.

Ex.—Happy-*est, happiest;* duty-*es, duties;* day-*s, days.*

(*a.*) Before the terminations *ly* and *ness,* some words, as *shy, dry,* do not change the final *y*. To prevent doubling *i*, the *y* is not changed when the suffix begins with *i*.

Ex.—Marry-*ing, marrying.*

For the same reason, the *e* being dropped by Rule II., in *die, lie, tie, vie,* the *i* is changed to *y*.

Ex.—*Dying, lying, tying, vying.*

(*b.*) The *f*, in words ending in *f* or *fe*, is often changed to *v*, when the suffix begins with a vowel.

ORTHOGRAPHY—COMPOUND WORDS. 35

Ex.—*Life,* by (**28,** 2,) *lif,*—plural *liv-es, lives.*

(c.) From *lay, pay, say,* and *stay,* though *y* is preceded by a vowel, we have *laid, paid, said,* and *staid.* So from *day,* we have *daily;* and from *gay, gaily* and *gaiety;* though better written *gayly* and *gayety.*

29. Exercise.

1. *Change by rule, and prefix* ANTI *to* arctic; CON *to* temporary, laborer, extensive, location, mend, mix, mingle, nomen, relative; AD *to* scribe, credit, firm, fluent, legation, rest, point, ply, tempt; IN *to* religious, legal, legible, liberal, mature, noble, perfect, pertinent, penitent, potent, prove, relevant; EN *to* body, broil; OB *to* position, press, cur, fend; SUB *to* cession, fix, fumigation, fusion, gest, press, render; SYN *to* pathetic, logistic; EX *to* centric, flux; DIS *to* fuse, late.

2. *Apply the preceding rules by adding* ING, ED, *or* ER, *to* beg, sit, dig, dim, bed, dog, let, bet, prefer, transfer, forget, dispel, propel, befit, control, travel, level, counsel; love, compile, receive, leave, grieve, confine, define. *Add* ABLE *to* peace, change, sale; LY *to* able, disagreeable, conformable, idle, noble; FUL *to* skill, will; ES, ED, *or* ING, *to* duty, lily, glory, story, history, beauty, beautify, amplify, rectify.

3. *Correct the following, and explain your corrections:*—

Beding, beting, wifes, debared, abhorent, alkalioid, gloryous, citys, fanciful, tarriing, carriing, dutyful, bountyful, handsomeest, bloting, fameous, agreeabley, incompatibley.

COMPOUND WORDS.
30. Formation of Compound Words.

1. Compound words usually follow the orthography of the *primitive* words of which they are composed.

2. In compounds which are closely united (**23,** 4), *full* and *all* drop the final *l.*

Ex.—*Handful, careful, fulfil, always, although, withal.*

But in those compounds which are merely temporary, the *ll* is retained.

Ex.—*Full-faced, chock-full, all-wise.*

3. When possessives are compounded with other words, they often drop the apostrophe.

Ex.—*Herdsman, helmsman* (**185,** 11, *a*).

4. *Chilblain, welcome, welfare,* and *fulfil,* drop one *l; shepherd, wherever,* and *whosoever,* drop an *e;* and *wherefore* and *therefore* assume an *e*.

31. Exercise.

1. *Correct the errors in the following examples, and give the rule by which each correction is made:—*

Wil, kniting, frized, clif, peacable, bur, stil, manumited, buieth, occuring, differring, begg, knel, bels, mobb, bigotted, whigism, gass, coquetish, swiming, cryeth, spyed, shily, shuned, veryest, maiest, interruptting, spoonful, al-powerful, allways, somthing, stilyards, defering, prevailling.

QUESTIONS.—What is Grammar? What is English Grammar? To what does it relate? Into how many parts is it divided? Of what does Orthography treat? Etymology? Syntax? Prosody? What is an elementary sound? How many elementary sounds are there in the English language? How are they divided? Of what do vocals consist? Subvocals? Aspirates? How are vocals divided? What is the long sound? The short? How are the subvocals divided? Describe the continuous; the explosive; the semivocals. Which aspirates are breathings? How formed? What is said of the remaining subvocals and aspirates? Give the pairs called correlatives or cognates. What are the first four pairs? The remaining ones? Why are they called mutes? Give the liquids. Why so called? Pronounce, in order, the words in the table, then give the sound of the element in Italics. What is a letter? How many letters are there in the English alphabet? What is the name of a letter? The power? How are letters divided, in respect to *form,—sound,—application?* How are capitals used? What letters are called vowels? Consonants? Repeat the rules for the use of capitals. Italics. When have we a combination of letters? What is a diphthong? A proper diphthong? An improper diphthong? A triphthong? A proper triphthong? An improper triphthong? When are two consonants said to unite? What may unite with a vowel sound? What is a syllable? How many syllables has every word? How are the consonants applied? Repeat the *Caution.* Divide the words in the first part of Exercise 12 into syllables. Of what does a word, when considered in reference to its sound, consist? What is a word of one syllable called? Of two syllables? Of three syllables? Of four or more syllables? What is accent? What words have an accent? Which may the accented syllable be? Give an example of a primary and a secondary accent. Mention the significant parts of a word. What is a root? A prefix? A suffix? Define a primitive word. A derivative. A compound. Define spelling. Give the rules for spelling primitive words. Give the rules for applying prefixes. For suffixes. For compound words.

ETYMOLOGY.

32. Definitions.

1. **Etymology** treats of the classification, the derivation, and the various modifications of words.

2. A word is the sign of an idea, and is either spoken or written.

33. Classes of Words.

1. According to their *meaning* and *use*, words are divided into eight classes, called *Parts of Speech*.

REMARKS.—Words are divided, according to their *sounds* in pronunciation, into *monosyllables, dissyllables, trisyllables*, and *polysyllables* (21); according to their *significant parts*, into *primitive, derivative,* and *compound* (23). So far as the treatment of roots, prefixes, and suffixes pertains to the simple union of syllables into complete words, it belongs to Orthography. It becomes, however, a department of Etymology when the modifying influence of the significant elements is considered.

2. Words which vary their forms in *construction* are called *declinable*. Those which do not vary them are *indeclinable*.

Ex.—Friend, friend-*s;* love, lov-*ed* (declinable); but, as, upon (indeclinable).

PARTS OF SPEECH.
34. Parts of Speech defined.

1. In English, there are eight parts of speech,—the *Noun*, the *Adjective*, the *Pronoun*, the *Verb*, the *Adverb*, the *Preposition*, the *Conjunction*, and the *Interjection*.

2. A *noun* is the name of an object.

Ex.—*Fruit, Henry, Boston.*

The word *noun* is derived from the Latin "nomen," *a name*. All words which are the names of *persons, animals, places,* or *things,* material or immaterial, are nouns.

3. An *adjective* is a word used to limit or qualify a noun.

Ex.—*Good, faithful, this, some.*

Adjective (derived from the Latin "adjectus," *added to*, i.e. to a noun) is a term applying to a large class of words which are added to nouns to express their qualities or to define them.

Ex.—*Worthy* citizens; *this* book.

Those words which are united to nouns answering such questions as *What? What kind? How many?* are adjectives.

4. A *pronoun* is a word which takes the place of a noun.

Ex.—*I, he, you, who.*

The word pronoun (derived from the Latin "pro," *for*, and "nomen," *a name*) applies to a small number of different words; yet any noun may be represented by a pronoun. The noun, the adjective, and the pronoun are intimately connected: the first is the *name of* an object; the second expresses the *properties* of an object; the third may take the *place* of the first.

5. A *verb* is a word which expresses *being, action,* or *state.*

Ex.—*Be, read, sleep, is loved.*

Nothing can be affirmed without a verb. The term is derived from the Latin "verbum," *the word,* i.e. the important word: it designates a large class of words.

6. An *adverb* is a word used to modify the meaning of a *verb,* an *adjective,* a *participle,* or another *adverb.*

Ex.—*Quickly, first, far.*

Adverb (from the Latin "ad" and "verbum," *added to a verb*) is the name given to those words which are added to verbs, adjectives, or other adverbs, to denote *time, place, manner,* &c.

7. A *preposition* is a word used to show the relation between a noun or a pronoun and some other word.

Ex.—*From, upon, on, with.*

This part of speech includes a small list of words which are used to denote the relations of *place, time, cause, manner, property, quality,* &c. It is called a preposition (from the Latin "*præ,*" *before,* and "*positio,*" *a placing; a placing before*) from the circumstance of its being commonly placed before the object with which it is always associated.

8. A *conjunction* is a word used to connect sentences, or the parts of sentences.

Ex.—*And, but, or.*

The conjunction includes but a small number of words, which are used to join the parts of a sentence: it is derived from the Latin "conjunctus," *joined together.*

9. An *interjection* is used to express some strong or sudden emotion of the mind.

Ex.—*O! alas!*

The term interjection (from the Latin "interjectus," *thrown between*) is applied to a few words that do not enter into the structure of a sentence, but are thrown in at pleasure.

10. The noun, the pronoun, the adjective, the verb, and the adverb are *declinable;* the rest are *indeclinable.*

NOUNS.
35. Definition and Distinctions.

1. **A noun** is the name of an object.

Ex.—*House, tree, Boston, goodness.*

REMARK.—The word *object,* as here used, should be carefully distinguished from the same term employed in Syntax to denote the complement of the transitive verb. It here denotes every species of existence, material or immaterial, which may be considered independently or alone; and is opposed to the term *attribute,* which always represents something dependent upon, belonging to, or inherent in, an object. An attribute, when regarded as an object to the mind, that is, when *abstracted* from that to which it belongs, becomes an object of itself. The *name* of such an attribute is a noun, and is usually derived from the word denoting the attribute.

Ex.—*Good, good-ness; bright, bright-ness.*

2. Whenever a word, a syllable, a letter, or a symbol of any kind is spoken of as an object, it is a noun.

Ex.—*We* is a personal pronoun. *Un* is a prefix. *A* is a vowel. + is the sign of addition. , is a comma.

3. So, when a phrase, or a clause of a sentence, is used to denote an object, it becomes a noun.

Ex.—*To see the sun* is pleasant. *That you have wronged me* doth appear in this.

REMARK.—The noun is often called a *substantive*. All phrases or clauses, when used as nouns, and even pronouns, are called *substantives*.

36. Proper and Common Nouns.

1. Nouns are divided into two classes,—*proper* and *common*.

2. A *proper* noun is the name of an individual object.

Ex.—*James, Erie.*

Such plural names as *Romans, Alps, Azores*, are commonly considered proper nouns, because a whole group is regarded as an individual.

3. A *common* noun is a name which applies to each individual of a class of objects.

Ex.—*Man, boy, house.*

4. As a proper noun denotes simply an individual by itself, whenever it is made to represent an individual as belonging to a class, it becomes a common noun.

Ex.—"He is the *Cicero* of his age," *i.e.* a distinguished *orator*.

Still, when the same name, as *Thomas*, happens to be given to several persons, but to each individually by itself, it is as truly a proper name as though it had been given to one alone.

5. Common nouns, on the contrary, may become proper, when, by personification or special use, the object named is regarded as an individual.

Ex.—O *Justice*, thou art fled to brutish beasts, and men have lost their reason. The *Common*. The *Park*.

6. Under the head of common nouns are commonly reckoned *collective, abstract*, and *verbal* nouns.

7. A **collective** noun is one which, in the singular, denotes more than one object.

Ex.—*Army, family, flock.*

8. An **abstract** noun is the name of a *quality* or of an *action*, considered apart from the object to which it belongs.

Ex.—*Goodness, virtue, wisdom, movement.*

9. A **verbal** noun is a *participle* used as a noun.

Ex.—He was convicted of *stealing.*

REMARK.—The *infinitive* is a kind of verbal noun: as, " *To see* the sun is pleasant."

10. Nouns which denote *substance* or *kind*, without reference to an individual, are common nouns.

Ex.— *Wood, grass, music, earth, algebra.*

37. Exercise.

1. *Tell which of the following words designate objects, and which properties; then select the nouns:—*

Horse, old, good, peach, vine, heavy, hard, strong, hill, star, empty, ocean, hilly, wright, William, European, engine, road, stile, rose, upright, smoke, balloon, oyster, sea, chariot, wild, hungry, farm, evil.

2. *Select the nouns in the following sentence:—*

As soon as the sun was seen coming over the hills, the farmer aroused the laborers from slumber, who, with their scythes on their shoulders, and pitchforks in their hands, marched gayly to the field to begin the labors of the day.

3. *Tell which of the following nouns are common, and which are proper:—*

Posterity, virtue, Rome, tea, Nero, Cicero, Germany, Paris, pomp, sunshine, meadow, Pekin, gulf, Medici, astronomy, Darius, father, calico, London, dungeon, district, Japan.

4. *Tell which of the following common nouns are abstract, which are collective, and which are verbal:—*

Army, tasting, goodness, heat, harmless, rising, sailing, wisdom, flock, wonder, teaching, energy, frankness, freedom, multitude, teething, shutting, dulness, company.

5. *Change the following names of properties into abstract nouns:—*

Good, cheerful, diligent, rapid, dark, strong, heavy, lovely, brilliant, beautiful, flaming, brave, swift, solid, easy. Thus, good*ness*.

6. *Write the names of fifteen objects in this room. Select all the nouns from page — in your Reader.* (*Let the teacher assign the page.*)

7. *Fill the blanks in the following examples with nouns of your own selection:—*

——— is short. ——— are strong. ——— have fallen. ——— is a quadruped. ——— were destroyed. ——— will decay. ——— will rise at six o'clock. ——— is the king of beasts. ——— was the father of his country. ——— was a tyrant. ——— were overthrown in the Red Sea. ——— mourned for Absalom. ——— shine at night.

38. Properties of Nouns.

To nouns belong the properties of *person, number, gender,* and *case.*

39. Person of Nouns.

1. **Person** is that property of a noun or a pronoun which shows the relation of the speaker to the object (**35,** Rem.) spoken of.

2. The object spoken of may be—(1) the *speaker himself,* (2) the person *spoken to,* or (3) a party neither speaking nor spoken to, but merely *spoken of.* Hence,—

3. There are three persons,—the *first,* the *second,* and the *third.*

4. The *first* person denotes the speaker.

Ex.—*I, John,* saw these things.

Remark.—Observe, here, that "*I*" denotes the one spoken of, as well as the one speaking.

5. The *second* person denotes the person spoken to.

Ex.—*Children,* obey your parents.

Here *ye* or *you* understood, meaning *children,* denotes the party spoken to, and also that spoken of.

6. The *third* person denotes the person or thing spoken of.

Ex.—*Thomas* did not come. The *harvest* is abundant.

Here *Thomas* and *harvest* represent *merely* the party spoken of.

ETYMOLOGY—PERSON OF NOUNS. 43

REMARK.—The first or the second person as such, *alone*, is never *represented* in any sentence. Yet every sentence presupposes a first, a second, and a third person. It is the last of these only which rightfully demands expression. The third person *must* be expressed. Hence, when the first or the second becomes also the third, it is for that reason that it claims a place in the sentence. But the mere *name* of the speaker or the hearer would represent him only as the party *spoken of*. It requires, therefore, the word *I* or *you* to represent him both as *speaking* and *spoken of* or *spoken to* at the same time.

7. A noun in the first or the second person is never used as the subject or the object of a verb, but may be put in apposition with either, for the purpose of explanation.

Ex.—I, *Paul*, beseech you. The salutation of me, *Paul*.

8. The names of inanimate objects are in the second person when the objects to which they apply are spoken to. Objects thus addressed are personified, and are treated as though they were actual hearers.

Ex.—And I have loved thee, *Ocean*.

40. Exercise.

1. *Tell the person of the nouns in the following sentences:—*

Nero was a tyrant. Children, obey your parents. Philip, thou art a man. Delays are dangerous. His praise, ye brooks, attune. The ferryman took us safely across the river. Keep thy heart with all diligence. King Philip was the last of the Wampanoags. "Let my country be thine," said his preserver. Seest thou a man diligent in his business? he shall stand before kings. Babylon, how art thou fallen! I, Daniel, was grieved in my spirit.

2. *Fill the blanks in the following expressions; tell the person of the noun or the pronoun inserted:—*

———— was executed for murder. ———— art the man. The lady lost ———— purse and all ———— contents. ———— are willing to remain. ———— has strangely ended. ———— delight in surf bathing. The father called ———— sons and ———— daughters around ————. The duke was esteemed for ———— uprightness, and the duchess beloved for ———— kindness. Art ———— a spirit of earth or air? ———— wast wrong to urge me so.

41. Number of Nouns.

1. **Number** is that property of a noun (or a pronoun) which distinguishes one object from more than one.

2. Nouns have two numbers,—the *singular* and the *plural*.

3. The *singular* number denotes but one object.

Ex.—*Horse, river, nation.*

4. The *plural* denotes more than one object.

Ex.—*Horses, rivers, nations.*

42. Regular Formation of the Plural.

1. The plural of nouns is *regularly* formed,—

(*a.*) By adding **s**, when the singular ends with a sound that can unite or coalesce with *s*.

Ex.—*Book, books; tree, trees.*

(*b.*) By adding **es**, when the singular ends with a sound that cannot coalesce with *s*.

Ex.—*Box, boxes; church, churches.*

2. When *es* is added, *s* has the sound of *z*.

Ex.—*Fox, foxes; branch, branches.*

When *s* only is added, it has the sound of *z* when it unites or coalesces with a vowel.

Ex.—*Folio, folios; flea, fleas.*

It follows the rule (**15**, 3) for the combination of consonants when it follows a consonant; that is, it is *s* aspirate when it unites with an aspirate.

Ex.—*Hat, hats; cap, caps; surf, surfs; clock, clocks.*

It is *s* subvocal (or *z*) when it follows a subvocal.

Ex.—*Lad, lads; log, logs; ball, balls; farm, farms; fan, fans; war, wars.*

3. The *s* or *es* adds a syllable when it does not coalesce with the final syllable of the singular.

Ex.—*Church, church-es; race, rac-es; cage, cag-es.*

The *s* or *es* does not add a syllable when it coalesces with the final syllable.

Ex.—*Work, works; echo, echoes.*

43. Irregular Formation of the Plural.

1. When the final *s*, contrary to the rule (**42**, 2), is subvocal, after the aspirate sounds *f, fe*, the *f* must be changed (**15**, 3) into its correlative *v*.

Ex.—*Loaf, loaves; life, lives; sheaf, sheaves; thief, thieves.*

When *s* is aspirate, as in the plural of *dwarf, brief, scarf, reef, chief, grief, kerchief, handkerchief, gulf, surf, turf, serf, proof, hoof, roof, safe, fife, strife,* the *f* is not changed. *Staff,* when meaning a stick, has *staves* for its plural; when meaning a set of officers, it has *staffs*. The plural of *wharf,* in the United States, is *wharves;* in England, *wharfs*.

2. The *s* added to *th* aspirate is also subvocal (except in *truth, youth,* and, it may be, a few other words), and would cause a similar change in the orthography of the plural, were not the correlative (6) also represented by *th*.

Ex.—*Oath, oaths; bath, baths.*

3. Most nouns ending in *o* preceded by a consonant, add *es*, notwithstanding *s* alone would coalesce with *o* (**42**, 1).

Ex.—*Cargo, cargoes.*

Zero, canto, grotto, quarto, junto, duodecimo, octavo, solo, portico, tyro, halo, piano, memento, add only *s*. Yet by some writers *es* is added.

Nouns ending in *o* preceded by a vowel, follow the general rule.

Ex.—*Folio, folios; cameo, cameos.*

4. Nouns ending in *y* preceded by a consonant (**28**, 3), change *y* into *ies*.

Ex.—*Glory, glories; mercy, mercies.*

Formerly these words in the singular ended in *ie*. Their plurals were then formed regularly.

Ex.—*Glorie, mercie.*

Nouns ending in *y* preceded by a vowel, form the plural regularly.

Ex.—*Day, days; key, keys.*

5. The following plurals are very irregular:—

Man, men; woman, women; ox, oxen; goose, geese; child, children; foot, feet; louse, lice; mouse, mice; cow, formerly *kine; tooth, teeth.*

6. Some nouns have both a regular and an irregular plural; but the two forms have usually different significations.

Ex.—*Brother, brothers* (of the same family); *brethren* (of the same society); *die, dies* (stamps); *dice* (cubes used in gaming); *genius, geniuses* (men of genius); *genii* (spirits); *index, indexes* (tables of reference); *indices* (signs in algebra); *pea, peas* (distinct seeds); *pease* (quantity); *penny, pennies* (coins); *pence* (a sum, or value).

7. Names of substances, and most abstract nouns, commonly have no plural form.

Ex.—*Gold, cider, flax, milk, tar, goodness, darkness.*

When different *kinds* of the substances are referred to, the plural form is used.

Ex.—*Waters, wines, teas.*

8. In compound words, if the word denoting the principal idea is placed first, it is changed to form the plural.

Ex.—*Court-martial, courts-martial; cousin-german, cousins-german; hanger-on, hangers-on.*

But if the principal word is placed last, the final word is changed.

Ex.—*Handful, hand-fuls.*

Both parts, being (apparently) equally prominent, are changed in *man-servant, woman-servant,* and *knight-templar.*

Ex.—*Men-servants, women-servants, knights-templars.*

9. Letters, marks, figures, and signs are pluralized by adding '*s*.

Ex.—The *s's;* the *i's;* the **'s;* the 9*'s;* the + *'s.*

10. When other parts of speech are used as nouns, their plurals are formed regularly.

Ex.—The *ifs* and *buts.* The *whys* and *wherefores.* At *sixes* and *sevens.*

11. Many nouns from foreign languages retain their original plurals.

ETYMOLOGY—NOUNS—NUMBER. 47

EXAMPLES.—Antithesis, antitheses; arcanum, arcana; automaton, automata; axis, axes; bandit, banditti; basis, bases; beau, beaux; cherub, cherubim; criterion, criteria; crisis, crises; datum, data; desideratum, desiderata; encomium, encomia; effluvium, effluvia; erratum, errata; ellipsis, ellipses; focus, foci; formula, formulæ; genus, genera; hypothesis, hypotheses; madame, mesdames; magus, magi; memorandum, memoranda; medium, media; minutia, minutiæ; metamorphosis, metamorphoses; monsieur, messieurs; nebula, nebulæ; phenomenon, phenomena; radius, radii; seraph, seraphim; stimulus, stimuli; stratum, strata; stamen, stamina; vortex, vortices.

44. Plural of Proper Names.

1. SINGLE NAMES.—The proper name of an individual object has no plural.

2. When several of the same name or family are spoken of together, the name takes the plural form.

Ex.—The *Tudors;* The twelve *Cæsars.*

3. So, also, the proper names of *races, communities,* and *nations,* are plural.

Ex.—The *Indians;* The *Jesuits;* The *Romans.*

4. The plurals of proper names are formed, as a general rule, according to the analogy of common names.

Ex.—*Canada, Canadas; Jew, Jews; Ptolemy, Ptolemies.*

5. COMPLEX NAMES.—When two or more names, applied to the same individual, stand in a sort of apposition to each other, they are generally considered as one complex name, and are made plural by varying the last only.

Ex.—The *George Washingtons.* May there not be Sir *Isaac Newtons* in every science?—*Watts.*

6. A TITLE AND A NAME.—When a title, as Miss, Mrs., Mr., Messrs., Gen., Capt., or Dr., is prefixed to a proper name, usage has not been uniform in the formation of the plural. Sometimes the *title,* sometimes the *name,* and sometimes *both,* have been varied.

Ex.—The *Misses Brown;* The *Miss Thompsons;* The *Misses Winthrops.*

7. In all these cases, the relative prominence of the name and title, for the most part, determines the plural form. Thus,—

(*a.*) When the *name* is made prominent, that alone, and not the title, takes the plural form. In speaking of three persons by the *name* of Brown, we should say (**44,** 2), "The three Browns;" thus distinguishing them from the *Smiths,* or those of any other name. Now, with this idea uppermost, if we wished also to distinguish them as young ladies, we should add, *incidentally,* the distinctive title,—"*the three Miss Browns.*" So, the *Dr. Smiths.*

(*b.*) When the *title* is to be made prominent, that alone should be varied. Thus, if we should speak of three persons, and say, *the three Misses,* we should distinguish them, as ladies, from so many gentlemen; in the same way we say, *the two Drs., the three Generals.* If now, with the title prominent, we would incidentally add the name, we should say, (1) if the names were *different,* "the three *Misses Brown, Atwood, and Putnam;*" (2) if the *same,* "*the three Misses Brown,*" and especially so without the numeral; as, "the *Misses Brown.*" In the former of these cases, if the *name* were prominent, we should say, "Miss *Brown,* Miss *Atwood,* and Miss *Putnam.*"

(*c.*) When two titles are made equally prominent, they are both varied.

Ex.—The *Lords Bishops* of Durham and St. David's; The *Knights Baronets* (**43,** 8).

And so it would seem, by the same law, that, when a *title* and a *name* are made equally emphatic, they should both be varied. Thus, the *Misses* Winthrop, in distinction from the *Messrs.* Winthrop; and the *Misses Winthrops,* in distinction from the *Messrs. Mortons.* Yet usage seems to be nearly uniform in placing the plural name after *Mrs,*—as, "the *Mrs. Whites,*"—and the plural title before the names, when persons of different names are mentioned together; as, "the *Misses* Wilson and Everett; *Messrs.* Little and Brown."

45. Remarks on the Number of Nouns.

1. NOUNS WITHOUT A PLURAL.—Proper nouns, except as in (**44,** 2, 3), and nouns denoting substance (**43,** 7), except when different sorts are expressed, have no plural.

Ex.—*Gold, grass, wine.*

2. NOUNS WITHOUT THE SINGULAR.—The following nouns have no singular: *scissors, vespers, ashes, clothes, billiards, ides, vitals, bellows, drawers, nippers, tongs, shears,* &c. *Lungs, bowels,* and some others, have a singular denoting a part of the whole. *Embers, oats, literati, antipodes, intestines,* are seldom used in the singular.

3. The following words are plural in respect to their original form, but singular or plural in respect to their meaning: *alms, amends, news, riches, pains* (meaning *effort*), *odds, wages, molasses, series, suds, corps, measles, tidings, mumps, rickets, nuptials;* as also the names of some of the sciences; as, *mathematics, ethics, optics, statics, mechanics, mnemonics.*

NOTE.—*News* is now regarded as singular; so also are *measles* and *molasses*, although they have the plural form.

4. NOUNS EITHER SINGULAR OR PLURAL.—Some nouns are alike in both numbers.

Ex.—*Deer, sheep, swine, vermin, hose, fry, trout, salmon, brace, couple, dozen, yoke, gross.*

46. Exercise.

1. *Tell which of the following nouns are singular, and which are plural:*—

Daughter, day, chairs, watches, apple, pears, stars, oats, coat, goose, oxen, nails, inkstand, horn, darkness, hearts, hoof, books, bundle, scissors, news, trout, milk, purity, chimneys, automata, beaux, genus.

2. *Write the plural of the following nouns, and give the rule for the termination:*—

Work, example, lady, oak, horse, hope, box, stratagem, ferry, leaf, storm, bird, bond, thief, sex, day, filly, half, watch, iron, vinegar, turkey, canto, tomato, potato, spoonful, knight-templar, step-father.

3. *Tell the singular of the following:*—

Heroes, pence, strata, teeth, dies, memoranda, children, mice, hypotheses, messieurs, brethren, scissors, seraphim, axes, snuffers, errata, cherubim, sheep, formulæ, swine, solos, flies, knives, riches, mottoes, octavos, courts-martial, inkstands, indices, dozen, genii, wharves.

4. *Correct the following plurals, and give the rule or remarks for the correction:*—

Negros, folioes, vallies, dutys, thiefs, yokes, calfs, phenomenons, criterions, mans, turkies, flys, father-in-laws, grottoes, son-in-laws, cups-full, echoes.

47. Gender of Nouns.

1. **Gender** is a distinction of nouns in regard to sex.

2. There are three genders,—the *masculine*, the *feminine*, and the *neuter*.

3. Nouns which denote males are of the *masculine* gender.

Ex.—*Man, king, hero.*

4. Nouns which denote females are of the *feminine* gender.

Ex.—*Woman, queen, mother.*

5. Nouns which denote neither males nor females are of the *neuter* gender.

Ex.—*Tree, rock, paper.*

6. Some nouns denote either males or females.

Ex.—*Parent, child, cousin, friend, neighbor.*

These are sometimes said to be of the *common* gender; but, as the gender of such nouns may generally be determined by the connection, there seems to be no necessity for the distinction. In case the gender is not so determined, such nouns may be called masculine.

7. By a figure of speech, called Personification, the masculine or feminine gender is applied to inanimate objects: thus, we say of a ship, "*She* sails well;" of the sun, "*He* rises in the east." The use of this figure imparts peculiar beauty and animation to language. "*Her* flag streams wildly, and *her* fluttering sails pant to be on their flight." "The meek-eyed morn appears, *mother* of dews."

8. In speaking of the inferior animals, and sometimes even of infants, the distinction of sex is not observed.

Ex.—And it became a *serpent*, and Moses fled from before *it*. The *child* was lying in *its* cradle.

But in speaking of animals distinguished for boldness, size, or any other marked quality peculiar to the male, we attribute to them the masculine gender, even when the sex is not known.

Ex.—The eagle is the *king* of birds.

9. Collective nouns, if they convey the idea of unity, or take the plural form, are *neuter*.

Ex.—The army, on *its* approach, raised a shout of defiance.

But if they convey the idea of plurality without the plural form, they take the gender of the individuals which compose the collection.

Ex.—The jury could not agree upon *their* verdict.

10. When the sexes are distinguished by different words (48, 1), the masculine is used to include both sexes.

Ex.—Jenner conferred a great benefit on *man*.

48. Methods of distinguishing the Sexes.

1. By using different words:—

EXAMPLES.—Bachelor, maid; beau, belle; boar, sow; boy, girl; brother, sister; buck, doe; bull, cow; cock, hen; drake, duck; earl, countess; father, mother; gander, goose; horse, mare; husband, wife; king, queen; lad, lass; lord, lady; male, female; man, woman; nephew, niece; ram, ewe; son, daughter; stag, hind; uncle, aunt; wizard, witch; dog, bitch; monk, nun; hart, roe; master, mistress; Mister, Mistress (Mr., Mrs.); papa, mamma; sir, madam; sloven, slut; steer, heifer; youth, damsel; swain, nymph.

(*a.*) Some masculine nouns have no corresponding feminines.

Ex.—*Baker, brewer, porter, carrier.*

While some feminine nouns have no corresponding masculines.

Ex.—*Laundress, seamstress.*

2. By a difference of termination:—

EXAMPLES.—Abbot, abbess; actor, actress; administrator, administratrix; adulterer, adulteress; ambassador, ambassadress; author, authoress; baron, baroness; bridegroom, bride; benefactor, benefactress; count, countess; czar, czarina; dauphin, dauphiness; deacon, deaconess; director, directress; don, donna; duke, duchess; emperor, empress; executor, executrix; governor, governess; heir, heiress; hero, heroine; hunter, huntress; host, hostess; instructor, instructress; Jew, Jewess; landgrave, landgravine; lion, lioness; marquis, marchioness; monitor, monitress; patron, patroness; poet, poetess; priest, priestess; prince, princess; prophet, prophetess; shepherd, shepherdess; tailor, tailoress; testator, testatrix; tiger, tigress; tutor, tutoress; viscount, viscountess; widower, widow; god, goddess; giant, giantess; negro, negress; songster, songstress; sorcerer, sorceress; sultan, sultana.

3. By joining some distinguishing word:—

EXAMPLES.—Land*lord*, land*lady;* gentle*man*, gentle*woman;* pea*cock*, pea*hen; he*-goat, *she*-goat; *man*-servant, *maid*-servant; *male* child, *female* child; *cock*-sparrow, *hen*-sparrow; grand*father*, grand*mother;* English*man*, English*woman;* mer*man*, mer*maid;* school*master*, school*mistress*.

49. Exercise.

1. *Tell which of the following nouns are masculine, which feminine, and which neuter:—*

Picture, walnut, duchess, Spaniard, letter, sailor, queen, priest, curtain, lioness, nun, captain, widow, wizard, deacon, hospital, banner, brother, countess.

2. *Give the feminine gender of the following nouns:—*

Man, abbot, horse, hero, tiger, heir, prophet, Jew, male, lord, widower, husband, beau, uncle, host, poet, gander, sultan, master, king, bridegroom, prince, nephew, duke.

3. *Give the masculine gender of the following:—*

Empress, mother, sister, marchioness, woman, she-goat, electress, witch, doe.

4. *Fill the blanks in the following examples; the first five with common nouns in the masculine gender:—*

——— is patient. ——— loves his sister. ——— reigns king of beasts. ——— exposes his wares for sale. ——— should venerate the old. *The next five with proper or common nouns in the feminine gender:* ——— was Queen of England. ——— entertained her guests with grace. ——— was a distinguished poetess. ——— was the nightingale of Sweden. ——— loves her offspring. *The next five with collective nouns, and tell the gender:* ——— met at the house of a friend. ——— brought in a verdict. ——— were appointed by the chair. ——— must obey its leaders. ——— listened with delight.

5. *Select the nouns in the following example; tell the class, person, number, and gender of each noun:—*

       Thou too sail on, O Ship of State!
       Sail on, O Union, strong and great!
       Humanity, with all its fears,
       With all the hopes of future years,

Is hanging breathless on thy fate!
We know what Master laid thy keel,
What workmen wrought thy ribs of steel.—*Longfellow.*

50. Case of Nouns.

1. **Case** denotes the relation of a noun or a pronoun to other words.

2. There are three cases,—the *nominative*, the *possessive*, and the *objective*.

3. The *nominative* case is the simplest form of the noun, and is commonly used as the subject of a proposition.

Ex.—*George* speaks. The *door* was shut.

4. Besides being the subject of a proposition, the nominative case may be used—1st, as the attribute of a proposition; 2d, to identify the subject or the attribute; 3d, it may be independent of any other word.

Ex.—(1st.) Peter was an *apostle*. The stars are *suns*. (2d.) Milton, the *poet*, was blind. It was John, the beloved disciple. (3d.) *Henry*, attend to your studies. *Mary*, are you ready?

5. The *possessive* case denotes the relation of property or possession.

Ex.—*David's* harp.

6. The possessive singular of nouns is regularly formed by adding an apostrophe (') and the letter s to the nominative.

Ex.—*Man's, David's.*

7. When the plural ends in *s*, the apostrophe only is added.

Ex.—*Boys', ladies'.*

But the (') and *s* are added when the plural ends in any other letter than *s*.

Ex.—*Men's, women's, brethren's.*

8. The possessive termination ('s) in the singular is evidently a contraction of the Anglo-Saxon or Old English genitive *es* or *is*.

The (') in the plural is a modern invention used to denote the possessive case. In Lord Grey's letter to the Prince of Wales, written in the latter part of the twelfth or the first of the thirteenth century, are these expressions:—"Our liege *Lordes* pryve seal;" "The *Kynges* commaundement;" "The *Erles* ground."

9. When the singular ends in *s*, or in a letter or combination of letters having the sound of *s*, and the addition of a syllable would be harsh, the poets and some prose writers add the (') only.

Ex.—*Peleus'* son, *goodness'* sake, *conscience'* sake, *Moses'* seat, *cockatrice'* den.

REMARKS.—Some difference of opinion prevails among writers respecting the form of the possessive in other cases where the singular ends in *s*, some adding the (') only, and some the (') and *s*. Thus, we have *Adams' Express*, or *Adams's Express; Otis' Letters*, or *Otis's Letters*. The weight of authority is in favor of the additional *s*, whenever the laws of euphony will admit; especially if a syllable is added in pronouncing the word; as, *Bates's Sermons*, *Barnes's Notes*.

10. In nouns whose singular and plural are alike (45, 4), the apostrophe should precede the *s* in the singular, and follow it in the plural.

Ex.—*Deer's, deers'; sheep's, sheeps'.*

REMARKS.—For the sound of the apostrophic *s*, and the increase of syllables, see (42, 2, 3.) The use of the apostrophe and *s* to mark the plural of letters and signs (43, 9) has no connection with case.

11. When a noun follows a transitive verb or a preposition, it is in the *objective* case.

Ex.—Thomas opened his *knife*. The bird sat on the *tree*.

12. The *nominative* case answers the question *Who?* or *What?* as, "*Who* writes?" "*John* writes."—"*What* alarms him?" "The *storm* alarms him." The *possessive* case answers the question *Whose?* as, "*Whose* book have you?" "I have my *brother's* book." The *objective* case answers the question *Whom?* or *What?* as, "*Whom* do you see?" "I see the *captain*."—"On *what* does he stand?" "He stands upon the *deck*."

13. The possessive case may be known by its form. But the forms of the nominative and the objective are alike: hence they must be determined by their relation to other words.

ETYMOLOGY—DECLENSION OF NOUNS. 55

51. Declension of Nouns.

The **declension** of a noun is its variation to denote number and case.

EXAMPLES.

1. Boy.

	Singular.	Plural.
Nom.	Boy,	Boys,
Pos.	Boy's,	Boys',
Obj.	Boy;	Boys.

2. Fly.

	Singular.	Plural.
Nom.	Fly,	Flies,
Pos.	Fly's,	Flies',
Obj.	Fly;	Flies.

3. John.

	Singular	Plural.
Nom.	John,	*Wanting.*
Pos.	John's,	
Obj.	John.	

4. Goodness.

	Singular.	Plural.
Nom.	Goodness,	*Wanting.*
Pos.	Goodness',	
Obj.	Goodness.	

52. Exercise.

1. *Put the following nouns in Italics into the possessive case, and let each expression be written on your slates, thus:—*

The *carpenter* axe.   The *carpenter's* axe.

Abraham son.   *David* harp.   *Moses* law.   *Adams* Arithmetic. *Webster* Dictionary. The *coachman* dog barked at the *herdsman* sheep. The *lion* roar aroused the *shepherd* dog. The *farmer* corn was destroyed by his *neighbor* cow.

2. *Give the rule for forming the possessive case.*

3. *Write the following nouns in the possessive plural, and place some appropriate noun after them, thus:—*

The *tailors'* shears. The *men's* apartment.

Tailor, seaman, captain, doctor, brother, valley, folly, alley, ally, hero, arch, child, director, president, sheep.

53. Parsing.

1. *Parsing* consists,—

(1.) In telling the *part of speech*.

(2.) In telling its *properties* or *accidents*.

(3.) In pointing out its *relation* to other words, and giving the *rule* for its construction.

2. In parsing a *noun*,—
(1.) Say it is a *noun*, and why.
(2.) *Common* or *proper*, and why.
(3.) Of the *first*, the *second*, or the *third person*, and why.
(4.) Of the *singular* or the *plural number*, and why.
(5.) Of the *masculine*, the *feminine*, or the *neuter gender*, and why.
(6.) Of the *nominative*, the *possessive*, or the *objective case*, and why.
(7.) The *rule* for construction.

NOTE.—The pupil who has been thoroughly drilled in the Introduction may be able to introduce this third element of parsing, if the teacher choose. The Rules of Syntax will of course be anticipated, if applied here. The teacher can omit or use the rules, as he may think best.

54. Exercise.

MODELS FOR PARSING NOUNS.

Washington, the successful general, was also a true patriot.

Washington is a *noun*,—it is the name of an object; *proper*,—it is the name of an individual object; *third person*,—it denotes the person spoken of; *singular number*,—it denotes but one; *masculine gender*,—it denotes a male; *nominative case*,—it is the subject of the proposition "Washington was a patriot," according to Rule I.: "A noun or pronoun, used as the subject of a proposition, must be in the nominative case."

General ... is a *noun* (why?); *common* (why?); *third person* (why?); *singular number* (why?); *masculine gender* (why?; *nominative case*, and is put in *apposition* with *Washington*. Rule VI.: "A noun or pronoun, used to *explain* or *identify* another noun or pronoun, is put by apposition in the same case."

Patriot ... is a *noun* (why?); *common* (why?); *third person* (why?); *singular number* (why?); *masculine gender* (why?); *nominative case* (why?); it is used as the attribute of the proposition, "Washington was a patriot." Rule II.: "A noun or pronoun, used as the attribute of a proposition, must be in the nominative case."

2. *John, bring me Fanny's History, that book lying on the desk.*

John .. is a proper noun, second person, singular number, masculine gender, and nominative case independent. Rule X.: "The nominative case independent, and the interjection, have no grammatical relation to the rest of the sentence."

Fanny's is a proper noun, third person, singular number, feminine gender, possessive case (why?), and limits *History*. Rule VII.: "A noun or pronoun, used to limit another noun by denoting possession, must be in the possessive case."

History is a common noun, third person, singular number, neuter gender, objective case, and is the object of *bring*. Rule VIII.: "A noun or pronoun, used as the object of a transitive verb, or its participles, must be in the objective case."

Book .. is a common noun, third person, singular number, neuter gender, objective case, and is put in apposition with *History*. Rule VI.

Desk .. is a common noun, third person, singular number, neuter gender, objective case, and is the object of the preposition *on*. Rule XIV.: "A noun or pronoun, used as the object of a preposition, must be in the objective case."

3. *Select the nouns in the following examples, and parse them according to the forms given above:—*

The first land discovered by Columbus was an island, to which he gave the name of San Salvador. King Agrippa, believest thou the prophets? In truth, the proper rest for man is change of occupation.

In autumn there is no sudden blight of youth and beauty; no sweet hopes of life are blasted, no generous aim at usefulness and advancing virtue cut short. The year is drawing to its natural term, the seasons have run their usual course; all their blessings have been enjoyed, and all our precious things are cared for.—*Cooper.*

> One moment I looked from the hill's gentle slope,
>   All hushed was the billow's commotion,
> And methought that the light-house looked lovely as Hope,
>   That star on life's tremulous ocean.—*Moore.*

> Land of the beautiful and brave,
> The freeman's home, the martyr's grave,
> The nursery of giant men,
> Whose deeds are linked with every glen!
>   My own green land for ever!—*Whittier.*

Attention makes the genius; all learning, fancy, and science depend upon it.—*Wilmott.*

4. *Let the whole class parse these or other words on the slate, thus:—*
Washington is N. p. 3d, s. m. nom. R. I.
Fanny's is N. p. 3d, s. f. pos. R. VII.
Desk is N. c. 3d, s. n. obj. R. XIV.

ADJECTIVES.
55. Definitions.

1. An **adjective** is a word used to limit or qualify a noun.

Ex.—A *good* school; a *diligent* boy; *this* table; *ten* men; *the* box.

All words which have the construction of the adjective are here considered under the head of adjectives. The article, like the adjective, belongs to the noun; it has the same construction as the adjective, and is hence placed among adjectives.

2. Every *adjective* is a dependent or subordinate word, and must belong to some noun or pronoun as its principal.

3. When the noun or pronoun to which the adjective belongs has been previously used in the same sentence, or is some indefinite word, as, *person, some one,* or *some thing,* it may be omitted.

Ex.—I will give you *this* book, if you will give me *that* [book]. The kingdom of heaven suffereth violence,(and the *violent* [persons] take it by force.

An adjective belonging to a noun understood or omitted, takes the place of the latter, and is said to be an *adjective used as a noun.*

56. Classes of Adjectives.

1. *Adjectives* are divided into two classes.—*limiting* and *qualifying*.

2. A **limiting** adjective is used to *define* or *restrict* the meaning of a noun, without expressing any of its qualities.

Ex.—*The* house; *five* books; *this* pen; *many* men.

3. *Limiting* adjectives are divided into three classes,—*articles*, *pronominal adjectives*, and *numeral adjectives*.

57. Articles.

1. The particular limiting adjectives, **the**, and **a** or **an**, are called **articles**.

2. *The* is called the **definite** article, because it points out some particular thing.

Ex.—*The* desk; *the* sun.

3. *A* or *an* is called the **indefinite** article, because it does not point out any particular thing.

Ex.—*A* pen; *an* orchard.

4. **An** is used before a vowel sound, and **a** before a consonant sound.

Ex.—*An* apple; *a* pin; *an* hour; *a* union; *an* honor.

Although the article is intimately connected with the limitation of nouns, it is to be regarded rather as the *sign* of limitation than as itself a limiting word. When one says, "*The* man," *the* gives notice to the hearer that some particular man is regarded in the mind of the speaker. He will point out, by limiting or individualizing, who that particular man is. *A* or *an*, again, is a *sign* that the speaker, in regarding a multitude of objects of the same kind, thinks of one, but no specific or particular one. The noun may be limited to show what class or description of objects is meant, but not to show any particular individual. *A* or *an*, however, may be said to limit whenever it prevents a noun from being used in its widest sense.

Ex.—*Man* = the whole human race; *a* man = one man, but no particular one.

The, again, may be said to extend the meaning of a noun in the singular, when it is used in such examples as these: "*The* horse" = all horses. "*The* dog," &c.

5. The article has the construction of the limiting adjective, and is to be parsed like it.

A or *an* is used before nouns in the singular; *the*, before nouns in the singular or plural.

6. Usually no article is needed before nouns used in the *whole extent* of their signification, or nouns denoting an *individual*, whether belonging to a class or not (**36, 4**).

Ex.—*Man* is mortal. *Gold* is precious.

58. Exercise.

Point out the articles in the following examples; tell which are definite and which are indefinite:—

The hat, a book, a knife, a box, an heir, an ox, a plough, an orchard, an industrious man, an honest man, a good citizen, a hill, a huge round stone, the enemy, the union the ewe, a university.

59. Pronominal Adjectives.

1. Those limiting adjectives which may, without the use of the article, represent a noun understood, are called **pronominal adjectives.**

Ex.—*That* (book) is his; *this* is yours.

2. The principal pronominal adjectives are *this, that, these, those, former, latter, which, what, each, every, either, neither, some, one, none, any, other, another, all, whole, such, much, both, few, fewer, fewest, first, last, little, less, least, many, more, most, own, same, several, sundry, certain, divers, enough.*

3. When such adjectives represent a noun understood, they are generally called *pronouns*. They may more properly be called *limiting adjectives* (*pronominal adjectives*) used as nouns.

Ex.—*This* is my book.

The articles never represent a noun understood.

4. Qualifying adjectives may also represent a noun when understood; but the article must be prefixed.

Ex.—*The good* are happy.

5. *All* is sometimes a noun.

Ex.—He robbed me of my house, my goods, my home, my *all*.

Both is frequently a conjunction.

Ex.—I *both* saw and heard him.

6. Among the pronominal adjectives may be distinguished,—

(1.) **Distributives**, or those which point out objects taken singly.

They are *each, every, either, neither*.

(2.) **Demonstratives**, or those which point out objects definitely, showing *which* is meant.

They are *this, that, these, those, former, latter, same*.

(3.) **Indefinites**, or those which point out objects indefinitely.

They are *some, one, none, all, any, whole, such, other, another*.

(4.) **Reciprocals**, or those which are reciprocally related.

They are *each other, one another*.

REMARK.—The *possessives* of the personal pronouns are by some reckoned as pronominal adjectives; namely, *my, mine, our, ours, thy, thine, your, yours, his, her, hers, its, their, theirs*. It is better to regard them as the possessive case of the pronouns.

7. *These, those, all, many, both, few, fewer, fewest, several, sundry*, usually require a noun in the plural.

Ex.—*These* days; *those* plants.

8. *Either* and *neither* are used with reference to two things only. When more than two objects are referred to, *any* and *none* should be used.

Ex.—Take *either* road; both are bad enough; and *neither* will suit you. *Any* of the four plans will meet with favor.

9. *This* refers to the nearer or last-mentioned object; *that*, to the more remote or first-mentioned.

10. *One* and *other* are declined thus:—

	Sing.	Plur.		Sing.	Plur.
Nom.	One,	Ones,	*Nom.*	Other,	Others,
Pos.	One's,	Ones',	*Pos.*	Other's,	Others',
Obj.	One;	Ones.	*Obj.*	Other;	Others.

60. Exercise.

1. *Point out the pronominal adjectives in the following sentences:*—

This rule is preferable to that. These scholars are more studious than those. The former plan has yielded to the latter. Each exercise was well written. Every accused one was acquitted. The first method is better than the last. Many of our hopes are blasted. Few men are of the same mind. Much remains to be said upon all these points. Our own wishes must often be yielded to those of others. More were present than were expected. Little hope was entertained of his recovery. Neither remark was just. The same course was pursued by several of the members. Much harm arises from imprudence. "Unto me, who am less than the least of all saints."

61. Numeral Adjectives.

1. **Numeral adjectives** are those which express number; as, *one, two, three, first, second,* &c.

2. Numeral adjectives are divided into,—

Cardinal, which denote *how many.*

Ex.—*One, two, three,* &c.

Ordinal, which show *which one of a series.*

Ex.—*First, second, third.*

Multiplicative, which show repetition.

Ex.—*Twice,* or *twofold, thrice,* or *threefold,* &c.

3. When a numeral is used as a noun, the cardinal, like the pronominal adjective, takes no article; while the ordinal has the article prefixed.

Ex.—*Two* only were present. The *third* was lost.

62. Exercise.

1. *Apply cardinal numbers to the following nouns; change them to the plural, if necessary:—*

Peach, berry, box, match, cork, shoe, penny, mouse, goose, woman, court-martial, tooth, brother-in-law, handfuls, stratum, index, stamen, cherub, phenomenon.

2. *Correct the following plurals, and apply to each any numeral greater than one or first:—*

Oxes, calfs, sheeps, deers, geeses, 9s, 7s, fs, cherubims, seraphims, swines, vallies, loafs, chimnies, journies, studys, commander-in-chiefs, heros, soloes, grottoes, ladys, spoonsful, trouts, dozens.

63. Qualifying Adjectives.

1. A **qualifying** adjective is one which limits the meaning of a noun, by denoting some *property* or *quality*.

Ex.—A *virtuous* man; a *running* horse.

2. To this class of adjectives belong the participles, which have the *signification* of the verb and the *construction* of the adjective.

3. When the participle is placed before the noun which it modifies, it is called a *participial adjective*.

Ex.—The *rising* sun.

When it is placed after the noun, and is itself limited by other words, it is parsed as a participle.

Ex.—The sun *rising* in the east.

4. When a qualifying adjective represents an object understood, either definite or indefinite, the article *the* must be placed before it.

Ex.—The wise [persons]; the benevolent [ones]; the beautiful, the good, and the true.

When a quality is used abstractly, the adjective is changed to an abstract noun.

Ex.—Wise, wis*dom*; beautiful, beau*ty*.

64. Comparison of Adjectives.

1. **Comparison** is the variation of the adjective to express different degrees of the quality which it denotes.

The variation may take place in the *meaning* only; as in *generous; very, rather, too, somewhat, quite generous; more generous, most generous;* or in both *meaning* and *form;* as in clear, clearer, clearest.

2. There are three degrees of comparison,—the *positive*, the *comparative*, and the *superlative*.

3. The **positive** denotes a quality without comparison.

Ex.—*Righteous, pleasant.* The pen is *long.* The street is *long.* The Atlantic cable is *long.*

Had *pen, street,* and *Atlantic cable* been compared in respect to *length*, we should have had *long, longer, longest.*

4. The **comparative** expresses a higher or a lower degree than the positive.

Ex.—The sun is *larger* than the moon. The march was *less difficult* by night than by day.

5. The **superlative** expresses the highest or the lowest degree of the quality.

Ex.—The dog is the *most faithful* of animals. The miser is the *least esteemed* of men.

6. In respect to **intensity,** comparison may show *equal* or *unequal* degrees.

Ex.—Monday will be as *convenient* as Tuesday. Truth is *stranger* than fiction. The *sweetest, wildest* land on earth.

7. In respect to the **terms** compared, it may show,—

(1.) That *two* objects, qualities, or conditions are contrasted in the *comparative* degree, and *one*, with *two more*, or *all others*, in the superlative.

Ex.—*George* is older than his *brother*, or is the older of the *two*. He is more *prosperous* than *scrupulous*. Many animals are more active *by night* than *by day*. Of *all jewels*, the diamond is the *most precious*.

(2.) That **different objects** may possess the same quality in equal or in unequal degrees.

Ex.—*Snow* is as white as *wool*. *Wool* is whiter than *hemp*. This *tree* is the tallest of *all* (the *trees*).

(3.) That, in **different circumstances,** the same quality may belong to the same object in equal or in unequal degrees.

Ex.—Our commander was as self-possessed *in danger* as *in safety*. The Asiatic cholera is more prevalent *in autumn* than *in winter*, and usually most prevalent *in summer*.

(4.) That **different qualities** may belong to the same object in equal or in unequal degrees.

Ex.—The aid was as *timely* as *acceptable*. The servant was *more skillful* than *willing*.

(5.) That **different qualities** may belong to *different objects* in equal, but rarely, if ever, in unequal, degrees.

Ex.—*He* was as *agreeable* as his *opponent* was *offensive*. Scarcely, with propriety, He was more agreeable than his opponent was offensive.

8. In respect to **form,** comparison may take place,—

(1.) *Without any change* of the adjective, as in comparison of equality, or when an adverb is applied to vary the meaning.

(2.) By a *change of termination,*—warm, warmer, warmest.

65. Formation of the Comparative and the Superlative.

1. The comparative of monosyllables is regularly formed by adding **r** or **er,** and the superlative by adding **st** or **est,** to the positive.

Ex.— *Wise, wiser, wisest; bold, bolder, boldest.*

REMARK.—Dissyllables in *le* and *y*, and some others, are compared like monosyllables; as, *noble, nobler, noblest; worthy, worthier, worthiest.*

2. The comparative of most adjectives of more than one syllable (sometimes of one only) is formed by prefixing **more** or **less,** and the superlative by prefixing **most** or **least,** to the positive.

Ex.—*Industrious, more industrious, most industrious; beautiful, less beautiful, least beautiful.*

3. The following adjectives are compared irregularly:—

Positive.	Comparative.	Superlative.
Good,	better,	best.
Bad, Evil, Ill,	worse,	worst.
Little,	less [lesser],	least.
Much, Many,	more,	most.
Far,	farther,	farthest.
Forth (*obsolete*),	further,	furthest.
Near,	nearer,	nearest *or* next.
Late,	later,	latest *or* last.
Old,	older *or* elder,	oldest *or* eldest.
Fore,	former,	foremost *or* first.

4. Adjectives terminating in *ish* indicate the possession of a quality in a lower degree than the positive; as, *bluish,* approaching in color to *blue.*

5. The meaning of the adjective is also varied by the addition of such adverbs as *somewhat, rather, slightly, a little, too, very, greatly,*

exceedingly, &c.; that of the comparative and the superlative, by such words as *much, far, vastly, altogether, by far*, &c.

Ex.—*Rather* weak tea. Eclipse is *much* the better horse.

6. Several adjectives in the superlative degree are formed by adding *most* to *up, upper, nether, in, inner, hind, hinder, out* (contracted to *ut*), *outer, further, hither, top, bottom;* as, *upmost, uppermost, nethermost*, &c.

7. Adjectives derived from proper names, numerals, those referring to position, material, and form, and those having an absolute signification, are seldom, if ever, compared.

Ex.—*German, Spanish, seven, sixth, perpendicular, level, square, woollen, icy.*

With the exception of *much, few, first, last, little, less, least, many, more, most,* the pronominal adjectives are not compared.

8. Many adjectives denoting *place* or *situation* are deficient in some of the degrees: thus, *further, furthermost* or *furthest, hither, hithermost, nether, nethermost, under, undermost,* want the positive. *Northern, northernmost; rear, rearmost,* and others, want the comparative. *Inferior, superior, junior, major, anterior, posterior, prior, ulterior, senior, minor,* are directly from the Latin, and have neither the positive nor the superlative.

66. Exercise.

1. *Tell which of the following words are adjectives:—*

Ice, cold, soft, water, this, little, chair, knob, arise, brave, diligent, inkstand, lamp, many, former, light, white, match, rough.

2. *Tell which of the following adjectives are limiting, and which are qualifying:—*

Strong, twenty, faithful, green, this, first, an, old, former, yellow, every, such, wonderful, timid, sweet, any, fifth, the, soft, those, pure, ripe, tough.

3. *Tell which of the following adjectives are of the positive, which of the comparative, and which of the superlative degree:—*

Braver, more acceptable, eldest, less useful, worst, better, most honorable, strongest, sadder, more plentiful, least worthy, last, good.

4. *Compare the following adjectives:—*

Bright, active, handsome, wise, sad, able, just, diligent, beautiful, good, excellent, dutiful, little, serene, fruitful, large, warm, lovely.

5. *Apply limiting adjectives to five common nouns; qualifying adjectives in the positive degree to five common nouns of the masculine gender; qualifying adjectives in the comparative degree to five common nouns of the feminine gender; qualifying adjectives in the superlative degree to five nouns of the neuter gender, plural number.*

67. Models for Parsing.

1. In parsing an adjective,—
(1.) Tell what part of speech it is. Why?
(2.) Tell what kind of adjective. Why?
(3.) Compare it, and give the degree (if a qualifying adjective).
(4.) Tell to what noun it belongs.
(5.) Give the rule.

2. The *faithful* man will be rewarded.

Faithful is an *adjective;* it is used to limit or qualify a noun; *qualifying,*—it denotes quality; *compared,*—positive, *faithful,* comparative, *more faithful,* superlative, *most faithful;* in the *positive* degree; and belongs to *man,* according to Rule V.: "An adjective or a participle must belong to some noun or pronoun."

3. Her house is *larger* than mine.

Larger . is an *adjective* (why?); *qualifying* (why?); *compared,*—positive, *large,* comparative, *larger,* superlative, *largest;* in the *comparative* degree; it shows that one of two objects has a higher degree of the quality than the other; and belongs to *house,* according to Rule V.

4. She is *worthy* of the highest praise.

Worthy is an *adjective* (why?); *qualifying* (why?); *compared,*— positive, *worthy,* comparative, *worthier,* superlative, *worthiest;* in the *positive* degree, and belongs to *she.* Rule V.

Highest is an *adjective* (why?); *qualifying* (why?); *compared,*—positive, *high,* comparative, *higher,* superlative, *highest;* in the *superlative* degree; it shows the highest degree of the quality; and belongs to *praise,* according to Rule V.

The ... is a *definite article* (why?), and as a limiting adjective it belongs to *praise*, according to Rule V.

5. *Three* birds were killed.

Three .. is a *numeral adjective* (why?); *limiting* (why?); it belongs to *birds*, according to Rule V.

6. Give me *this* apple, and I will give you *that*.

This .. is a *pronominal adjective, singular number* (59, 6, 2), and limits *apple*, according to Rule V.

That .. is a *pronominal adjective, singular number*, and is used to limit the noun *apple*, understood;—or it is used as a *noun*, instead of *apple*, of the *third person, singular number, neuter gender, objective case*, and is the object of the verb *give*, according to Rule VIII.

7. The field of combat fills the *young* and *bold;*
The solemn council best becomes the *old.—Pope.*

Young . is an *adjective;* it belongs to *persons*, understood; or it is used as a *noun*, of the *third person, plural number, masculine gender, objective case*, and is the object of *fills*, according to Rule VIII.

Point out the ADJECTIVES *in the following examples, and parse them according to the above forms:—*

The passionate are like men standing on their heads; they see all things the wrong way.

There are two ways of arriving at the highest personal liberty; one is to have few wants, and the other is to have abundant means of satisfying them.

Shining characters are not always the most agreeable.

Mental pleasures never cloy; unlike those of the body, they are increased by repetition.

The beautiful strikes us as much by its novelty as the deformed itself.—*Burke.*

>Stone walls do not a prison make,
>Nor iron bars a cage.
>Minds innocent and quiet take
>That for a hermitage.

9. *Parse the* NOUNS *and the* ADJECTIVES *in the following examples:*

Rarely in public office, he (Rufus Choate) was still a public man in the largest sense; all were proud of him. The old honored him, the young loved him, and both old and young admired him.

> How sweetly come the holy psalms
>   From saints and martyrs down,—
> The waving of triumphal palms
>   Above the thorny crown!
> The choral praise, the chanted prayers
>   From harps by angels strung,
> The hunted Cameron's mountain airs,
>   The hymns that Luther sung!—*Whittier.*

PRONOUNS.

68. Definitions and Distinctions.

A pronoun is a word which takes the place of a noun.

Ex.—The farmer ploughs *his* field; *he* reaps *his* wheat, and gathers *it* into *his* barn.

1. The pronoun takes the place of the noun, not merely to be a substitute for it, or to avoid a disagreeable repetition, but to represent it in some important relation.

Sometimes it is used to avoid *repetition,* as when a noun in the *third person,* with its modifications, would occur frequently in a sentence; sometimes it is employed to avoid *misapprehension* or *ambiguity,* as when the first or the second person becomes the object *spoken of* (**39,** 8, Rem.); sometimes to introduce an *adjective expression* to modify the noun, as when by means of a relative and its clause we restrict the meaning of a noun; sometimes to represent the noun as the subject of *inquiry,* as when the interrogatives are used.

2. The relations which the pronoun may represent are,—

(*a.*) That of the *object* spoken of to the *speaker.*

In this relation the object may be either the speaker himself, the one spoken to, or the one spoken of. Hence the *first,* the *second,* and the *third person* (**39, 8**), and the pronouns *I, thou,* and *he, she, it;* and hence, too, the name *personal.*

(*b.*) That of the *object* to some modifying *circumstances.*

Ex.—A fortress *which* stands on a hill is a conspicuous object.

Here we employ the pronoun *which,* incidentally to denote the object *fortress,* but *chiefly* to *join* to it the circumstance of its position as that which renders it conspicuous. Hence the pronouns *who, which, that,* and *what;* and hence, too, the name *relative.*

(*c.*) That of an *object* to the speaker as an *inquirer.*

Here, again, the object is *incidentally* represented by the pronoun (its name being unknown), and that for the special purpose of making it a subject of *inquiry*. Hence we have *Who? Which?* and *What?* and the name *interrogative*.

(*d.*) That of the *object* to the speaker, as something *known* or *unknown, mentioned* or *not mentioned*.

The personal pronouns of the third person, and all the relative pronouns, are employed when an object is supposed to be not only *known*, but to have been *previously mentioned*. The personal pronouns of the first and the second person are used when the object is *known* (by its presence) but has not (necessarily) been *previously mentioned*. The interrogative pronouns are used when the object is neither *known* nor has been *previously mentioned*.

3. The **antecedent** is the noun or substantive expression for which a pronoun stands.

Ex.—The *world* in *which* they are placed, opens with all its wonders upon their eyes.

4. The antecedent may be a phrase or an entire proposition.

Ex.—*To believe the report, which* is the thing you desire, would be offensive to one of the noblest of men. *The servant opened the window, which* was strictly forbidden.

The term *antecedent*, however, usually means something more than the noun which the pronoun represents; it denotes the leading term of a relation, and implies a subsequent term. Hence it is more especially used in the case of a relative pronoun, which is employed to show a relation between its antecedent noun and some following circumstance. The personal pronoun bears no such syntactical relation to its antecedent.

5. The object represented by the personal pronouns of the first and the second person is always supposed to be present, and, consequently, the antecedent noun is seldom given; that of the third person is usually expressed. Sometimes, however, a personal or an interrogative pronoun is employed without an antecedent, and so limited by a relative and its clause as to give to the whole the effect of a single name.

Ex.—"*He who sways the minds of men by his eloquence,*" i.e. the orator, "*exerts the highest human power.*" "*Who, that marks the fire still sparkling in each eye,* but would deem their bosoms burned anew?"

6. Sometimes the antecedent pronoun, in such cases, is omitted, or is included in the relative.

Ex.—"*Who* would be free, themselves must strike the blow;" that is, *they who*. "*Who* steals my purse steals trash;" that is, *he who*.

7. The pronoun stands not merely for a noun, but for a noun in its syntactical relation, and also as restricted by modifying words.

Ex.—"We saw the little deformed boy who watched at the gate, and pitied him;" i.e. *the little deformed boy who watched at the gate.*

8. The antecedent, as the term indicates, is something *going before;* but, as an interrogative pronoun inquires for an object as yet unknown, the antecedent cannot be a preceding noun. The pronoun, therefore, must agree in person, number, and gender, not necessarily with the noun in the answer,—the *subsequent,*—but with a noun which the speaker conceived to be the name of the object (however erroneous his thought might be) when he uttered the question.

Ex.—*What* is there? Ans. A *friend.*

Here *what* evidently refers to *thing* or *animal,* being equivalent to *what thing.* It would have been *who,* had the speaker known the character of the object inquired for.

69. Classes of Pronouns.

1. Pronouns are divided into three classes,—*personal, relative,* and *interrogative.*

2. To these classes some grammarians add *adjective pronouns.* It is true that certain limiting adjectives may take the place of nouns; as, *this, that, these, those, each, all,* &c. So, any qualifying adjective, preceded by an article, may stand for a noun in the same way; as, *The good, the wise, the prudent;* but a noun, in both cases, is properly understood. Hence they should be disposed of alike, —that is, as adjectives used as nouns.

3. To pronouns, like nouns, belong *Person, Number, Gender,* and *Case.*

70. Personal Pronouns.

1. A **personal** pronoun is used both to represent a noun, and to show whether it is of the *first,* the *second,* or the *third* person.

2. **I** (plural, **we**) is of the *first* person; **thou** (plural, **ye** or **you**) is of the *second* person; **he, she,** and **it** (plural, **they**) are of the *third* person, masculine, feminine, and neuter, respectively.

3. The personal pronouns of the first and the second person

represent the speaker or the hearer. The gender is supposed to be known, and is not indicated by the form of the pronoun; while that of the third person is represented by one of the forms *he, she*, or *it*.

4. **It** is often used in a vague sense, as the subject of verbs descriptive of the weather; as, "It rains." "It thunders." It is used as an expletive,—(1) as the object of a verb; as, "Come and trip *it* as you go;" (2) to introduce a sentence whose subject is placed after the predicate. "*It* is pleasant *to see the sun.*" "*It* has been ascertained *that water is composed of oxygen and hydrogen.*" *It* is used as subject to represent a noun or a pronoun as attribute, of any number, gender, or person; as, "It is *I.*" "It is *they.*" "It is *James.*" "It is *she.*"

5. Formerly, **thou** was used in addressing a single individual, and a corresponding form of the verb was used; as, "Thou singest;" but gradually *you* has come to take its place, till the use of *thou*, except in the solemn or poetic style, is now wholly discontinued. *You*, therefore, is both singular and plural in its application, but the verb does not change its form; it invariably takes the plural form; as, "You (meaning one) *write,*" not *writest.*

6. The compound personal pronouns are,—first person, *myself* (plural, *ourselves*); second person, *thyself, yourself* (plural, *yourselves*); third person, (*masculine*) *himself,* (*feminine*) *herself,* (*neuter*) *itself,* (plural, *themselves*).

7. The compound personal pronouns are sometimes, but seldom, used as the subject of a proposition, though they are often used in apposition with it.

Ex.—He *himself* knows not whereof he affirms.

8. When used as the object of a transitive verb, they are called *reflexive*, because the act of the agent falls back upon himself.

Ex.—The boy struck *himself.*

71. Exercise.

1. *Substitute the nouns and their modifying words for the pronouns in the following sentences:—*

At this time, the commander of the American forces and *his* army took post at Harlem; *he* now sought to ascertain the state of *his* enemy's forces on Long Island. Captain Nathan Hale volunteered *his* services; *he* entered the British army in disguise. On *his* return, *he* was apprehended and sent to the cruel Marshal Cunningham, by *whom he* was ordered to execution without a trial.

Edward carelessly lost his books on his way to school; he tried to excuse himself to his teacher for his deficiency in his lessons, but she required him to prepare them after school, and recite them to her.

72. Declension of the Personal Pronouns.

1. The personal pronouns are thus declined:—

FIRST PERSON.

	Singular.	Plural.
Nom.	I,	We,
Pos.	My *or* mine,	Our *or* ours,
Obj.	Me,	Us.

SECOND PERSON.

	Singular.	Plural.
Nom.	Thou,	Ye *or* you,
Pos.	Thy *or* thine,	Your *or* yours,
Obj.	Thee,	You.

THIRD PERSON, *Masculine.*

	Singular.	Plural.
Nom.	He,	They,
Pos.	His,	Their *or* theirs,
Obj.	Him,	Them.

THIRD PERSON, *Feminine.*

	Singular.	Plural.
Nom.	She,	They,
Pos.	Her *or* hers,	Their *or* theirs,
Obj.	Her,	Them.

THIRD PERSON, *Neuter.*

	Singular.	Plural.
Nom.	It,	They,
Pos.	Its,	Their *or* theirs,
Obj.	It,	Them.

First Person.

	Singular.	Plural.
Nom.	Myself,	Ourselves,
Pos.	———	———
Obj.	Myself,	Ourselves.

Second Person.

	Singular.	Plural.
Nom.	Thyself, yourself,	Yourselves,
Pos.	———	———
Obj.	Thyself,	Yourselves.

Third Person.

	Singular.			Plural.
	Masc.	*Fem.*	*Neut.*	
Nom.	Himself,	Herself,	Itself,	Themselves,
Pos.	———	———	———	———
Obj.	Himself,	Herself,	Itself,	Themselves.

2. Of the possessives, *my, thy, her, our, your, their,* are used when the noun is expressed; *mine, thine, hers, ours, yours,* and *theirs* (in modern style), when it is understood, and the latter must be changed to the former whenever the noun is supplied. "That book is *yours;* this is *mine.*" "That book is *your* book; this is *my* book."

3. When *mine, thine,* &c. are used as in the above example, they seem to perform a double office: first, to represent the speaker, the hearer, or the person spoken of, as a possessor; and, secondly, like other limiting or qualifying words, when the noun is understood, to represent or stand for that noun, not as a pronoun does, but as an adjective (69, 2). Thus, we say, "*This* [book] is an arithmetic; *that* [book] is a geography." "The *violent* [persons] take it by force." "*Mine* [my task] was an easy task." Properly, neither of the above words is a noun. The first three are adjectives used to limit the noun understood, which follows them, and the last a personal pronoun in the possessive case, used to limit the noun *task*, understood. If it is proper to say that *this, that,* or *violent* is used as a noun, it is equally so of the word *mine*, not in its pronominal, but in its adjective office. It is then, strictly, a pronoun in the possessive, governed by some noun understood, but may, like an adjective, be parsed as that noun, in the nominative or the objective case.

73. Exercise.

1. In parsing a pronoun,—

  (1.) Tell what part of speech it is. Why?

ETYMOLOGY—PERSONAL PRONOUNS. 75

(2.) Tell what kind of pronoun. Why?
(3.) Tell what its antecedent is. Why?
(4.) Decline it.
(5.) Give the person, number, gender. Why?
(6.) Rule for person, number, gender. Why?
(7.) Case and construction.
(8.) Rule for construction.

NOTE.—In parsing, let the pupil follow this order, and, as soon as possible, without any question from the teacher. The pronoun is parsed very much like the noun.

2. *Study the following models for parsing:—*

David brought *his* book, and laid *it* on the table.

His . is a *pronoun;* it takes the place of a noun; *personal;* it is used both to represent a noun, and to show whether it is of the first, the second, or the third person; it refers to *David* for its antecedent; (singular, nominative *he,* possessive *his,* objective *him;* plural, nominative *they,* possessive *their* or *theirs,* objective *them;*) it is of the *third person, singular number, masculine gender,* because its antecedent is (Rule III.: "A pronoun must agree with its antecedent in *gender, number,* and *person*"); *possessive case,* and is used to limit *book,* by denoting possession, according to Rule VII. (Repeat it.)

It ... is a *pronoun* (why?); *personal* (why?); it has *book* for its antecedent; (decline it;) it is of the *third person, singular number, neuter gender,* because its antecedent *book* is (Rule III.), *objective case,* and is the object of *laid:* Rule VIII. (Repeat the rule.)

The messenger *himself* revealed the treachery.

Himself is a *pronoun* (why?); *compound,* composed of *him* and *self;* it has *messenger* for its antecedent; *third person, singular number, masculine gender,* because its antecedent is (Rule III.), *nominative case,* and used to identify or explain *messenger,* according to Rule VI.

3. *Parse the* PERSONAL PRONOUNS *in the following sentences:—*

Can it be that America, under such circumstances, can betray herself? that she is to be added to the catalogue of republics, the inscription upon whose ruins is, "They were, but they are not!" Forbid it, my countrymen! forbid it, Heaven!—*Story.*

It is a noble faculty of our nature which enables us to connect our thoughts, our sympathies, and our happiness, with what is distant in place or time.— *Webster*.

His praise, ye winds that from five quarters blow,
Breathe soft or loud; and wave your tops, ye pines.—*Milton*.

Love took up the glass of Time, and turned it in his glowing hands,
Every moment, lightly shaken, ran itself in golden sands.—*Tennyson*.

Not theirs the blame who furnish forth the treat,
But ours who throng the board and grossly eat.—*Sprague*.

4. *Give the class, the person, the number, the gender (when it can be determined by the form), and the case of the following pronouns:*—

I, he, his, hers, mine, you, thou, they, them, us, we, myself, himself, they, herself, me, themselves, ourselves, my, thee, your, thine, herself, yourselves.

74. Relative Pronouns.

1. A **relative** pronoun is used both to represent a preceding noun or pronoun, called the *antecedent*, and to connect with it a dependent proposition.

Ex.—Those *who* wish for favors must assist others.

Relative adverbs are commonly called *conjunctive adverbs*. By analogy, we ought to have *conjunctive* instead of *relative* pronouns.

2. The relative pronoun, when used only as such, follows the antecedent; as, "All *that* I have is yours;" when used both as a limiting adjective and a pronoun, it always precedes it; as, "I will give you *what* money I have."

3. The following distinctions will show the difference between a relative and a personal pronoun:—

(*a.*) The relative refers to an object always known, and either previously mentioned, or so clearly implied as to need no mention; the personal pronouns refer always to an object known,—in the third person to an object previously mentioned, but in the first and the second person to an object not previously mentioned.

(*b.*) The personal pronouns have a distinct form for each grammatical person; *I* for the first, *thou* or *you* for the second, and *he, she,* or *it* for the third. The relative pronouns do not change their form to represent person.

(*c.*) The essential difference is seen in the *relations* which they denote (see **68,** 2), and in their use in construction. The personal pronoun may represent the subject of an independent sentence,—that is, one expressing a thought; the relative shows a dependent *adjective* relation; as, "He is present." "Which is important." The first is a complete sentence; the second needs some word, as *measure* (which is important), on which it may depend.

75. Simple Relatives.

1. The **simple** relatives are *who, which, that,* and *what.*

2. **Who** is used to represent *persons;* **which** and **what,** to represent *things;* and **that,** to represent both *persons* and *things.*

3. The antecedent of a relative pronoun is not only the word for which the pronoun stands, but is the leading or antecedent term of a relation, of which the clause introduced by the relative is the subsequent term; it is that on which the relative clause depends, and is either a *definite* or an *indefinite* object.

4. **Who, which,** and **that** usually refer to a *definite* antecedent.

Ex.—The *man* who came. The *horse* which died. The *tree* that fell.

In the sentence, "Who steals my purse steals trash," *who* refers to an indefinite antecedent.

5. *What* may refer either to a *definite* or an *indefinite* antecedent.

Ex.—I gave him *what* money he wanted (definite). I gave him *what* he wanted (indefinite).

When the antecedent is indefinite, the relative stands alone, some indefinite word, like *thing* or *things*, being understood.

6. *What* is both a relative pronoun and a limiting adjective, and is equivalent as adjective to *that* or *those,* as relative to *which,* and, consequently, has a double construction.

NOTE.—In disposing of *what*, we should not parse *that* and then *which,*— two words not given,—but *what* itself, calling it a *relative pronoun.* (**77,** 6.)

When the antecedent is definite, *what* should be parsed—(1) as an adjective; (2) as a relative pronoun; as, "He gave me *what* books I wanted." Here *what* as limiting adjective *belongs* to *books,*—as relative pronoun *relates* to books. When the antecedent is indefinite, the noun "thing" or "things" may be supplied, making this case the same as above; or, it may be taken—(1) as an adjective in the sense of *that* or *those,* but used as a noun (69, 2); it practically then becomes both antecedent and relative; (2) as a relative in the sense of *which,* relating to *itself* in the sense of *thing* or *things;* as, "He gave me *what* I wanted," that is, "He gave me *what* (ant. = *that*) *what* (rel. = *which*) I wanted." The two methods are practically the same. The former, from its perfect identity with the case of a definite antecedent, will be the more easily understood. (77, 5, 6.)

7. What is,—

(*a.*) A *relative*—(1) when it can be changed into *that which;* as, "It is *what (that which)* I wanted;" (2) when it both limits and relates to a noun; as, "What ore was found, was very poor," = *That* ore *which* was found, &c.

(*b.*) An *interrogative* pronoun when used alone (belonging to an indefinite object) to ask a question; as, "What [things] do you want?"

(*c.*) An *interrogative* adjective when used to limit a noun (a definite object), and also to ask a question; as, "What excuse does he render?"

(*d.*) An *interjection* when it denotes an exclamation; as, "What! have you come?"

(*e.*) An *adverb* when it is equivalent to *partly;* as, "The year before, he had so used the matter, that, *what* by force, *what* by policy, he had taken from the Christians above thirty castles."

8. That is,—

(*a.*) A *relative* only when *who* or *which* can be substituted for it; as, "He *that (who)* getteth wisdom loveth his own soul." "What private grief they have, alas! I know not, *that (which)* made them do it."

(*b.*) A *pronominal adjective* when it limits a noun, expressed or understood; as, "*That* book."

(*c.*) A *subordinate conjunction* when it joins a dependent clause to some part of a principal; as, "I know *that* my Redeemer liveth."

9. When *that* is used as the object of a preposition, the latter is always placed at the end of a clause; and *that* must be changed to *whom* or *which* whenever the preposition precedes.

Ex.—It was James that I depended upon, = upon whom I depended.

10. *As,* by an ellipsis of the relative, after *such, many,* or *same,* seems to take its place, and may be regarded as a relative, though, properly speaking, it is never a relative.

Ex.—The Lord added to the church daily such *as* [were those who] should be saved.

76. Compound Relatives.

1. The **compound** relatives are *whoso, whoever, whosoever, whichever, whichsoever, whatever,* and *whatsoever.*

2. These are formed from the simple relatives by adding the adverbs *ever, so,* and *so-ever.*

What, on account of its *double* construction (75, 6), has been erroneously regarded as a compound pronoun.

3. **Whoever** and **whosoever** refer to some indefinite antecedent, as, *he, person, any one,* and are equivalent to *any one who.*

Ex.—*Whoever* hopes a faultless piece to see.

In all other respects they are parsed like *who, whose, whom.*

4. **Whichever** and **whichsoever** refer to a definite object, to which they belong as adjectives.

Ex.—*Whichever* way you take will lead to the city.

They are equivalent to *any — which.*

5. **Whatever** and **whatsoever** belong, as adjectives, either to a definite or an indefinite object, and relate, as pronouns, to the same (75, 5).

Ex.—We are interested in *whatever* occupation you follow. *Whatsoever* is more than these cometh of evil.

They are equivalent to *that — which,* or *any thing — which.*

6. The relative and interrogative pronouns are thus declined:—

	Sing. and Plu.	*Sing. and Plu.*
Nom.	Who,	Which,
Pos.	Whose,	Whose,
Obj.	Whom.	Which.

That and *what* have no variation. *Whoever* and *whosoever* are declined like *who.*

77. Exercise—Models for Parsing.

1. The man *who* is faithfully attached to religion will be upright.
Who .. is a relative pronoun. (Why?)

(1.) As a pronoun, it has *man* for its antecedent; nominative *who,* possessive *whose,* objective *whom;* plural the same; third person, singular number, masculine gender, because its antecedent is (Rule III.: Repeat it), nominative case, and is used as the subject of the proposition, "who is attached." (Rule I.: Repeat it. See **172**.)

(2.) As a relative or connective, it joins the subordinate proposition, "who is faithfully attached to religion," to the antecedent *man*. Rule XV.: "Subordinate connectives are used to join dissimilar elements."

2. Cherish true patriotism, *whose* root is benevolence.

Whose is a relative pronoun. (Why?)

(1.) As a pronoun, it has *patriotism* for its antecedent; nominative *which*, &c.; third person, singular number, neuter gender (Rule III.: Repeat it), possessive case, and is used to limit *root*, by denoting possession. (Rule VII.: Repeat it.)

(2.) As a relative or connective, it connects the subordinate proposition, "whose root is benevolence," to the antecedent *patriotism*. (Rule XV.: Repeat it.)

3. Compassion is an emotion of *which* we should never be ashamed.

Which is a relative pronoun. (Why?)

(1.) As a pronoun, it represents *emotion* as its antecedent (decline, and give person, number, gender: Rule III.), objective case, and is used as the object of the preposition *of*. (Rule XIII.: Repeat it: **197**.)

(2.) As a relative or connective, it joins the subordinate proposition, "of which we should never be ashamed," to the antecedent *emotion*. (Rule XV.)

4. Here is the sofa *that* he sat upon.

That.. is a relative pronoun. (Why?)

(1.) As a pronoun, it has *sofa* for its antecedent (decline, and give person, number, gender: Rule III.), objective case, and used as the object of the preposition *upon*. (Rule XIV. See **75**, 8.)

(2.) As a relative or connective, it connects the subordinate proposition, "that he sat upon," to the antecedent *sofa*. (Rule XV.)

5. I have ascertained *what* lesson we must learn.

What. is a relative pronoun, used also as an adjective. (1.) As an adjective, it belongs to *lesson*, according to Rule V. (**172**.)

ETYMOLOGY—RELATIVE PRONOUNS. 81

(2.) As a pronoun, it has *lesson* for its antecedent, and is of the third person, singular number, neuter gender, according to Rule III.; objective case, and is the object of *must learn*, according to Rule VIII. (172.)

(3.) As a relative or connective, it joins the subordinate proposition, "what we must learn," to the antecedent *lesson*. (Rule XV.)

6. I know *what* will be done.

What. is a relative pronoun, used also as an adjective.

(1.) As an adjective, it belongs to some noun, as *thing* (*what thing*), understood, and should be parsed as above (**75**, 6); or, as an adjective, it is used for the noun, which it represents (**55**, 3), in the third person, singular number, neuter gender, objective case, and the object of *know*. (Rule VIII.)

(2.) As a pronoun, it relates to *thing* understood, or to *what*, its representative, for its antecedent, and is of the third person, singular number, neuter gender (Rule III.); nominative case, and the subject of *will be done*. (Rule I.)

(3.) As a relative or connective, it connects the subordinate proposition, "what will be done," to *thing*, or to *what*, its representative. (Rule XV.)

7. He has lost *whatever* fortune he had.

Parse "whatever" *according to the first model* (5) *for* "what."

8. *Whoever* fails must try again.

Supply the antecedent (**76**, 3), *and parse as in Model* 1.

9. *Parse the* RELATIVES *in the following examples:—*
A dauntless soul erect who smiles on death.—*Thomson.*
Call imperfection what thou fanciest such.—*Pope.*
Whoever seeks the good of others, will himself be blest.
Whatsoever he doeth, shall prosper.

But that which gave the brightest lustre not only to the eloquence of Chatham, but to his character, was his loftiness and nobleness of soul. He loved fame, but it was the fame that follows, not the fame that is run after; not the fame that is gained by the little acts that bring forward little men, but the fame that a minister will and must wring from the very people whose prejudices he despises, and whose passions he controls.—*Mahon.*

> For the structure that we raise,
> Time is with materials filled;
> Our to-days and yesterdays
> Are the blocks with which we build.—*Longfellow.*

10. *Tell what part of speech "that" is in the following examples* (**75,** 8):
Thoughts that breathe and words that burn.
That is the same man that we met before.
I do not deny that you may be right.
I will send the articles that you asked for.
I hope that that boy that stole that purse will be punished.
He said that that "that" that that boy, that sat on that seat, parsed yesterday was not à pronoun.
It is not from my lips that that strain of eloquence is this day to flow.— *Webster.* ✗

78. Interrogative Pronouns.

1. An **interrogative** pronoun is used both to represent a noun, and to ask a question.

Ex.— *Who* art thou, Lord? *What* shall this man do?

2. The interrogatives are *who*, used to inquire for persons; *which*, for persons and things; and *what* (usually) for things.

Ex.— *Who* gave thee that authority? *Which* house does he live in? *What* have I to do with thee?

3. When a *definite* object is inquired for, *what* and *which* are interrogative adjectives used to limit the name of the object inquired for.

Ex.— *What* books do you want? *Which* road shall we take?

When an *indefinite* object is inquired for, the interrogative takes its place, or belongs to it, understood (**59,** 3).

Ex.— *What* (thing) do you want?

The difference between *who, which,* and *what* as interrogatives will appear in the following example, in which *who* asks for the *name, which* for the *individual,* and *what* for the *occupation.*

Ex.— *Who* did that work? Mr. Jones. *Which* Jones? John Jones. *What* is he? A printer.

4. When an interrogative sentence is quoted, and incorporated into another sentence, it loses much of its interrogative character; the interrogative pronoun becomes a connective, and, as the incorporated clause is an unanswered question, the pronoun refers to some person or thing both *unknown* and *unmentioned.* It may, therefore, be called an *indefinite interrogative pronoun.*

Ex.— *Who* is concealed in the garden?

The name has not been mentioned; and although he may be a familiar friend, yet, as the *concealed one*, he is unknown. The answer, therefore, must be, "I do not know *who* is concealed in the garden." *Who* is here (1) an *indefinite interrogative pronoun*, third person, singular number (shown by the verb), masculine gender, nominative case, &c.; and (2) a subordinate connective, joining the subordinate proposition, "who is concealed in the garden," to *know*. (Rule XV.) Compare this with "I do not know *him who* is concealed in the garden." Here *who* should be parsed as a relative pronoun having *him* for its antecedent.

5. Besides *pronouns*, various interrogative adverbs are used in asking questions (**134**, 7); as, *Why? Where? When? How?*

79. Exercise.

1. *Point out the interrogative pronouns in the following examples:—*
Who has learned his lesson? Which seat do you prefer? What have you found in the garden? For what are you punished? Whose school do you attend? Who went with you? Whom do you follow? Which way has she gone?

2. *Tell which of the above examples are pronouns, and which interrogative adjectives.* (See **78**, 3.)

3. *Tell which of the following pronouns are relative, and which interrogative:—*
He whose image thou art. From what fountain flowed their light? What title dost thou bear? Whose genius had angelic wings. What readiest way would bring me to the place? Who found the flower? I am he whom ye seek. He found the book for which I sent him. Of whom do you speak? That which was lost is found.

4. *Models for parsing interrogatives:—*

Who shall separate us from the love of Christ?

Who . is a *pronoun* (why?); interrogative (why?); its *antecedent* (subsequent) is not expressed (**68**, 8); nominative *who*, possessive *whose*, objective *whom;* plural, the same; *third person, singular number, masculine gender,* because its antecedent (subsequent, *no one* implied) is (Rule III.: Repeat it), *nominative case,* and used as the subject of the proposition, "who shall separate." (Rule I.: Repeat it.)

Whose books have you found?

Whose is an *interrogative pronoun;* nominative *who,* &c. (*person, number,* and *gender* depending upon the object conceived of as the answer (**68, 8**), *possessive case*, and is used to limit *books* by denoting possession. (Rule VII.: Repeat it.)

What seek ye?

What. is an *interrogative pronoun;* indeclinable; *third-person* (*number* and *gender* depending upon the object conceived of as the answer), *objective case*, and used as the object of the verb *seek*. (Rule VIII.: Repeat it.)

What lesson shall we learn?

What. is a *pronominal adjective, used interrogatively*, or an *interrogative adjective*, and belongs to *lesson*, for which it inquires. (Rule V.)

I know not *who* is there.

Who. is an (1) *indefinite interrogative pronoun*, having properly no antecedent, but referring to some unknown person previously inquired for, *third person, singular number* (shown by the verb), *masculine gender* (**47**, 6), &c.; and (2) a subordinate connective, joining the subordinate proposition, "who is there," to *know*. (Rule XV.)

5. *Parse the* NOUNS, *the* ADJECTIVES, *and the* PRONOUNS, *in the following examples:*—

A great mistake, which is too common, especially among those who have experienced many trials and difficulties in life, is, that happiness is to be found in rest. But, as has been pointedly remarked, that man is most restless who is most at rest.—*Buckminster*.

An ill book well written is like poisoning a fountain that runs forever; a man may do mischief this way, it may be, as long as the world lasts. He is a nuisance to future ages, and lays a snare for those who are yet unborn.—*Jeremy Collier*.

Mark but my fall, and that that ruined me.
Cromwell, I charge thee, fling away ambition!
By that sin fell the angels.—*Shakspeare*.

Motionless torrents! silent cataracts!
Who made you glorious as the gates of heaven
Beneath the keen full moon? Who bade the sun
Clothe you with rainbows?—*Coleridge*.

Ay! Heaven had set one living man
  Beyond the pedant's tether;
His virtues, frailties, He will scan
  Who weighs them all together!—*Holmes*.

VERBS.
80. Definitions and Distinctions.

1. A **verb** is a word which expresses *being, action,* or *state;* as, *be, read, sleep, is loved.*

2. It is the characteristic property of the verb to *affirm* what it expresses. Yet the being, action, or state may be *affirmed, assumed,* or *used abstractly.*

Ex.—George *runs.* George *running. To run.*

Thus, when an *affirmation* is made, the verb, being either the predicate or copula of the proposition, is used *predicatively,* and is said to be *finite;* when the action of the verb is *assumed,* it takes the construction of the *adjective,* or is used *adjectively,* that is, is joined to the subject, and is called a *participle;* when it is used *abstractly,* it is separated from the subject, and, being unlimited by its person or number, it is said to be *infinitive (unlimited).*

3. **Affirm,** as here used, includes an *absolute* declaration; as, "Mary learns;"—a *conditional* statement; "If Mary learns;"— an *interrogation;* "Does Mary learn?"—a *petition;* "May Mary learn?"—a *command;* "Mary, learn."

4. If a word is a verb only when it *affirms* being, action, or state, neither the participle nor the infinitive is a verb. These can be included in the verb only by defining it as *expressing action,* &c. They are really both participles, being derived from the verb and partaking of its meaning.

5. The abstract or substantive verb is the pure verb BE, called the *copula,* having no other power or value than to assert some attribute of a noun.

When the attribute expresses a *quality* or *class,* this verb or an equivalent must always be used; as, "Lead *is* heavy;" but when the attribute is an *action,* it may blend with the verb *be,* and then both become one word; as, "The sun *is rising.*" "The sun *rises.*" The combined form then takes the name of verb, and undergoes inflections to represent *voice, mode, tense, number,* and *person;* in all other cases, the verb *to be* undergoes these variations.

6. A verb is called *attributive,* when to the pure verb it joins an attribute.

The verb *to be* is attributive whenever it is used to assert existence; as, "There *was* a man sent from God." When thus used, the verb is commonly followed by its subject, and preceded by the expletive "there," which serves no other purpose than to introduce the sentence and indicate this peculiarity of the verb.

7. Every finite verb represents some *person* or *thing* as acting or existing in a certain state; and that which represents this *person* or *thing* is called the *subject*.

Ex.—*Frank* plays. *She* sleeps.

81. Exercise.

1. *Point out the verbs and their subjects in the following examples:—*

The clouds vanish. The vapor rises. The plant lives. Flowers die. Children sing. They stand. Can you see? Here they are! The ice melts.

2. *Write appropriate verbs for the following nouns as subjects:—*

Samuel, the pen, the book, flowers, we, oceans, moon, the earth, forests, the king, Victoria.

3. *Write appropriate nouns as subjects for the following verbs:—*

Rules, is, thinks, hopes, learns, shine, grow, dig, revolve, sits, fears, blossom, arise, sink.

4. *Point out the verbs on page — in your Reader, and tell the subjects.*

Note.—Let the teacher assign this lesson.

82. Verbs classified by their Use.

1. Verbs are divided, according to their *use*, into *transitive* and *intransitive*.

2. A **transitive** verb receives or requires an object to complete its meaning.

Ex.—The servant opened the *door*. What walls can guard *me*, or what shades can hide [me]?—*Pope.*

3. An **intransitive** verb neither receives nor requires an object to complete its meaning.

Ex.—The sun *rises*. The horse *runs*.

4. Verbs may be divided, on account of their relation to the subject, into,—

(*a.*) The *abstract* or *substantive* verb BE, which represents no attribute of the subject whatever (**80.** 5).

(*b.*) *Attributive* or *mixed* verbs, in which an attribute denoting an action or a state of the subject is blended with the copula; as, *runs,* = *is running;* *is* being the copula, and *running* the attribute.

5. Attributive verbs, including also the copula *to be*, have been divided, with reference to the subject, into,—

(*a.*) **Active verbs,** or those which represent the subject in an *active* state.

(*b.*) **Passive verbs,** or those which represent the subject in a *passive* state; that is, in such a state as to *receive* or suffer an action.

(*c.*) **Neuter verbs,** or those which represent the subject in *neither* of these states; that is, a state in which it neither acts nor receives the effect of an action.

REMARK 1.—But this distinction has little to do with the construction of language. It is the relation of the verb to a succeeding term, the *object*, that renders a classification important. This division is retained in the dictionaries, and the learner should understand, in consulting a dictionary, that *v. a.* = *verb active*, after a verb, is equivalent to *transitive, v. n.* = *verb neuter*, to *intransitive*. Thus, *run, fly, walk,* though they represent the subject in a very active state, are marked *v. n.*

REMARK 2.—The terms *transitive* and *intransitive* have been generally adopted by recent grammarians, as best suited to the purpose of construction. Although the idea of an act originating in an agent and "passing over" to an object seems inapplicable to such verbs as *have, possess, receive, acquire,* and many others, still the terms, as defined above, are liable to little or no objection.

REMARK 3.—The subdivision of verbs into *active-transitive* and *active-intransitive* is not only needless, but partial in its application. The distinction is made to apply exclusively to *active* verbs; whereas it may apply as well to *neuter* as to *active* verbs. In the sentence, "The son *resembles* his father," no one will maintain that *resembles* is any more an active verb than *sleeps*. Yet it is transitive; and, to be consistent, we ought to have *neuter-transitive* and *neuter-intransitive*. By omitting the words *active* and *neuter* altogether, we have a practical division, and one of universal application.

6. The *object* or *complement* of the transitive verb stands as an answer to the question *What?* or *Whom?* with the verb.

Ex.—The ox eats (*what?*) hay, grass, oats, corn, &c. The boy found (*whom?*) his father, his mother, &c.

To determine whether a verb is transitive or intransitive, we have only to use this test: ask with it the question *What?* or *Whom?* and if, in its signification *as used* in the example in question, it has, as answer, a noun or a pronoun meaning a *different* thing from the subject, or if one is obviously required to complete the meaning intended, it is transitive; otherwise it is intransitive.

7. When the noun or the pronoun thus added means the same person or thing as the subject, it is not the object, but is a *predicate-nominative*, and the verb is either intransitive, or transitive in the passive voice. All such verbs perform the office of the copula, and are hence called *copulative* verbs. These are *be* (*the simple copula*), *become, seem, appear, stand, walk*, and other verbs of *position, motion,* and *condition;* the passive verbs *is called, is named, is styled, is appointed, is constituted, is elected, is chosen, is made, is esteemed, is reckoned,* and others.

8. A transitive verb in a proposition necessarily implies three terms,—a *subject,* a *predicate,* and an *object.*

Ex.—Cæsar (*sub.*) crossed (*pred.*) the Rubicon (*obj.*).

An intransitive verb requires but two terms,—a subject and a predicate; as, "The tempest (*sub.*) rages" (*pred.*).

9. Many verbs are transitive in one signification, and intransitive in another.

Ex.—It *breaks* my chain. Morning *breaks* in the east.

When the object is not necessarily implied, it is better to consider such verbs intransitive, and not transitive, because an object, in some other possible signification of the verb, *may* be supplied; as, "She sings beautifully" (intransitive). "She sings soprano" (transitive).

10. Some verbs, usually intransitive, become transitive when used with a causative signification.

Ex.—The train usually runs at the rate of twenty-five miles an hour; but they *ran* a train (caused it to run) at the rate of forty.

Some verbs become transitive when they take an object after them of a kindred signification; as, "He ran a *race.*" "They played a *game.*"

83. Exercise.

1. *Tell which of the following verbs are transitive, and which intransitive:*—

Anna loves her mother. The golden gates open. The moon silvers the distant hills. Mary has found her ring. Eleanor writes poetry. The snow melts. The dew fetters break. The innocent lamb dies. The child plays. The fragrant flowers bloom. She received a letter. Does Paul live there?

2. *Write an appropriate subject and object for each of the following verbs:—*

Rings, learn, find, hide, fears, remembers, inflicts, receives, lift, hears, renews, reviews, write.

MODEL.—The *sexton* rings the *bell.*

3. *Point out the transitive and the intransitive verbs in the following examples; also the subject of each verb, and the object, if it has one:—*

Oh, spare me, that I may recover strength before I go hence and be no more.

Awake! arise! or be forever fallen!

Hannibal passed through Gaul, crossed the Alps, came down into Italy, and defeated several Roman generals; but he could not conquer the count r, nor take the city of Rome.

Let me die the death of the righteous, and let my last end be like his.

Hands of angels hidden from mortal eyes, shifted the scenery of the heavens; the glories of night dissolved into the glories of the dawn. The blue sky now turned more softly gray; the great watch-stars shut up their holy eyes, the east began to kindle, and soon the whole celestial concave was filled with the inflowing tides of the morning light.—*Everett.*

> The shadow of departed hours
> Hangs dim upon thine early flowers;
> Even in thy sunshine seems to brood
> Something too deep for solitude.—*Hemans.*

84. Verbs classified by their Form.

1. Verbs are divided, according to their *form*, into *regular* and *irregular.*

2. A **regular** verb is one which forms its past tense and past participle by adding **ed** (**28, 2**) to the present tense.

Ex.—Love, lov*ed*, lov*ed;* gain, gain*ed*, gain*ed.*

3. An **irregular** verb is one which does *not* form its past tense and past participle by the addition of **ed** to the present tense.

Ex.—*See, saw, seen; write, wrote, written.*

4. A **defective** verb is one in which some of the parts are wanting.

Ex.—*May, might; shall, should; will, would* (participle wanting).

5. An **auxiliary** verb is one which is employed in the conjugation of other verbs.

Ex.—*Have*, in *have* loved; *will*, in *will* love; *may*, in *may* love.

6. An **impersonal** verb is one by which an action or a state is asserted independently of any particular subject.

Ex.—It *rains*. It *snows*. It *lightens*. It *thunders*.

85. Exercise.

1. *Point out the verbs in the following examples; tell whether they are regular or irregular, transitive or intransitive.* (See list of irregular verbs.)

Where shall a man go to avoid pain and sickness?

If thine enemy hunger, feed him; if he thirst, give him drink.

All that the Father giveth me, shall come to me.

Canst thou bind the sweet influences of the Pleiades? or loose the bands of Orion?

I impeach him (Warren Hastings) in the name of the English nation, whose ancient honor he has sullied.—*Burke.*

Far as the breeze can bear, the billows foam,
Survey our empire, and behold our home.—*Byron.*

2. *Write five sentences containing regular transitive, and five containing irregular transitive verbs. Draw a line under the verb and its object.*

MODEL.

REG. TRANSITIVE.　　　　　　IRREG. TRANSITIVE.
Mr. Brown *has incurred* a great *debt.*　The child *led* the blind *man.*

3. *In the same way, write five sentences containing regular intransitive, and five containing irregular intransitive verbs.*

86. Properties of Verbs.

To verbs belong *voice, mode, tense, number,* and *person.*

87. Voice.

1. **Voice** is that form of the transitive verb which shows whether the subject *acts* or is *acted upon*.

2. There are two voices,—the *active* and the *passive*.

3. The **active** voice represents the subject as *acting*.

Ex.—John *struck* William.

Here *John* is the subject, and *John* performs the act.

4. The **passive** voice represents the subject as *acted upon*.

Ex.—William *was struck* by John.

Here *William* is the subject, but he does not act: he only *receives* the act, or is *acted upon;* that is, *is passive*, which means *suffering* or *receiving* an act, the subject or receiver, meanwhile, being in an inactive state.

Only transitive verbs can properly have a passive voice.

5. Any sentence, having for its predicate a transitive verb, may be transformed by changing the active to the passive voice, or the passive to the active. The same meaning, or nearly the same, will be expressed in either case.

Ex.—The locusts *devoured* (active) the grass. The grass *was devoured* (passive) by the locusts.

Strictly speaking, the ideas of *active* and *passive*, though manifesting themselves in the form of the verb, are not attributes of the verb, but of the persons or things connected with it: the one *performs* the act, the other *receives* or *suffers* it. If the active one is made the subject of the sentence, the verb is said to be in the *active voice;* if the passive one is made the subject, the verb is said to be in the *passive voice*.

6. The following are all the possible cases which can occur:—

(*a.*) *One* and the same person or thing may represent both relations, —the *active* and the *passive*.

Ex.—*He* struck *himself.* *She* struck *herself.* *It* destroyed *itself.* *You* struck *yourself.* *I* struck *myself.* (See Personal Pronoun, **70**, 7, 8.)

(*b.*) *Two* different persons or things may be employed to represent these relations.

(1.) One may be simply active, and the other simply passive.

Ex.—*George* struck *William*, = *William* was struck by *George.*

(2.) Each may be, at the same time, both active and passive.

Ex.—*They* struck *each other*, = *They* struck, each [struck] the other. (See **183,** 8.)

(*c.*) *Three* different persons or things may be employed; one active, and two passive.

(1.) One may act, another suffers the act, while the third stands as that to which the act is tending.

Ex.—*He* (act.) gave *me* (tending to) a *book* (pass.) *He* told *me* his *history*, = His *history* was told *me* by *him*, = *I* was told his *history* by *him*.

(2.) One acts, another is acted upon, and thereby transformed or made into the third (**187,** 9).

Ex.—They made *him* an *officer*, = He was made an *officer* by *them*, = An officer was made of *him* by *them*.

In this case there are but two *different* persons or things. The second and third denote the same individual.

7. The use of the passive voice enables us,—

(*a.*) To *conceal* the agent.

Ex.—The deed was performed, I must not tell by whom.

(*b.*) To give *prominence* to an event, or to *state* it when the agent is *unknown*.

Ex.—Letters were introduced at an early period.

(*c.*) To preserve the *unity* of a sentence which the use of the active voice would destroy.

Ex.—The ore was mined, shipped to England, and smelted in less than six months.

Observe, here are at least three different agents.

8. We use the active voice when we wish to make the agent prominent.

Ex.—*Moses* conducted the Israelites out of Egypt.

9. Some intransitive verbs, when accompanied by the preposition following, admit of a passive form.

Ex.—They *laughed at* him, = He was *laughed at*.

So, when a verb takes two objects, one *direct* and the other *indirect*, the latter is sometimes made the subject of the verb in the passive voice (**187,** 12).

Ex.—I told *him* a story, = *He* was told a story.

10. Certain intransitive verbs, as *come, arrive, fall, rise,* &c., admit of a passive form, yet with an intransitive signification, as will be seen by observing that the *agent* or *actor,* not the *object,* is the subject of the sentence in either form.

Ex.—Babylon *is fallen* (has fallen).

This idiom is less common now than formerly, and may be regarded as an imitation of the French or the German form of similar verbs.

88. Exercise.

1. *Tell which of the following verbs are in the active voice, and which in the passive:*—

The moon gives a pleasant light. The book was written by my father. The song of the bird is heard in the grove. Leverrier discovered a new planet. How doth the little busy bee improve each shining hour! Knowledge gives power. The heavens declare the glory of God.

2. *In the above sentences, change the verbs in the active voice into the passive, and the verbs in the passive voice into the active.*

3. *Write five sentences containing regular, and five containing irregular verbs in the passive voice.*

MODEL.

REG. PASSIVE.	IRREG. PASSIVE.
Charles I. *was beheaded.*	The grass *was mown.*

4. *Select the verbs in the following examples, tell whether they are regular or irregular, transitive or intransitive, of the active or the passive voice:*—

The thunders of heaven are sometimes heard to roll in the voice of a united people.

In the battle of Solferino, four hundred thousand men are said to have been engaged.

I care not what mines are opened in the mountains of Siberia, or in the sierras of California; wheresoever the fountains of the golden tide may gush forth, the streams will flow to the regions where educated intellect has woven the boundless network of the useful and ornamental arts.—*Everett.*

'Tis finished.—Their thunders are hushed on the moors;
Culloden is lost, and my country deplores:
But where is the iron-bound prisoner? Where?
For the red eye of battle is shut in despair.—*Campbell.*

89. Mode.

1. **Mode** is the *manner* in which the action, the being, or the state is asserted.

2. Mode does not show the manner of the action or state, but the manner of its assertion. It may be asserted as a *reality*, or as something *imagined* that *may*, *can*, or *must* take place, or as something *imagined* or *supposed* which is placed under a condition, or as something *desired*. The manner of the action or state is expressed by means of limiting words; as, "The soldier *fought* (a reality) *bravely*" (manner of the act); "The soldier *may fight* (something imagined) *bravely*" (manner of the supposed act).

3. The infinitive is not properly a mode of the verb (**80**, 2); for, since it does not assert action at all, it cannot be said to have any *manner* or *mode* of assertion. The same may be said of the participle. In fact, the infinitive is a participle, partaking of the properties of the noun and the verb, as the (so called) participle partakes of the properties of the adjective and the verb (**80**, 4). It is inserted here in conformity with established usage, but may be called *the infinitive*,—not the infinitive mode.

4. There are commonly reckoned five modes,—the *indicative*, the *potential*, the *subjunctive*, the *imperative*, and the *infinitive*.

5. The **indicative** mode asserts a thing as *actually existing*. (See 10, below.)

Ex.—James *loves*. William *was struck*. *Has* he *come?*

6. The **potential** mode asserts the *power, liberty, permission, necessity,* or *duty* of acting, or of being in a certain state.

Ex.—We *can sing*. You *may write*. *Must* he *read?* They *should obey* the law. *Can* you *do* it?

7. The **subjunctive** mode asserts a thing as *conditional* or as *doubtful*.

Ex.—If he *leave* me. Though he *slay* me.

8. The **imperative** mode asserts a *command*, an *entreaty*, or a *permission*.

Ex.—*Write*. *Go* thou. *Be admonished*.

9. The **infinitive** represents the action or state as an abstract noun.

Ex.—*To write*. *To be seen*.

10. The indicative mode is used in principal propositions, and is employed to represent what is *actual*, *real*, or *absolute*. It may be used in interrogative or exclamatory sentences.

Ex.—Has he arrived? The villain has fired the dwelling!

It is often used in subordinate propositions, but always to represent what is actual; as, "I know *that* he discovered (actually) the plot."

11. The potential mode is also used in principal propositions, not, however, to represent the actual, but that which, at the time of speaking, exists, or is supposed to exist, only in *idea*,—that which is merely *imagined* or *thought of*.

Ex.—A storm *may* arise. (*Actually* there is no storm.) Can he write? How can you persist?

The *ideal* act or state, however, is supposed to have some relation to *reality*. It *can* become a reality; that is, there is no impossibility in the way of its realization; no ability is wanting: it *may* become a reality; that is, *permission* is granted, or in the final result *perhaps* it will be a reality: it *must* become actual; that is, a *necessity* or an *obligation* exists. This mode may be used in interrogative, exclamatory, or supplicatory sentences; as, "Can he leave the city in safety?" "He may be assassinated." "May the truth be victorious!" It may be used in subordinate propositions, but always to represent what is *ideal* or what has not been *realized;* as, "He says that I may (I *do* not now) attend school."

12. The potential may be known by the auxiliaries, *may, can, must, might, could, would, should*. (See **113.**)

13. The subjunctive mode is used exclusively in subordinate propositions, and hence its name ("sub," *under*, and "jungo," *I join*). It is joined to the verb of the principal proposition by the subordinate conjunctions, *if, though, although, lest, except, that, save that, unless, provided that,* and some others; they impart the idea of *doubt, contingency,* or *conditionality.*

Whatever of futurity may be implied in the subjunctive, is to be accounted for either from the fact that any thing that is conditional or contingent is *yet* to be realized (if ever), or from the influence of a suppressed auxiliary, such as *shall* or *should*, which imparts (though understood) the idea of futurity; as, "Though he (should) slay me, yet will I trust in him."

14. The subjunctive represents an ideal act, or a real act conceived only as an idea, and places it under a condition accompanied with more or less doubt. As to a distinctive form of the subjunctive, it can scarcely be said to have any, unless it be found in the present tense, or the present and past of *to be;* and in all such cases (with the single exception of *were*, in examples like "If it *were*,"

"If I *were*"), by supplying an ellipsis, they may be referred to the forms of the indicative future or the past potential.

Ex.—If it rain, we shall not leave, = If it *should* rain, &c. Till one greater man restore (*shall* restore) us, and regain (*shall* regain) the blissful seat, sing, heavenly muse.

> The majority of writers, at present, employ the forms of the indicative present; as, "If it rains;" "If he leaves." Hence the subjunctive may be regarded as borrowing its forms from the indicative and the potential mode. Indeed, as a *form* of the language, it is now but little used. "The subjunctive is evidently passing out of use; and there is good reason to suppose that it will soon become obsolete altogether."—*Geo. P. Marsh.*

15. The imperative mode is used in principal propositions. It is the mode which expresses *will* or *desire*. It may usually be known by the omission of the subject.

Ex.—*Read* (thou); *write*.

The force of this mode, under the same form, depends upon the relation of the parties. If a superior speaks imperatively to an inferior, it is a command; if an equal to an equal, it is an exhortation or an entreaty; if an inferior to a superior, it is a prayer or a supplication. The imperative is made subordinate only in a direct quotation; as, "God said, Let there be light." It is often elegantly put for a conditional clause; as, "Let but the commons hear this testament, and they would go and kiss dead Cæsar's wounds," = Could the commons, &c., or, If the commons could but hear, &c.

16. The infinitive is used in abridged propositions, and hence is wholly dependent, being incorporated as an element of another proposition. It does not assert any thing; it is not limited by the number and the person of a subject, and hence its name (**so**, 2), *infinitive*, = *unlimited*, in distinction from *finite*, which is applied to all verbs used in construction with their subjects, and thereby limited by the number and person of the latter.

17. The infinitive is used as an abstract noun; yet it may be associated with the subject from which it has been abstracted.

Ex.—The soldier *faints* (finite); for the *soldier to faint* (infin.). He *goes; for him to go;* we told *him to go*.

90. Exercise.

Tell the mode of each of the verbs in the following examples; also the kind of verb:—

Where wast thou when I laid the foundations of the earth? declare, if thou hast understanding.

Then said Jesus to his disciples, If any man will come after me, let him deny himself, and take up his cross, and follow me.

We can converse with a picture, and find an agreeable companion in a statue.—*Addison.*

> Daughter of Faith! awake, arise, illume
> The dread unknown, the chaos of the tomb.—*Campbell.*

> And out again I curve and flow,
> To join the brimming river;
> For men may come, and men may go,
> But I go on forever.—*Tennyson.*

PARTICIPLES.
91. Definition and Distinctions.

1. A **participle** is a word having the signification of a verb, but the construction of an adjective.

Ex.—We found him *lying* on the ground. *Having written* his letter, he sent it to his friend.

2. The participle is so called because it participates or partakes of the properties of the verb and the adjective. It is the attributive (**80, 4, 5**) part of the verb alone; it is the being, action, or state deprived of the power of assertion; and therefore, when joined without the copula to the noun whose attribute it expresses, it must be assumed (not predicated) (**205, 2**), just as an adjective is assumed under similar circumstances. It has the meaning of the verb and is modified like the verb, but is used like the adjective.

3. The participle is not a distinct part of speech, but is derived directly from the verb,—the present by adding *ing*, the past by adding *ed*, to all regular verbs, and the perfect by prefixing to the past the auxiliary *having*.

92. Classes of Participles.

1. There are, properly, two participles,—the *present* and the *perfect*.

Ex.—*Reading, having read; (being) loved, having been loved.*

2. These two participles correspond to the present and the perfect tense of the verb. They are used in abridged propositions: the former, when the pro-

position before its abridgment was in the present, the past, or the future tense; the latter, when it was in either of the perfect tenses. See abridged propositions (**167, 2**).

3. There are, however, three forms, commonly called participles,—the *present*, the *past*, and the *perfect*.

Ex.—

	Pres.	*Past.*	*Perf.*
ACTIVE VOICE,	Loving,	Loved,	Having loved.
PASSIVE VOICE,	(Being) loved,	Loved,	Having been loved.

4. The passive participle *loved* does not necessarily denote past time. Of itself, it simply denotes the reception of an act, complete or incomplete. The time depends upon that of the verb with which it is associated.

REMARK 1.—The form called the *past participle* may have been once the passive participle, having the same form. If so, it has now wholly lost its original signification, and, strictly speaking, has lost its character as a participle. It never partakes of the properties of the adjective; it is never used to limit a noun, like that part of speech; it is never used alone in participial constructions,—that is, where the participle, with the words depending upon it, takes the place of a subordinate proposition; it is always found in the predicate, either of complete or abridged propositions, and is connected with some form of *have ;* as, *have loved, had loved, having loved ;* it has an active signification, and always denotes a past, completed act, and belongs as well to intransitive as to transitive verbs.

REMARK 2.—The passive participle of the same form, on the contrary, is limited to transitive verbs, has always a passive signification, may denote as well present as past time; it may have the participial construction, or, with the copula, may form the *passive verb* in all the modes and tenses.

5. Participles, in their appropriate use, take the place of dependent propositions, and consequently represent time in the same manner as the propositions from which they are derived. As the verb of the dependent clause dates from the time expressed by the principal verb, and not from that of the speaker, the participle may be present, with a past, a present, or a future act.

Ex.—I saw a man *walking;* I see a man *walking;* I shall see a man *walking.*

So, again, the participle may denote a past act, completed at the time of a past, a present, or a future act.

Ex.—*Having ploughed* his field, the farmer *sowed, sows, will sow,* the seed.

93. Present Active Participle.

1. The **present active** participle denotes an action or a state present and in progress at the time represented by the principal verb.

Ex.—We *find, found,* or *shall find* him *sitting* in a chair.

2. This participle always ends in *ing:* it has an active signification, and may be used,—

(*a.*) **To abridge a dependent proposition.**
Ex.—I saw a man *walking in the meadow,* i.e. *who was walking,* &c.

(*b.*) **As an adjective.** It is then placed before the noun.
Ex.—The *roaring* billows.
When thus used, it is called a *participial adjective.*

(*c.*) In the **progressive form** of the verb.
Ex.—I am *reading.*

(*d.*) **Gerundively,** to denote a concomitant act,—came *how?*
Ex.—The Son of man came *eating* and *drinking.*

(*e.*) As a **noun,**—(1) Wholly so, with *the* preceding, and *of* following.
Ex.—The *reading* of the law.

(2.) In the construction of the noun with the modifications of the verb.
Ex.—The eye is never satisfied with *beholding* the stupendous works of the Creator.

3. Though this participle is usually active, it sometimes has a passive signification. When an object is undergoing a progressive change, and we wish to express this as a continuous reception of the act, our language is deficient in appropriate forms. Good writers have resorted to the use of the active participle, giving it a passive signification.

Ex.—The house is *building.* New efforts are *making* for the extension of this trade.—*Webster.* This new tragedy was *acting.*—*Everett.*

Recent writers of some distinction have adopted the forms, "The house is *being built;*" "Preparations are *being made.*" It is not the province of the grammarian to dictate as to questions of usage, but to admit and explain whatever good, national, and reputable usage sanctions. When subjected to these tests, it must be said of such forms, that they are by no means adopted by the best writers as good English, they are not sanctioned by the best grammarians, and they are of too recent origin to be regarded as idioms of the language.

94. Present Passive Participle.

1. The **present passive** participle denotes the reception of an act at the time represented by the principal verb.

Ex.—He *lives, lived, will live, loved* by all.

2. This participle may be used as an adjective, or, with the copula, to form the passive verb.

Ex.—A *refined* taste *is possessed* only by the *cultivated*.

When preceded by *being*, it may be used as a noun.

Ex.—By *being involved* in one wrong act, he was soon lost to all the appeals of his friends.

95. Perfect Participles, Active and Passive.

1. The **perfect active** participle denotes an action or a state completed at the time represented by the principal verb.

Ex.—*Having finished* his speech, he *sat* down.

2. The **perfect passive** participle denotes the reception of an act past and completed at the time represented by the principal verb.

Ex.—*Having been driven* from home, he enlisted in the army.

3. The perfect participles are never used like the present, with the copula, to form the predicate. They may be used as verbal nouns.

Ex.—He was accused of *having obtained* goods on false pretences.

96. The Participle predicated or assumed.

1. The action or the state expressed by the participle may be either *predicated* or *assumed* (**205**, 2).

Ex.—The horse *is running* through the street. The horse *running* through the street.

2. The participle, when the act is predicated, constitutes, with the copula, or auxiliary *have*, a form of the verb. The present participle is used in the *progressive form* (**109**, 1) or imperfect

tenses; the past, in the *complete form*, or the perfect; the passive, in the *passive form*.

Ex.—The farmer *was ploughing* his field. The farmer *had ploughed* his field. The field *was ploughed* by the farmer.

3. The participle, when the act is assumed, is equivalent to a subordinate clause; as, "The boat which sails on yonder lake is propelled by steam," = The boat *sailing* on yonder lake is propelled by steam. (See **205**, 2.)

97. Exercise.

1. *Write the participles of the following verbs:—*

Find, obey, ride, grow, lie, lay, sit, set, lose, loose, load, steal, arrive, suppose, happen, come, do, take, run.

2. *Use each of the above participles in a short sentence.*

Models.—*Finding* his mistake, he left. The source of the river *being found*, the travellers returned home. *Having found* the owner, he restored the ring.

3. *Point out the* PARTICIPLES *in the following examples; tell what kind of participle each one is, and name the verb from which it is derived:—*

Let the last feeble and lingering glance of my dying eyes rather behold the gorgeous ensign of the Republic, now known and honored throughout the earth, still full high advanced,—its arms and trophies streaming in their original lustre, not a stripe erased or polluted, nor a single star obscured.—*Webster*.

One wave rises, and, having reached its destined limit, falls gently away, and is succeeded by yet another.—*Story*.

   Then shook the hills, with thunder riven;
   Then rushed the steeds to battle driven;
   And, louder than the bolts of heaven,
    Far flashed the red artillery.—*Campbell*.

  The warriors on the turrets high,
  Moving athwart the evening sky,
   Seemed forms of giant height.
  Above the gloomy portal arch,
  Timing his footsteps to a march,
   The warder kept his guard,
  Low humming, as he paced along,
  Some ancient border-gathering song.—*Scott*.

98. Tense.

1. **Tense** primarily denotes the *time* of an action or an event, in its relation to the moment of speaking.

2. In reference to the time of speaking, an action or an event may be *present, past,* or *future*.

Ex.—I *ride;* I *rode;* I shall *ride*.

3. The **tense-form** of the verb denotes also the *state* of an action or an event with reference to its *continuance*.

4. An action or an event is,—

Indefinite, when (**109,** 5) it is viewed at the *commencement* as one event, *complete in itself*, without reference to its *progress* or *completion*.

Ex.—I *love;* I *loved;* I *shall love*.

Progressive, when (**109,** 9) it is contemplated in its progress as *going on*, without regard to its *commencement* or *completion*.

Ex.—I *am writing;* I *was writing;* I *shall be writing*.

Perfect or **completed**, when the attention is directed to its *end* or *completion*, without reference to its *commencement* or *progress*.

Ex.—I *have written;* I *had written;* I *shall have written*.

Perfect progressive, when regard is had to both the *progress* and the *completion*, and not to the *commencement*.

Ex.—I *have been writing;* I *had been writing;* I *shall have been writing*.

REMARK.—As the *passive voice* denotes the *reception* of an act, it expresses an event which may be regarded as indefinite, progressive, or completed (**110**).

99. Divisions of Time.

1. In each of the three divisions of time—the *past*, the *present*, and the *future*—we distinguish a **point** and a **period**.

REMARK.—By a "point" is not meant the least possible division of time, but any portion taken without regard to its duration. Thus, the time of speaking may really be a period. The point is referred to by *when, as, the moment;* whereas the period is referred to by *while, during which, how long*.

2. The **point** of time denotes either *the time of speaking*, as the first and principal point of reference, or a *specified date* in either of the periods.

Ex.—I have written a letter *to-day* since *twelve o'clock*.

Here, observe the time of speaking,—*now;* the event,—*past* as to the moment of speaking,—*have written,*—but *present* as to its completion in the present period,—*to-day;* also a specified date,—*twelve o'clock.*

I had written a letter *last month* before the *15th.*

Here we have the time of speaking,—*now;* the past event,—*had written;* also the past period, including the time of its completion,—*last month;* and the specified date,—*the 15th.*

I shall have written a letter before the mail leaves.

Here the future period is indefinite.

3. The **period** is a *definite* or an *indefinite* portion of time, either *past, present,* or *future.*

Ex.—Last month, last year; this century, this age; next week, next quarter.

The indefinite present is any assumed portion of time; while the indefinite past or future extends from the present without limit. It is important to observe that a present period includes the time of speaking, and also the time of the completion of an act; that the past or the future period excludes the time of speaking, but includes the time of the completion, and usually a second date to which the latter is referred.

4. Tenses which receive this second point of reference are called *relative tenses;* while those which have only a single reference to the speaker are called *absolute tenses.*

5. Each division has two tenses,—an *absolute* and a *relative.* There are, therefore, six tenses,—three absolute and three relative; as (absolute), "I *write,*" "I *wrote,*" "I *shall write;*" (relative), "I *have written*" (some time to-day or this year), "I *had written*" (before the boat sailed), "I *shall have written*" (at noon).

6. The absolute tenses take their names from the division of time to which they belong. Thus, we have the *present* tense, the *past* tense, the *future* tense. The relative tenses affix to the name of the tense the word *perfect,* which refers not so much to the *time* as to the *completion* of the act. Thus, we have the *present perfect,* the *past perfect,* and the *future perfect.*

Strict analogy would give us, for the *progressive* forms, *I am writing, I was writing, I shall be writing,* present, past, and future *imperfect* tenses.

100. Tenses in the Indicative Mode.

The tenses of the indicative are,—the *present,* the *present perfect;* the *past,* the *past perfect;* the *future,* the *future perfect.*

These tenses have their characteristic significations only in the indicative mode.

101. Present Tense.

1. The **present** tense represents what takes place in present time.

Ex.—I *see;* I am *seeing;* I *do see;* I am *seen.*

By present, here, is meant the present of the speaker or the writer. The present of the hearer is the same as that of the speaker; but that of the reader is not the same as that of the writer.

2. This tense may be used to denote an action or an event,—

(1.) As in itself *complete* at the *precise moment* of speaking; as, "I *see it;*" "I *feel* the *heat;*" "I *perceive* your meaning;" *i.e.* when the event is *instantly* perceived and mentioned. Compare with (3), below.

(2.) As *incomplete* at the *precise moment* of speaking; as, "I am *writing;*" "The boy *is studying.*"

(3.) As a *habit* or a *custom* in a *limited period* assumed as present; as, "He *reads* seven languages;" but not at the time of speaking, nor forever.

(4.) As a *universal truth* during an *unlimited period;* as, "Vice produces misery;" "God *is just;*" and that regardless of the time of speaking, and forever.

(5.) As if *present,* though really in the past or future,—to represent a thing *more vividly,* or to make it present to another future event.

Ex.—Hark! *heard* ye not those hoofs of dreadful note? *Sounds* not the clang....—*Byron.* They *rally,* they *bleed* (as *now* seen in vision) for their kingdom and crown.—*Campbell.* We *will pay* him when he *comes* (*shall come*). Matthew *traces* (*has traced*) the descent of Joseph; Luke *traces* (*has traced*) that of Mary.

102. Present Perfect Tense.

1. The **present perfect** tense represents a past event as completed in present time.

Ex.—I *have seen;* I *have been seeing;* I *have been seen.*

In this tense, **present-perfect,** observe that a period—*this* day, *this* year, the *present* age (hence the prefix *present*)—embraces the time of *finishing* an act (hence *perfect*), and also a subsequent time of *speaking* of it (hence a present and a past *within* the period). (See 99, 2, 3.)

NOTE.—Be careful to distinguish *present* meaning the period, from *present* meaning the time of speaking.

2. This tense may be used,—

(1.) To denote an act *completed* in the assumed present, with only an implied reference to the time of speaking.

Ex.—"He *has learned* his lesson,"—the *fact* remains till now.

(2.) To denote an act spoken of as *completed*, but continuing till the time of speaking, either in *itself* or in its *effects*.

Ex.—"Jupiter has revolved around the sun for ages,"—the *fact* and the *act* continue. "The culprit *has been imprisoned* for ten years,"—the *act* was completed, and the *condition* remains till *now*.

(3.) To denote an act completed in a future period, to correspond with a future event.

Ex.—They *will be dissatisfied* before they *have remained* a month.

103. Past Tense.

1. The **past** tense represents what took place in time wholly past.

Ex.—I *saw;* I *was seeing;* I *was seen.*

In this tense, the time of *speaking* is the present; that of the *act* or the *event*, a period wholly past.

2. This tense is used to denote an act or an event,—

(1.) As in itself *complete*, begun and ended in a past period absolutely, or with reference to a specified time.

Ex.—He *wrote* a letter; He *wrote* a *letter at noon yesterday.*

This is the Latin *perfect*, or the Greek *aorist*.

(2.) As *incomplete* at, before, or after a past time mentioned.

Ex.—He *was riding* by, *at, before*, or *after* noon.

This is the true Latin *imperfect*.

(3.) As a *custom* or *habit* belonging to a past *period*.

Ex.—He *braided* lace at intervals.

104. Past Perfect Tense.

1. The **past perfect** represents a past event as completed in time wholly past.

Ex.—I *had seen;* I *had been seeing;* I *had been seen.*

NOTE.—Observe the difference between the past and the past perfect. "I *wrote* a letter yesterday." Here the act is spoken of as complete in itself, that is, *begun, continued,* and *finished* (but without reference to either, 98, 4), in the period *yesterday.* "I *had written* a letter yesterday at twelve o'clock." Here the act is spoken of *as completed* at a specified time in the period *yesterday.*

2. This tense is used only when the present, or time of *speaking*, is separated from a *period* wholly past, and the time of an act is at or before a *specified time* in this period.

Ex.—"He *had written* his letter before noon;" that is, He *had* (in a past period) *written* (finished the act) *before noon* (specified time in the period).

105. Future Tense.

1. The **future** tense represents what will take place in future time.

Ex.—I *shall see;* I *shall be seeing;* I *shall be seen.*

2. In this tense, as in the others, an event may be represented as in itself *complete, incomplete,* or as a *custom.*

Ex.—He *will write;* He *will write* before *noon.* They *will be marching* before the *dawn.* The lion *shall eat* straw like the ox.

106. Future Perfect Tense.

1. The **future perfect** tense represents an event as completed in future time.

Ex.—I *shall have seen.*

NOTE.—Observe that in all the perfect tenses *four* different times are, or may be, distinguished:—a *period,* past, present, or future (sometimes named, oftener not); the *time of completing* something in any one of the periods; the *time of speaking,* always in the present period; a *specified time,* always in the same period as the event.

Ex.—"I *have* (time of speaking) *caused* (time of completing) the bells to be rung *before twelve* (specified time) *to-day* (present period)." So, "I *had caused,* &c., *yesterday.*" "I *shall have caused,* &c., *to-morrow.*"

2. This tense differs from the simple future as the past perfect differs from the past. It represents an act *as completed,* and refers to a specified time in some future period.

Ex.—I *shall have written* a letter *at twelve to-morrow.*

107. Tenses in all the Modes.

1. The subjunctive mode has *six tenses,*—the same as the indicative.

2. The potential mode has *four tenses,*—the present, the present perfect, the past, and the past perfect.

3. The infinitive has *two tenses,*—the present and the perfect.

4. The imperative has only *one tense,*—the present.

5. Tense in the subjunctive mode does not usually mark time with the same exactness as in the indicative. Thus,—

(*a.*) In conditional clauses, if the thing spoken of denotes something *actual* or taken as actual, the tense-form usually denotes the true time.

Ex.—If it *rained,* I did not know it.

But if it refers to something merely hypothetical or supposed, the past tense represents present time, and the past perfect represents past time.

Ex.—If I *were going* now (but I cannot), I should ride. If I *had had* an opportunity yesterday (but I had none), I should have spoken to him.

(*b.*) The verb *to be* has a distinct form for the present and the past tense used hypothetically and denoting present time (**89,** 13).

Ex.—If it *be* true. If I *were* not Alexander, I would be Diogenes.

(*c.*) *Were* in this use cannot stand for *would be,* or *would have been,* although in other uses it may.

Ex.—It *were* an impossibility to raise the requisite sum,—*would be.*

Had, in like manner, is used for *would,* or *would have.*

Ex.—I *had* rather be a dog, and bay the moon, than such a Roman. It *had* been better for him if he had pursued the opposite course.

6. The tenses in the potential mode have by no means the signification which their *names* denote.

(*a.*) The present denotes present *possibility, permission, ability,* or *necessity* to perform an act sometimes *present* and sometimes *future.*

Ex.—We *may (now) go (to-morrow).* You *can (now) write (now).* He must *(now)* leave *(now, to-morrow, next week).*

(*b.*) The present perfect generally denotes a present *possibility, necessity,* &c. that a past act was performed.

Ex.—I *must* have written (= it *is* now undeniable that I *wrote*) (yesterday).

(c.) The past denotes,—

(1.) A past *possibility*, &c. to perform an act.

Ex.—Can you write? I *could* write yesterday.

(2.) A *custom*.

Ex.—He *would* often sit the entire evening without uttering a word.

Would and *might* are now seldom, if ever, used to denote past time.

(3.) It denotes the present *possibility*, &c. when followed by a conditional clause.

Ex.—I *might* or *could* go (now) if I would. I *should* or *would* go (now) if I could.

(4.) It denotes a *future possibility*, &c.

Ex.—I shall not go; but if I *should go* (hereafter), I *could* (hereafter) walk.

(5.) It denotes a universal duty without reference to time.

Ex.—Children *should obey* their parents.

(d.) The past perfect denotes usually a past *possibility*, &c., but by no means a past completed act. It usually implies the non-performance of the act. Thus: I *could have assisted* you (yesterday) if you had desired it, = I was able to assist you, but you did not desire it, and I *did not do* it.

7. The infinitive has but two tenses,—the present and the perfect. They denote, the former an indefinite or a progressive, and the latter a completed, state of the act.

Ex.—*To write; To be writing. To have written; To have been writing.*

(a.) The infinitive, like the participle, may be connected with any mode or tense of the principal verb.

(b.) The present infinitive denotes a time either present or future with reference to that of the principal verb, and not necessarily present with the speaker.

Ex.—I *intend to write*. I *intended to write*. I *had intended to write*. I *shall begin to write*.

(c.) The perfect denotes a past act completed at the time denoted by the principal verb.

Ex.—She *is said to have sung*. She *was thought to have written*. She *will be known to have done it*.

8. The imperative has only the present tense, which denotes the time of *giving* a command; the time of its performance is future.

ETYMOLOGY—VERBS—FORMS.   109

108. Exercise.

1. *Tell the* TENSES *of the following verbs:—*

Did you hear the lecture? He listened earnestly. I hope to find the study interesting. It will not rain. Ralph had intended to go. I have heard the Irish orator. We saw the constellation of the Southern Cross. Richard will have learned his lesson by the time we wish to leave. I shall have finished my work when Sarah comes. The child cried. Was the view pleasant? Are the notes of the nightingale sad? Had Anne read the book? The hills were covered with snow.

2. *Tell the* TENSES *of the following verbs; also those which denote the* RECEPTION *of an act, which the* PROGRESS, *which the* COMPLETION *of an act, and which an act* COMPLETE *in itself:—*

The paper is published in Boston. Is he planting the seed? Has Frank been drawing? I shall be allowed to go. When will Caroline go to ride? Have they been to the concert? My brother is teaching. Happiness will be her portion. Sorrow is the common lot. Have you been taught to sing? Had his wife heard the good news? I wish to go. I will not be denied. He shall not forget the penalty. Flowers bloom. Our friends will have gone when you come. Joseph tore the book. What shall I do? William has gained the prize. Have you been to Europe? Fanny has been learning to skate. The clock has struck. Washington was never known to tell a lie. He had been promoted. You do not think so. You will learn to know her better. It shall not be. The general is deceived. Charles has fallen from the tree. He broke his arm. Louisa was carrying the package. He shall be immortal who liveth till he be stoned by one without fault.

109. Forms of the Verb.

1. The **forms** of the verb are its various changes to express the *time* and *state* (**98**, 1, 3) of an act in the several modes and tenses.

2. *Transitive* verbs may have four forms,—the *common*, the *emphatic*, the *progressive*, and the *passive*.

Ex.—I *love;* I *do love;* I *am loving;* I *am loved.*

3. The emphatic form is confined to the present and past indicative, and the present imperative. The other forms are extended through all the modes and tenses.

4. *Intransitive* verbs may have three forms,—the *common*, the *emphatic*, and the *progressive*.

Ex.—I *sit;* I *do sit;* I *am sitting.*

5. The *common* (indefinite) form represents an act indefinitely, as a custom, or as completed, without reference to its progress.

Ex.—I *love;* I *loved;* I *shall love;* I *have loved.*

6. The variations of this form in the second and the third person, as seen in the terminations *est* and *eth*, belong to what is called the *solemn style*. They are found in the Scriptures, in forms of prayer, in poetry, and in various sacred books.

7. The *emphatic* form represents an act with emphasis.

Ex.—I *do write;* I *did write.*

8. This form is used in interrogative or negative sentences without emphasis.

Ex.—Do *you write?* Did *you write?* I *do write.*

9. The *progressive* form represents the *progress* of an unfinished act.

Ex.—I *am writing.*

10. In the perfect tenses, it represents the *completion* of a progressive act.

Ex.—I *have been writing;* I *shall have been writing.*

11. The *passive* form represents the reception of an act.

Ex.—I *am loved;* I *was loved;* I *shall be loved.*

12. The perfect tenses of this form are used when we wish to represent the *completion* of a *passive* state.

Ex.—I *have been honored;* I *had been honored;* I *shall have been honored.*

The following table gives the form for each division of time, with a description of the state of the act:—

110. Forms for each Division of Time.

I. Present.

Time.	Act.	Example.
1. Present.	Complete in itself.	He *writes.*
2. "	Progressive incomplete.	He *is writing.*
3. "	Completed.	He *has written.*
4. "	Progressive completed.	He *has been writing.*
5. "	Emphatic.	He *does write.*
6. "	Passive or received.	The letter *is written.*
7. "	Progressive received.	The house *is building.*
8. "	Passive completed.	The letter *has been written.*

ETYMOLOGY—VERBS—AUXILIARIES. 111

II. Past.

Time.	Act.	Example.
1. Past.	Complete in itself.	He *wrote*.
2. "	Progressive incomplete.	He *was writing*.
3. "	Completed.	He *had written*.
4. "	Progressive completed.	He *had been writing*.
5. "	Emphatic.	He *did write*.
6. "	Passive or received.	The letter *was written*.
7. "	Progressive received.	The house *was building*.
8. "	Passive completed.	The letter *had been written*.

III. Future.

1. Future.	Complete in itself.	He *will write*.
2. "	Progressive incomplete.	He *will be writing*.
3. "	Completed.	He *will have written*.
4. "	Progressive completed.	He *will have been writing*.
5. "	Passive or received.	The letter *will be written*.
6. "	Progressive received.	The house *will be building*.
7. "	Passive completed.	The letter *will have been written*.

111. Auxiliaries.

1. **Auxiliary verbs** are those which are used in conjugating other verbs. They are,—

PRES. *Do, be, have, shall, will, may, can, must.*
PAST. *Did, was, had, should, would, might, could,* ———

2. The auxiliaries were originally *principal verbs;* and some of them are still used as such.

3. The auxiliary verbs are used to form the modes and tenses of other verbs, and to give to the forms in which they are used the shades of meaning peculiar to their original signification.

4. In the early stages of the language, these verbs were undoubtedly used as principal verbs followed and modified by the infinitive of what is now called the principal verb; as, *may go, can* read, *must* sing; like the Latin *Possum scribere,* or the French *Je puis aller,* or the German *Ich kann schreiben.* Finally, the subordinate infinitive came to be regarded as the principal verb, and that on which it depended became its auxiliary.

5. The auxiliaries should be regarded merely as *relation-words,* or words used to show relations of *time* and *mode,* as the preposition is used to show relations of *time, place, origin, cause, manner, property, material,* &c. In fact,

all words used to show a relation of whatever nature—such as *prepositions*, *relative pronouns*, and *conjunctive adverbs*—are a species of auxiliary. In the progress of language, these auxiliaries have increased, and in the same ratio the inflection of the principal word has diminished. An exact and familiar acquaintance with their various uses is essential to a correct knowledge of the language. (See **113**, below.)

6. The auxiliaries, as such, have only two tenses,—the *present* and the *past*,—except *must*, which has no variation. They may be thus represented:—

112. Conjugation of the Auxiliaries.

	\<th colspan="3"\>Singular.			\<th colspan="3"\>Plural.		
	1st Per.	2d Per.	3d Per.	1st Per.	2d Per.	3d Per.
	I.	*Thou.*	*He.*	*We.*	*You.*	*They.*
Present.	Am	art	is	are	are	are
	Do	dost	does	do	do	do
	Have	hast	has	have	have	have
	Will	wilt	will	will	will	will
	Shall	shalt	shall	shall	shall	shall
	May	mayst	may	may	may	may
	Can	canst	can	can	can	can
	Must	must	must	must	must	must
Past.	Was	wast	was	were	were	were
	Did	didst	did	did	did	did
	Had	hadst	had	had	had	had
	Would	wouldst	would	would	would	would
	Should	shouldst	should	should	should	should
	Might	mightst	might	might	might	might
	Could	couldst	could	could	could	could

113. Signification of the Auxiliaries.

1. The auxiliaries, deriving much of their force from their original significations, give their own shades of meaning to the tense-form into which they enter.

2. **Be**, from the Saxon "beon," *to be fixed, to exist*, denotes *existence*.

As an auxiliary, it is the *copula*, used (**80**, 5) to join an attribute to, and assert its existence in, the subject; as, "The heat *is* oppressive."

3. **Do**, from the Saxon "don," *to do*, denotes *action*.

As an auxiliary, it is used chiefly to give *intensity* of meaning to the action of the principal verb. This it does especially in affirmative sentences, and, to some degree, in negative. But, in interrogative sentences it is little more than a sign of interrogation; as, "I *do* try;" "I *did* go;" "He *did* not speak;" "*Do* you hear it?"

4. **Have**, from the Saxon "habban," *to have*, denotes *possession*.

As an auxiliary, it retains its original meaning in the idea of *completion;* as if an act was not fully possessed by its subject until completed. It seems to have acquired this meaning thus:—In "I have treasures concealed," *have* denotes possession, and is separated from "concealed;" in "I have concealed treasures," it still denotes possession, but is brought into connection with "concealed;" whereas, in "I have concealed the treasures," it is brought into intimate relation with "concealed," which passes from a passive to an active signification; and here we have the idea of possession or *completion* of the act.

5. **Shall**, from the Saxon "scealan," *to be obliged*, and **will**, from the Saxon "willan," *to determine*, have,—

(*a.*) A *complex signification*, when a future event is made to depend upon the determination, resolution, or volition of a personal agent (either the actor or another).

Ex.—He *shall* go (I so resolve); I *will* go (I myself so resolve).

(*b.*) A *simple signification*, denoting mere futurity, when a future event is wholly or chiefly independent of *volition* or *resolution.*

Ex.—It *will* rain (whatever you or I may resolve); I *shall* be overtaken (independent of my will).

In this case the speaker merely *predicts* or expresses an *opinion*. The past tenses *should* and *would* are used with the same or nearly the same significations.

The following rules apply to *shall* and *will.*

6. RULE I.—*When the person who resolves or predicts is not mentioned, the speaker or* FIRST *person is always understood in affirmative, and the hearer or* SECOND *in interrogative sentences.*

Ex.—You shall go. (*I* will it.) Shall he go? (Do *you* will it?) It will rain. (*I* predict it.) Will it rain? (Do *you* predict it?)

7. RULE II.—WILL *should be used when the resolution and the action are attributed to the* SAME *person, and* SHALL *when they are attributed to* DIFFERENT *persons.*

Ex.—I will go. (I myself resolve.) Will you go? (Do you yourself resolve?) He will go. (He himself resolves.) He shall go. (I resolve.) They have determined that you shall go. Shall he go? (Do you resolve?)

8. RULE III.—SHALL *should be used when the prediction and the action are both attributed to the* SAME *person, or in any case, provided the action be attributed to the* FIRST *person; and* WILL *should be used when the prediction and the action (except in the case of the first person) are attributed to* DIFFERENT *persons.*

Ex.—You will be promoted. (I predict it.) I shall teach, or be a teacher. (I, he, you, or they, predict it.) Will he teach? (Do you predict it?) Will it rain? (Do you think so?) It will rain. (I think so.)

Shall is used in animated discourse, contrary to the last part of Rule III., when the speaker offers an implied pledge that his prediction *shall* be fulfilled; as, "When the precepts of the gospel shall have been thoroughly inwrought into the lives of men, then *shall* war be known only in history."

9. **May,** from the Saxon "magan," *to be strong,* expressed the primary idea of *power,* and implied a personal agency from *without,* employed to remove all *hindrance.* Hence the idea of *permission.*

10. **Can** is from the Saxon "cunnan," *to know,*—that is, an intellectual power *within* one's self. Hence the idea of *ability.*

11. **Must** is from the Saxon "motan," *to be able,*—that is, to be impelled by a power coming—not from any personal agency *without,* as in case of *may,* nor *within,* as in case of *can*—but from the nature, constitution, or fitness of things. Hence the idea of *necessity,* and, in a moral point of view, *obligation.*

NOTE.—It will be seen that *may, can,* and *must* agree in the idea of *power,*—hence the term *potential,*—but they differ in the *source* of it. As auxiliaries, they retain much of their original meaning. *May* expresses, in general, *permission;* as, "You *may* visit the country."

12. *May* sometimes denotes *possibility,* and implies *doubt;* as, "It *may* rain;" "He *may* have written;" sometimes a petition; as, "*May* it please you."

13. *Might* and *could* also express in past time the same general meaning as in the present; as, "I know I *may* or *can* go." "I knew I *might* or *could* go."

14. *Might, could, should,* and *would* are used in conditional sentences, *might* in one clause answering to *could* in the other, when *power, ability,* or *inclination* is implied; as, "He *might* sing, if he *could* or *would.*" So, "He *could* sing, if he *would.*" "He *would* sing, if he *could.*" Sometimes the conditional clause is omitted. "He *might* write." "He *could* write." "He *would* write." In all these examples a *present possibility, liberty,* &c. is referred to. When *past time* is referred to, we use the *past perfect* tense; as "He might have written, if he *would* (have written)".

114. Exercise.

1. *In the following sentences, do* SHALL *and* WILL *resolve, or predict?*—

I will go to the party. You shall not leave the room. It will be a sad day for him. He shall do as I tell him. Eugene will come to see me. I shall go to see my sister. I shall see him to-morrow. In the day that thou eatest thereof, thou shalt surely die. Thou wilt show me the path of life. He will be elected. Perhaps I shall find my book. I will fear no evil. I will dwell in the house of my God forever. Shall I go to ride? Will Florence do it? In spite of all your objections, I will do it. The sun will shine. The clock will strike. Shall you go to the lecture? When will the time come? Will the earl do well?

2. *Correct the following examples by giving and explaining the right use of* SHALL *and* WILL:—

I will receive a letter when my brother comes. If they make the changes, I do not think I will like them. Will we have a good time if we go? Perhaps you shall find the purse. I will be unhappy if you do not come. I will be afraid if it is dark. Surely goodness and mercy shall follow me, and I will dwell in the house of the Lord forever. I resolve that he will return with me. I will be obliged to you. I will be punished. What sorrow will I have to endure! The moon shall give her light. Will I write? He is resolved that Mary will go. If we examine the subject, we will perceive the error. I will suffer from poverty; nobody shall help me. When shall you go with me? Where will I leave you?

3. *Study the following Models for Analysis, and explain the auxiliaries:*—

We are marching. . . . . *Are* is an auxiliary verb, denotes present time, and asserts a thing as actual; *marching* is a present participle, denoting a progressive act: hence *are marching* is the present tense, indicative mode, progressive form.

I do write. . . . . *Do* is an auxiliary verb, denotes the present tense, asserts a thing as actual, and imparts emphasis; *write* denotes the simple act: hence *do write* is the present indicative, emphatic form.

He will sing. . . . . *Will* is an auxiliary verb, denotes future time (simply predicts), and asserts a thing as actual; *sing* denotes the simple act: hence *will sing* is in the future tense, indicative mode.

He has conquered. . . . *Has* is an auxiliary verb, denotes present time, is a sign of completed action, and asserts a thing as actual; *conquered* is the past participle of *conquer*, denoting a completed or perfect act: hence *has conquered* is the present perfect, indicative.

I had been writing. . . . *Had* is an auxiliary verb, denotes past time, is a sign of completion, and with *been* asserts a thing as actual; *been* is the past participle of the auxiliary *to be*, and is used to denote completion; *writing* is the present participle of *write*, formed by adding *ing* (28, 2), and denotes a progressive act: hence *had been writing* is the past perfect progressive, indicative.

They will have fought. *Will* is an auxiliary verb; it denotes future time (simply predicts), and asserts a thing as actual; *have* is a sign of completion; hence *will have* is the sign of future completion; *fought* is the past participle of *fight;* it denotes completion: hence *will have fought* is the future perfect tense, indicative.

I may read. . . . . *May* is an auxiliary verb; it denotes present time, asserts a thing as imagined or thought of (not as actual), and gives permission, or expresses doubt; *read* denotes the simple act *now* in contemplation: hence *may read* is the present potential, common form.

If he is detained. . . . . *Is* is an auxiliary verb, denotes present time, and of itself asserts a thing as actual, but, under the influence of *if*, asserts a thing as doubtful and conditional: *detained* is a passive participle, denoting the reception of an act: hence *is detained* is the present passive, subjunctive.

4. *In the same manner analyze the following examples:—*

The tempest has passed. The sun was rising. I shall be satisfied. The sailor would have been discharged, if he had not given a satisfactory excuse. The boys were anxious to go. Leolio hoped to have finished the work before the storm approached. Go to the prison. Write an answer. The letter may have been delayed. If you should write a correct lesson, you would be commended.

5. *Write three examples of the emphatic indicative past; three of the progressive past perfect; four of the progressive potential past perfect; also any other which your teacher may give.*

6. *Tell the* MODE, *the* TENSE, *and the* FORM *of each of the following verbs:—*

Shepherd, lead on. Sweet is the breath of morn. These are thy works. He will be coming. Silence filled the courts of heaven. Thus far shalt thou go. He leads them forth through golden portals. Truth, crushed to earth, shall rise again. Do thou in secret pray. If thy brother die, he shall live again. By that time he will have been reaping his wheat. They must go to rest. He has been studying his lesson. The sun will have set when I reach home. He sunk to repose where the red heaths are blended.

115. Uses of the Auxiliaries. Formation of Tenses.

1. The auxiliaries may combine to form the tenses,—

(*a.*) With **participles**.

Ex.—I *am writing;* He *was loved;* We *have written.*

(*b.*) With **infinitives** (**111, 4**).

Ex.—I *may write;* They *shall read.*

(*c.*) With both united.

Ex.—I *may have learned.*

2. In the indicative mode they combine as follows:—

(*a.*) Abs. tenses. Present.
- **Do love,** emp. form,—inf. and *do, dost, does.*
- **Am loving,** prog. form,—pres. part. and *am, is, art, are.*
- **Am loved,** pas. form,—past part. and *am, is, art, are.*

- (a.) Abs. tenses. (*Continued.*)
  - Past.
    - **Did love,** emp. form,—inf. and *did, didst.*
    - **Was loving,** prog. form,—pres. part. and *was, wast, were.*
    - **Was loved,** pas. form,—past part. and *was, wast, were.*
  - Future.
    - **Shall love,** com. form,—inf. and *shall, shalt, will, wilt.*
    - **Shall be loving,** prog. form,—inf. of *be,* and pres. part. with *shall, shalt, will, wilt.*
    - **Shall be loved,** pas. form,—inf. of *be,* and pas. part. with *shall, shalt, will, wilt.*

- (b.) Rel. tenses.
  - Pres. perf.
    - **Have loved,** com. form,—past part. and *have, hadst, has.*
    - **Have been loving,** prog. form,—past part. *been,* and pres. part. with *have, hast, has.*
    - **Have been loved,** pas. form,—past part. *been,* and pas. part. with *have, hast, has.*
  - Past perf.
    - **Had loved,** com. form,—past part. and *had, hadst.*
    - **Had been loving,** prog. form,—past part. *been,* and pres. part. with *had, hadst.*
    - **Had been loved,** pas. form,—past part. *been,* and pas. part. with *had, hadst.*
  - Fut. perf.
    - **Shall have loved,** com. form,—inf. of *have,* and past part. with *shall, shalt, will, wilt.*
    - **Shall have been loving,** prog. form,—inf. of *have,* past part. of *been,* and pres. part. with *shall, shalt, will, wilt.*
    - **Shall have been loved,** pas. form,—inf. of *have,* and past part. *been,* and pas. part. with *shall, shalt, will, wilt.*

3. In the potential mode they combine as follows:—

- (a.) Abs. tenses.
  - Present.
    - **May love,** com. form,—inf. and *may, mayst, can, canst, must.*
    - **May be loving,** prog. form,—inf. of *be,* and pres. part. with *may, mayst, can, canst, must.*
    - **May be loved,** pas. form,—inf. of *be,* and pas. part with *may, mayst, can, canst, must.*
  - Past.
    - **Might love,** com. form,—inf. and *might, mightst, could, couldst, should, shouldst, would, wouldst.*

ETYMOLOGY—VERBS—TENSE-FORMS.

(a.) Abs. tenses. *(Continued.)*

Past. *Continued.*
- **Might be loving,** prog. form,—inf. of *be,* and pres. part. with *might, mightst, could, couldst, would, wouldst, should, shouldst.*
- **Might be loved,** pas. form,—inf. of *be,* and pas. part. with *might, mightst, could, couldst, would, wouldst, should, shouldst.*

(b.) Rel. tenses.

Pres. perf.
- **May have loved,** com. form,—inf. of *have,* and past part. with *may, mayst, can, canst, must.*
- **May have been loving,** prog. form,—inf. of *have,* past part. *been,* and pres. part. with *may, mayst, can, canst, must.*
- **May have been loved,** pas. form,—inf. of *have,* past part. *been,* and pas. part. with *may, mayst, can, canst, must.*

Past perf.
- **Might have loved,** com. form,—inf. of *have,* and past part. with *might, mightst, could, couldst, would, wouldst, should, shouldst.*
- **Might have been loving,** prog. form,—inf. of *have,* past part. *been,* and pres. part. with *might, mightst, could, couldst, should, shouldst, would, wouldst.*
- **Might have been loved,** pas. form,—inf. of *have,* past part. *been,* and pas. part. with *might, mightst, could, couldst, should, shouldst, would, wouldst.*

4. With the exception of the distinctive form in the present and the past (**107,** 5, 6), the subjunctive mode has the same tense-forms as the indicative or the potential, with *if, unless, though,* &c., prefixed.

Ex.—*If I love; if I may love.*

5. The imperative mode has but one tense, the *present,* which is used generally without the subject expressed, and in all the four forms of the verb.

Ex.—*Study; be thou studying; be thou loved; do write.*

6. The infinitive mode has two tenses,—the *present* and the *perfect*. The *present* is used in the *common,* the *progressive,* and the *passive* forms of the verb, and is formed by prefixing "*to*" to the simple verb for the common form, "*to be*" to the present participle for the progressive form, and "*to be*" to the passive participle for the passive form.

Ex.—*To write; to be writing; to be written.*

The *perfect* is used in the *common*, the *progressive*, and the *passive* form of the verb, and is formed by prefixing *to have* to the past participle of the verb for the common form,—*to have been* to the present participle for the progressive form,—and *to have been* to the passive participle for the passive form.

Ex.—*To have written; to have been writing; to have been written.*

7. The *present* participle is formed by adding *ing* to the simple verb.

Ex.—Read-*ing*.

The *past* participle is formed for regular verbs by adding *ed* to the simple verb (**28, 2**).

Ex.—Honor-*ed; honored.*

The *perfect* participle is formed by prefixing *having* to the past participle of the verb for the common form,—*having been* to the present participle for the progressive form,—and *having been* to the passive participle for the passive form.

Ex.—*Having written; having been writing; having been written.*

116. Number and Person of the Verb.

1. The **number** and **person** of the verb are properties which show its agreement with the subject. Like the subject, the verb has two numbers and three persons.

2. The *first* person singular, and the *first*, the *second*, and the *third* person plural, of the present tense indicative, in all verbs (*am, are, was, were,* excepted) are alike. The *second* person singular is like the first, except in the solemn or ancient style, when it is formed by adding *st*, or *est*, to the first person. The *third* person singular is formed from the first, by adding *s* or *es;* in ancient style it ends in *eth.*

Ex.—Thou lov*est* me not. He pray*eth* best who lov*eth* best.

Verbs ending in *y* preceded by a consonant, change *y* into *i*, and add *es*, to form the third person singular; as, *try, tries.*

3. By a figure of *enallage* (**216, 7**), the second person plural of the pronoun and the verb is substituted, in conversational, common, and familiar style, for the second person singular.

Ex.—Hubert, *you are* sad, = Hubert, *thou art* sad.

NOTE.—The tendency among some grammarians to omit from their paradigms, as obsolete, the forms of the second person singular, is to be regretted.

To say nothing of these forms in the prose of the past few centuries, much of which is read at the present time, we have them in all kinds of poetry, ancient and modern, in the Scriptures, and in religious books: especially in prayer, *thou*, as the *pronomen reverentiæ*, is in daily use. There can be no objection to give the plural *you* for the singular as an example of the common form; but the other should not be omitted.

4. The imperative mode has usually only the second person.
Ex.—Go thou.

In some languages the imperative has also a form for the first person plural and the third person singular and plural. A few examples seem to occur in English; as, "Rise thy sons;" "Be it decreed." Most of these cases, however, can be explained by supplying an ellipsis; as, "Let thy sons rise;" "Let it be decreed."

117. Conjugation.

1. The **conjugation** of a verb is the regular arrangement of its several *modes, tenses, voices, numbers, and persons*.

2. The only tenses which change their termination are the *present* and the *past;* as sit, sit*test*, sit*s*, sat, sat*test;* tarry, tarr*iest*, tarr*ies*, tarr*ied*, tarr*iedst*. All other changes are made by means of auxiliaries.

3. In adding *s* or *es*, observe the same rules as in the formation of the plural of nouns; as, play, play*s;* fly, fl*ies;* go, go*es*. So, also, observe the rules (**28**) for the changes of the radical verb; as, drop, drop*ped* (Rule I.); reply, repl*ied* (Rule III.).

4. The **principal parts** of a verb are the *present indicative*, the *past indicative*, and the *past participle*.

EXAMPLES.

Present.	Past.	Past Participle.
Explain,	explained,	explained.
Rely,	relied,	relied.
Write,	wrote,	written.
Shine,	shone,	shone.
Hurt,	hurt,	hurt.

118. Exercise.

1. *Give the principal parts of the following verbs:*—

Sail, smile, see, shut, close, open, burn, glaze, gild, turn, try, reform, renew, take, leave, make, build, hope, fold, alter, correct.

2. *Study the following Models:—*

> Thou hast gone to thy rest.

Hast gone .. is a *verb*—it expresses being, action, or state; irregular—it does not form its past tense and past participle by adding *ed;—principal parts*—pres. *go*, past *went*, past part. *gone; intransitive*—it does not receive or require an object to complete the meaning; *common form*—it represents an act as completed without reference to its progress; *indicative mode*—it asserts a thing as actual; *present perfect tense*—it expresses an action completed in present time; *second person, singular number*, to agree with its subject *thou*.

Abbreviated form:—

Hast gone .. is an *irreg. intransitive* verb,—*go, went, gone,* indicative mode, present perfect tense, 2d person, sing. number, to agree with its subject *thou*. Or, for the slate, thus:—is a v. ir. int. ind.—pres. perf.—2d per. sing.

3. *In the following examples, explain the* VERBS *in the same manner:—*

We read of that philosophy which can smile over the destruction of property, of that religion which enables its possessor to extend the benign look of forgiveness and complacency to his murderers; but it is not in the soul of man to bear the lacerations of *slander*.

> "Lord, and what shall this man do?"
>   Ask'st thou, Christian, for thy friend?
> If his love for Christ be true,
>   Christ hath told thee of his end:—
> This is he whom God approves,
> This is he whom Jesus loves.—*Keble*.

And the raven, never flitting, still is sitting, still is sitting
  On the pallid bust of Pallas, just above my chamber-door;
And his eyes have all the seeming of a demon's that is dreaming,
  And the lamplight o'er him streaming throws his shadow on the floor,
And my soul from out that shadow that lies floating on the floor,
  Shall be lifted—nevermore!—*E. A. Poe.*

119. Conjugation of the Verb TO BE.

INDICATIVE MOOD.

PRESENT TENSE.

Singular.	Plural.
1. I am,	We are,
2. Thou art,	(Ye *or*) You are,
3. He is;	They are.

PRESENT PERFECT TENSE.

1. I have been,	We have been,
2. Thou hast been,	You have been,
3. He has been;	They have been.

PAST TENSE.

1. I was,	We were,
2. Thou wast,	You were,
3. He was;	They were.

PAST PERFECT TENSE.

1. I had been,	We had been,
2. Thou hadst been,	You had been,
3. He had been;	They had been.

FUTURE TENSE.

1. I shall *or* will be,	We shall *or* will be,
2. Thou shalt *or* wilt be,	You shall *or* will be,
3. He shall *or* will be;	They shall *or* will be.

FUTURE PERFECT TENSE.

1. I shall *or* will have been,	We shall *or* will have been,
2. Thou shalt *or* wilt have been,	You shall *or* will have been,
3. He shall *or* will have been;	They shall *or* will have been.

POTENTIAL MODE.

PRESENT TENSE.

1. I may be,	We may be,
2. Thou mayst be,	You may be,
3. He may be;	They may be.

PRESENT PERFECT TENSE.

Singular.	Plural.
1. I may have been,	We may have been,
2. Thou mayst have been,	You may have been,
3. He may have been;	They may have been.

PAST TENSE.

1. I might be,	We might be,
2. Thou mightst be,	You might be,
3. He might be;	They might be.

PAST PERFECT TENSE.

1. I might have been,	We might have been.
2. Thou mightst have been,	You might have been.
3. He might have been;	They might have been.

SUBJUNCTIVE MODE.

PRESENT TENSE.

1. If I am,	If we are,
2. If thou art,	If you are,
3. If he is;	If they are.

PRESENT PERFECT TENSE.

1. If I have been,	If we have been,
2. If thou hast been,	If you have been,
3. If he has been;	If they have been.

PAST TENSE.

1. If I was,	If we were,
2. If thou wast,	If you were,
3. If he was;	If they were.

PAST PERFECT TENSE.

1. If I had been,	If we had been,
2. If thou hadst been,	If you had been,
3. If he had been;	If they had been.

FUTURE TENSE.

1. If I shall *or* will be,	If we shall *or* will be,
2. If thou shalt *or* wilt be,	If you shall *or* will be,
3. If he shall *or* will be;	If they shall *or* will be.

ETYMOLOGY—VERBS—CONJUGATION.

FUTURE PERFECT TENSE.

Singular.   *Plural.*
1. If I shall *or* will have been,   If we shall *or* will have been,
2. If thou shalt *or* wilt have been,   If you shall *or* will have been,
3. If he shall *or* will have been.   If they shall *or* will have been.

SUBJUNCTIVE MODE. (*Subjunctive form.*)

NOTE.—Besides the forms already given, the subjunctive has another in the present and the past, peculiar to itself.

PRESENT TENSE.

Singular.   *Plural.*
1. If I be,   If we be,
2. If thou be,   If you be,
3. If he be;   If they be.

PAST TENSE.

1. If I were,   If we were,
2. If thou wert,   If you were,
3. If he were;   If they were.

IMPERATIVE MODE.

PRESENT TENSE.

Be, *or* Be thou;   Be ye *or* you.

INFINITIVE MODE.

Present Tense.   To be.
Present Perfect.   To have been.

PARTICIPLES.

Present. Being.   *Past.* Been.
Perfect. Having been.

COMMON STYLE.

Congugate the verb BE in the common style, thus:—

INDICATIVE MODE.

PRESENT TENSE.

Singular.   *Plural.*
1. I am,   We are,
2. You are,   You are,
3. He is;   They are.

PRESENT PERFECT TENSE.

Singular.	Plural.
1. I have been,	We have been,
2. You have been,	You have been,
3. He has been;	They have been.

In the same manner, let the learner go through all the tenses and modes.

Synopsis is a short view of the verb, showing its forms through the modes and tenses in a single number and person.

Synopsis of the verb BE, *in the first person, singular number.*

INDICATIVE MODE.

Present.	I am.	*Past Perf.*	I had been.
Pres. Perf.	I have been.	*Future.*	I shall be.
Past.	I was.	*Fut. Perf.*	I shall have been.

SUBJUNCTIVE MODE.

Present.	If I am.	*Past Perf.*	If I had been.
Pres. Perf.	If I have been.	*Future.*	If I shall be.
Past.	If I was.	*Fut. Perf.*	If I shall have been.

POTENTIAL MODE.

Present.	I may be.	*Past.*	I might be.
Pres. Perf.	I may have been.	*Past Perf.*	I might have been.

Here the *first person* ends; yet it is well for the pupil to give the imperative, the infinitive, and the participles.

IMPERATIVE MODE.

Present. Be thou.

INFINITIVE.

Present. To be.	*Perfect.* To have been.

PARTICIPLES.

Present. Being.	*Perfect.* Having been.

120. Exercise.

1. *In what mode and tense are the following* VERBS?—

I am. He has been. If I were. You can be. He might be. To have been. They were. He will have been. You might be.

ETYMOLOGY—VERBS—CONJUGATION. 127

She had been. You will be. To be. I must have been. Thou art. If he be. If you are. They might have been. We were. I had been. Thou wast. He is.

2. *Give a synopsis of* TO BE, in the IND., second person singular,—sec. per. plur.,—first per. plur.,—third per. sing.,—third per. plur. POT., third per. sing.,—sec. per. plur.,—third per. plur. SUB., sec. per. sing.,—sec. per. plur.,—third per. plur.,—first per. plur.

121. Conjugation of the Regular Verb TO LOVE.

ACTIVE VOICE.

INDICATIVE MODE.

PRESENT TENSE.

Singular.	*Plural.*
1. I love,	We love,
2. Thou lovest,	You love,
3. He loves;	They love.

PRESENT PERFECT TENSE.

1. I have loved,	We have loved,
2. Thou hast loved,	You have loved,
3. He has loved;	They have loved.

PAST TENSE.

1. I loved,	We loved,
2. Thou lovedst,	You loved,
3. He loved;	They loved.

PAST PERFECT TENSE.

1. I had loved,	We had loved,
2. Thou hadst loved,	You had loved,
3. He had loved;	They had loved.

FUTURE TENSE.

1. I shall *or* will love,	We shall *or* will love,
2. Thou shalt *or* wilt love,	You shall *or* will love,
3. He shall *or* will love;	They shall *or* will love.

FUTURE PERFECT TENSE.

1. I shall *or* will have loved,	We shall *or* will have loved,
2. Thou shalt *or* wilt have loved,	You shall *or* will have loved,
3. He shall *or* will have loved;	They shall *or* will have loved.

POTENTIAL MODE.

PRESENT TENSE.

Singular.
1. I may love,
2. Thou mayst love,
3. He may love;

Plural.
We may love,
You may love,
They may love.

PRESENT PERFECT TENSE.

1. I may have loved,
2. Thou mayst have loved,
3. He may have loved;

We may have loved,
You may have loved,
They may have loved.

PAST TENSE.

1. I might love,
2. Thou mightst love,
3. He might love;

We might love,
You might love,
They might love.

PAST PERFECT TENSE.

1. I might have loved,
2. Thou mightst have loved,
3. He might have loved;

We might have loved,
You might have loved,
They might have loved.

SUBJUNCTIVE MODE. (*Regular form.*)

PRESENT TENSE.

1. If I love,
2. If thou lovest,
3. If he loves;

If we love,
If you love,
If they love.

PRESENT PERFECT TENSE.

1. If I have loved,
2. If thou hast loved,
3. If he has loved;

If we have loved,
If you have loved,
If they have loved.

PAST TENSE.

1. If I loved,
2. If thou lovedst,
3. If he loved;

If we loved,
If you loved,
If they loved.

PAST PERFECT TENSE.

1. If I had loved,
2. If thou hadst loved,
3. If he had loved;

If we had loved,
If you had loved,
If they had loved.

FUTURE TENSE.

Singular.	Plural.
1. If I shall *or* will love,	If we shall *or* will love,
2. If thou shalt *or* wilt love,	If you shall *or* will love,
3. If he shall *or* will love;	If they shall *or* will love.

FUTURE PERFECT TENSE.

1. If I shall *or* will have loved,   If we shall *or* will have loved.
2. If thou shalt *or* wilt have loved,   If you shall *or* will have loved,
3. If he shall *or* will have loved;   If they shall *or* will have loved.

SUBJUNCTIVE MODE. (*Subjunctive form.*)

PRESENT TENSE.

1. If I love,	If we love,
2. If thou love,	If you love,
3. If he love;	If they love.

PAST TENSE.

1. If I loved,	If we loved,
2. If thou loved,	If you loved,
3. If he loved;	If they loved.

IMPERATIVE MODE.

Love, *or* Love thou.   Love, *or* Love you.

INFINITIVE MODE.

Present. To love.   *Perfect.* To have loved.

PARTICIPLES.

Present. Loving.   *Past.* Loved.
Perfect. Having loved.

PASSIVE VOICE.

INDICATIVE MODE.

PRESENT TENSE.

Singular.	Plural.
1. I am loved,	We are loved,
2. Thou art loved,	You are loved,
3. He is loved;	They are loved.

PRESENT PERFECT TENSE.

Singular.	Plural.
1. I have been loved,	We have been loved,
2. Thou hast been loved,	You have been loved,
3. He has been loved;	They have been loved.

PAST TENSE.

1. I was loved,	We were loved,
2. Thou wast loved,	You were loved,
3. He was loved;	They were loved.

PAST PERFECT TENSE.

1. I had been loved,	We had been loved,
2. Thou hadst been loved,	You had been loved,
3. He had been loved;	They had been loved.

FUTURE TENSE.

1. I shall *or* will be loved,	We shall *or* will be loved,
2. Thou shalt *or* wilt be loved,	You shall *or* will be loved,
3. He shall *or* will be loved;	They shall *or* will be loved.

FUTURE PERFECT TENSE.

1. I shall *or* will have been loved,	We shall *or* will have been loved,
2. Thou shalt *or* wilt have been loved,	You shall *or* will have been loved,
3. He shall *or* will have been loved;	They shall *or* will have been loved.

POTENTIAL MODE.

PRESENT TENSE.

1. I may be loved,	We may be loved,
2. Thou mayst be loved,	You may be loved,
3. He may be loved;	They may be loved.

PRESENT PERFECT TENSE.

1. I may have been loved,	We may have been loved,
2. Thou mayst have been loved,	You may have been loved,
3. He may have been loved;	They may have been loved.

PAST TENSE.

Singular.	Plural.
1. I might be loved,	We might be loved,
2. Thou mightst be loved,	You might be loved,
3. He might be loved;	They might be loved.

PAST PERFECT TENSE.

1. I might have been loved,   We might have been loved,
2. Thou mightst have been loved, You might have been loved,
3. He might have been loved;   They might have been loved.

SUBJUNCTIVE MODE. *(Regular form.)*

PRESENT TENSE.

1. If I am loved,   If we are loved,
2. If thou art loved,   If you are loved,
3. If he is loved;   If they are loved.

PRESENT PERFECT TENSE.

1. If I have been loved,   If we have been loved,
2. If thou hast been loved,   If you have been loved,
3. If he has been loved;   If they have been loved.

PAST TENSE.

1. If I was loved,   If we were loved,
2. If thou wast loved, If you were loved,
3. If he was loved;   If they were loved.

PAST PERFECT TENSE.

1. If I had been loved,   If we had been loved,
2. If thou hadst been loved, If you had been loved,
3. If he had been loved;   If they had been loved.

FUTURE TENSE.

1. If I shall *or* will be loved,   If we shall *or* will be loved,
2. If thou shalt *or* wilt be loved,   If you shall *or* will be loved,
3. If he shall *or* will be loved;   If they shall *or* will be loved.

FUTURE PERFECT TENSE.

1. If I shall *or* will have been loved,   If we shall *or* will have been loved,
2. If thou shalt *or* wilt have been loved,   If you shall *or* will have been loved,
3. If he shall *or* will have been loved;   If they shall *or* will have been loved.

SUBJUNCTIVE MODE. (*Subjunctive form.*)

PRESENT TENSE.

Singular.
1. If I be loved,
2. If thou be loved,
3. If he be loved;

Plural.
If we be loved,
If you be loved,
If they be loved.

PAST TENSE.

1. If I were loved,
2. If thou wert loved,
3. If he were loved;

If we were loved,
If you were loved,
If they were loved.

IMPERATIVE MODE.

Be loved, *or* Be thou loved;   Be loved, *or* Be you loved.

INFINITIVE MODE.

Present. To be loved.   *Perfect.* To have been loved.

PARTICIPLES.

Present. Being loved.   *Past* (passive). Loved.
Perfect. Having been loved.

122. Interrogative and Negative Forms.

1. A verb is conjugated *interrogatively* in the indicative and the potential mode, by placing the subject after it, or after the first auxiliary.

Ex.—IND., Do I love? Have I loved? Did I love? Had I loved? Shall I love? Shall I have loved? POT., Can I love? Can I have loved? &c.

2. A verb is conjugated *negatively* by placing the adverb *not* after it, or after the first auxiliary; but the negative adverb should be placed before the infinitive and the participles.

Ex.—IND., I love not, *or* I do not love. I have not loved. I loved not, *or* I did not love. I had not loved, &c. INF., Not to love. Not to have loved. PART., Not loving. Not loved. Not having loved.

3. A verb is conjugated *interrogatively* and *negatively*, in the

indicative and the potential mode, by placing the *subject*, and the adverb *not*, after the verb, or after the first auxiliary.

Ex.—Love I not? *or* Do I not love? Have I not loved? Did I not love? Had I not loved? &c.

123. Exercise.

1. *Tell the mode, the tense, the voice, the number, and the person of the following* VERBS:—

She has loved. I might love. We had loved. We had been loved. He may have loved. If I be loved. I love. He will love. He shall have loved. I have loved. They shall have loved. She is loved. We may be loved. You might have been loved. If I love. If they love. They may love. We will love. I had loved. Thou hast loved. Thou wilt have loved. I love. Thou art loved. He was loved. She will have been loved.

2. *Write or repeat a full conjugation of the following verbs:—*
Believe, defy, think.

3. *Conjugate the first of the above verbs interrogatively, the next negatively, and the third interrogatively and negatively.*

4. *Give a synopsis of either of the above verbs in either form, in the first, the second, or the third person.*

124. Synopsis—Progressive and Emphatic Forms— Verb Read.

NOTE.—The progressive form is the verb **be** joined to the **present participle.**

Ex.—**I am reading, I was reading.**

The passive form is the verb **be** joined to the **passive participle.**

Ex.—**I am pleased, I was pleased.**

☞ The pupil should be careful not to mistake the one for the other. In the emphatic form, the auxiliary *do* is added to the simple verb for the present, and *did* for the past. It is found only in the indicative and the imperative mode.

Verb **read**, *progressive.*—IND., I am reading, I have been reading, I was reading, I had been reading, I shall be reading, I shall have been reading. POT., I may be reading, I may have been reading, I might be reading, I might have been reading. SUB., If I am or

be reading, if I have been reading, if I was or were reading, if I had been reading, if I shall be reading, if I shall have been reading.
IMP., Be thou reading.   INF., To be reading, to have been reading.
PART., Reading, having been reading.

Verb **read,** *emphatic.*—IND., I do read, I did read.   IMP., Do thou read.

125. Exercise.

1. *Write or repeat a full conjugation of* write, lend, play, *in the progressive form.*

2. *Give a synopsis of either of the above verbs in the second and the third person, singular and plural.*

3. *Tell the difference between the progressive and the passive form.* (See Note above.)

126. Forms for each Division of Time combined.

THE VERB *TO MAKE.*

INDICATIVE MODE.

PRESENT TENSE.

	1st Sing.	2d Sing.	3d Sing.
	I	THOU	HE, SHE, IT,
1. Indef.	make,	makest,	makes.
2. Prog. incomp.	am making,	art making,	is making.
3. Compd.	have made,	hast made,	has made.
4. Prog. compd.	have been making,	hast been making,	has been making.
5. Emphatic.	do make,	dost make,	does make.
6. Passive.	am made,	art made,	is made.
7. Pas. prog.	——,	——,	is making.
8. Pas. compd.	have been made,	hast been made,	has been made.

	1st Plur.	2d Plur.	3d Plur.
	WE	YE or YOU	THEY
1. Indef.	make,	make,	make.
2. Prog. incomp.	are making,	are making,	are making.
3. Compd.	have made,	have made,	have made.
4. Prog. compd.	have been making,	have been making,	have been making.
5. Emphatic.	do make,	do make,	do make.
6. Passive.	are made,	are made,	are made.
7. Pas. prog.	——,	——,	are making.
8. Pas. compd.	have been made,	have been made,	have been made.

PAST TENSE.

	1st Sing. I	2d Sing. Thou	3d Sing. He, She, It,
1. Indef.	made,	madest,	made.
2. Prog. incomp.	was making,	wast making,	was making.
3. Compd.	had made,	hadst made,	had made.
4. Prog. compd.	had been making,	hadst been making,	had been making.
5. Emphatic.	did make,	didst make,	did make.
6. Passive.	was made,	wast made,	was made.
7. Pas. prog.	———,	———,	was making.
8. Pas. compd.	had been made,	hadst been made,	had been made.

	1st Plur. We	2d Plur. Ye or You	3d Plur. They
1. Indef.	made,	made,	made.
2. Prog. incomp.	were making,	were making,	were making.
3. Compd.	had made,	had made,	had made.
4. Prog. compd.	had been making,	had been making,	had been making.
5. Emphatic.	did make,	did make,	did make.
6. Passive.	were made,	were made,	were made.
7. Pas. prog.	———,	———,	were making.
8. Pas. compd.	had been made,	had been made,	had been made.

FUTURE TENSE.

	1st Sing. I	2d Sing. Thou	3d Sing. He, She, It,
1. Indef.	will make,	wilt make,	will make.
2. Prog. incomp.	will be making,	wilt be making,	will be making.
3. Compd.	will have made,	wilt have made,	will have made.
4. Prog. compd.	will have been making,	wilt have been making,	will have been making.
5. Emphatic.	———,	———,	———.
6. Passive.	will be made,	wilt be made,	will be made.
7. Pas. prog.	———,	———,	will be making.
8. Pas. compd.	will have been made,	wilt have been made,	will have been made.

	1st Plur. We	2d Plur. Ye or You	3d Plur. They
1. Indef.	will make,	will make,	will make.
2. Prog. incomp.	will be making,	will be making,	will be making.
3. Compd.	will have made,	will have made,	will have made.
4. Prog. compd.	will have been making,	will have been making,	will have been making.
5. Emphatic.	———,	———,	———.
6. Passive.	will be made,	will be made,	will be made.
7. Pas. prog.	———,	———,	will be making.
8. Pas. compd.	will have been made,	will have been made,	will have been made.

127. Irregular Verbs.

1. An *irregular* verb is one which does not form its past tense and past participle by adding *ed* to the present tense; as, *see, saw, seen; write, wrote, written.*

<small>The irregular verbs were much more numerous in the early history of the language than at present. The tendency in modern English is constantly to diminish the number of irregular formations: hence the numerous obsolete forms. Some of the present forms are derived from other verbs. *Went* comes from *wend*, and not from *go*. Philologists call the irregular the *strong*, and the regular the *weak* inflection.</small>

2. The following list contains the principal parts of the irregular verbs. Those verbs which are marked R. have also the regular forms. Those which are *italicized* are either obsolete or are becoming so, and should not be committed to memory. When the **R** is *dark-faced*, the regular form is preferred, and should be repeated first; *r.* in italics means regular but seldom used.

Present.	*Past.*	*Past Participle.*
Abide,	Abode,	Abode.
Arise,	Arose,	Arisen.
Awake,	Awoke, *r.*	Awaked.
Be *or* am,	Was,	Been.
Bear (*to bring forth*),	Bore, *bare*,	Born.
Bear (*to carry*),	Bore, *bare*,	Borne.
Beat,	Beat,	Beaten, beat.
Begin,	Began,	Begun.
Belay,	Belaid, R.	Belaid, R.
Bend,	Bent, *r.*	Bent, *r.*
Bet,	Bet, R.	Bet, R.
Bereave,	Bereft,	Bereft, *r.*
Beseech,	Besought,	Besought.
Bid,	Bid, bade,	Bidden, bid.
Bind, *Un-*	Bound,	Bound.
Bite,	Bit,	Bitten, bit.
Bleed,	Bled,	Bled.
Blend,	Blent, **R.**	Blent, **R.**
Bless,	Blest, **R.**	Blest, **R.**
Blow,	Blew,	Blown.
Break,	Broke, *brake*,	Broken, *broke*.
Breed,	Bred,	Bred.

Present.	Past.	Past Participle.
Bring,	Brought,	Brought.
Build, *Re-*	Built, *r.*	Built, *r.*
Burn,	Burnt, R.	Burnt, R.
Burst,	Burst,	Burst.
Buy,	Bought,	Bought.
Cast,	Cast,	Cast.
Catch,	Caught, *r.*	Caught, *r.*
Chide,	Chid,	Chidden, chid.
Choose,	Chose,	Chosen.
Cleave (*to adhere*),	Cleaved, *clave*,	Cleaved.
Cleave (*to split*),	Clove, cleft, *clave*,	Cleft, *cloven*, *r.*
Cling,	Clung,	Clung.
Clothe,	Clad, R.	Clad, R.
Come, *Be-*	Came,	Come.
Cost,	Cost,	Cost.
Creep,	Crept,	Crept.
Crow,	Crew, R.	Crowed.
Cut,	Cut,	Cut.
Dare (*to venture*),	Durst, R.	Dared.
Dare (*to challenge*), R.	Dared,	Dared.
Deal,	Dealt, *r.*	Dealt, *r.*
Dig,	Dug, *r.*	Dug, *r.*
Do, *Mis-, Un-, Out-*,	Did,	Done.
Draw,	Drew,	Drawn.
Dream,	Dreamt, R.	Dreamt, R.
Dress,	Drest, R.	Drest, R.
Drink,	Drank,	Drunk, drank.
Drive,	Drove,	Driven.
Dwell,	Dwelt, *r.*	Dwelt, *r.*
Eat,	Ate, eat,	Eaten, or *eat*.
Fall, *Be-*,	Fell,	Fallen.
Feed,	Fed,	Fed.
Feel,	Felt,	Felt.
Fight,	Fought,	Fought.
Find,	Found,	Found.
Flee,	Fled,	Fled.
Fling,	Flung,	Flung.
Fly,	Flew,	Flown.
Forbear,	Forbore,	Forborne.
Forget,	Forgot,	Forgotten, forgot.
Forsake,	Forsook,	Forsaken.

Present.	Past.	Past Participle.
Freeze,	Froze,	Frozen.
Freight,	Freighted,	Fraught, R.
Get, *Be-, For-*,	Got,	Got, gotten.
Gild,	Gilt, R.	Gilt, R.
Gird, *Be-, En-*,	Girt, R.	Girt, R.
Give, *For-, Mis-*,	Gave,	Given.
Go,	Went,	Gone.
Grave, *En-*,	Graved,	Graven, R.
Grind,	Ground,	Ground.
Grow,	Grew,	Grown.
Hang (*to take life*, R.)	Hung,	Hung.
Have,	Had,	Had.
Hear,	Heard,	Heard.
Heave,	Hove, R.	Hoven, R.
Hew,	Hewed,	Hewn, R.
Hide,	Hid,	Hidden, hid.
Hit,	Hit,	Hit.
Hold, *Be-, With-*,	Held,	Held, *holden*.
Hurt,	Hurt,	Hurt.
Keep,	Kept,	Kept.
Kneel,	Knelt, r.	Knelt, r.
Knit,	Knit, r.	Knit, r.
Know,	Knew,	Known.
Lade, *to load* (*to dip*, R.),	Laded,	Laden, R.
Lay,	Laid,	Laid.
Lead, *Mis-*,	Led,	Led.
Leap,	Leapt, R.	Leapt, R.
Learn,	Learnt, R.	Learnt, R.
Leave,	Left,	Left.
Lend,	Lent,	Lent.
Let,	Let,	Let.
Lie (*to recline*),	Lay,	Lain.
Lie (*to speak falsely*), R.	Lied,	Lied,
Light,	Lit, R.	Lit, R.
Lose,	Lost,	Lost.
Make,	Made,	Made.
Mean,	Meant,	Meant.
Meet,	Met,	Met.
Mow,	Mowed,	Mown, R.
Pass,	Past, R.	Past, R.
Pay, *Re-*,	Paid,	Paid.

ETYMOLOGY—VERBS—IRREGULAR. 139

Present.	Past.	Past Participle.
Pen (*to enclose*),	Pent, R.	Pent, R.
Prove,	Proved,	Proven, R.
Put,	Put,	Put.
Quit,	Quit, r.	Quit, r.
Rap,	Rapt, R.	Rapt, R.
Read,	Read,	Read.
Rend,	Rent,	Rent.
Rid,	Rid,	Rid.
Ride,	Rode, *rid,*	Ridden, *rid.*
Ring,	Rang, rung,	Rung.
Rise, *A-*,	Rose,	Risen.
Rive,	Rived,	Riven, R.
Run,	Ran, *run,*	Run.
Saw,	Sawed,	Sawn, R.
Say,	Said,	Said.
See,	Saw,	Seen.
Seek,	Sought,	Sought.
Seethe,	Sod, R.	Sodden, R.
Sell,	Sold,	Sold.
Send,	Sent,	Sent.
Set, *Be-*,	Set,	Set.
Shake,	Shook,	Shaken.
Shape, *Mis-*,	Shaped,	Shapen, R.
Shave,	Shaved,	Shaven, R.
Shear,	Sheared, (*shore, obs.*)	Shorn, R.
Shed,	Shed,	Shed.
Shine,	Shone, R.	Shone, R.
Shoe,	Shod,	Shod.
Shoot,	Shot,	Shot.
Show,	Showed,	Shown, R.
Shred,	Shred,	Shred. [shrunken.
Shrink,	Shrunk, shrank,	Shrunk *or*
Shut,	Shut,	Shut.
Sing,	Sang, sung,	Sung.
Sink,	Sunk, *sank,*	Sunk.
Sit,	Sat,	Sat.
Slay,	Slew,	Slain.
Sleep,	Slept,	Slept.
Slide,	Slid,	Slidden, slid.
Sling,	Slung, *slang,*	Slung.
Slink,	Slunk,	Slunk.

Present.	Past.	Past Participle.
Slit,	Slit, *r.*	Slit, *r.*
Smell,	Smelt, R.	Smelt, R.
Smite,	Smote,	Smitten, smit.
Sow (*to scatter*),	Sowed,	Sown, R.
Speak, *Be-*,	Spoke, *spake*,	Spoken.
Speed,	Sped, *r.*	Sped, *r.*
Spell,	Spelt, R.	Spelt, R.
Spend, *Mis-*,	Spent,	Spent.
Spill,	Spilt, R.	Spilt, R.
Spin,	Spun, *span*,	Spun.
Spit, *Be-*,	Spit, *spat*,	Spit.
Split,	Split, *r.*	Split, *r.*
Spoil,	Spoilt, R.	Spoilt, R.
Spread, *Be-*,	Spread,	Spread.
Spring,	Sprang, sprung,	Sprung.
Stand, *With-*, &c.,	Stood,	Stood.
Stave,	Stove, R.	Stove, R.
Stay,	Staid, R.	Staid, R.
Steal,	Stole,	Stolen.
Stick,	Stuck,	Stuck.
Sting,	Stung,	Stung.
Stride,	Strode, strid,	Stridden, strid.
Strike,	Struck,	Struck, stricken.
String,	Strung,	Strung.
Strive,	Strove,	Striven.
Strow, or Strew, *Be-*,	Strowed or *strewed*,	Strown, strewn.
Swear,	Swore, *sware*,	Sworn.
Sweat,	Sweat, R.	Sweat, R.
Sweep,	Swept,	Swept.
Swell,	Swelled,	Swollen, R.
Swim,	Swam, swum,	Swum.
Swing,	Swung,	Swung.
Take, *Be-*, &c.,	Took,	Taken.
Teach, *Mis-*, *Re-*,	Taught,	Taught.
Tear,	Tore, *tare*,	Torn.
Tell,	Told,	Told.
Think, *Be-*,	Thought,	Thought.
Thrive,	Throve, R.	Thriven, R.
Throw,	Threw,	Thrown.
Thrust,	Thrust,	Thrust.
Tread,	Trod,	Trodden, trod.

Present.	Past.	Past Participle.
Wake,	Woke, R.	Woke, R.
Wax,	Waxed,	Waxen, R.
Wear,	Wore,	Worn.
Weave,	Wove,	Woven.
Wed,	Wed, R.	Wed, R.
Weep,	Wept,	Wept.
Wet,	Wet, R.	Wet, R.
Whet,	Whet, R.	Whet, R.
Win,	Won,	Won.
Wind,	Wound, R.	Wound.
Work,	Wrought, R.	Wrought, R.
Wring,	Wrung,	Wrung.
Write,	Wrote,	Written.

Note.—Many of the words in the list are irregular to the eye, not to the ear. The preference is one of orthography. Thus, *rapt* and *rapped* are pronounced alike; so, also, *drest, dressed, blest, blessed,* and others. Sometimes the difference in sound is that of *t* and its correlative *d*,—*dwelt, dwelled, spelt, spelled.* Besides the words in the list, there are a few forms which are seldom found except in the poets or in the older usages of the language. The following *very rarely* have a regular past and past participle:—*Grind, lay, pay, shake, slide, sweep, string, strive, wind, wring.*

Betide has (obs.) *betid*; *bide* has (obs.) *bided*; *creep* has (obs.) *crope*; *curse* has sometimes *curst*; *dive* has (obs.) *dove, diven*; *heat* has (colloquial) *hĕat*; *plead* has (improperly) *plĕad*; *reave* (itself little used) has *reft*, R.; *shear* has (obs.) *shore*; *show* has (obs.) *shew, shewn*; *strow, strew,* or (obs.) *straw,* has *strowed, strewed,* (obs.) *strawed, strawn, strewn*; but it may now be regarded as a regular verb,—*strew, strewed, strewed.*

128. Exercise.

1. *Give the past and the past participle* of teach, sing, write, read, hurt, sit, arise, take, beat, tell, &c. &c.

2. *Give the present and the past for the following past participles:*— Thrown, sworn, swum, built, spoken, stolen, &c. &c.

3. *Correct the following examples, and give the number and person of each:*—

The blossoms have fell from the trees. Mary come to school in haste. Sarah's exercise is wrote badly. The thief stoled the money and telled a falsehood about it. The lake is froze hard. Charles has took the wrong course. The bell ringed loud. The soldiers fit bravely. She did not git the premium. The exercise is wrote badly. James has not spoke the truth. A sad misfortune has befell him. The carriage was drawed by four horses. Being weary, I laid down, and ris much refreshed. The ball was throwed too high. I see the soldiers when they come. The wind has blowed the fruit from the trees, and broke the branches. He sit down upon the bank. The cattle were drove to pasture. After he had strove many times, he winned the prize. The bee stinged Nellie badly. Edwin has took my knife. The sky has wore a cloudy aspect for several days. She singed the song well. The cars have ran off the track. Grandmother has weaved the cloth beautifully. Who teached him grammar? These apples have growed very fast. He clinged to the mast. He give me some money. Anna stringed the beads quickly. The vessel has hove in sight. She springed a leak. The stone smit him in the face. The river has overflown its banks. I seen Harry when he done it.

129. Defective Verbs.

1. **Defective** verbs are those in which some of the principal parts are wanting.

2. They are *may, can, shall,* and *will,* which have the past tense, but no participles; *must* and *ought,* which have neither a past tense nor participles; *quoth,* which has neither a present tense nor participles.

3. When *must* refers to past time, it is used in the present-perfect tense.

Ex.—He must have left.

When *ought* refers to past time, it is followed by the perfect infinitive.

Ex.—He ought *to have written.*

4. *Quoth* is now seldom used, and only in the past tense, first and third person singular.

Ex.—Air, quoth he, thy cheeks may blow.

Beware formerly was written in two words:—"Of whom *be* thou *ware.*" It is used chiefly in the imperative mood.

Ex.—*Beware* of dogs.

130. Redundant and Impersonal Verbs.

1. A **redundant** verb has more than one form for its past tense or past participle.

Ex.—*Thrive, thrived* or *throve, thrived* or *thriven.*

2. An **impersonal** verb is one by which an action or a state is asserted independently of any particular subject.

Ex.—It rains. It snows.

3. *Methinks, methought, meseems, meseemed,* may be regarded as impersonal, or rather unipersonal, verbs.

Ex.—My father! methinks I see my father.

They are equivalent to *I think, I thought, It seems, It seemed to me.*

131. Exercise.

1. *Study the following models for parsing the verb:*—

(Full form.)

(1.) Give the part of speech, and tell why.
(2.) Tell whether it is regular or irregular, and why.
(3.) Give the principal parts.
(4.) Tell whether it is transitive or intransitive, and why.
(5.) Tell the voice and form, and why.
(6.) Tell the mode, and why.
(7.) Tell the tense, and why.
(8.) Inflect the tense.
(9.) Tell the number and person, and why.
(10.) Give the rule.

(Abbreviated form.)

(1.) It is a regular or irregular, transitive or intransitive, verb, (if transitive) active or passive form.
(2.) Principal parts.
(3.) Mode.
(4.) Tense.
(5.) Number and person.
(6.) Construction and rule.

EXAMPLES.

2. Sarah has written a letter.

Has written ... is a *verb* (why?); *principal parts* (pres. *write*, past *wrote*, past part. *written*); *transitive* (why?); *active voice* (why?); *common form* (why?); *indicative mode* (why?); *present-perfect tense;*—it is formed by prefixing *have*, which both denotes present time and is the sign of completion, to the past participle *written*, which denotes completion (*I have written, thou hast written, he has written; we have written, you have written, they have written*); *third person, singular number,* and agrees with its subject *Sarah*, according to Rule IV.: "The verb must agree with its subject in number and person."

3. She can play.

Can play ..... is a *verb* (why?); *regular* (why?); *principal parts; intransitive* (why?); *common form* (why?); *potential mode* (why?); *present tense* (why?); (analyze and inflect it); *third person, singular number* (why?). Rule IV.

4. America was discovered by Columbus.

Was discovered. is a *regular transitive verb, passive voice,*—or simply a *regular passive verb,*—the subject is represented as acted upon; (*discover, discovered, discovered*), *indicative mode* (why?); *past tense* (why?); (analyze (114, 3) and inflect it); *third person, singular number,* and agrees with its subject *America*, according to Rule IV.

5. I love to see the sun shine.

To see........ is an *irregular transitive verb, active voice,* &c., *infinitive mode* (why?); *present tense,* and limits *love,* according to Rule XVI.: "The infinitive has the construction of the noun," &c.

Shine .... is an *irregular intransitive verb* (*shine, shone, shone*), *infinitive mode, present tense,* and limits *see.*

6. If they were reading the book.

Were reading .. is an *irregular transitive verb, active voice, progressive form* (why?); *subjunctive mode* (why?), &c.

7. Has he come?

Has come..... is an *irregular intransitive verb, common form* (conjugated interrogatively), &c.

8. *Add an object, and change the following transitive verbs from the active to the passive voice:—*

Mary loved. They read. Henry lost. The children played. Augustus threw. Anna found. He rowed. Hear. The father punished. Jane broke. Give. Will you lend? (Thus: Mary loved the truth, = The truth was loved by Mary.)

9. *Change the following transitive verbs from the passive to the active form, and supply a subject when it is omitted:—*

America was discovered in 1492. Religious liberty was established in Rhode Island. Magna Charta was granted to the English. The Mexicans were defeated at Buena Vista. The king was concealed in the tree. The retreat of the Greeks was conducted very skilfully. A great battle was fought at Marathon. The Gunpowder Plot was discovered. King Charles was restored to the throne in 1660. Paradise Lost was written by Milton. The Messiah was written by a distinguished poet. (Thus: *Christopher Columbus* discovered America in 1492.)

10. *Parse the* VERBS *in the following examples; also the* NOUNS, *the* ADJECTIVES, *the* PRONOUNS, *and the* PARTICIPLES:—

In August, even, not a breeze can stir but it thrills us with the breath of autumn. A pensive glory is seen in the far, golden gleams among the shadows of the trees.—*Hawthorne.*

Reproach did not spare Braddock even in his grave. Still, his dauntless conduct on the field of battle shows him to have been a man of fearless spirit; and he was universally allowed to be an accomplished disciplinarian. Whatever may have been his faults and errors, he expiated them by the hardest lot that can befall a brave soldier, ambitious of renown,—an unhonored grave in a strange land, a memory clouded by misfortune, and a name forever coupled with defeat.—*Irving.*

Now, by the skies above us, and by our fathers' graves,
Be men to-day, Quirites,—or be forever slaves!—*Macaulay.*

Whatever changes be rung upon bells, they ought to be chimes.—*Willmott.*

The game is done! I've won, I've won!
Quoth she, and whistles thrice.—*Coleridge.*

────── Yet once, methought,
It lifted up its head, and did address
Itself to motion, like as it would speak.—*Hamlet.*

ADVERBS.
132. Definition.

1. An **adverb** is a word used to modify the meaning of a *verb*, an *adjective*, a *participle*, or another *adverb*.

Ex.—He leaves *quickly*. Washington was a *truly* great man. The judge, rising *slowly*, addressed the prisoner. I beg your pardon, I spoke *very* hastily.

REMARK.—When an idea, however expressed, is put in such relation to a verb, an adjective, a participle, or an adverb, as to represent some circumstance of *place, time, cause, manner,* or *degree,* it is adverbial, because it is placed in an adverbial relation in the sentence. The same idea placed in relation to a noun or a pronoun is of the nature of an adjective; as, "He who acts *uprightly* is an *upright* man;" "The *star rose in the east;*" "The star *in the east;*" "The eagle *which perched upon the cliff;*" "They saw the eagle *as it perched upon the cliff.*"

2. An adverbial idea may be expressed,—

(1.) By a **single word**, an *adverb*, having its relation determined by its termination, its position, or its meaning.

Ex.—'Tis *greatly* wise to talk with our past hours.

(2.) By a **noun** or a **pronoun**, having its relation expressed by a preposition.

Ex.—The affair was managed *with prudence,* = *prudently*. They gathered *around it.*

In this case, the *phrase* consisting of the preposition and the noun is said to be *adverbial.*

(3.) By a **proposition,** having its relation expressed by a conjunctive adverb.

Ex.—Speak *so that you may be understood* = *distinctly.*

Here the clause or proposition is adverbial.

3. Adverbs are usually abridged expressions taking the place of phrases consisting of a preposition and a noun.

Ex.—He lived *there,* = *in that place.* He conducted *wisely,* = *in a wise manner.*

4. Sometimes an adverb seems to qualify a noun, and thereby to partake of the nature of an adjective.

Ex.—I found the boy *only*.

5. Sometimes an adverb modifies a phrase, or an entire proposition.

Ex.—*Far* from home. The accident happened *directly* after we crossed the bridge.

133. Exercise.

1. *Point out the* ADVERBS *in the following sentences:—*

She sang sweetly. The wind moaned mournfully over her grave. O, lightly, lightly tread. The storm raged fearfully. When shall I see you again? They lived very happily. They were agreeably disappointed. Do you expect them to-morrow? She is continually changing her mind. It cannot be true. Perhaps I shall go. Doubtless it is true. George writes elegantly.

2. *Insert the following adverbs in sentences of your own:—*

Where, hopefully, soon, bravely, yes, surely, undeniably, sorrowfully, briefly, quite, below, above, ever, constantly, so, yet, although, no.

134. Classes of Adverbs.

1. **Adverbs** may be divided into four general classes,—adverbs of *place*, of *time*, of *cause*, of *manner*.

2. Adverbs of **place** answer the questions *Where? Whither? Whence?*

Ex.—Here, there, where, herein, therein, wherein, hither, thither, whither, hence, thence, whence, above, below, up, down, yonder, somewhere, nowhere, everywhere, away, aside, aloof, back, forth, off, far, aboard, ashore, aloft, aground, forwards, backwards, outwards.

3. Adverbs of **time** answer the questions *When? How long? How often?*

Ex.—Now, when, then, often, immediately, always, frequently, to-day, to-morrow, yesterday, ever, never, sometimes, lately, early, again, forever, soon, hitherto, seldom, rarely, after, ago, anon, hereafter.

4. Adverbs of **cause** answer the questions *Why? Wherefore?*

Ex.—Why, wherefore, therefore, then.

Causal relations are commonly expressed by *phrases* and *clauses.*

5. Adverbs of **manner** and **degree** answer the questions *How?* *How much?* They are generally derived from adjectives denoting quality.

Ex.—Faithfully, fairly, elegantly, so, thus, well, too, very, chiefly, quite, partly, wholly, amiss, scarcely, nearly, asunder, however, otherwise, together, just, less, much, least, enough, almost, asunder, headlong, generally, somewhat, excellently, gracefully.

6. **Modal** adverbs, or those which show the manner of the *assertion*, belong to this class.

Ex.—Yes, yea, verily, truly, surely, doubtless, forsooth, certainly, no, nay, not, perhaps, perchance, indeed, really, haply, possibly, probably, nowise, peradventure.

7. The adverbs *when, where, why, how,* &c., when used in asking questions, are called *interrogative* adverbs.

Ex.—*When* did he come?

8. Adverbs of manner are numerous. Most of them are formed from adjectives by adding *ly*.

Ex.—Bright, bright-*ly;* smooth, smooth-*ly*.

But when the adjective ends in *ly*, the *phrase* is commonly used.

Ex.—"In a *lovely* manner," instead of *lovelily*.

9. *There* is used as an expletive to introduce a sentence when the verb *to be* denotes existence. It is also sometimes used with the verbs *seem, appear, come, go*, and others.

Ex.—*There* are many men of the same opinion. *There* went out a decree from Cæsar Augustus.

In this use it has no meaning.

10. The adverb *so* is often used as a substitute for some preceding word or group of words.

Ex.—He is *in good business*, and is likely to remain *so*.

11. In colloquial use, some adverbs limit no particular word or words in the sentence, and are said to be used independently.

Ex.—*Well*, I will let you know, if I decide to go. *Why*, you told me so yourself.

135. Conjunctive Adverbs.

1. **Conjunctive adverbs** are those which express the

adverbial relation of a dependent clause, and connect it with the verb, the adjective, or the adverb which it modifies.

Ex.—I shall meet my friend *when* the boat arrives.

2. They are equivalent to two phrases, the one containing a relative pronoun, the other its antecedent.

Ex.—The lilies grow *where* the ground is moist, = The lilies grow *in that place in which* the ground is moist.

Here the phrase *in that place* modifies *grows*, and the phrase *in which* modifies *moist:* hence *where*, the equivalent of the two, modifies both. For the principal conjunctive adverbs, see (**143**, 18).

3. The words *therefore, wherefore, hence, whence, consequently, then, now, besides, likewise, also, too, moreover,* and some others, are adverbs, and at the same time are used—either alone or when associated with other connectives—to join propositions. But, unlike conjunctive adverbs, they connect coördinate and not subordinate clauses.

136. Exercise.

1. *Tell the class of the following adverbs:—*

Very, greatly, perhaps, therefore, below, to-morrow, when, there, purely, truly, always, continually, yesterday, why, sorrowfully, painfully, down, above, here, vainly, exceedingly.

2. *Point out the conjunctive adverbs in the following examples:—*

He will be prepared when the time arrives. The patriot answers whenever his country calls. Whither I go ye cannot come. It was for a long time uncertain where the gypsies originated. Newton, only by profound study, discovered why an apple falls to the ground. The Bible teaches us how to guide our steps aright. Make hay while the sun shines. When a man's coat is threadbare, it is easy to pick a hole in it.

137. Comparison of Adverbs.

1. Many adverbs, especially those denoting manner, admit of comparison.

Ex.—*Brightly, more brightly, most brightly; soon, sooner, soonest.*

2. When an adjective undergoes comparison, it usually shows that two or more *objects* are compared; but when an adverb undergoes the same change,

it shows that two or more *actions* or *qualities* are compared; as, "James *speaks* more fluently than George [*speaks*]."

3. The following adverbs are compared irregularly: *Ill* or *badly, worse, worst; little, less, least; far, farther, farthest; much, more, most; well, better, best.*

138. Exercise.

1. *Study the following outline for parsing adverbs:*—

To parse an adverb, tell,—
   (1.) What part of speech it is, and why.
   (2.) Compare it (where it admits of it), and tell what degree.
   (3.) Tell what it modifies.
   (4.) Give the rule.

2. The sun shines *brightly*.

Brightly ...... is an *adverb;* it modifies the meaning of the verb; it is compared (positive *brightly*, comparative *more brightly*, superlative *most brightly*); it is in the *positive degree*, and modifies the verb *shines*, according to Rule IX. (Repeat it.)

3. Mary writes *more elegantly* than her brother.

More elegantly . is an *adverb;* it modifies the meaning of the verb; it is compared (*elegantly, more elegantly, most elegantly*); it is in the *comparative degree*, and modifies the verb *writes*, according to Rule IX. (Repeat it.)

4. I will go *whenever* you wish.

Whenever ..... is a conjunctive adverb of time. (Why?)
   (1.) As an adverb it modifies both *will go* and *wish*, according to Rule IX.
   (2.) As a connective it connects the subordinate clause "whenever you wish" to *will go*. Rule XI.

5. *Parse the* ADVERBS *in the following examples; also the* ADJECTIVES, *the* VERBS, *and the* PRONOUNS:—

He (Sir Thomas More) stands unchangeably on the centre of eternal right; his head, majestically erect, gloriously lifted up to heaven, bends not before the shock, and his breast receives the tempest only to shiver it.—*Giles.*

No human fancy can take in this mighty space in all its grandeur, and in all its immensity; can sweep the outer boundaries of such a creation; or lift itself up to the majesty of that great and invisible arm, on which all is suspended.—*Chalmers.*

Hitherto shalt thou come, and no further; and here shall thy proud waves be stayed.

Where I could not be honest, I never yet was valiant.—*Shakspeare.*

When man is at peace with man, how much lighter than a feather are the heaviest metals in his hand!—*Sterne.*

>When Music, heavenly maid, was young,
>While yet in early Greece she sung,
>The Passions oft, to hear her shell,
>Thronged around her magic cell.—*Collins.*

>Yet where to find that happiest spot below,
>Who can direct, when all pretend to know?—*Goldsmith.*

PREPOSITIONS.
139. Definition.

1. A **preposition** is a word used to show the relation of a noun or a pronoun to some other word.

Ex.—The ship was seen *from* the citadel. He sailed *upon* the ocean *in* a ship *of* war.

2. The preposition always shows a relation between two terms,—an *antecedent* and a *subsequent*. The subsequent term is called the *object* of the preposition. The preposition and the object united form a dependent element of the sentence, having the antecedent term as its principal element.

3. The preposition and its object form a *phrase*. When the antecedent term is a noun, the phrase is of the nature of an adjective. When it is a verb, a participle, an adjective, or an adverb, the phrase is of the nature of an adverb (sometimes an indirect object).

Ex.—The rays *of the sun*, = *solar* rays. The case was conducted *with skill*, = *skilfully.*

4. The *object* of the preposition is not always a single word: it may be a *phrase* or a *clause.*

Ex.—The city was *about to capitulate* when Napoleon arrived. Much will depend *on who the commissioners are.*

5. The preposition is sometimes placed after its object.

Ex.—While its song, sublime as thunder, rolls the woods *along*.

The preposition and the object sometimes precede the word on which they depend.

Ex.—*Of* all *patriots*, Washington was the noblest.

140. List of Prepositions.

aboard,	before,	excepting,	till,
about,	behind,	for,	to,
above,	below,	from,	touching,
across,	beneath,	in, into,	toward,
after,	beside,	notwithstanding,	towards,
against,	besides,	of,	under,
along,	between,	on,	underneath,
amid *or*	betwixt,	over,	until,
amidst,	beyond,	past,	unto,
among,	by,	regarding,	up,
amongst,	concerning,	respecting,	upon,
around,	down,	round,	with,
at,	during,	since,	within,
athwart,	ere,	through,	without.
bating,	except,	throughout,	

1. A **complex** preposition consists of two words, and is parsed as a single word.

Ex.—*According to, as to, as far, out of, instead of, because of, off from, over against, round about, from among, from between, from around, from before,* and the like.

The first word of the phrase is sometimes parsed as an *adverb*. *According, contrary,* in the phrases *according to, contrary to,* are sometimes regarded as participles or adjectives modifying some noun in the sentence.

2. In such combinations as the following, *put in, go up, go down, cut through, pass by, climb up,* and others, the preposition may be parsed as an *adverb* when it is not followed by an object.

Ex.—The captain stood *in* for the shore. They rode *by* in haste.

3. Some words commonly employed as prepositions are occasionally used as adverbs.

Ex.—*Before, after, till, until, above, beneath, for, on, in,* &c.

So also some words commonly employed as adverbs or as conjunctions are sometimes used as prepositions.

Ex.—*But, save, despite,* &c.

Off is usually an adverb, but may be parsed as a preposition, when followed by an object. *Instead* is either a preposition or equivalent to a preposition and a noun, = *in stead.*

4. In such expressions as *a hunting, a fishing,* &c., if authorized at all, the *a* may be regarded as itself a preposition, or a contraction of *at, in,* or *on.*

141. Exercise.

1. *Study the following outline for parsing the preposition:*—

To parse a preposition, tell,—

    (1.) What part of speech, and why.
    (2.) Between what words it shows the relation.
    (3.) Give the rule.

2. He went *from* England *to* France.

From .. is a *preposition;* it is used to show the relation of a noun or a pronoun to some other word; it shows the relation of the noun *England* to the verb *went,* according to Rule XIII. (Repeat it.)

To .... is a *preposition;* it shows the relation of the noun *France* to the verb *went,* according to Rule XIII.

3. *Point out the* PREPOSITIONS *in the following sentences, and explain their relations:*—

He heard the birds sing in the morning. The buds are swelling in the sun's warm rays. The winds will come from the distant south. The bees gather honey from the flowers. I bring fresh showers for the thirsty flowers from sea and stream. I shall be Queen of the May. In the garden the crocus blooms. The hills are covered with a carpet of green. We shall have pleasant walks with our friends. We shall seek the early fruits in the sunny valley.

4. *Parse the* NOUNS, *the* PRONOUNS, *the* ADVERBS, *and the* PREPOSITIONS *in the following sentences:*—

  Humility mainly becometh the converse of man with his Maker,
  But oftentimes it seemeth out of place in the intercourse of man
    with man;

Yea, it is the cringer to his equal, that is chiefly seen bold to his God,
While the martyr whom a world cannot browbeat, is humble as a child before him.—*Tupper.*

>Of all the thoughts of God that are
>Borne inward unto souls afar
> Along the Psalmist's music deep,
>Now tell me if there any is
>For gift or grace surpassing this—
>" He giveth His beloved sleep."—*Mrs. Browning.*

CONJUNCTIONS.
142. Definition.

1. **A conjunction** is a word used to connect sentences or the parts of sentences.

Ex.—The horse fell over the precipice, *but* the rider escaped. The horse *and* rider fell over the precipice.

In the first example, *but* connects two sentences; in the second, *and* connects the two parts, *horse* and *rider*.

2. A pure conjunction forms no part of the material (152, 1) or substance of a sentence: its office is simply to unite the materials into a single structure.

3. Besides pure conjunctions, there is a large class of words which enter into the sentence as a part of its substance and at the same time connect different elements or parts.

Ex.—This is the pencil *which* I lost.

Here *which* is the object of *lost*, and at the same time connects the dependent clause, *which I lost*, to *pencil*. All such words are called *connectives*, or *conjunctive words*.

143. Classes of Connectives.

1. All connectives (whether pure conjunctions or conjunctive words) are divided into two classes,—*coördinate* and *subordinate*.

2. **Coördinate** connectives are those which join similar or homogeneous elements.

ETYMOLOGY—CONJUNCTIONS.

Ex.—*John* AND *James* were disciples.

Here *John* and *James* are similar in construction, and have a common relation to the predicate. Two elements are coördinate, and consequently demand a coördinate conjunction, when they are placed in the same relation or rank; as, "The insects devoured *leaves* and *blossoms.*" Here *leaves* is dependent on *devoured; blossoms*, also, is not only dependent, but has precisely the same sort of dependence as *leaves;* hence they are coördinate with each other. In the sentence, "The insects devoured the leaves greedily," *leaves* and *greedily* are both dependent on *devoured*, but they have not a *similar* dependence; hence they are not coördinate, and cannot be connected by *and*, or any other coördinate conjunction.

3. Coördinate connectives are always conjunctions, and may be divided into three classes,—*copulative, adversative,* and *alternative.*

4. **Copulative** conjunctions are those which add parts in harmony with each other.

Ex.—The day dawned, *and* our friends departed.

5. The copulative conjunctions are,—

(*a.*) *And*, a connective of the most general character, placing the connected parts in a relation of perfect equality, without modification or emphasis.

(*b.*) *So, also, likewise, too, besides, moreover, furthermore, now, hence, therefore, wherefore, consequently, even,* connectives associated with *and* expressed or understood, and used to give *emphasis* or some additional idea.

Ex.—Cromwell was a successful soldier; [*and*] *besides*, he was the greatest statesman of his age.

(*c.*) *Both — and; as well — as; not only — but; but also; but likewise; first — secondly:* these connectives are employed when we wish not only to make the second part emphatic, but to awaken an expectation of some addition.

Ex.—*Both* religion *and* reason condemn excess. *You might as well* deny me at once *as* begin to find excuses. *Not only* the wise and the learned, *but also* the common people, heard him gladly.

As these parts correspond to each other, these connectives are called *correlatives.*

6. **Adversative** conjunctions are those which unite parts in opposition to, or in contrast with, each other.

Ex.—The fish was brought to the shore, *but* plunged into the water again.

7. Adversative conjunctions are employed,—

(1.) When the second part is placed in opposition to the first.

Ex.—It does not rain, *but* it snows.

(2.) When the second part is placed in opposition to a supposed inference from the first.

Ex.—The army was victorious, *but* the general was slain.

Here, lest the inference should be that all was prosperous, the second clause preceded by *but* is added.

8. The adversative conjunctions are,—

(*a.*) *But*, which simply shows opposition without emphasis.

Ex.—I shall go, *but* I shall not walk.

(*b.*) *Yet, still, nevertheless, notwithstanding, however, now*, and some others, which are associated with *but*, either expressed or understood, and give emphasis or some additional idea.

Ex.—The delinquent has been repeatedly admonished, (*but*) *still* he is as negligent as ever.

9. **Alternative** conjunctions are those which offer or deny a choice between two things.

Ex.—Obey and live, *or* disobey and die. She can *neither* sing *nor* play.

10. The alternative conjunctions are,—

(*a.*) *Or*, which *offers*, and *nor* (*not or*), which *denies* a choice.

(*b.*) *Else, otherwise*, associated with *or* for the sake of emphasis.

(*c.*) *Either* and *neither*, correlatives of *or* and *nor*.

Ex.—We must fight *or* our liberties are lost. Thou desirest not sacrifice, *else* would I give it. *Neither* a borrower *nor* a lender be. *Either* the Turk *or* the Christian shall withdraw his forces.

11. Parts standing in a causal relation to each other are sometimes coördinate; but usually there are, in such cases, two connectives, one expressed and the other understood.

Ex.—The south wind blows, [*and*] *therefore* there must be rain.

12. **Subordinate** connectives are those which join dissimilar or heterogeneous elements.

Ex.—I shall go *when* the stage arrives.

Here, *when* joins the subordinate clause *when the stage arrives*, to the verb *shall go*. It is a part of the clause itself, being equivalent to *at the time at which.* Hence it should be introduced in naming the clause; but not so with the pure coördinate conjunctions.

13. The connected element is always a proposition; it is subordinate, and consequently demands a subordinate connective, because it becomes merely a limiting expression of the antecedent term on which it depends. It is unlike the part with which it is connected, in its form, in its relation or rank, and in its grammatical character.

14. A subordinate connective, like a preposition, always shows a relation of dependence. But the second term is a proposition instead of a noun or a pronoun.

15. Subordinate connectives are divided into three classes,—those which connect *substantive* clauses, those which connect *adjective* clauses, and those which connect *adverbial* clauses.

16. Substantive clauses containing a **statement (163,** 3) are connected by the conjunctions *that, that not,* and sometimes *but, but that.*

Ex.—Addison acknowledged *that* he would rather inform than divert his readers.

Substantive clauses containing an **inquiry** are connected by the interrogatives *who, which, what, where, whither, whence, when, how long, how often, why, wherefore, how.*

Ex.—I wish to know *where* we may look for redress.

17. Adjective clauses are connected by the relative pronouns *who, which, what, that, whoever, whosoever, whichever, whichsoever, whatever, whatsoever,* and sometimes the relative adverbs *why, when, where.*

Ex.—A writer *who* abuses the confidence of friends should be treated with contempt.

18. Adverbial clauses are joined to the principal element by,—

(1.) Connectives which denote **place:** these are, *where, whither, whence, wherever, whithersoever, as far as, as long as, farther than.*

Ex.—We feel that we are on the spot *where* the first scene of our history was laid.— *Webster.*

(2.) Connectives which denote **time:** these are, *when, while, whilst, as, before, after, ere, till, until, since, whenever, as long as, as soon as, the moment, the instant, as frequently as, as often as.*

Ex.—He scarce had ceased *when* the superior fiend
Was moving to the shore.—*Milton.*

(3.) Connectives which denote **causal** relations: these are the conjunctions *because, for, as, whereas, since, inasmuch* (causal), *if, unless, though, lest, except, provided, provided that* (conditional), *that, that not, lest* (final), *though, although, notwithstanding, however, whatever, whoever, while,* with the correlatives *yet, still, nevertheless* (adversative).

Ex.—A timid man shrinks from an enterprise *because* he fears a danger may be in the way.

(4.) Connectives which denote **manner:** these are, *as, just as, so — as, same — as* (correspondence), *so — that, such — that* (consequence), *as — as* (comparison of equality), *the — the, the — so much the* (proportionate equality), *than, more than, less than* (comparison of inequality).

Ex.—True politeness requires you to act as a kind heart dictates.

144. Exercise.

1. *Study the following outline for parsing conjunctions.*

In parsing a conjunction or connective, tell,—

   (1.) What part of speech, and why.
   (2.) To what class it belongs.
   (3.) What elements it connects.
   (4.) Give the rule.

2. Socrates and Plato were distinguished philosophers.

And ... is a *conjunction;* it is used to connect sentences, or the parts of sentences; *coördinate,* because it connects similar elements; it connects *Socrates* and *Plato,* according to Rule XI. (Repeat it.)

3. Wisdom is better than riches.

Than .. is a *conjunction* (why?); *subordinate,* because it connects dissimilar elements; it connects the proposition *than riches* (*are*) with *better,* according to Rule XVI. (Repeat it.)

4. We must *either* obey *or* be punished.

Either . is a *coördinate conjunction* (alternative), used to awaken expectation of an additional element, and also to introduce it with emphasis.

Or .... is a *coördinate conjunction* (alternative), and with its correlative *either* is used to connect the predicate *must be punished* with *must obey.* (Rule XI.: Repeat it.)

5. *Though* he slay me, *yet* will I trust in him.

Though is a *subordinate conjunction* (adversative), used to awaken expectation of an additional idea.

Yet ... is a *subordinate conjunction* (adversative), and, with its correlative *though*, is used to connect the subordinate clause *he slay me*, with the principal one *will I trust in him*, according to Rule XVI.

6. *Tell which of the following connectives are coördinate, and which are subordinate:—*

The pen and ink are poor. The horse and the rider were plunged into the water. If you come, I shall have the work in readiness. When the million applaud, seriously ask yourself what harm you have done. He knew that he had disobeyed instructions. That which cannot be cured must be endured. Take heed lest ye fall.

7. *Parse the* CONJUNCTIONS, *the* ADJECTIVES, *and the* VERBS, *in the following examples:—*

It is to the Union that we owe our safety at home, and our consideration and dignity abroad. Every year of its duration has teemed with fresh proof of its utility and its blessings; and, although our territory has stretched out wider and wider and our population spread further and further, they have not outrun its protection or its benefits.— *Webster.*

In a word, point us to the loveliest and happiest neighborhood in the world on which we dwell,—and we tell you that our object is to render this whole earth, with all its nations and kindreds and tongues and people, as happy as—nay, happier than—such a neighborhood.— *Wayland.*

Thy Hector, wrapped in everlasting sleep,
Shall neither hear thee cry, nor see thee weep.—*Pope.*

'Twas but a kindred sound to move;
For pity melts the heart to love.—*Dryden.*

INTERJECTIONS.
145. Definition.

1. An **interjection** is a word used to express some strong or sudden emotion of the mind.

Ex.—Alas! I then have chid away my friend.

2. As the interjection is not the sign of an idea, but merely an expression of emotion, it cannot have any definable signification or grammatical construction; but, as it is of frequent use in colloquial and impassioned discourse, it should not be omitted in parsing.

3. "Interjection" is derived from the Latin word "in" "jectus,"—*thrown between*, that is, between the parts of the sentence; but it is often placed at the beginning or at the end of a sentence.

4. The most common interjections are those expressing,—

Joy or **exultation**,—*hey, hurra, huzza.*
Surprise,—*aha, hah, ah.*
A wish for attention,—*ho, lo, halloo, hem.*
Aversion or **contempt**,—*fie, pshaw, pugh, tush, foh.*
Sorrow, grief, or **compassion**,—*alas, woe, alack, O.*
A wish for silence,—*hist, hush, mum.*
Languor,—*heigh-ho, heigh-ho-hum.*
Laughter,—*ha, ha, he, he.*

Some words used as interjections may be parsed as verbs, nouns, or adjectives; as in the sentence, "*Strange!* cried I,"—where *strange* is an adjective, and the expression is equivalent to "It is strange;" and in the sentence, "*Behold!* how well he bears misfortune's frowns!" *behold* is a verb in the imperative, equivalent to *behold ye.*

146. Exercise.

1. *Outline for parsing an interjection:*—

To parse an interjection, tell,—
    (1.) What part of speech, and why?
    (2.) Give the rule.

2. Hark! they whisper.

Hark. is an interjection (why?); it is used independently. Rule X.

3. *Parse all the words in the following examples:*—

Oh, say, what mystic spell is that which so blinds us to the sufferings of our brethren,—which deafens our ear to the voice of bleeding humanity, when it is aggravated by the shriek of dying thousands.—*Chalmers.*

> Woe worth the chase! woe worth the day!
> That cost thy life, my gallant grey.—*Scott.*

Oh, now you weep; and I perceive you feel
The dint of pity; these are gracious drops.
Kind souls! What! weep you when you but behold
Our Cæsar's vesture wounded! Look you here!
Here is himself, marred as you see, with traitors.—*Shakspeare.*

> Hail! holy light, offspring of heaven first-born,
> Or of the Eternal, co-eternal beam!—*Milton.*

> Unfading Hope! when life's last embers burn,
> When soul to soul, and dust to dust, return,
> Heaven to thy charge resigns the awful hour!
> Oh! then, thy kingdom comes! Immortal Power!
> What though each spark of earth-born rapture fly
> The quivering lip, pale cheek, and closing eye!
> Bright to the soul thy seraph hands convey
> The morning dream of life's eternal day!—
> Then, then, the triumph and the trance begin,
> And all the phœnix spirit burns within!—*Campbell.*

QUESTIONS FOR REVIEW.

What is Etymology?
What is a word?
How are words divided according to their meaning and use? According to their sounds? According to their significant parts?
What are declinable words? Indeclinable?
How many parts of speech are there? Name them. Define each. What part of speech is *un*, in the sentence "*Un* is a prefix"? Why? What is a proper noun? A common noun? A collective noun? An abstract noun? A verbal noun?
Give an example of a noun of each kind.
What are the properties of the noun?
What is Person? Define each person.
When is a noun in the first or second person?
What is Number? Define each number.
Give the rule for forming the plural of nouns regularly.
How do nouns ending in *f* or *fe* form the plural? Nouns ending in *o*? Nouns ending in *y*? What nouns have a very irregular plural?
What nouns have no plural?
Give the rule for the plural of compound nouns.
How are other parts of speech used as nouns pluralized?
What is the rule for the plural of single names? Of complex names? Of a title and name?
Mention three nouns that have no singular. Three that are either singular or plural. Three that are alike in both numbers.
What is Gender? How many genders are there? Define each. How can inanimate objects become masculine or feminine? Name the three modes of distinguishing the sexes.
What is Case? How many cases are there? Define each. How is the possessive regularly formed? When is the apostrophe only added? How may you know the nominative case? The possessive? The objective?
What is Declension? Parsing?
What is an Adjective? Name the two classes. The three kinds of limiting adjectives.
How many Articles are there? Define each. When is each used? When is no article needed?
What is a Pronominal Adjective? Name the principal ones. What are distributives? Demonstratives? Indefinites? Reciprocals? Name the classes of Numeral Adjectives.
What is a Qualifying Adjective? A Participial Adjective?
What is Comparison? Define the three degrees.
What may comparison show in respect to *intensity*? The *terms*?
Give the rule for forming the comparative and superlative of monosyllables. Of words of more than one syllable. Mention five adjectives compared irregularly. What adjectives are not compared?
What is a Pronoun? What four relations does the pronoun represent? What is the Antecedent? Into what three classes are pronouns divided? What properties have pronouns in common with nouns?
Define and name the Personal Pronouns. Name the different uses of It. Of Thou and You. Name the compound personal pronouns. Decline the pronouns. Where do you use *My* and *Mine?*
What is a Relative Pronoun? How does the relative differ from the personal pronoun? Name the simple relatives. What can you say of What? Of That? Name the compound relatives, and give the rule for forming them.
Define and name the Interrogative Pronouns. What besides pronouns are used in asking questions?
What is a Verb? What is the meaning of *affirm?* What can you say of Be? When is a verb attributive? Define the *subject*. How are verbs divided according to their *use?* Define a Transitive Verb. An Intransitive. What do you mean by an Active, Passive, and Neuter Verb? What can you say of this distinction? What is the *object* of a transitive verb? Can the same verb be both transitive and

ETYMOLOGY—QUESTIONS FOR REVIEW.

intransitive? How are verbs divided according to their *form?* Define a Regular Verb, an Irregular Verb, a Defective, an Auxiliary, an Impersonal. — What properties belong to verbs? What is Voice? Define the Active voice. The Passive. What verbs can have the passive voice? What are the uses of the passive voice? Of the active?

What is Mode? Define each mode. What modes are used in principal propositions? What one in subordinate propositions? What one in abridged propositions?

What is a Participle? Why so called? What is the mode of forming the participles? How many Participles are there? How many forms? Define the Present Active Participle. Name the uses of it. What can you say of the form "is being built," and the like?

Define the Present Passive Participle; the Perfect Active; the Perfect Passive. When is the participle predicated? When assumed?

What is Tense? What are the four ways of considering an action or event? What is meant by a *point* of time? A *period?* What are *relative* tenses? Absolute? How many of each?

Define the Present Tense in the indicative mode. How is it used? The Present Perfect. How used? The Past Tense. How used? The Past Perfect. How used? The Future. The Future Perfect.

How many tenses has each mode? What is the signification of the tenses in the Subjunctive mode? In the Potential? In the Infinitive? In the Imperative?

What are the *forms* of the verb? Name and define each. Give the form for each division of time.

What are Auxiliary Verbs? Name them. For what are they used? Conjugate them. What is the signification of *be?* Of *do?* Of *have?* Of *shall* and *will?* Give the rules for the use of shall and will. What is the signification of *may?* of *can?* of *must?* Show how the auxiliaries combine to form the tenses of the Indicative mode. Of the Potential mode.

→What are the Number and Person of the verb? How do you distinguish them?

What is the Conjugation of the verb? The Principal Parts? Conjugate the verb *be* in all the modes and tenses. Conjugate the verb *love.* How is a verb conjugated interrogatively? Negatively? Give the list of Irregular Verbs. Name the Defective Verbs. What is a Redundant Verb?

What is an Adverb? Name the three ways of expressing an adverbial idea. Adverbs of Place answer what questions? Adverbs of Time? Adverbs of Cause? Adverbs of Manner and Degree? What are Modal Adverbs? What are Conjunctive Adverbs? What adverbs admit of comparison?

What is a Preposition? What do you mean by the *object* of the preposition? What constitutes a *phrase?* What is a Complex Preposition?

What is a Conjunction? What is the office of conjunctions? Name the two classes of connectives. How many classes of coördinate connectives are there? What are Copulative Conjunctions? Name them. Adversative Conjunctions? When are they used? Name them. Alternative Conjunctions? Name them.

What are Subordinate Connectives? Name the three classes. How are substantive clauses connected? Adjective clauses? Adverbial clauses?

What is an Interjection? Name the most common.

SYNTAX.

147. Preliminary Development—Sentence-Making.

1. **Syntax** treats of the construction of sentences.
2. A **sentence** is a thought expressed in words.

Ex.—The flowers fade. The sun is shining. The boy heeded not his father's advice. Socrates was unmoved when the sentence of death was pronounced against him.

Syntax signifies *putting together*. Thus, the words in these examples are put together,—but in such a manner as to *say*, *affirm*, or *assert* something. If joined thus,—the fading flowers, the shining sun, the boy heeding not his father's advice, Socrates unmoved, &c.,—they would not *say*, *tell*, or *assert* any thing: *i.e.* they would not *express a thought*.

3. To express a thought, we must **say something** of **some object.**

Ex.—The moon is rising in the east.

The *object* here is the *moon;* we *say* of it, *is rising*. When we *say* or *assert* something, as we do here, it is implied that we *know* or *believe* what we say,—or we speak *as if* we *knew* or *believed* what we said. If we know of the *rising*, but do not know what *object* is rising, we can still speak, but so as only to *intimate* what we know, and *seek for* what we do not know. Thus, "*What* is rising?" If ignorant of the act, but not of the object, we should say, "*What* is the moon *doing?*" If we did not know the *place*, we should say, "*Where* is the moon rising?" Thus, a sentence may express *knowledge*, or *ignorance*. It may also express our feelings or desires. "How beautifully the moon is rising in the east!" "Give me that book."

4. The **subject** represents that of which something is said or affirmed.

Ex.—The *trees* grow; the *clouds* are beautiful; —— is reading; —— is coming; —— was beheaded. Is —— the capital?

Let the pupil point out the subjects, and supply appropriate ones in place of the blanks.

5. The **predicate** represents that which is said or affirmed.

SYNTAX. 165

Ex.—The house *is built;* the rain *is falling;* the boy ———; the duck ———; the daisy ———. Will Walter ———?

REMARK.—The predicate is sometimes used to *deny, ask for, command,* or *exclaim;* and the term *say, affirm,* or *assert* applies to either case (**80, 3**).

Observe that in these examples we say only *one* thing of *one* object.

6. We may say **one thing** of several objects, or **several things** of one object.

Ex.—Lilies, roses, asters, hyacinths, and dahlias *bloom.*
The bird *chirps, sings, hops, builds a nest, lays eggs, and feeds her young.*

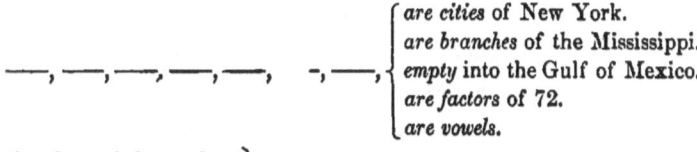

The days of the week
The parts of a tree
The seasons of the year
The States of the Union
} are ——, ——, ——, ——, ——, ——, ——.

Let the blanks be filled by the pupil. The two cases may then be combined, thus:—"The oranges, apples, lemons, peaches, and pears, are ripe, mellow, sweet, juicy, and delicious."

7. A sentence expresses,—

(1.) An **indefinite** thought, when the subject or the predicate is a general term without limitations.

Men formed.

Any word, as a common noun, a verb, a participle, or an adjective, is a *general term* when it can apply to any number of individuals. Thus, an adjective, as *white,* may apply to many objects, as, *white* house, *white* snow, *white* birds, &c.; the verb *run* may express the action of many objects; a common noun, as *men,* in the example above, may belong to many classes; there may be *few* or *many, old* or *young, rich* or *poor, good* or *bad, strong* or *weak, brave* or *cowardly, wise* or *unwise,* &c. The verb *formed* has nothing joined to it to show *what, where, when, how,* or *why* they *formed.*

(2.) A **definite** thought, when the subject and the predicate are properly limited.

To limit the subject, we may join to it,—

(a.) The **definite article,** to show that some *particular* men are intended.

The men formed.

(*b.*) A **numeral adjective,** to restrict the *number.*

The *twenty* men formed.

(*c.*) A **qualifying adjective,** to show *what kind,* and thereby to exclude all others.

The twenty *young* men formed.

(*d.*) An **adjective expression,** to point them out by showing how they were regarded.

The twenty young men **who were the pride of the town formed.**

To limit the predicate, we may join to it,—

(*a.*) An **adverb,** to determine the *time.*

The men .... **immediately** formed.

b.) A **noun,** to show *what* they formed.

The men .... immediately formed a **combination.**

(*c.*) An **adverbial expression,** to show *why* they formed a combination.

The men .... immediately formed a combination, **that they might free the people from these nightly invaders.**

Thus we have the definite thought intended, namely,—

The–twenty–young–**men**–who were the pride of the town–immediately–**formed**–a combination–that they might free the people from these nightly invaders.

Observe, here,—

(1.) We have *one* subject and *one* predicate (6, above).

(2.) That each, to become definite, must have many added words.

(3.) As the thought becomes more and more definite, the sentence becomes more and more extended, and the *definite thought* is obtained from the *indefinite thought* by various modifications.

8. A **modifier** is a word or a group of words joined to a term to limit, extend, or in some way to determine, its application.

Ex.—**Men,**—*ten* men, *all* men, *the* men *of the last century;* **seek**—*the lost*—*diligently*—*in every place.*

9. The subject, the predicate, and the modifiers of each, form the elements of the sentence.

Ex.—*Charles's*—**resignation**—**filled**—*all Europe*—*with astonishment.*

Observe, here and above, that some elements are *single words* and some are *groups,* and that each expresses an *idea.*

10. The uniting of elements into a sentence is called **construction,** or **synthesis;** the separation of a sentence into its elements is called **analysis.**

REMARK.—As a sentence is a *thought* and its *expression*, so its elements are *ideas* and their *expressions*. The first steps in analysis should be guided by the prominent ideas which constitute the thought. In the final analysis, all expressions should be reduced to *single words*. Hence,—

11. Syntax is naturally divided into syntax of *sentences*, syntax of *elements*, and syntax of *words*.

148. Exercise.

In the following examples, point out the subject and the predicate, and unite them to form the indefinite thought; then point out the modifiers of the subject, explaining the limitations; then the modifiers of the predicate in the same manner, and show how the definite thought is expressed:—

The clouds are gathering. Humboldt wrote Kosmos. The fashions change. Madeira has a fine climate. Do all birds migrate? The wind is east. The weathercock is rusty. Cæsar crossed the Rubicon. The Rubicon is an Italian river. Coleridge wrote "The Ancient Mariner." The drone is an idle, lazy bee. The best tobacco grows in Cuba. A continent is a large island. Thimble is derived from thumb. Humility is a graceful ornament.

Travellers can ascend, by a winding road, to the top of Mt. Washington. The climate of Florida is favorable to invalids. A man's word should be kept sacred. Solon, the Athenian lawgiver, lived about six hundred years before Christ. There is through all nature a regular succession of events. Montaigne, the entertaining French essayist and philosopher, travelled on horseback, from his chateau in France, through Germany and Switzerland, into Italy. Apicius, a Roman glutton, having spent seven and a half million dollars in the gratification of his palate, and finding he had but three hundred thousand dollars left, killed himself for fear of dying of hunger. A basket, left on the ground and overgrown by acanthus, suggested the Corinthian capital. The Giant-killer with the familiar name has the whole heart of the boy.

When I look upon the tombs of the great, every emotion of envy dies within me. The sumptuous cities which have lighted the world since the beginning of time, are now beheld only in the pictures of the historian or the poet. Whenever the queen bee goes forth to take the air, many of the small bees attend upon her, guarding her before and behind. Longfellow, in the "Psalm of Life," one of his best-known poems, says that our hearts, like muffled drums, are beating funeral marches to the grave. The life of Agricola, the Roman general who conquered Britain, was written by his son-in-law Tacitus, the celebrated Latin historian. The Venetians, while under Austrian rule, were a nation in mourning. Absence of mind which is the result of (thinking of something else is quite different) from absence of mind which is the result of thinking of nothing at all.

SYNTAX OF SENTENCES.

149. Sentences classified by their Use as a Whole.

1. Sentences considered as a whole are,—

(1.) **Declarative**, or those which declare something as real and absolute, or as possible, probable, obligatory, or necessary.

Ex.—I have found favor in the sight of the king. It may rain. We should pay our debts. The work must be done.

The declarative sentence forms the main body of every species of composition. It may be positive or negative; its mode may be indicative or potential.

(2.) **Interrogative**, or those which ask a question.

Ex.—Doth my father yet live? Can a mother forget her child?

Interrogative sentences are used either to obtain information or gain assent; as, "Who opened the door?" "Doth God pervert judgment?"

An interrogative sentence is *direct* when it can be answered by *yes* or *no*; *indirect* when it is introduced by an interrogative (78, 2, 5) and cannot be answered by *yes* or *no*; as, "Will you ride to town to-day?" "Who is walking in the garden?"

(3.) **Imperative**, or those which express a command, an entreaty, an exhortation, or a prayer.

Ex.—Let justice be done. Do extricate my suffering friend. Let love be without dissimulation. Thy kingdom come.

An imperative sentence is determined in character by the rank of the parties involved (89, 15).

(4.) **Exclamatory**, or those which express emotion.

Ex.—The foe has come! Was it not strange! Make haste!

SYNTAX—CLASSIFICATION OF SENTENCES. 169

Exclamatory sentences are often fragmentary, partaking of the nature of interjections; as, "Strange!" "Impossible!" "To arms!"

2. A **mixed** sentence is one which is composed of two different classes.

Ex.—Give me a place to stand, and I will move the world. They entered indeed upon the work; but why did they not continue?

150. Sentences classified by their Propositions.

1. All sentences consist either of a single proposition or of two or more united propositions, and are divided into,—

(1.) **Simple sentences,** or those which contain but one proposition.

Ex.—The wind blows. Will you heed the warning? Obey your parents. How feeble is man!

(2.) **Complex sentences,** or those which contain at least two propositions, one of which is principal, and one or more subordinate.

Ex.—When the wind blows, the trees bend. As they advanced, they heard the sound of music. You speak like one who has never felt the pangs of separation.

(3.) **Compound sentences,** or those which contain at least two principal propositions.

Ex.—The wind blows, and the trees bend. His wish still continued, but his hope grew less.

2. A **proposition** is the combination of a subject and a predicate. (See **147,** 4, 5, and Rem.)

Ex.—Trees—grow. The moon—is bright. The hour—has arrived.

3. A proposition is—

(1.) A **sentence (147,** 2), when, independently and alone, it expresses a thought of the speaker.

Ex.—The mists of the morn have passed away. Coming events cast their shadows before.

(2.) An **element** of a sentence, when it expresses a mere *idea* (**147,** 10, Rem.) or part of a thought.

Ex.—I know *that my Redeemer liveth.* The things *that are before us* require attention. *Though I cannot teach courage,* I must not learn cowardice.

Observe that a sentence is always a proposition, either alone or combined with another, but a proposition is not always a sentence. In complex sentences, at least one proposition is used to express merely an *idea.* In compound sentences, at least two propositions are used to express *thoughts.*

4. A proposition used as a sentence is a *simple sentence,* however much it may be extended to express a definite thought. (**147, 7.**)

But a proposition used as an element, like all other elements (**156**), is *simple* only as it expresses the most general idea without limitations.

Ex.—To the skeptic—all—the—**events**—of all the ages of the world —**are**—but a—**crowd**—of useless and indigested materials.—*Buckminster.* I suspected **that sleep had robbed** (*simple*)—me—of some part of my powers (*complex element*).

5. Among united propositions, that one is—

(1.) The **principal** proposition, which contains the principal or leading assertion; and is that on which the subordinate depends.

Ex.—When spring comes, *the flowers will bloom.*

The **subordinate** proposition, which, by means of a connective, depends upon some part of the principal.

Ex.— *When spring comes,* the flowers will bloom.

6. United propositions are called *clauses.*

A sentence containing but one proposition (**150,** 1) cannot be said to have clauses. A clause is always a proposition; but a proposition is not always a clause.

7. Two united propositions are—

Similar principal propositions, when both express kindred thoughts of the speaker; or

Similar subordinate propositions, when they express elements of the thought kindred in construction (**153,** 3).

Ex.—Talent is power, [but] tact is skill. I cannot tell *when he came, nor when he went.*

Dissimilar propositions, when one expresses a thought of the speaker, and the other a mere element of the thought, or when any two express elements of the thought unlike in their construction or relations.

Ex.—He *who assumes the guidance of others,* should govern himself.

If we take no account of our sins on the day—on which they are committed—can we hope—**that they will recur** to us at a more distant period,—**that we shall watch** against them to-morrow,—or **that we shall gain** the strength to resist them, which we will not implore?— *Channing.*

Observe in this complex sentence that the principal clause, "Can we hope," is not similar to any of the others; that the subordinate clauses marked by the bold type are alike dependent upon "hope," and are similar to each other; that any one of these, compared with any of the other subordinate clauses, has a different construction.

REMARK.—These distinctions lay the foundation for the division of sentences into *simple, complex,* and *compound* (**1**, (1), (2), (3), above). A *simple* sentence has but one proposition; a *complex,* two or more dissimilar propositions; and a *compound,* two or more similar propositions. It should be borne in mind that two or more mere subordinate propositions, whether similar or dissimilar, can never form a sentence.

8. **Entire sentences,** by some affinity in the thoughts expressed, are united into paragraphs either by *conjunctions* or by simple *succession.*

Ex.—Her (Athens's) power is, indeed, manifested at the bar, in the senate, in the field of battle, in the school of philosophy. *But* these are not her glory.

As an example of *succession,* observe the paragraph from Patrick Henry, below.

151. Exercise.

Point out the declarative, the interrogative, the imperative, and the exclamatory sentences in the following examples. Construct or select others like them. Change any of them from one class of sentence to another; that is, turn the declarative into interrogative, or the interrogative into declarative.

NOTE.—The learner should first read the sentence attentively, and then consider whether, as a whole, it declares something, asks a question, expresses a command, or utters an exclamation.

Thou shalt not take the name of the Lord thy God in vain. Though he slay me, yet will I trust him. What think ye of Christ? Whose son is he? Would God I had died for thee, O Absalom! my son! my son! Is this a dagger that I see before me? The way was long, the wind was cold. Strike! till the last armed foe expires!

Great Hierarch! tell thou the silent sky,
And tell the stars, and tell the rising sun,
Earth, with her thousand voices, praises God.—*Coleridge*.

They tell us, sir, that we are weak,—unable to cope with so formidable an adversary. But when shall we be stronger? Will it be the next week, or the next year? Shall we gather strength by irresolution and inaction? Sir, we are not weak, if we make a proper use of those means which the God of nature hath placed in our power. The battle, sir, is not to the strong alone: it is to the vigilant, the active, the brave. If we were base enough to desire it, it is now too late to retire from the contest. The war is inevitable, —and let it come. Our brethren are already in the field. Why stand we here idle? Is life so dear, or peace so sweet, as to be purchased at the price of chains and slavery? Forbid it, Almighty God! I know not what course others may take; but as for me, give me liberty, or give me death!—*Patrick Henry*.

Tell which of the foregoing or of the following sentences are SIMPLE, *which are* COMPLEX, *and which are* COMPOUND. *In the foregoing paragraph, tell what sentences are connected by* CONJUNCTIONS, *and what by* SIMPLE SUCCESSION. *What relation of thought can you see?*

In the production of order, all men recognize something sacred. Decide not by authoritative rules, when they are inconsistent with reason. Though he were as rich as Crœsus, still would man be dissatisfied with his condition. Pope had perhaps the judgment of Dryden, but Dryden certainly wanted the diligence of Pope. The emperor Augustus was a patron of the fine arts. Good and evil are inseparable companions; but the latter often hides behind the back of the former. Tell me when it was that you felt yourself most strongly inclined to go astray.

SYNTAX OF ELEMENTS.
152. Definition and Division.

1. The **elements** of a sentence are its component parts, each standing for an *idea* and its relation to some other idea.

Ex.—The **shepherd**—**gave**—the alarm—when he discovered the approach of the wolf.

Here we have the *person*, the *action*, the *object*, and the *time*,—four distinct elements (**147,** 9).

SYNTAX—ELEMENTS. 173

2 Every element, considered—

(1.) As a **whole**, is *principal* or *subordinate*,—*substantive*, *adjective*, or *adverbial*.

The first two distinctions refer to the *rank* of the united elements; the last three, to their *grammatical value* as parts of speech. This use of an expression as a *whole* for any grammatical purpose resembles that of the parenthesis in algebra.

(2.) As to its **component parts**, is a *word*, a *phrase*, or a *clause*, —*simple*, *complex*, or *compound*.

The first three have reference to the *form* of the element; the last three, to its *relation to*, or *union with*, other elements.

153. Principal, Subordinate, and Independent Elements.

1. The **principal** elements are the *essential* parts of the sentence,—namely, the subject and the predicate (**147**, 4, 5).

Ex.—The—seasons of the year—bring—each its peculiar pleasures.

2. The **subordinate** elements are those which depend upon and modify the principal. They are the *adjective*, the *objective*, and the *adverbial* element.

Ex.—*Coming*—events—cast—*their shadows*—*before*.

The subject and the predicate are of the first rank; elements depending on them are of the second; while elements depending upon these are of the third' and so on. It is best, however, to consider a *sentence* as having only *five* elements,—two principal, the *subject* and the *predicate*, and three subordinate, the *adjective*, the *objective*, and the *adverbial*. All elements below the second rank are to be regarded as parts of a complex element of the sentence.

3. Two principal or two subordinate elements are **coördinate** when they have a similar construction.

Ex.—*Peter* and *John* went up to the temple. We were employed *early* and *late*. He could not tell *where he was* or *what he had done*.

Observe that *Peter* and *John* have a similar construction; so, also, *early* and *late*, and *where he was* and *what he had done*. Two elements may have the same rank (*coördinate*), but not a similar construction. Thus, "The boy studies—*grammar—diligently*." Here *grammar* and *diligently* are of the same order of dependence,—that is, they are both of the second rank,—yet they are not coördinate, because they have dissimilar constructions. For the same reason, the subject and the predicate are not coördinate, though both are principal elements.

15*

4. Of two united elements differing in rank, the principal *governs*, and the subordinate *limits*.

Ex.—Now **launch** the *boat* upon the wave.

Here *launch* is principal, and governs *boat;* while *boat* is subordinate, and limits *launch*.

REMARK 1.—The *government* of the principal element is of two kinds. It may cause the subordinate element to *agree* with itself, in which case it is called *concord*,—or it may cause it to take some particular *case, mode*, or *tense*, in which case it is called *government;* as, "*These* (not *this*) books;" "He *walks*" (not *walk*); "I am *he*" (not *him*). The government may be effected *directly;* as, "*Solomon's* temple;" "We saw *him;*" or *indirectly*, by means of a *connective;* as, "The temple *of Solomon;*" "We looked *at him*."

REMARK 2.—The subordinate element *limits* the principal by *restricting* or extending its application. (See **147**, 7.)

REMARK 3.—Coördinate elements neither *govern* nor modify each other.

5. Coördinate elements are connected by coördinate conjunctions (**143**, 3).

Ex.—Youth is bright *and* lovely. Then build anew, *or* act it on a plain.

6. A subordinate element is joined to its principal by a subordinate connective (**143**, 12).

Ex.—Shall I be frighted, *when* a madman stares?

REMARK.—The preposition is a subordinate connective, and is used to connect a subordinate to a principal element; as, "A man *of wisdom;*" "O Cassius, you are yoked *with a lamb.*" When the subordinate element is a single word, no connective is used; as, "A *wise* son maketh a *glad* father."

7. An **independent** element is one which stands in no grammatical relation to the parts of the sentence.

Ex.—You wrong me, *Brutus*. *Why, man*, he doth bestride the narrow world like a Colossus.

REMARK.—The independent element may be the nominative independent, the interjection, or an adverb used independently.

154. Substantive, Adjective, and Adverbial Elements.

1. An element in any of its forms is *substantive, adjective*, or *adverbial*, when, as a whole, it has the construction and use of the part of speech for which it is named.

Ex.—**Substantive.**—*Birds* devour *insects*. *To live happily* requires *obedience* to all the *laws* of our *being*. *That the mind is under any necessity to adopt this or that mode of action* is denied.

Adjective.—The *best* books were selected. *Wisdom's* ways are ways *of pleasantness*. The lesson *which was assigned* was too long.

Adverbial.—The wind blew *briskly*. The voice of the Lord was heard *in the garden*. Who shall decide *when doctors disagree?*

REMARK.—These three kinds of elements enter in to form the principal and the subordinate parts of the sentence.

2. The subject (**147, 4**) is always substantive: it is either a word or a group of words answering the question *Who?* or *What?*

Ex.—*Bees* buzz. *He* rides. *To be* contents his natural desire. *Who invented letters* is not certainly known.

3. The predicate, in its attribute, may be either substantive or adjective, and is a word or a group of words answering the question *What is said?*

Ex.—The day *dawns*. The affair *is to be investigated*. The only objection to the credibility of miracles *is, that they are contrary to general experience.*—*Buckminster.*

Observe that the predicate stands, in every case, as answer to the question *What is said?* of the subject. As the predicate contains the copula and the attribute, the latter only can become a group of words.

4. The adjective element may be either substantive or adjective, and is a word or a group of words added to the subject (or to the noun or the pronoun in any relation) to show *what kind, what one, how many, whose.*

Ex.—*White* clouds are seen in the west. *These* hands have ministered to my necessities. Peter *the hermit*. The proposition *that the whole is equal to all its parts* is a self-evident truth. *Wisdom's* ways are ways *of pleasantness.*

5. The objective element is substantive, and is a word or a group of words added usually to a verb, answering the question *What? Whom? To, for, or of what or whom?*

Ex.—The boy opened the *door*. He gave *me a book*. I perceived *that I lost the sense of song*.

REMARK.—The *direct* object answers the question *What?* or *Whom?* The *indirect* answers the question *To, for, or of what or whom?* The *attributive* answers the question *What? In what state?* or *To do what?* as, "They made the *man—a servant—idle,—work.*" The *double* or *combined* object consists usually of the direct and the attributive.

6. The **adverbial element** is any word or group of words (**132,** 2) added to a verb, a participle, an adjective, or an adverb, answering the question *When? Where? Why? How? How much?* &c.

Ex.—We approached *very slowly*. They came *in the spring*. They stopped *when the night overtook them*.

155. Forms of the Elements—Words—Phrases—Clauses.

1. A **single word,** expressing an *idea* without a connective (**153,** 6, Rem.), is an element of the *first class.*

Ex.—Constant—boasting—always—betrays—incapacity.

REMARK.—When such a word depends upon one of the subordinate elements, it is of the third rank, and, though an element of the first class, it is an element of an element,—that is, forms part of a complex element; as, "We hoped to find *employment.*"

2. A **phrase,** having one word to represent an *idea,* and another to show its *relation,* is an element of the *second class.*

Ex.—A statue *of marble—was chiselled—by the artist.*

REMARK 1.—Any group of words not containing an assertion is a phrase; as, "very earnestly;" "quite favorably;" but here each word expresses an *idea.* A *phrase,* as used in the analysis of sentences, is restricted to a group of words having one word to show a *relation,* and another, either alone or modified, to express an *idea;* as, "*at dawn;*" "*at early dawn.*"

REMARK 2.—When a phrase depends upon one of the subordinate elements, it is still an element of the second class, but not a sentence-element (**153,** 2); as, "A popular poet had the post *of honor.*"

All phrases, as a whole, are either *substantive, adjective,* or *adverbial* (**152,** 2).

Every simple phrase should be separated into its two parts; and every complex or compound phrase, into its simple elements. For a full discussion of Phrases, see Analysis, Chap. II.

3. A **clause,** having a proposition to represent an *idea,* and some word to show its *relation,* is an element of the *third class.*

Ex.—Satan, *whom now transcendent glory raised above his fellows,* spake.

Observe that a clause, like a phrase, is always a group of words; but, unlike a phrase, it always contains a proposition.

SYNTAX—ELEMENTS. 177

A word, a phrase, or a clause, is a sentence-element only when it is used as the subject, the predicate, or the part directly dependent upon one of these; otherwise, it is but an element of an element.

156. Simple, Complex, and Compound Elements.

1. A **simple** element is a word, a phrase, or a clause, without addition or modification.

Ex.—An *honest* man; a man *of honesty;* a man *who is honest.*

2. The simple subject is called the *grammatical* subject the simple predicate, the *grammatical* predicate.

The same distinction might be made in the other elements. Thus, we have the *simple* or *grammatical* adjective, objective, or adverbial element.

3. A **complex** or **logical** element is an expression containing a simple or a grammatical element with all its modifications.

4. In this case, the grammatical or leading element is called the *principal element*, or *basis*, and gives its own name and properties to the whole group.

Thus, in the sentence, "They improved the opportunities which they enjoyed," the objective element is "the opportunities which they enjoyed;" *opportunities* is the basis, limited by the adjective clause "which they enjoyed."

REMARK.—In complex elements, the simple parts unite subordinately (**153**, 4). An element may be subordinate to one and principal *to* another; as, "They discovered huge *masses* of ice." Here "masses" is *subordinate* to "discovered," and *principal* to the phrase "of ice."

5. A **compound** element consists of two or more simple or complex elements joined together coördinately.

Ex.—*Exercise* and *temperance* strengthen the constitution.

157. Exercise.

1. *Separate the following sentences into their* ELEMENTS (**155**, 1, 2, 3), *so as to represent the prominent* IDEAS:—

The trees are leafless. A life of prayer is a life of heaven. The Swiss love liberty. He was not clad in costly raiment. Henry

M

begged that they would come to his assistance. His parents mourned his untimely death. He labored diligently to complete the work. The quality of mercy is not strained. Simon, son of Jonas, lovest thou me? He jests at scars that never felt a wound. How sweet the moonlight sleeps upon this bank! Let me stand here till thou remember it. Peace, tranquillity, and innocence, shed their mingled delights around him. Approach and behold, while I lift from his sepulchre its covering.

2. *Tell which are* PRINCIPAL, *and which* SUBORDINATE.

3. *Point out the* SUBJECTS, PREDICATES, ADJECTIVE, OBJECTIVE, *and* ADVERBIAL *elements.*

4. *Tell which are* SUBSTANTIVE, *which* ADJECTIVE, *and which* ADVERBIAL.

5. *Tell which are* SIMPLE, *which* COMPLEX, *and which* COMPOUND.

6. *Tell which are* WORDS, *which* PHRASES, *and which* CLAUSES.

7. *Separate the following sentences into their* ELEMENTS (**154**), *and tell the* RANK *of each.*

Soft stillness and the night become the touches of sweet harmony.

> The man that hath not music in himself,
> Nor is not moved with concord of sweet sounds,
> Is fit for treasons, stratagems, and spoils.

Now the bright morning star, day's (harbinger, comes dancing from the east)

All the triumphs of truth and genius over prejudice and power, in every country and in every age, have been the triumphs of Athens.

> (The way was long—the wind was cold,
> The minstrel was infirm and old.)

8. *Separate the following sentences into their elements, and describe each element in full.*

Regard the rights of property. Columbus died in ignorance of the real grandeur of his discovery. On Prague's proud arch the fires of ruin glow. The credulity which has faith in goodness is a sign of goodness. The noble Brutus hath told you Cæsar was ambitious. We stand the latest, and, if we fail, probably the last, experiment of self-government by the people. (We have begun it under circumstances of the most auspicious nature) We are in the vigor of youth. (Our growth has never been checked) by the oppressions of tyranny. The Atlantic rolls between us and any formidable foe.

> Lochiel, Lochiel, beware of the day
> When the Lowlands shall meet thee in battle array.

ELEMENTS COMBINED.—CONSTRUCTION AND ANALYSIS.

I. SIMPLE SENTENCES.—SINGLE WORDS.

158. Elements joined without a Connective.

1. The **simplest** possible sentence contains only two elements,—a *subject* and a *predicate*.

Model 1.—Time flies. Here, *time* and *fly* combine to form the simple declarative sentence (**149,** 1) *Time flies,* of which—

Time. is the simple subject; it represents that of which something is affirmed, and

Flies. is the simple predicate; it represents what is affirmed.

Time is to be parsed as in (**54**); *flies,* as in (**131,** 1). Let the following examples be analyzed in a similar manner. Let the pupil mark the changes in the words (fly = *flies*) as they enter into combination, and the changes in the classification of the sentences.

Ex.—Roses fade. Children play. I laugh. You read. She writes. They run. He sings. We ride. Jesus wept. God reigns.
Who came? What comes? Which fails? Understandest thou? Know ye?
Come [*thou* or *you*]. Learn. Study. Go. Wait. They come! Hasten! Arise!

2. The **complex** or **logical** subject is formed by joining to the simple subject—

(1.) A **single word,** as an *adjective* element.

Model 2.—These *men came.* Here *this, man,* and *come* unite and form a declarative sentence, of which—

Men . . . . . . is the simple subject (why?).
Came . . . . . is the simple predicate (why?).

These ..... is the simple adjective element; it is a word joined to the subject to limit its application (**147, 7**). Parse it by (**67, 6.**)

These men is the *complex* subject; it is the simple subject with its modifications (**156, 3**).

Ex.—Five dogs barked. What trees fell? The ink fades. A cat plays. Which boys study? Every star shines.

Old trees decay. Wise men err. Hot water scalds. Good scholars learn. Cold winter comes. Queen Mary reigned. General Scott conquered. Prince Eugene commanded.

Mary's mother wept. Wellington's renown increased. William's invention failed. Our door creaks. His term ends.

(2.) By joining **two or more words** *directly* to the subject.

In this case, one word usually modifies the subject, as limited by the other; as, two *old men*.

Model 3.—What two *travellers returned?* This is an interrogative sentence; it is used to ask a question. **Travellers** is the simple subject, and **returned** is the simple predicate. *Travellers* is limited by **two**, which shows how many are considered together (parse *two* by **67, 5**); it is further limited by **what**, which asks for some particular *two travellers*. **What two travellers** is the complex subject. Parse *what* as in (**79**).

Ex.—The first dawn appeared. The second class recites. The twelve Cæsars reigned. Many a gem sparkles.

Every new lesson varies. Any good book instructs. Several old houses fell. Which smooth button shines? Those two young men agree. Many a serious struggle arose. Those bright, cheerful days return.

The apostle Paul (**54, 1**) labored. The martyr Stephen died. Jacob's (**54, 2**) eldest son Reuben returned.

(3.) By forming a **complex adjective element,** and joining it to the subject.

Model 4.—Very strange *reports arose*. A simple sentence,—it contains but one proposition; declarative,—it is used to declare something as a fact.

Reports .... is the simple subject (why?).
Arose .... is the simple predicate (why?). The subject is limited by
Very strange ...... a complex adjective element of the first class, used to show what kind of reports arose.

SYNTAX—ELEMENTS. 181

Strange .... is the *basis*, or *leading* element (**156**, 4), and is itself an element of the first class (parse it as in **67**, 2); it is limited by

Very .... a simple adverbial element of the first class, used to express *intensity*.

Very strange reports is the complex subject.

Ex.—A truly great man appeared. Too many competitors entered. Exceedingly heavy rains fell.

The old man's daughter left. The bright sun's rays illumine. The shepherd's dog barked.

Arnold, the base traitor, escaped. Elizabeth, Henry's daughter, delayed. Peter, Christ's bold disciple, denied.

3. The **complex** or **logical** predicate is formed by joining to the simple predicate—

(1.) A **single word** as an *objective* element.

Model 5.—*The boy gathered* **nuts.** A simple declarative sentence, of which **boy** is the simple, and **the boy** the complex subject; **gathered** is the simple, and *gathered nuts* the complex predicate. *Gathered* is limited by **nuts**,—a simple objective element of the first class, used to show *what* the boy gathered. Parse **boy** as in (**54**, 2, *history*.)

Ex.—Cæsar conquered Gaul. Attila invaded Rome. Whom seest thou? What have you? Which has he? We write sentences.

(2.) A **single word** as an *adverbial* element.

Model 6.—*The bells ring* **merrily.** A simple declarative sentence, having **bells** for the simple subject, **the bells** for the complex subject; having also **ring** for the simple predicate, and **ring merrily** for the complex predicate. **Bells ring** expresses the indefinite thought; the bells *ring merrily*, the definite thought. *Ring* is limited by **merrily**, a simple adverbial element of the first class, showing *how* the bells ring. Parse **merrily** as in (**138**, 2.)

Ex.—The shadow moves onward. Where standest thou? Who came here? Go forward. Come hither. The coach arrived yesterday. He changes often. They ride occasionally. Why came ye? The campaign opened vigorously. The curtains hang gracefully.

(3.) By joining *two or more* words *directly* to the predicate.

As a model, combine Models 5 and 6.

Ex.—Give me flowers. They lent him money. I wrote him letters. The teacher appointed Charles monitor. They called him traitor. Jesus made the water wine.

They raise oranges there. Study the lesson faithfully. The master taught him thoroughly. He never found it. He utters the syllables distinctly.

In the case of *combined objects*, as in, "They elected *him commander,*" each is joined to the predicate, while at the same time they are joined together. Analyze thus:—The predicate *elected* is limited by the double object *him commander*, which is used to complete its meaning, the *direct* object *him* answering the question **Whom?** and the *attributive* answering the question **What?** They elected (*whom?*) They elected him (*what?*) The attributive object is called by many the *factitive* object,—that into which the direct object *is made*.

(4.) By first forming a **complex objective** or a **complex adverbial element.**

Model 7.—*The tropical islands yield* **delicious spices.** This is a simple declarative sentence, of which

Islands..is the simple subject, and .

Yield.. is the simple predicate. *Islands yield* expresses the *indefinite* or *unlimited* thought. *Islands* is limited by **the** and **tropical,** two simple adjective elements of the first class. *The tropical islands* is the *complex* or *definite* subject. *Yield* is limited by *delicious spices,*—a complex objective element of the first class, of which *spices* is the basis, and is limited by *delicious*, a simple adjective element of the first class.

Ex.—The monk led a desolate life. The merchant gained a handsome profit. He recognized his mother's voice. He kept his word. Herod beheaded John the Baptist. She plays very skilfully. Read Shakspeare very attentively. The general managed his troops most adroitly.

4. A sentence may have connected with it an independent element.

Model 8.—**Plato,** *thou reasonest well.* A simple declarative sentence (why?).

Plato is the *independent element,*—the *compellative*: it represents the person to whom the words are addressed, and forms no part of the sentence *thou reasonest well.* Parse it as in (**54,** 2.)

REMARK.—The subject and the predicate may both become complex in any of the foregoing ways. Let it be observed that no sentence in all the preceding examples, though it contains any or all of the five elements, has a connective of any kind. The pupil should carefully apply the models in the following exercise.

SYNTAX—SIMPLE SENTENCES. 183

159. Exercise.

The lightning glares. This old mountain still stands. Speak the truth. God gives every bird its food. A wise man sometimes changes his mind. Rushed the bold eagle exultingly forth. The refreshing showers soon revived the drooping plants. The distinguished historian Xenophon skilfully conducted the dangerous retreat. Leonidas, the brave Spartan hero, gallantly defended the narrow pass.

> The soft hautboy's melting trill
> Confessed the magic master's skill.

II. SIMPLE SENTENCES.—PHRASES.

160. Elements joined by some Auxiliary or by a Preposition.

1. A *phrase* (**155**, 2) is,—

(1.) *Inseparable;* as, to read, to walk, to have learned; or,—
(2.) *Separable;* as, in town, is base, over mountains.

Here, in parsing *to read, to walk*, &c., we call the whole expression a verb,—*the infinitive*. But in parsing *in town, is base*, &c., we must separate each into two parts,—*preposition* and *object*, *copula* and *attribute*. But in such phrases as *may be done*, we should parse the phrase as a whole, yet should distinguish between the *auxiliary* as the *relation-word*, and the *principal verb* as the *idea-word*.

2. The parts of a separable phrase are,—

(1.) The **connective**, expressing a relation,—namely, the *copula*, the *auxiliary*, or the *preposition*.

(2.) The **word expressing an idea**,—namely, the *attribute*, denoting the *class, quality, action*, or *condition* of the subject; the *principal verb*, denoting the *state* (**98**, 3) of the act or the event (**98, 113, 114, 115**); or the *object*, denoting the *person* or the *thing* named.

REMARK.—Here the learner finds the first kind of *connectives* not improperly called *term-connectives*, inasmuch as they join, not propositions, but usually a subordinate to a principal term.

3. The subject or the predicate may be a **phrase**, or an element of the second class.

Model 9.—To steal is base. Here the two phrases *to steal* and *is base* unite and form a simple declarative sentence.

Observe, here we cannot say that *steal* is the simple subject, modified by *to*, but both must unite to form the subject in its simplest state. So of *is base*.

To steal is the simple subject (why?); an element of the second form or class, because it has one word, *steal*, to express an idea, and another, *to*, to represent its relation.

Parse *to steal* as an irregular intransitive verb, present tense,—used as a noun in the nominative case, and subject of the proposition.

is base. is the simple predicate (why?); it is of the second class, having the attribute *base* to express the predicated idea, and *is*, the copula (**so**, 5), to predicate it and connect it with the subject. Parse *is* and *base*.

REMARK.—The subject only may be a phrase,—the predicate only,—or both together; as, *To forgive* ennobles. *Night is approaching. To betray is infamous.*

Ex.—To love exalts. The ceremony was performed. Silence is impressive. To err is human. To forgive is divine.

Her desire is to leave. To love is to obey. The lady is in grief. His intention is to return. To rob is to plunder.

4. The complex subject may be formed by joining to the simple subject,—

(1.) A *simple phrase* as an adjective element.

Model 10.—Fields of grain *were waving*. Here the single word *fields*, and the two phrases *of grain* and *were waving*, unite and form a simple declarative sentence, of which

Fields .... is the simple subject (why?); an element of the first class.

Were waving . is the simple predicate; a phrase of which *were* is the copula and *waving* is the attribute. *Fields*, the subject is limited by the simple adjective-phrase *of grain;* *of* is the connective, and *grain* is the object.

Parse *of* by (**141**, 2,) and *grain* as in (**54**, 2, last model.)

Ex.—Many works on history were carefully consulted. Days of fasting were often appointed. Bouquets of flowers were presented.

(2.) By *two or more* adjective elements of the first or the second class, each joined to the subject.

Ex.—The first settlers at Plymouth were called Puritans. Huge waves of the ocean overwhelmed the ship. The dawn of light appeared.

(3.) By a **complex phrase** as an adjective element.

Compare Models 4 and 10.

Ex.—An army confident of success is invincible. Paul, the Apostle to the Gentiles, was imprisoned. The father of the lost prince never smiled. A visit from a friend in Boston is soon expected. A jailer of the Dauphin of France was named Simon.

5. The **complex predicate** may be formed by joining to the simple predicate,—

(1.) A *simple phrase* as an objective or an adverbial element.

For models, see 10 for the *form*, and 3 for the relation.

Ex.—He hopes to succeed. I am trying to learn. The watch needs to be repaired. We spoke to him. They gave money to the poor. He failed of the opportunity. The fruit fell from the tree. The express will come from Boston. In the morning it flourisheth. Come on Monday. Can you write in cipher? The Greeks succeeded by stratagem.

(2.) By *two or more* elements of the first or the second class, added directly to the simple predicate.

Compare Models 10 and 6.

Ex.—They urged me to go. The doves besought the hawk to defend them. I heard the cannon [to] roar. He bade me tell you. They made the prisoner stand up. My cousin gave a book to me. The dispatch informed me of my brother's arrival. Throw the ball to me. The teacher promised a reward to the best scholar. We heard their songs in the grove. Did you learn to sing in childhood?

(3.) By two or more elements of the first or the second class, joined together, and then joined to the predicate.

See Models 6 and 7.

Ex.—We found large masses of ice. The party made a tent of boughs. The general gave the command to the colonel of the regiment. The arrangement was made for the child of my brother. The savages came from their hidden retreats. They hope to reach home safely. The air was filled with the fragrance of the flowers. Moses stood on the summit of Pisgah. The city was situated at the head of the bay.

161. Exercise.

The massy trunks are cased in the pure crystal. The relation of sleep to night appears to have been expressly intended by our benevolent Creator. In every period of life, the acquisition of knowledge is one of the most pleasing employments of the human mind. Hope, the charmer, lingered still behind. (Men apt to promise are apt to forget) This hour's work will breed proscriptions. (Many actions apt to procure fame are not conducive to our ultimate happiness) The brilliant flowers of the tropics bloom from the windows of the green-house. The hermit trimmed his little lamp. His troops moved to victory with the precision of machines. A ship incurs guilt by the violation of a blockade. (A sea of blood gushed from the gaping wound.) (Oh that those lips had language)!

III. COMPLEX SENTENCES.—SUBORDINATE CLAUSES.

162. Elements joined by a Subordinate Connective.

1. The subject may be a substantive **clause**, or an element of the third class.

Model 11.—**That you have wronged me,** *doth appear in this.* Here the substantive clause *that you have wronged me,* the phrases *doth appear,* and *in this,* unite and form a complex (**150**) declarative sentence, of which the substantive clause

That you have wronged me is the subject, and
Doth appear .... is the simple predicate.
Doth appear in this ...... is the complex predicate.

The subject is a substantive clause, having
That .... as its connective, used here without an antecedent term (**201,** 3).
You .... is the subject (why?), and
Have wronged .... is the simple predicate. Hence
That you have wronged ... is the basis, or unmodified element.

Wronged is limited by
Me .... a simple objective element of the first class.

Parse *That* as in (**144,** 3.) Observe, there is no principal element on which it can depend, since the whole clause occupies the highest place in the sentence.

Ex.—That the truth will finally prevail cannot be questioned, (= It cannot be questioned that the truth will finally prevail.) Who wrote Junius's Letters is uncertain. When Congress will adjourn is a question. Where the thief concealed the goods has been ascertained. Why will he persist? is often asked. How he lives on such a pittance is a mystery. Whether the clouds will pass away is doubtful.

SYNTAX—COMPLEX SENTENCES.

2. The predicate may consist of the copula and a substantive clause.

As a model, see 11 for the clause and 9 for its relation.

Ex.—My desire is that the difficulty may be adjusted. Our hope is that an entire change of his habits may restore his health. His objection was that the requisite means could not be easily obtained.

Let the pupil change all the examples in this section 1 and 2 to equivalent ones introduced by *it* (**173, 4**).

3. The complex subject may be formed by joining to the simple subject an adjective clause.

At the same time, it may be limited by a word or a phrase.

Model 12.—*Lines* **which are drawn parallel to each other** *will never meet*. In this example, the single word *lines*, the clause *which are drawn parallel to each other*, the phrase *will meet*, and the word *never*, combine and form the complex declarative sentence, of which

Lines .... is the simple subject (why?).
Will meet ..... is the simple predicate (why?).
Lines which are drawn parallel to each other is the complex subject (why?).
Will never meet . is the complex predicate (why?).
    Lines is limited by
Which are drawn parallel to each other, an adjective clause or element of the third class, of which
Which .... is the subject and the connective, and
Are drawn parallel is the predicate, of which the copulative (**82, 7**) verb *are drawn* is the connective, and *parallel* is the attribute. The attribute is limited by *to each other* (**187**, 1, *b*), an indirect objective element of the second class.

Ex.—Evils which cannot be cured must be endured. Rays which fall perpendicularly upon the earth are called vertical. Who steals my purse steals trash. The unwearied pains which he took to accomplish his plans insured their success. Peter the Hermit, who preached the first crusade, was a native of Amiens, in France. The dreams of Joseph, who was the favorite son of Jacob, were the occasion of much ill will. The stream which flows from the mountain-range that bounds the valley on the east, takes its name from an early custom of the inhabitants.

REMARK.—The learner will readily see that the complex subject may be formed by joining to the simple subject several single adjective *words*, *phrases*, or *clauses*, or that any of these may be first joined to each other, forming a complex adjective element, which may be united to the subject. Let him be careful to show that the *leading element* always determines the name (adjective) and class of the whole complex element. Thus, in the last example the adjective element is of the third class; in the one before it, of the second class.

4. The complex predicate may be formed by joining to the simple predicate an *objective* or an *adverbial* clause.

Here, also, modifying *words* or *phrases* may be employed besides the limiting clause; and they may be joined directly to the simple predicate, or to each other, forming a complex element of the first, the second, or the third class. As a model for the clause, see Model 12; as a model for its relation, see Model 5 or 6.

Ex.—I at first believed that all these objects existed within me. During this moment of darkness I imagined that I had lost the greatest part of my being. By this exercise I soon learned that the faculty of feeling was expanded over every part of my frame.—*Buffon*.

He closed his career before he had completed his thirty-sixth year. Place the package where it will not be injured. Had he reformed, I would have assisted him, as I encouraged him to hope. If such be the character of the youthful mind, am I to ask you what must be the appearances of riper years? When the farmer came down to breakfast, he declared that his watch had gained half an hour in the night. The views which we have now unfolded show that a vigorous action of the mind is dependent upon a healthful condition of the physical functions.

163. Direct and Indirect Discourse—Quotations.

1. Discourse is,—

(1.) **Direct,** when originally uttered as a thought of its author, or when afterwards quoted by the speaker, *without change*, as the already uttered words of the author.

(2.) **Indirect,** when *narrated* for the author with only such changes as shall make it the adopted language of the speaker.

Ex.—"I will obey your orders:"—the thought of the author.

Direct.	Indirect.
I said, "I will obey your orders," =	I said that I would obey, &c.
You said, "I will obey your orders," =	You said that you would obey my orders.
He said, "I will obey your orders," =	He said that he would obey my orders.

In this last case, instead of *my* we might have *her, your, his, our, their,* to correspond to the party to whom the pledge was made.

2. The quoted part is used *substantively*, and appears as a substantive clause most commonly in the objective.

3. All substantive clauses may be divided into those containing,—

(1.) A **statement** or a **command.**

Ex.—Many suppose *that the planets are inhabited.* The captain gave the order, "Shoulder arms."

(2.) An **inquiry.**

Ex.—Let me ask *why you have come.*

4. In quoting a statement of another *directly*, we should indicate the quotation by the marks, or the use of the capital, without a connective. But in quoting *indirectly*, the quotation-marks are omitted, and the connective *that* should be employed.

Ex.—God said, Let there be light, and there was light. St. John says that God is love.

5. In quoting an inquiry of another, two cases may occur:—

(*a.*) The interrogative may be a *direct* question (**149,** 1), without an interrogative word; or,

(*b.*) It may be an *indirect* question, with an interrogative pronoun or an adverb for a connective (**78,** 5).

6. When a direct or an indirect question is quoted *directly*, the quoted part should begin with a capital, or receive the quotation-marks, having the interrogation point at the close.

Ex.—They inquired, *Will he certainly come?* He asked, "*How long must we wait?*"

7. When a direct question is quoted indirectly, the connective *whether* (sometimes *if*) is used, the quotation-marks are omitted, and a period is placed at the close; as, "He asked *whether the time had arrived.*" When an indirect question is quoted *indirectly*, the interrogative word becomes the connective, and the sentence closes with the period, the quoted part having no quotation-marks; as, "They asked *where we were to stop.*"

8. The quoted passage, whether direct or indirect, may form either of the five elements of the sentence, except the adverbial.

EXAMPLES.—"*Will he do it?*" is the question;" "The question is, *Will he do it?*" "The question, '*Will he do it?*' has not yet been answered." "He said *that he would do it.*"

REMARK.—It should be observed that the interrogation point follows all interrogative clauses when quoted directly, and is omitted after all such clauses when quoted indirectly. The case in this last remark must not be confounded with that in which the principal clause is interrogative; as, "Shall I tell where we met with encouragement?" "Do you ask me who I am?"

9. The clause which is generally the leading one may take,—

(*a.*) A prominent position; as, "*They say* that they have bought it."

(*b.*) An intermediate position; as, "For all that, *said the pendulum*, it is very dark here."

(*c.*) A position wholly subordinate; as, "He left, *as he told me*, before the arrival of the steamer."

164. Exercise.

1. *Separate the following sentences into their elements, and point out the quotations:*—

Then Judah came near unto him, and said, O my lord, let thy servant, I pray thee, speak a word in my lord's ears. "Punctuality," replied Washington, "is an angel virtue." "Tell me, my son," said he, "did you ever hear of any who are called ungrateful?" Try the spirits, whether they be of God. He asked whether they were friends or foes. "Why have you come so late?" was the prompt inquiry. The question, "Where shall the funds be obtained?" seemed not to have entered their minds. Let me ask you if your resolutions are as firm as when you first set out in the spiritual life. The Scriptures inform us how we may obtain eternal life. It is natural to man, as Patrick Henry eloquently said, to indulge in the illusions of hope. I am not to discuss the question whether the souls of men are naturally equal. But I would ask, does the recollection of Bunker's Hill, Saratoga, and Yorktown afford no pleasure?

2. *Show which quotations are* DIRECT, *and which are* INDIRECT.

3. *Show which contain* STATEMENTS *or* COMMANDS, *and which* INQUIRIES.

IV. COMPOUND SENTENCES.—PRINCIPAL CLAUSES.

165. Elements joined by a Coördinate Conjunction.

1. The elements of a compound sentence are principal propositions.

SYNTAX—COMPOUND SENTENCES.

Remark.—Each principal proposition may have any of the preceding forms of elements, and hence may by itself be a complex sentence.

Model 13.—*I was hungry, and ye gave me no meat.* In this sentence the two independent propositions *I was hungry* and *ye gave me no meat* unite and form a compound declarative sentence, of which *I was hungry* is the first clause, and *ye gave me no meat* is the second, being joined to the first coördinately by the conjunction *and*.

Analyze each clause as a simple sentence by the preceding models, and parse *and* by (144, 2.)

EXAMPLES.

I. Copulative Clauses.

Without emphasis, with a *single* connective.—The rain is over, **and** the sun shines.

Second clause emphatic, by means of an associated connective.—She sings, *and,* **besides,** she plays skilfully.

Emphatic by correlative.—**Not only** am I instructed by this exercise, **but** I am **also** invigorated.

II. Adversative Clauses.

Opposition or contrast.—He did not return to his parents, **but** he persisted in wandering among strangers.

Limitation or restriction.—The army was victorious, **but** the general was slain.

Emphatic opposition or restriction.—The delinquent has been repeatedly admonished, **but still** he is as negligent as ever.

III. Alternative Clauses.

Offering or denying a choice.—Surrender, **or** take the consequences. He cannot ride, **nor** will he walk.

With emphasis.—**Either** he will love the one, and hate the other; **or else** he will hold to the one, and despise the other.

IV. Causal Clauses.

The south wind blows, [and] **therefore** it will rain.

Component parts complex.—When he rose, every sound was hushed; and when he spoke, every eye was fixed upon him. You take my house, when you do take the prop that doth sustain my house; you take my life, when you do take the means whereby I live.

V. CONTRACTED SENTENCES.

166. Common Part omitted.—Compound Elements.

1. A **compound** sentence may be *contracted* to a sentence *partially compound*, by using but once all elements common to the full propositions, and uniting all others.

Thus, *Heaven* **shall pass away**, and *earth* **shall pass away**, = *Heaven and earth* shall pass away. Observe that the contracted sentence has only a compound subject.

Model 14.—**Exercise** *and* **temperance** *strengthen the constitution.* It is a contracted declarative sentence, derived from the compound sentence, *Exercise strengthens the constitution, and temperance strengthens the constitution*, by omitting the common part in the first proposition.

Exercise and temperance . . is the compound subject, and
Strengthen . . . . is the simple predicate, and
Strengthen the constitution is the complex predicate. *Exercise* and *strengthen* are connected by the coördinate conjunction **and**, because they are equal in rank and have a similar construction, being both equally subjects of the proposition. **Strengthen** is of the plural number (Rule XII). Parse *and* and *strengthen*.

EXAMPLES.—**Subjects compound.**—Virtue and vice form a strong contrast to each other. To soothe thy sickness, and to watch thy health, shall be my pleasure. That their poetry is almost uniformly mournful, and that their views of nature were dark and dreary, will be allowed by all who admit the authenticity of Ossian.

Predicates compound.—No fascinated throng weep, and melt, and tremble at his gate. The present life is not wholly prosaic, precise, tame, and finite. His direction was, that the patient should take a great deal of exercise, that his diet should be very carefully attended to, and that every thing of an exciting nature should be avoided.

Adjective element compound.—Wise and good men are frequently unsuccessful. The parting of Hector and Andromache is beautifully described by Homer. That faith which is one, which renews and justifies all who possess it, which confessions and formularies can never adequately express, is the property of all alike.

Objective element compound.—Behold my mother and my brethren. It teaches us to be thankful for all favors received, to love each other,

and to be united. He found that every thing was changed, that strangers inhabited the home of his childhood, and that he was alone in the world.
Adverbial element compound.—The boy studied diligently and faithfully. With trembling limbs and faltering steps, he departed from his mansion of sorrow. When a few more friends have left, a few more hopes deceived, and a few more changes mocked us, we shall be brought to the grave, and shall remain in the tomb.

167. Subordinate Clause Abridged.—Abridged Propositions.

1. A **complex** sentence may be contracted by *abridging* its subordinate clause.

Thus, from the sentence, "*When peace of mind is secured*, we may smile at misfortune," we obtain the contracted sentence, "*Peace of mind being secured,* we may smile at misfortune." The expression in italics conveys the same, or nearly the same, meaning as the full proposition: it is called an *abridged proposition.*

REMARK.—A proposition is *abridged* when it loses its copula, or when its predicate retains only its attribute, whatever may be the number of words or syllables remaining. The remaining expression is called an abridged *proposition,* even though it contains no assertion to indicate both its changed form and its relation to the primitive form.

2. A subordinate clause is abridged by dropping its connective, and changing the predicate into a *participle* or an *infinitive.*

Ex.—To an American (*who visits Europe* =) *visiting Europe*, the long voyage he has to make is an excellent preparative. I am glad *that I find you well,* = I am glad *to find you well.*

REMARK.—The *participle* is employed usually to abridge adjective and adverbial clauses, and the *infinitive* (sometimes the participle) to abridge *substantive* clauses. In many cases the copula is dropped and the attribute alone remains, in apposition, or as an attributive object.

3. The *subject* is dropped when it has already been expressed in the principal clause. Otherwise it must be retained, either in the nominative, the possessive, or the objective case.

4. Abridged propositions may be divided into two classes,—*participial forms,* and *infinitive forms.*

I. PARTICIPIAL FORMS.

Model 15.—*A ship* **gliding over the waves** *is a beautiful object.*

It is a *contracted complex sentence*, or a simple sentence *derived* from the complex sentence, "A ship *which glides over the waves* is a beautiful object," by abridging its subordinate clause.

Ship . . . . is the simple subject, and
A ship gliding over the waves is the complex subject.
Is object . . . . is the simple predicate: *is* is the copula, and *object* is the attribute.
Is a beautiful object . . . . . . is the complex predicate (point out the modifications of *object*).

The subject, *ship*, is limited by "gliding over the waves," a complex adjective element of the first class; it is equivalent to "which glides over the waves" (an adjective element of the third class), and is, therefore, an abridged proposition, obtained by dropping the subject and connective "which," and changing "glides," the predicate, into the participle "gliding."

EXAMPLES.

Subject nominative retained.—*When shame is lost*, all virtue is lost, = *Shame being lost*, all virtue is lost.

Predicate nominative retained.—*That one should be a servant to the whole public* is no easy task, = *Being a servant to the whole public* is no easy task.

Both retained.—*Since a youth is their leader*, = *A youth being their leader*, what can they do?

Observe, where a clause denotes a causal relation, or some accompanying circumstance, as in the last example, the abridged expression does not come under the governing influence of any word in the principal clause: hence both the subject nominative and the predicate nominative are as it were *absolved* from any grammatical regimen; they are, hence, in the *nominative absolute*.

Subject changed to the possessive.—I was not aware *that he lived in the city*, = I was not aware of **his** *living in the city*.

Here the full clause and the abridged expression are under the regimen of *aware, or aware of* in the principal clause. Observe, however, that this governing word has no control over *his*, which is wholly under the government of *living*.

The same with pred. noun unchanged.—I was not aware *that he was a foreigner*, = I was not aware of **his** being a **foreigner**. I was not aware of **its** being **he**.

Here *his*, itself a subordinate element (**153,** 4, Rem.), has no power over *being a foreigner*, its principal (**153,** 1). Hence, though *being a foreigner* is governed by *of*, *foreigner* alone is governed neither by *of* nor *being*. Like the case above, it is *absolved* from any government, and is *pred. nom. absolute*. Similar to this is the case of the nominative after the expletive *there* when the proposition is abridged. "Was this owing to *there* being twelve primary **deities** among the Gothic nations?" Here the abridged expression is under the regimen of *owing to*, but *deities* is not governed by *to*. In the full form, *deities* is the subject:—"Was this owing to *the fact* that there were twelve primary *deities*," &c.

Subject and pred. changed to the objective.—We regarded *him* as being a good *writer*. He intrusted his son to a *gentleman* named *Edric*. I saw that the **chrysalis** *was becoming* a **butterfly,** = I saw the **chrysalis** *becoming* a **butterfly.**

Here, as in many other cases, there is a difference of meaning between the two forms. In this case the usual form for abridgment is the infinitive. In fact, the participle is equivalent to the infinitive. The subject is changed to the objective, and the predicate noun takes the same case.

Subject dropped.—*As we were walking by the sea-shore*, we discerned the light of the burning ship, = *Walking by the sea-shore*, &c. When we arrived at the gate, we found the porter asleep, = *On arriving at the gate*, &c.

II. INFINITIVE FORMS.

Model 16.—*The officer commanded* **him to retire.** It is a simple sentence, derived by contraction from the complex sentence, The officer commanded *that he should retire*.

Officer . . . . is the simple subject, and
The officer . . . . is the complex subject.
Commanded . . . . is the simple predicate, and
Commanded him to retire is the complex predicate. *Commanded* is limited by *him to retire*, a double object, of which **him** is the *direct* and **to retire** the *attributive* object.

Observe, in the full form, that the whole clause is the only object, while in the abridged form the subject becomes the direct object, and the predicate, still holding its relation to it as attribute, is the attributive object.

EXAMPLES.

Subject retained in the objective.—We taught *them to read*. We wish *that you would* stay, = We wish *you to stay*.

Here the subject should be dropped when it is the same as that of the principal clause. I wish *to go*; not, I wish *me to go*.

Predicate noun retained in the nominative.—*To be a* **king** *is to be a* **sovereign.**

Subject and predicate retained in the objective.—I believed *that he was an honest man,* = I believed **him** *to be an honest* **man.** For **him** *to be such a* **spendthrift** was wholly inexcusable.

The abridged expression, the term of a comparison.—The bed is shorter *than that a man can stretch himself in it.—Bible.* = The bed is shorter *than for a man,* &c.

Here the subjects are unlike.

My friend was so elated *as that he forgot his appointment,—as to forget,* &c. The soldiers desired nothing more *than that they might know where the enemy was,—than to know,* &c.

Here the subjects of the two clauses are alike.

An incorporated interrogative sentence.—I knew not *what I should do,* = *what to do.*

REMARK.—In the same manner we have *whom to send, when to go, when to stop, how to proceed.* The connectives *what, where, when,* &c., by Rule 3, above, should be dropped; but, as they are a part of the substance of the sentence, they must be retained. Were they *merely* connectives, they would be dropped.

VI. TRANSFORMATION OF SENTENCES.—EQUIVALENT ELEMENTS.

168. Equivalent Elements.

1. A sentence is **transformed** when it undergoes a change in the form of any of its elements, without any material change in the meaning; the new forms of the elements, which express the same or nearly the same meaning, are called *equivalents.*

Ex.—*After he had discovered Hispaniola,* Columbus returned to Spain, = *Having discovered Hispaniola,* Columbus returned to Spain. Here the subordinate clause denoting time is exchanged to an equivalent abridged proposition denoting time (see **167**).

2. We may change the form of a sentence,—

(*a.*) By *altering the grammatical construction* of any of its elements;
(*b.*) By *causing or supplying an ellipsis;*
(*c.*) By *transposing* any element to another part of the sentence.

SYNTAX—EQUIVALENT ELEMENTS. 197

3. The grammatical construction of an element may be altered by changing,—

(1.) The **voice** of the verb.

Ex.—Columbus *discovered* America, = America *was discovered* by Columbus.

(2.) The **class** from one of the first class (**155**, 1, 2) to one of the second, or from one of the second to one of the first.

Ex.—A *morning* ride is refreshing, = A ride *in the morning* is refreshing.

(3.) A **complex sentence** to a simple one (a *contracted complex*), by abridging its subordinate clause.

Ex.—When the shower had passed, we resumed our journey, = The shower having passed, we resumed our journey.

(4.) A **simple sentence** to a complex, by expanding any of its elements into a proposition.

Ex.—A *merciful* man is merciful to his beast, = A man *who is merciful* is merciful to his beast.

(5.) A **complex sentence** to a compound, by raising the subordinate clause to an equal rank with the principal, and changing the subordinate connective to a coördinate.

Ex.—*When* spring comes, the flowers will bloom, = The spring will come, *and* the flowers will bloom.

(6.) A **compound sentence** to a complex, by depressing one of its propositions into a subordinate rank.

Ex.—Man has a moral sense, and therefore he is an accountable being, = Since man has a moral sense, he is an accountable being.

(7.) A question for gaining assent (**149**, 2, Rem.) may be changed into a declarative sentence, or a declarative sentence may be changed into a question for gaining assent.

Ex.—Will he plead against me with his great power? = He will *not* plead against me with his great power.

(8.) Its **whole construction**, by entirely remodelling it.

Ex.—That which agrees with the will of God should please us, = We should be pleased with whatever is agreeable to the will of our heavenly Father.

(9.) A **compound sentence** to a *partial compound*.

Ex.—Bacon was a distinguished writer, Shakspeare was a distinguished writer, and Butler was a distinguished writer, = Bacon, Shakspeare, and Butler were distinguished writers.

(10.) Any **contracted compound sentence,** to a complete compound.

Ex.—The king and queen were absent, = The king was absent, and the queen was absent.

4. The arrangement of the elements is the *position* which they take in the sentence.

5. There are two kinds of arrangement,—the *natural* or *grammatical*, and the *inverted* or *transposed*.

6. In a proposition, by the natural order, the subject is placed before the predicate; the adjective element is placed before the noun when of the first class, but after the noun when of the second or third; the objective element is placed after the verb which governs it; and the adverbial element commonly follows the objective element.

Ex.—The good boy studied his geography attentively. The kingdom of Sardinia is situated in the south of Europe.

7. An element is *transposed* whenever it is placed out of its natural order.

Ex.—*Great* is Diana of the Ephesians. Copernicus *these wonders* told. *Wisely* were his efforts directed.

8. When the verb "to be" predicates existence, the subject is not only transposed, but its place is supplied by the expletive "there" (**134**, 9). So when a phrase or a clause as subject (**160**, 1; **162**, 1) is transposed, its place is supplied by "it" used as an expletive (**70**, 4).

169. Exercise.

1. *Use the active for the passive, and the passive for the active, in the following examples, supplying the agent where omitted:*—

Wellington is buried in Westminster Abbey. Not a drum was heard, nor a funeral note. Energy of purpose awakens powers before unknown. Can Honor's voice provoke the silent dust? Three of your armies, O Romans, have been slaughtered by Mark Antony. I give my hand and my heart to this vote.

2. *In the following, change any element of the first class to one of the second; and the reverse:*—

A marble statue was placed in the grove. Achilles was a Grecian hero. The siege of Troy lasted ten years. In dreams his song of triumph [he] heard. Strike the golden lyre again. Last came Joy's ecstatic trial.

3. *Change the following complex sentences to simple or contracted complex sentences, by abridging the subordinate clauses:—*

A man who is deceitful can never be trusted. When the orator had finished, the assembly retired. Heard ye the whisper of the breeze, as soft it murmured by? He declares that she is a slave of his. This is the man who deserves commendation. He went to Egypt that he might see the pyramids.

4. *Expand the italicized elements into clauses:—*

The crocuses, *blooming in the garden*, attracted the bees. Hannibal, *the Carthaginian general*, conquered the Romans in four battles. We told him *to leave*. Cæsar should have perished on the brink of the Rubicon *before attempting to cross it*.

> Perhaps in this neglected spot is laid
> Some heart *once pregnant with celestial fire*.

5. *Supply the words omitted by ellipsis:—*

> All nature is but art, unknown to thee,
> All chance, direction which thou canst not see;
> All discord, harmony not understood;
> All partial evil, universal good.

6. *Arrange the elements in their natural order:—*

Great is Diana of the Ephesians. Welcome thou art to me. To each honor is given. In fearless freedom he arose. Whom ye ignorantly worship, him declare I unto you.

7. *See if the following can be improved by transposing any element:—*

I would be Diogenes, were I not Alexander. The parting soul relies on some fond breast. That is the question,—to be, or not to be. Then the hills shook, riven with thunder. When creation began we know not.

170. Directions for Analysis of Sentences and Elements.

Sentences.—1. Read the sentence, and determine by its meaning whether it is *declarative, interrogative, imperative,* or *exclamatory*.

2. Determine the *leading assertion*, and point out the subject and the predicate.

3. If any of the parts are inverted, *arrange* them in the natural order.

4. If necessary, supply ellipses.

5. Find all the separate words or groups of words which express distinct ideas added to the subject, and show in what way they modify it.

6. In the same manner dispose of all the additions to the predicate.

7. If neither the subject, nor the predicate, nor any of the additions to either, contains a proposition, the sentence is *simple*.

8. But if either contains a proposition, the sentence is *complex*.

9. If the sentence contains two or more independent assertions, it is *compound*, and should first be separated into its component parts, each of which should be analyzed as a simple or a complex sentence.

10. If the subject, the predicate, or any of the additions to either, contains two coördinate parts, the sentence is a *partial compound*, and should be analyzed like a simple sentence, with the exception of the compound part: this should be named as a *compound element*, and then resolved into its component parts.

11. If the subject, the predicate, or any of the additions to either, contains a *participle*, or an *infinitive* equivalent in its use to a dependent proposition, the sentence is a *contracted complex*, and should be analyzed like a simple sentence. Yet the part derived by abridging a dependent clause (**167**, 2) should be named, and its equivalent proposition given.

Elements.—1. Resolve the sentence as in **170**; and then, regarding each part as an element, classify it as in (**155**.)

NOTE.—This analysis gives the office and relation of all the subordinate ideas and of all the words in the sentence; that in **170** gives the relation of all the prominent ideas.

2. If any element contains but one word, it is completely reduced, and may then be parsed.

3. If an element containing more than one word is simple (**156**, 1), it must be a *phrase* or a *clause*, and is to be still further analyzed by pointing out,—

(*a.*) The *connective*, showing what parts it joins.

(*b.*) The part which expresses the *idea:*—in case of the phrase, a *word;* in case of the clause, the *subject* and the *predicate*.

4. If an element is complex or compound, reduce it to its simple elements, and then proceed as in 2 or 3 above.

5. In case of a complex element, point out and dispose of the *principal element*, or *basis* (**156**, 4), then each of the others in the order of their rank.

6. In case of a compound element, separate it into its component simple elements, point out and classify the coördinate conjunction which joins them, and then dispose of each as in 2 or 3 above.

7. Thus the sentence is reduced by simple and methodical steps to the parts of speech which enter into it.

REMARK.—It will not, generally, be best to parse *all* the words. It is a good exercise for the pupil to name them in the order of their *rank*, from the subject or the predicate to that which holds the lowest rank. The teacher can best judge what ones should be parsed.

171. General Exercise in Analysis.

REMARK.—The learner who has carefully studied the preceding development of the elements of the sentence is now prepared to analyze and form an English sentence, from the simplest, with which he began, up to the most complicated. Let him examine the following model and apply the general principles of analysis to the examples in this exercise. It will not always be best to separate the elements into their parts. Let the learner name them, and give their general effect in the sentence.

Model 17.—"The Cynic who twitted Aristippus by observing that the philosopher who could dine on herbs might despise the company of a king, was well replied to by Aristippus, when he remarked that the philosopher who could enjoy the company of a king might also despise a dinner of herbs."

This is a complex sentence, containing seven clauses,—one principal, and six subordinate.

(1.) *The Cynic was well replied to by Aristippus,*
(2.) *Who twitted Aristippus by observing,*
(3.) *That the philosopher might despise the company of a king,*
(4.) *Who could dine on herbs,*
(5.) *When he remarked,*
(6.) *That the philosopher might also despise a dinner of herbs,*
(7.) *Who could enjoy the company of a king.*

The first is the principal clause, and the others are subordinate.
Cynic is the subject of the principal clause.
Was replied to is the predicate.
The subject, *Cynic*, is limited by "who twitted Aristippus by observing," &c., a complex adjective element of the third class; "who" is the connective and subject, "twitted" is the predicate, and is limited, first, by "Aristippus," a simple objective element of the first class, and also by "by observing that the philosopher might despise the company of a king," a complex adverbial element of

the second class; "by observing" is the basis, "by" is the connective, and "observing" is the object; "observing" is limited by "that the philosopher might despise the company of a king," a complex objective element of the third class, of which "that" is the connective; "philosopher" is the subject, and is limited by "who could dine on herbs," an adjective element of the third class; "might despise" is the predicate, and is limited by "the company of a king," a complex objective element of the first class.

The predicate, *was replied to*, is limited, first, by "well," a simple adverbial element of the first class, and by "by Aristippus," an adverbial element of the second class, and also by the clause "when he remarked that the philosopher," &c., a complex adverbial element of the third class, of which "when" is the connective, "he" is the subject, and "remarked" is the predicate; "remarked" is limited by "that the philosopher," &c., a complex objective element of the third class, of which "that" is the connective, "philosopher" is the subject, "the philosopher who could enjoy the company of a king" is the logical subject, "might despise" is the predicate, and "might also despise a dinner of herbs" is the logical predicate; the subject, "philosopher," is limited by the clause "who could enjoy the company of a king," a complex adjective element of the third class, of which "who" is the connective and subject, "could enjoy" is the predicate, and is limited by "the company of a king," a complex objective element of the first class; the predicate "might despise" is limited by "a dinner of herbs," a complex objective element of the first class, of which "dinner" is the basis, and is limited by "of herbs," a simple adjective element of the second class.

Model 18.—Brief Method.

Cynic, ... the *subject*, is limited by the expression **who twitted Aristippus . . . king,** used to *identify* the *Cynic*, by stating what he *did* and *said*.

Was replied to, the *predicate*, is limited,—
(1.) By **well,** showing the *fitness* of the reply.
(2.) By **by Aristippus,** showing *by whom* the reply was made.
(3.) By **when he remarked . . . dinner of herbs,** used to show the *reply itself*, rather than the *time* of it.

Analyze the following sentences according to the models:—

Most men know what they hate; few what they love.
He who openly tells his friends all that he thinks of them, must

expect that they will secretly tell his enemies much that they do not think of him.

That nations sympathize with their monarch's glory, that they are improved by his virtues, and that the tone of morals rises high when he that leads the band is perfect, are truths admitted with exultation and felt with honest pride.

Highly elated by his unexpected good fortune, he returned home. Saving carefully the fruits of his labor, he at length was able to purchase a farm.

A pretended patriot, he impoverished his country.

How is it that tyranny has thus triumphed,—that the hopes with which we greeted the French Revolution have been crushed,—that a usurper plucked up the last roots of the tree of liberty and planted despotism in its place?

Revolutions which are acted out in a day have often been years or centuries in preparation.

>   Why did Wolsey, near the steps of fate,
>   On weak foundations raise the enormous weight?
>   Why, but to sink beneath misfortune's blow
>   With louder ruins to the gulf below?

Will you believe that the pure system of Christian faith which appeared eighteen hundred years ago, in one of the obscurest regions of the Roman empire, at the moment of the highest mental cultivation and of the lowest moral degeneracy; which superseded at once all the curious fabrics of pagan philosophy; which spread almost instantaneously through the civilized world, in opposition to the prejudices, the pride, and the persecution of the times; which has already had the most beneficial influence on society, and has been the source of almost all the melioration of the human character; and which is now the chief support of the harmony, the domestic happiness, the moral and intellectual improvement of the best part of the world: will you believe, I say, that this system originated in the unaided reflections of twelve Jewish fishermen on the Sea of Galilee, with the son of a carpenter at their head?

Join subordinate elements to the following indefinite sentences, and thereby convert them into definite ones:—

>   Messenger brought.
>   Will the pupil remember?
>   Men understood.
>   Poet says.
>   History was traced.

SYNTAX OF WORDS.

In the syntax of words we recognize a **regular,** an **incorrect,** and a **peculiar** use.

I. REGULAR USE.
172. Rules of Construction.

A **rule** of syntax is a statement of the law which governs the *form* and the *use* of a word in construction.

Rule I.—A noun or a pronoun used as the **subject** of a proposition must be in the nominative case.

Rule II.—A noun or a pronoun used as the **attribute** of a proposition must be in the nominative case.

Rule III.—A **pronoun** must agree with its antecedent in person, number, and gender.

Rule IV.—The **verb** must agree with its subject in person and number.

Rule V.—An **adjective** or a **participle** must belong to some noun or pronoun.

Rule VI.—A noun or a pronoun used to **explain** or **identify** another noun or another pronoun, is put by apposition in the same case.

Rule VII.—A noun or a pronoun used to limit another noun by denoting **possession,** must be in the possessive case.

Rule VIII.—A noun or a pronoun used as the **object** of a transitive verb, or its participles, must be in the objective case.

Rule IX.—**Adverbs** are used to limit verbs, participles, adjectives, and other adverbs.

Rule X.—The nominative case **independent,** and the in. jection, have no grammatical relation to the other parts of the sentence.

Rule XI.—**Coördinate** conjunctions are used to connect similar elements.

Rule XII.—When a verb or a pronoun relates to two or more nouns connected by a coördinate conjunction,—

(1.) If it agrees with them taken **conjointly,** it must be in the *plural number.*

(2.) But if it agrees with them taken **separately,** it must be of the same number as the noun or the pronoun which stands next to it.

(3.) If it agrees with **one,** and **not** the other, it must take the number of that one.

Rule XIII.—A **preposition** is used to show the relation of its object to the word on which the latter depends.

Rule XIV.—A noun or a pronoun used as the **object** of a preposition must be in the objective case.

Rule XV.—**Subordinate** connectives are used to join dissimilar elements.

Rule XVI.—The **infinitive** has the construction of the *noun,* with the signification and limitations of the verb, and, when dependent, is governed by the word which it limits.

Rule XVII.—**Participles** have the construction of *adjectives* and *nouns,* and are limited like *verbs.*

RULES, CAUTIONS, AND REMARKS.

173. The Subject.

1. **Rule I.**—A noun or a pronoun used as the *subject* of a proposition must be in the nominative case.

Ex.—*Cæsar* conquered Gaul. *I* have found a man *who* professes to teach all *that* is necessary to be known.

A **letter,** a **symbol,** a **phrase,** or a **clause,** when used as the subject, is a noun in the nominative singular.

Ex.—*A* is a vowel. + is the sign of addition. *To steal is base. That you have wronged me* doth appear in this.

A noun or a pronoun, as the subject of an abridged proposition, is in the—

Nominative absolute with a participle (**167, 4, Ex.**) when its case depends upon no other word; but in the

Objective with an infinitive when its case depends upon a verb or a preposition.

Ex.—*Shame being lost,* all virtue is lost. They requested *him to leave. For you to be released,* and *for me to be burdened,* is obviously unjust.

2. A noun or a pronoun is in the nominative when used,—

(1.) As **subject** (**147, 4**).
(2.) As **predicate** (**147, 5**).
(3.) In **apposition** with the subject or the predicate (**183**).
(4.) As the **compellative** (**158**, Model 8).
(5.) As subject or predicate of an abridged proposition (**167, 4**).
(6.) In headings, titles, and unfinished sentences.

3. The subject is usually **omitted,**—

(1.) In the imperative mode, in which case it is always a pronoun of the second person, even when the compellative is expressed.

Ex.—Son, arise. Go, my friend.

(2.) After *but, when, while, if,* and *though;* also after comparisons made by *as* and *than.*

Ex.—We shall go, *if* [it is] possible. Though poor, luxurious; though submissive, vain. There is no heart but [*what* or *it*] must feel them. The disaffection was spread far wider than was supposed.

4. The proper **position** of the subject is before the predicate; but it is placed after either the verb or its auxiliary,—

(1.) In the imperative mode, in direct questions, in exclamatory sentences, in suppositions without a connective, in sentences arranged for rhetorical effect, and in the governing clause of a direct quotation.

Ex.—*Go ye* into all the world, and *preach* [*ye*] the gospel to every creature. *Doth* my father yet live? How *is* the great fallen! *Were* I not Alexander, I would be Diogenes. Great *is* Diana of the Ephesians. *It* is natural to man, *said* Patrick Henry, to indulge in the illusions of hope.

(2.) When the subject of a sentence is a phrase or a clause. The vacant place of the subject is then filled by the expletive "it," a word adapted to this idiom, but not necessary to the construction.

When the subject is before the predicate, the expletive should not be used. The following sentence, therefore, is wrong:—"That the soul be without knowledge, *it* is not good." The following sentences are faulty for want of the expletive, because *which*, the object of the infinitive subject, is erroneously made subject of the following verb. "Why do ye that *which* [it] is not lawful *to do* on the sabbath days?" "We have done that which [it] was our duty *to do*."

5. The *object* of the verb in the active voice becomes its subject in the passive voice.

Ex.—John granted the *Magna Charta,* = The *Magna Charta* was granted by John.

CAUTION I.—*Never use the objective as the subject of a finite verb.* Say, "*I* did it,"—not "*Me* did it."

NOTE.—This caution should be specially heeded in the construction of subjects consisting of a personal pronoun used jointly with a noun or another pronoun, in the use of the relative and interrogative pronouns, in the use of a noun or a pronoun as a term of comparison after *than* or *as*, and in the answers to questions. See examples under Incorrect Use.

174. Exercise.

1. *Analyze the following examples, and parse the* SUBJECTS:—

Those who would give the highest training to the mind must furnish to it deeds of excellence, tales of heroism. How beautiful an object is a tree, growing, with all its foliage, freely and fairly on a sheltered lawn! Ye hills, lift up your voices; let the shaggy woods upon your summits wave with adoration. Has reason fled from our borders? Have we ceased to reflect? There is great economy in giving pleasure to children. A trifling gift, a little kindness, goes a great way, and is long remembered. It is natural for man to indulge in the illusions of hope. To err is human; to forgive, divine. It was said that fifty guineas had been paid for a single ticket. It was determined to examine witnesses at the bar of the Commons. The doves besought the hawk to defend them. The captain commanded his company to march.

MODEL I.—"Happiness depends upon the prudent constitution of the habits."—*Paley.*

This is a simple sentence, containing three sentence-elements.

The subject is "happiness;" the predicate, "depends;" and the adverbial element, "upon the constitution of the habits."

REMARK.—In this and in the following models the teacher can best judge whether or not the pupil needs more practice in minute analysis. If sufficient skill has already been acquired, it is recommended that *only* the sentence-elements be pointed out (**171,** Mod. 18), with their mutual influence upon each other,—except in *rare* constructions, or when the pupil fails to comprehend the true relations of the parts.

Happiness is a common noun, third, sing., neut., nom., and is used as the subject. (Rule I.)

MODEL II.—"It is evident that his conduct was directed by a profound policy."—*Macaulay.*

This is a complex sentence. Arranged in the natural order, it would be, "That his conduct was directed by a profound policy is evident." (**168,** 4, 2.) In either form it contains two general elements:—the subject, "That his conduct was directed by a profound policy;" the predicate, "is evident."

The subject is a substantive clause, third, sing., neut., and in the nominative case, by Rule I. *a.*

For the use of *that*, see **201,** 3. This clause is also represented by the expletive "it" (**70,** 4), of the same person, number, gender, and case as the clause, and is grammatically pleonastic, but is essential to this arrangement of the true subject (see 4, above), and is used to introduce the sentence in an agreeable way.

MODEL III.—"The patriots not dispersing, Pitcairn ordered his men to fire."

This is a simple sentence, having abridged propositions for its elements. It is derived, by contraction, from the complex sentence, "As the patriots did not disperse, Pitcairn ordered that his men should fire."

The subject is "Pitcairn;" the predicate, "ordered;" objective element, "his men to fire;" and the adverbial element, "the patriots not dispersing."

The subject is not modified. The predicate is modified by the double object "his men to fire." (**187,** 10.) "Men" is the *direct*, and "to fire" the *attributive*, object. The combination is derived from the objective proposition "that his men should fire,"—"men" being the subject, and "should fire" the predicate.

SYNTAX—NOUN AS ATTRIBUTE. 209

"Men" is a common noun, third-person, plural number, masculine gender, and is logically the subject of "to fire" (see **173,** 1); but, since the proposition is abridged, it becomes, with "to fire," the object of "ordered." "To fire" is a regular intransitive verb, in the infinitive, present tense, and is used as a noun to form the attributive object of "ordered."

The predicate is further modified by "the patriots not dispersing," an abridged expression equivalent to "as the patriots did not disperse," and is used to show the *occasion* or *reason* for the order. In the full form, it would be connected with "ordered" by "as;" but in the abridged form it is grammatically (not logically) (**167,** Ex.) set free, and hence is said to be absolute,—"patriots," the subject, still remaining in the nominative, by Rule X., *d.*

2. *Construct or select examples to illustrate the subject in either form, as given in the models.*

175. A Noun or a Pronoun as Attribute.

1. **Rule II.**—A noun or a pronoun used as the *attribute* of a proposition must be in the nominative case.

Ex.—I am *he.* I, who walk *queen* of the gods.

(*a.*) A **letter,** a **mark,** a **phrase,** or a **clause,** used substantively as the attribute of a proposition, is a noun in the nominative case.

Ex.—That letter is *h.* To purloin is *to steal.* A fourth mistake in relation to happiness is, *that we make our provision only for the present world.*—*Buckminster.*

(*b.*) A noun or a pronoun used as the attribute in an abridged proposition, after the participle or the infinitive of the copula, must agree in case with the subject, or with any *equivalent* of the subject to which the abridged expression may be joined, except when the subject is changed to the possessive or is wholly dropped from the sentence: it then remains in the *predicate nominative absolute.*

EXAMPLES.—(1.) In the **nominative,** after a participle, to agree with its subject; as, "You being the *captain*, I must obey," = Since you are the captain, &c.

(2.) In the **objective**, after the participle, to agree with an equivalent of the subject; as, "Ananias descended with the elders, and with a certain *orator* [who was] named *Tertullus;*" *who*, the true subject, being dropped, by **167**, 3.

(3.) In the *objective* case, after the infinitive, to agree with the subject; as, "I believed *him* to be a *traitor*," = I believed *that he was a traitor*.

(4.) In the *nominative absolute*, after the participle, preceded by the possessive of the subject; as, "I was not aware of *his* being a *foreigner*," = I was not aware that *he was a foreigner*.

(5.) In the *nominative absolute*, after the participle or the infinitive, the subject of the full proposition having no equivalent, and being wholly dropped from the sentence; as, "To be a *king* is to be a *sovereign;*" "Being a *scholar* is not being an *idler*." See a parallel construction of the predicate adjective (**181**, 20).

REMARK.—A noun or a pronoun is the *attribute* of a proposition when it is used with the copula, or any copulative verb (**82**, 9), to form the predicate. It usually denotes the same person or thing as the subject, and when it denotes a person it agrees with the subject not only in *case*, but in *gender* and *number*. In the case of copulative verbs, the predicate seems to have two attributes,—the one the participle or attributive part of the verb, and the other the following noun or adjective; as, "He was *called John;*" "The boy was *made sick*."

2. **It**, used in a vague sense, not unlike the algebraic symbol for an unknown quantity, is made the subject representing a noun or a pronoun as attribute in any number, person, or gender; as, "It is *I;*" "It is *they;*" "It is *James;*" "It is *she;*" "It is clear *that the enemy has crossed the river.*"

3. The number and the person of the verb are affected by the subject, and not by the predicate noun.

Ex.—Apples *are* fruit. His meat *was* (not *were*) locusts and wild honey.

4. After the copulative verbs *regard, consider, reckon, name*, and some others, the connective "as" precedes the attribute when the verb is passive, and the attributive object when it is active, to denote the *capacity* in which the subject or the direct object is to be taken.

Ex.—He was regarded *as* an able *advocate*, = They regarded him *as* an able *advocate*.

SYNTAX—NOUN AS ATTRIBUTE. 211

5. The predicate nominative is commonly placed after the verb, and the subject nominative before it; but in questions, both direct and indirect, in poetry, and in sentences arranged for rhetorical effect, this order is often changed.

Ex.—Is it *I?* *Who* is *he?* And *I* thy *victim* now remain. I was *eyes* to the blind, and *feet* was *I* to the lame.

6. The subject may be a noun, and the attribute a clause; or the subject may be a clause, and the attribute a noun. **Will he do it?** is the *question*. The *question* is, **Who will put the bell upon the cat?** (163, 6.)

CAUTION I.—*Never use the objective as the attribute after a* FINITE *verb, nor the nominative after an* INFINITIVE *preceded by its objective subject.* Say, "It is *I*,"—not "It is *me;*" "I knew *it* to be *him*,"—not "I knew *it* to be *he*."

CAUTION II.—*Avoid constructions in which the thing denoted by the subject is falsely identified by the attribute.* Say, "The *noun James* is the NAME of the actor,"—not "The *noun James* is the *actor*."

176. Exercise.

1. *Analyze the following sentences, and parse the* ATTRIBUTES:—

John was called the beloved disciple. Rhetoric, logic, and grammar are three arts that should always walk hand in hand. Embarrassed, obscure, and feeble sentences are generally, if not always, the result of embarrassed, obscure, and feeble thought. What is man, that thou art mindful of him? He returned a friend, who came a foe. It still remains a monument of his greatness. Warsaw was the capital of Poland. Mecca is regarded by the Mohammedans as a holy city. The inhabitants of the Arabian desert are styled Bedouins.

A second mistake upon the subject of happiness is, that it is to be found in prosperity. The truth is, that of the objects of human acquisition, very few are, beyond a certain limit, even the means of happiness. To be an Englishman in London, a Frenchman in Paris, a Spaniard in Madrid, is no easy matter; and yet it is necessary. I did not dream of its being he. Do you take it to be her? For him ever to become a correct writer is out of the question. Widowhood is the state of being a widow. A second objection raised against our Lord's being the Son of God and King of Israel, was taken from his mean condition.

MODEL I.—"Talent is something, but tact is every thing."—*London Atlas.*

Analyze.—This is a compound sentence, &c. (See Model 13.)

Something is a common noun, of the third, sing., neut., and in the nom. case, being used as the attribute of the proposition "Talent is something," according to Rule II. (Repeat it.)

In the same manner parse "*thing*," in the second clause.

MODEL II.—"The reason is, that the outward signs of a dull man and a wise man are the same."—*Sydney Smith.*

Analyze as in Model, 162, 2.

"That," in this case, may be considered as joining the clause as a dependent element to the subject, while the copula joins it only as a *predicated* element. If the clause were *assumed* of the subject, "that" would be the only connective. Thus, "The reason *that the outward signs*," &c. The preposition has a similar connection when a *phrase* becomes the attribute; as, "The boy *is in the field.*" Compare "The boy *in the field.*"

MODEL III.—"It is almost as hard a thing to be a poet in despite of fortune, as it is in despite of nature."—*Cowley.*

This is a complex sentence, consisting of one principal and one subordinate clause. It is introduced by the expletive "it," which is disposed of as in Model II., **174.** Arranged grammatically, it stands, "To be a poet in despite of fortune, is almost as hard a thing as it is in despite of nature." The logical subject is "to be a poet in despite of fortune;" the logical predicate is "is almost as hard a thing as [to be a poet] is in despite of nature." The grammatical subject is "to be a poet," and is limited by the complex phrase "in despite of fortune." This is an adverbial element, since it limits not "poet," but the whole idea, "to be a poet." The copula is "is," the simple attribute, "thing;" it is parsed as in Model I. The attribute "thing" is limited by "a," and by "as hard as [to be a poet] is in despite of nature," a complex adjective element; it is of the first class, since the basis is "hard;" it is complex, since the basis is limited by "as [to be a poet] is in despite of nature," which shows a comparison between two things, or the two conditions of being a poet, and would be a comparison of equality, but for the effect of "almost." In the subordinate clause, "as" is the connective, and joins the adverbial clause to "hard;" the connection is strengthened by the correlative adverb "as" in the principal clause. The subordinate clause is introduced by the expletive "it," and, when completed and arranged grammatically, stands, "[to be a poet] in despite of nature is [hard]." This clause is analyzed like the principal clause.

Poet is a part of the grammatical subject of both clauses: "to be" is not the grammatical subject, since it no more expresses an *idea* than does the copula (**80, 5**). The *simple* idea is, "to be a poet."

Poet is a common noun, third pers., sing., masc., nom., and is used as the attribute of an abridged proposition, namely, "That one should be a poet in despite of fortune, &c.," = "To be a poet in despite of fortune, &c." The subject "one" is entirely dropped from the sentence in abridging the proposition; and hence, by Rule II., 1, *b*, "poet" is in the predicate nominative absolute. See **167, 4**, Model 16, Ex.

2. *Construct, analyze, and parse examples of your own similar to the preceding.*

177. Agreement and Construction of the Pronoun.

1. **Rule III.**—A pronoun must agree with its antecedent in person, number, and gender.

Ex.—Those *who* are most consistent are not more unlike to others than *they* are to *themselves*.

(*a*.) A pronoun relating to a collective noun in the singular is put in the neuter singular when the noun denotes *unity*, but in the masculine or feminine plural when it denotes *plurality*.

Ex.—A civilized people has no right to violate *its* solemn obligations because the other party is uncivilized. The committee, having made *their* report, were discharged.

(*b*.) A pronoun relating to an antecedent consisting of coördinate terms, agrees with it, by Rule XII. (See, also, **195**, 1, *a*, *b*, &c.)

2. Interrogative pronouns commonly refer to objects unknown to the speaker; and hence the person, number, and gender must be *assumed* till the person or thing inquired for becomes known.

Although the pronoun may not agree with the *true* antecedent, it does agree, by rule, with the *assumed;* and consistency should be preserved in every reference to it. The following sentence is wrong:—" Who *was* not charmed with the music *they* heard?" *Was* should be changed to *were*, or *they* to *he*. Again, a pronoun relating to a singular antecedent limited by *many a* is commonly put in the plural; as, " I have heard *many an act* of devotion in my life, had Heaven vouchsafed me grace to profit by *them*."—*Scott*.

3. The pronoun **it** is used,—

(*a*.) *Without an antecedent*,—(1) when employed as in **173**, 4; (2) as an *expletive*.

Ex.—*It* is good *for me to be afflicted*. Come trip *it* as you go.

(*b*.) *When the antecedent is a young child or an animal*, the sex of which is disregarded.

Ex.—The true friend of the child is he who regards *its* future wellbeing. The raccoon feeds chiefly by night, keeping in *its* hole during the day.

4. A pronoun sometimes refers (apparently contrary to the general rule) to a noun taken from its ordinary signification.

Ex.—We studied *Woodbridge's Elements* of Geography on *its* first appearance before the public. When we say *books* is a noun, we classify *it*,—that is, the *word*,—not the *objects* themselves. Herod, *which* (not *who*) is another name for cruelty.

5. The English language being destitute of a pronoun of the third person, which may apply equally to either sex, an erroneous use of *they*, referring to *person, any one*, or *some one*, has been adopted even by respectable writers to conceal the gender, or to avoid an awkward use of *he* or *she*.

Thus: "If any one would test these rules for the preservation of health, *they* (*he* or *she*) must persevere in all states of the weather." The want of such a pronoun is still more apparent when the speaker has a definite person before his mind and wishes to conceal the gender: thus, "The person who gave me this information desired me to conceal —— name." When the person referred to belongs to an assemblage known to be composed wholly of males or wholly of females, the masculine or feminine pronoun should be used accordingly. But when the person belongs to an assemblage of males and females, usage has sanctioned the employment of a masculine pronoun: thus, "Is any among you afflicted? let *him* (not *them*,—not *her*) pray."

6. When things or animals are personified, they should be represented as persons by the pronouns employed.

Ex.—Next *Anger* rushed, *his* eyes on fire. The wolf *who* from the nightly fold fierce drags the bleating prey.

7. The pronoun usually follows its antecedent; but sometimes it is placed first.

Ex.—Hark! *they* whisper; angels say.

8. Relative and interrogative pronouns are usually placed at the beginning of their clauses, even though the order of construction would assign them some other position.

Ex.—Paternus had but one son, *whom* he educated himself.

9. The relative in the objective is sometimes omitted.

Ex.—Here is the present [which] he gave me.

The antecedent is not unfrequently omitted.

Ex.—[He] Who steals my purse steals trash.

The antecedent is sometimes a part of a sentence, and sometimes a possessive.

Ex.—The boy closed the blinds, *which* darkened the room. Supreme authority, strictly speaking, is only *His* who created the universe.

10. The *construction* of the pronoun is independent of its antecedent, and is like that of the noun in similar relations.

It may be,—

In the *nominative case*, as subject of a finite verb, *nominative absolute*, *possessive case*, or in the *objective case*, governed by a transitive verb or by a preposition; as, "They *who* speak." "We ordered the horses to be harnessed, *which* being done, we commenced our journey." "He hastened to the palace of his sovereign, into *whose* presence his hoary locks and mournful visage soon obtained admission." "The person *whom* I saw." "*Whom* did you take him to be?" "The man *whom* they call the janitor." "This is the rule to *which* we called his attention."

REMARK.—In disposing of a personal pronoun, two rules should be given, —one for its agreement, and one for its construction; in disposing of a relative, we should add to these the rule for it as a connective; and in case of *what*, *whatever*, or *whatsoever*, still another, to explain its use as an adjective.

11. The relative *which* formerly referred as well to persons as to things.

Ex.—Our Father *which* art in heaven.

It was sometimes preceded by the definite article; as, "In *the which* ye also walked sometime."—*Bible.* When used interrogatively, *which* may refer to persons; as, "*Which* of the two was the wiser man?"

12. The relative pronoun is,—

(*a.*) *Restrictive*, when it introduces a clause which restricts like an adjective the general idea denoted by the antecedent.

Ex.—The coffee *which* grows in Java = *Java* coffee = is of an excellent quality.

(*b.*) *Explanatory*, when it simply resumes the idea expressed by the antecedent, either in its full extent or as previously defined, and adds another thought.

Ex.—He gave me a book, which he requested me to read, = He gave me a book, *and* he requested me to read *it*.

REMARK.—When used *restrictively*, it often has, prefixed to the antecedent, a *correlative*, such as *the, this, that, these, those;* the adjective clause becomes a necessary addition to the antecedent, to complete the limitation intimated by these words. When used in an *explanatory* way, the relative introduces an additional proposition, and is equivalent to *and he, and she, and it, and they*.

That, what, and *as* are always used restrictively. *Who* and *which* may be either restrictive or explanatory.

13. When the relative is governed by a preposition, it is generally best to place the latter at the beginning of the clause.

Ex.—"This is the subject *to* which he alluded,"—not "which he alluded *to*."

But when the relative *that* is thus governed, the preposition is always placed at the end; as, "Here is the last bridge *that* we shall come *to*." It is better not to employ *that* when the governing preposition is understood: yet sometimes it is so used; as, "In the day *that* thou eatest thereof, thou shalt surely die."

14. The compound relatives *whoever, whoso, whosoever, whichever, whichsoever, whatever,* and *whatsoever,* show that the antecedent—

(1.) Is taken **universally**,—that is, in the full extent of its application.

Ex.—*Whoever* seeks shall find, = *Any one* who seeks shall find.

(2.) Is to be **understood**, especially in the compounds of *who* and *what;* and hence these words must either have a double construction, or an antecedent must be supplied.

Ex.—The soldiers made proclamation that they would sell the empire *to whoever* [*any one who*] would purchase it at the highest price.

15. The words *what, whatever,* and *whatsoever* combine in one word both the *relative* and its *correlative*.

REMARK.—They are equivalent to *the, this, that, these,* or *those — which:* hence they perform the office of a limiting adjective, and at the same time that of a relative pronoun; and hence, too, unlike all other relative pronouns, they are placed before the antecedent (except as in 17, below) when expressed (**75,** 5, and **76,** 3). Sometimes the simple *what* is separated from the affix by the antecedent; as, "*Whatsoever* plague, *whatsoever* sickness, there may be, *what* prayer and supplication *soever* be made by any man."—1 Kings viii. 37, 38. (See **77**, 5, 6, 7.)

16. *Whoever, whatever, whichever, whichsoever,* and *whatsoever* are often used to introduce and connect an *adversative* subordinate clause. (See Anal. **327**, *b*.)

Ex.—Whatever you may say, he persists in doing it.

In this case an adversative preposition is understood to govern the antecedent; as, "*Whatever* useful or engaging endowments we possess, virtue is requisite in order to their shining with proper lustre," = *Notwithstanding all those* useful or engaging endowments *which* we possess, &c. Here *endowments* is governed by *notwithstanding*, and *which* by *possess*. It is an error to say, as some do, that *whatever*, here, is simply an adjective; for then we should have no relative word to connect the clauses. In like manner we have "*What* time I am afraid, I will trust in thee," = *At what* time, &c.

17. *Whatever* and *whatsoever* are often used to express *universality* (15) emphatically.

Ex.—I have no confidence *whatever* in the proposed measure.

Here, as in comparisons after *than* or *as*, the subject or the attribute of the subordinate clause being given, the rest is to be supplied; as, "I have no confidence whatever [it may be] in the proposed measure." It is an error here to suppose that *whatever* is a *mere* adjective, or is like the emphatic personal pronoun *himself*, as in the following:—"The declarations contained in them [the Scriptures] rest on the authority of *God himself;* and there can be no appeal from them to any authority *whatsoever*" [that authority may be]. Care should be taken, in these difficult constructions, not to make a pleonastic use of a personal pronoun or other word. The following sentence is faulty:—"*Whatsoever* he saith unto you, do *it;*" omit *it*.

18. When interrogative clauses are quoted indirectly (**163**, 7), the interrogative pronoun is used indefinitely, having only an implied antecedent (2, above).

Ex.—*What* shall I do? I know not *what* I shall do.

Here the whole clause is the object of *know*, and *what* of *shall do*. When such clauses are abridged,—thus, "I know not *what* to do,"—the whole expression "what to do" is the double object of *know*, and *what* is the object of "to do." So, "I know not *whom* to send."

19. The relative *that* is always restrictive, and should be used,—

(1.) After the interrogative *who*.

Ex.—*Who that* marks the fire still sparkling in each eye, &c.

(2.) After an adjective in the superlative degree.

Ex.—He was the *last that* left.

(3.) After *very, all, same.*

Ex.—This is the *very* book *that* I want. Is not this *all that* you ask? He is the *same* person *that* I took him to be.

(4.) When the relative refers to an antecedent denoting both persons and things.

Ex.—Here are the *persons* and *papers* that were sent for.

20. Instead of *in which, by which, of which,* &c., the equivalent relative adverbs *where, when, whereby, whereof,* &c. are used, like the pronoun, to join an adjective clause to its antecedent.

Ex.—We discovered the place *where the goods had been concealed.*

CAUTION I.—*Avoid the use of a noun and a pronoun as subject or object of the same verb, unless great emphasis is required.* Say, "The *boy* did it,"—not "The boy *he* did it."

CAUTION II.—*Avoid the use of a plural pronoun having a singular antecedent.* Say, "Let every one attend to *his* (not *their*) work."

CAUTION III.—*In the use of a pronoun, avoid ambiguity in its reference to an antecedent.* Say, "A boy *who* deceives his father will regret it,"—not "If a boy deceives his father, *he* will regret it."

CAUTION IV.—*In arranging nouns or pronouns of different persons, a pronoun of the second person should be placed before one of the first or the third;* as, "*You* and *he* and *I*,"—not "*I* and *he* and *you*."

Yet, in confessing a fault, it is more generous for the speaker to put himself first.

CAUTION V.—*Avoid the use of* who *when speaking of animals and inanimate objects, and of* which *when speaking of persons.* Say, "The cat *which* mews,"—not "*who* mews." "The stranger *who* came,"—not "The stranger *which* came."

CAUTION VI.—*Avoid a change of number, or a change of pronouns, when reference is made to the same antecedent in the same sentence.* Say, "I know *you*, and I love *you* too,"—not "I know *thee*, and I love *you* too."

CAUTION VII.—*A pronoun relating to an antecedent consisting of co-ordinate terms of different persons or genders, should agree with the first person rather than the second or the third, and with the second rather than the third, and with the masculine gender rather than the feminine.* Say, "You and Charles are learning *your* lesson,"—not "*their* lesson." "If a man smite the eye of his *servant*, or the eye of his *maid*, that it perish, he shall let *him* [not *her*, nor *them*] go free for *his* eye's sake."—*Bible.*

178. Exercise.

1. *Analyze the sentences, and parse the pronouns, in the following examples:—*

Ye, therefore, who love mercy, teach your sons to love it too. Other sheep I have, which are not of this fold. This is the friend of whom I spoke. He who had no mercy upon others is now reduced to a condition which may excite the pity of his most implacable enemy. At sea, every thing that breaks the monotony of the surrounding expanse attracts attention. That life is long which answers life's great end. He is the friend whose arrival is daily expected. The board of health have published their report. The committee, who were divided in opinion, will discuss the question more fully at their next meeting. It is the undaunted bravery and the wild impetuosity of the Zouaves that render their charges so formidable. All this took place when the vice and ignorance which the old tyranny had generated, threatened the new freedom with destruction. One or the other must relinquish his claim. Either Jane or Julia will perform her task.

MODEL I.—"Hastings advanced to the bar and bent his knee."—*Macaulay.*

Analyze as in Model 14 (166), and parse *his* thus:—

His is a personal pronoun, of the third person, singular number, masculine gender, according to Rule III. (repeat it); in the possessive case, limiting "knee." Rule VII.

MODEL II.

"Thus urged the chief; a generous *troop* appears,
Who spread *their* bucklers, and advance *their* spears."

Pope.

Let the learner analyze this compound sentence, and parse *their* as in the preceding model, giving as a rule 177, 1, *a.*

Who is a relative pronoun; as a pronoun it has *troop* for its antecedent, a collective noun in the singular denoting plurality, and is of the third person, plural number, masculine gender, by 176, 1, *a,* and in the nominative case, by Rule I.

Observe that *troop* first denotes *unity,* since *appears* is singular; and then it denotes *plurality,* as shown by *who* and *their.*

Model III.—"I wish, after all I have said about *wit* and *humor*, I could satisfy myself of *their* good effects upon the character and disposition."—*Sidney Smith.*

This is a complex declarative sentence, of which *I* is the subject, and *wish* the predicate of the principal clause. Let the learner point out all the modifications of the predicate, and parse the pronouns.

Their is a personal pronoun, of the third person, plural number, neuter gender, and agrees with its antecedent "wit and humor," whose coördinate terms are taken conjointly, by **177**, 1, *b*, or Rule XII., and is in the possessive case, by Rule VII.

179. The Verb as Predicate.

1. **Rule IV.**—The **verb** must agree with its subject in person and number.

Ex.—I *am.* Thou *art sitting.* We *have come.*

(*a.*) A verb agreeing with a collective noun in the singular is put in the singular when the noun denotes *unity,* but in the plural when it denotes *plurality.*

Ex.—A *detachment* of two thousand men *was sent* to support the left wing. The council *were divided* in their opinion.

(*b.*) A verb agreeing with a subject consisting of coördinate terms, is singular or plural, according to Rule XII. (See **195**, 1, *a, b, c.*)

To the general rule that the verb must agree in number and person with any subject, according as it denotes *unity* or *plurality* of idea, there are, properly, no exceptions. In the following examples, "Ten head o. cattle *were* feeding;" "Five *yoke* of oxen were ploughing;" "Fifty *sail* of vessels were seen," the rule **177**, 1, *a,* is properly applicable. So, in case of the apparent exception in which the title of a book is plural, the mind is fixed upon the *treatise* itself as *one thing:* thus, "Wayland's *Elements* of Political Economy *was* published in 1837." Here "Elements of Political Economy" is the same as "*Treatise* upon the Elements," &c. So, again, a *phrase* or a *clause* (**173**, 1, *a*) used as a subject is to be regarded as *one thing,* requiring the verb to be in the third person singular. But when a phrase expressive of a combination of numbers is regarded as denoting separate units rather than a single number, the verb should be plural; as, "Three times three *are* nine."

2. The nominative and the verb after *many a* or *many an* should be in the singular number.

Ex.—Full *many a* flower is born to blush unseen.

3. The subject of verbs in the imperative mode is *thou,* or *ye* or *you,* and is usually omitted.

The subject is often to be supplied after comparisons with *than* or *as.* (See **173,** 3.)

Ex.—John has more fruit than [*what = that which*] can be gathered in a week. It is as broad as [it is] long.

4. In such inverted interrogative sentences as, *Who am I? Who is he? Who are you? What am I? Who art thou? Is it I? Is it he? Is it thou?* the attribute should not be taken for the subject, which alone controls the person and number of the verb.

CAUTION I.—*Avoid all such ungrammatical expressions as,* "*Says I;*" "*Thinks I;*" "*Thinks says I;*" "*I hears him,*" &c.

CAUTION II.—*Never use a plural verb with a singular subject, though the latter be modified by a noun in the plural.* Say, "Each of his brothers *is* (not *are*) well."

CAUTION III.—*Be careful not to use the* WRONG VERB, *as,* **set** *for* **sit, lay** *for* **lie, come** *for* **go;** *or the* WRONG FORM, *as,* **done** *for* **did, wrote** *for* **written,** &c.; *or the* WRONG TENSE, *as,* **see** *for* **saw, give** *for* **gave;** *or* IMPROPER CONTRACTIONS, *as,* **ain't** *for* **are not,** &c.

180. Exercise.

1. *Analyze and parse the following examples:*—

The Connecticut River was first explored, as far as Hartford, by Adrian Block. The sun was setting upon one of the rich, glassy glades of the forest. Those who have ever witnessed the spectacle of the launching of a ship of the line, will perhaps forgive me for adding this to the examples of the sublime objects of artificial life. Ferdinand and Isabella were seated, with their son, Prince John, under a superb canopy. The nobility were haughty and exacting. The people take the matter into their own hands. Society is not always answerable for the conduct of its members.

MODEL I.—"After a brief interval, the sovereigns requested of Columbus a recital of his adventures."—*Prescott.*

Analyze according to Model (**162,** 3, 4), and parse *requested* thus:—

Requested is a regular transitive verb; *principal parts,*—pres. re-

quest, past *requested*, past participle *requested;* indicative mode, past tense, third person, plural number, and agrees with "sovereigns," according to Rule IV. (Repeat it.)

MODEL II.—"Why do the heathen rage, and the people imagine a vain thing?"—*Bible.*

This is a compound interrogative sentence, consisting of two coördinate clauses joined by "and." Analyze them separately.

Do rage is a regular intransitive verb, emphatic form, indicative mode, present tense, third person, plural number, and agrees with "heathen," according to Rule IV., *a*. In the same way parse "do imagine."

MODEL III.—"Gold, silver, and copper abound in South America."

Follow Model 14 (**166**, 1), and parse *abound* thus:—

Abound is a regular intransitive verb, indicative mode, present tense, third person, plural number, and agrees with its compound subject, according to Rule IV., *b*, or Rule XII.

2. *Construct similar examples of your own.*

181. The Adjective as Modifier and as Predicate.

1. **Rule V.**—An adjective or a participle must belong to some noun or pronoun.

Ex.—The *guilty* man; the man was *guilty.*

(*a.*) An adjective or a participle used as the *attribute* of a proposition, belongs to the subject.

Ex.—The tree is *tall.* To see the sun is *pleasant.* Where the funds will be obtained is *doubtful.*

(*b.*) An adjective or a participle used to *modify* a noun, belongs to the noun which it modifies.

Ex.—*An upright* judge. *Five* boxes. *The good old* man.

(*c.*) Adjectives denoting *number* agree in number with the nouns they limit.

Ex.—*This* book. *These* trees. *Ten* men.

(*d.*) The article *a* or *an* belongs to nouns in the singular number, except before *few*, *hundred*, or *thousand;* and *the*, to nouns either singular or plural.

Ex.—*A* man. *An* hour. *The* desk. *The* pens. *A few* men.

2. The appropriate use of the adjective is to restrict the application of a noun.

The adjective thus used is always a dependent term, having the restricted noun as its principal.

3. A noun may be restricted or limited in its application,—

(1.) Without affecting any of its properties; as, "*Two* men." "*These* books."

(2.) By designating some *property* or *quality;* as, "*Good* men." "*Industrious* boys."

(3.) By *identifying* it; as, "Paul *the Apostle.*" "Peter *the Hermit.*"

(4.) By representing it as an object *possessed;* as, "*David's* harp."

The first two limitations are effected by *adjectives;* the last two, by *nouns* or *pronouns* performing the office of the adjective.

4. Any word, or group of words, employed to limit a noun, is an *adjective element;* that is, it is of the nature of an adjective.

Ex.—*Industrious* men. Men *of industry.* Men *who are industrious.*

5. Limiting adjectives, when used in connection with qualifying, are generally placed first.

Ex.—*The* old man. *This* valuable hint. *Ten* small trees.

When two limiting adjectives are used, one of which is an article, the latter is usually placed first; as, "*The* ten commandments." But after *many, such, all, what,* and *both,* the article stands next to the noun; so, also, after adjectives preceded by *too, so, as,* or *how;* as, "*Many a* man." "*Such a* man." "*All the* boys." "*What a* boy." "*Both the* girls." "*Too great, as great, so great, how great, a* man." "*Half a* dollar."

6. The article should be,—

(1.) **Omitted**,—(*a.*) Before *proper* nouns, *abstract* nouns, and nouns denoting *substance* or *material,* when used in their general signification.

Ex.—*Patience* is a Christian virtue. *Gold* abounds in Colorado. *Wood* is becoming scarce.

(*b.*) Before the participle used as a noun, with the limitations of the verb.

Ex.—The ancients erred in *supposing* the earth a vast plane.

(*c.*) Before a common noun used in the full extent of its signification.

Ex.—*Man* is mortal. *Woman* is justly appreciated only in civilized countries. The lizard is a kind of *reptile*.

REMARK.—Contrary to this rule, *the* is often used before a noun in the singular to denote the *whole* class, and must be distinguished from the cases in which *the* points out an *individual object*, by a careful attention to the connection. Thus, we have *the horse, the bee, the oak, the ash, the dahlia. The horse* is a noble animal. *The horse* is lame. Go to *the ant*, thou sluggard. *The ant* was drowned in the cup.

(*d.*) Before a noun denoting a mere title, or a name used as a word.

Ex.—Ye call me *Master* and *Lord*. *Acorn* is derived from *ac*, oak, and *corn*, grain.

(*e.*) Before any common noun already limited by one of the definitives *any, each, either, every, much, neither, no* or *none, some, this, that, these,* or *those,* or by any other words which make its meaning sufficiently definite.

(2.) **Inserted,**—(*a.*) Before a *common noun* used to denote an *individual object*, or any *number of individual objects* definitely referred to.

Ex.—*The* rose which blooms by the wall.

(*b.*) Before *adjectives* used as nouns.

Ex.—None but *the brave* deserves *the fair*.

(*c.*) Before *participles* used wholly as nouns.

Ex.—For *the edifying* of the church.

(*d.*) Before *proper nouns* in the plural, *abstract nouns*, and nouns denoting *substance* or *material* when used with specific reference to an individual example (6, 1, *a*, above).

Ex.—*The* Websters. *The* twelve Cæsars. Ye have heard of *the* patience of Job. *The* wood is sufficiently dry.

7. The article, if required at all by the preceding rules, should,—

(1.) Be **repeated,**—(*a.*) Before each *noun* of a coördinate combination, when the objects, by some correspondence or contrast, or by some limitation not common to all, are specially distinguished.

Ex.—The soldiers did not inquire for *the number*, but *the place*, of the enemy.

Here the contrast requires the repetition of the article.

Ex.—England, during the interval between *the* Protectorate and *the* restoration of the Stuarts, was virtually governed by General Monk.

Here the omission of *the* before *restoration* would refer the *Protectorate* and the *restoration* alike to the Stuarts.

(*b.*) Before each part of a coördinate combination employed as an *adjective element* (166, 1, Ex.), when the parts apply to objects individually different, yet of the same name.

Ex.—"*The* northern and *the* southern boundary,"—two very different boundaries. "*A* Bancroft's, *a* Lossing's, and *a* Goodrich's history,"—three different books. "We had pleasant companions, *an* Englishman, *a* Scotchman, and *a* German,"—each a companion, but three men.

REMARK.—By a common usage, justified by standard authority, the article may be placed before the first adjective *only*, when the noun is put in the plural at the end of the series; as, "*The* first, second, and third regiments." It is here supposed that the hearer will distribute the adjectives properly. The rule just given, though it sometimes renders the construction somewhat formal, secures precision in the application of the adjectives; while the omission of the article leaves their application doubtful, and hence sometimes endangers the perspicuity of the sentence.

(2.) **Not be repeated,**—(*a.*) Before any of the foregoing combinations when the nouns, as in (*a*), do not express a correspondence or a contrast, or have a common limitation, or the modifiers, as in (*b*), belong to a common object.

Ex.—"*The* men, women, and children of the party suffered alike,"—each being of the party. "Give me *the* ripe red and mellow peaches,"—each being ripe, red, and mellow. "He bought *a* Wheeler and Wilson's sewing-machine,"—one machine of two patentees. "Dr. Kane, *the* scholar, naturalist, and explorer,"—one man with three characteristics.

(*b.*) Before the second term of a comparison, where both refer to the same person or thing.

Ex.—He was *a* better speaker than writer.

8. *Many*, followed by *a* (*an*), though implying *plurality*, is followed by a noun in the singular.

Ex.—*Many a* man, = *Many men.*

9. When two numerals precede a noun, one singular and the other plural, the plural should generally be placed next to the noun.

Ex.—"The first *two* lines,"—not "The two *first* lines."

In such expressions as, "*Five yoke of oxen*," "*Ten head of cattle*," "*Fifty sail of vessels*," the plural adjective belongs to a noun in the singular, but used collectively to convey the idea of plurality.

P

10. When objects are contrasted, *that* refers to the first and *this* to the last mentioned.

Ex.—Wealth and poverty are both temptations: *that* tends to excite pride; *this*, discontent.

11. By a peculiar use, *the — the*, primarily articles, belonging to some noun understood, as *part*, are used with comparatives, to denote proportionate equality, and are to be regarded as conjunctive adverbs used to join two clauses.

Ex.—*The* more I see it, *the* better I like it.

12. The adjective is often used as a noun, the noun to which it belongs being understood.

Ex.—*The good* are respected.

On the other hand, the noun is often used as an adjective.

Ex.—*Gold beads.*

13. One adjective often limits the complex idea expressed by another adjective and a noun.

Ex.—Two *old* horses.

So, again, in combined numbers, and in some few other cases, one adjective limits another.

Ex.—Five hundred thousand. A *bright red* apple.

14. The predicate adjective following *copulative verbs* generally denotes some property of the subject, either already possessed by it, or acquired through the action of the verb.

Ex.—The boy was made *sick*. The bread was baked *brown*. The fruit tastes *sweet*.

15. A participle, an adjective, or even a noun, in the predicate, yet referring to the subject, is often used somewhat adverbially to express an accompanying action. Although it does not show the manner of the action, it shows *how* or *with what* it is accompanied.

Ex.—The Son of man came *eating* and *drinking*. The maiden sat there *sad*. He came *as a spectator*.

16. When two objects or sets of objects are compared, the comparative degree is generally used.

Ex.—"George is *taller* than William," or, "is the *taller* of the two." Our *oranges* are sweeter than *yours*.

17. When more than two objects are compared, the superlative degree is used.

Ex.—Achilles was the *bravest* of the Greeks.

18. When the comparative degree is used, the latter term should always *exclude* the former.

Ex.—New York is larger than any other city of the United States. He was wiser than his brothers.

But when the superlative is used, the latter term should always *include* the former.

Ex.—Rhode Island is the smallest of the United States.

19. *Each, one, either,* and *neither* belong to nouns in the third person singular. Hence, when used as nouns, verbs and pronouns should agree with them accordingly.

Ex.—Each of his brothers is (not *are*) well.

Either and *neither* have reference to *two* things only; *each, every,* and *any,* to *more* than two. *All* refers to the individuals of a whole taken collectively; while *each, every,* and *any* refer to them when taken distributively. The following sentence is wrong, because the individuals should be taken collectively: —" Every term in the series is alike." Say, "*All* the terms are alike."

20. An adjective after the participle or infinitive of the copula is sometimes used *abstractly*, referring, it may be, logically (but not grammatically) to some indefinite object.

Ex.—To be *good* is to be *happy*.

21. An adjective may belong to an adverb, to a phrase, or to a clause used as a noun.

Ex.—*This* once. (Here " once" is equivalent to "one time.") To deceive is *criminal*. That youth and vigor must pass away is *undeniable*.

22. The reciprocal *each other* should be applied to *two* objects; *one another*, to *more* than two.

Ex.—" Righteousness and peace have kissed *each other*,"—not "*one another*." These various tribes have been at war with *one another*.

CAUTION I.—*Never use* A *before the sound of a vowel, nor* AN *before the sound of a consonant*. Say, "*An* apple,"—not "*A* apple."

CAUTION II.—*Avoid the use of a plural adjective to limit a singular noun*. Say, "**This** sort of people,"—not "**those sort**."

CAUTION III.—*Avoid the vulgar use of* THEM *for* THOSE, *and* THIS HERE, *or* THAT 'ERE, *for* THIS, *or* THAT. Say, "*Those* books,"—not "*Them* books;" "*This* chair,"—not "*This 'ere* chair."

CAUTION IV.—*Avoid the use of the adjective for the adverb*. Say, "Speak *promptly*,"—not "*prompt*."

CAUTION V.—*Avoid the use of the superlative degree when two objects are compared, or of the comparative when more than two are compared.* Say, "The *wiser* of the two,"—not "The *wisest* of the two;" "The *wisest* of them all,"—not "The *wiser* of them all."

CAUTION VI.—*Avoid the use of double comparatives and superlatives.* Say, "This is the *unkindest* cut of all,"—not "the *most unkindest* cut of all."

CAUTION VII.—*Avoid the use of the article before a title or name used merely as a word.* Say, "He is called *captain*,"—not "*the captain*."

CAUTION VIII.—*Avoid the use of the article before the second noun, when the same object is compared in two different capacities.* Say, "He is a better teacher than *poet*,"—not "*than a poet*."

182. Exercise.

1. *Analyze the following examples, and parse the adjectives:*—

The yellow sunflower by the brook in autumn beauty stood. Life is real, life is earnest. The influence of such pursuits is ennobling. He was a good man, and a just. He was a burning and a shining light. These opportunities, improved as they should be, must produce the desired results. The hopes of the whole family were centred on him. His resources were inexhaustible. To insult the afflicted is impious. Pity the sorrows of a poor old man, whose trembling limbs have borne him to your door. That he should refuse such a proposition, was not unexpected. Every thing which is false, vicious, or unworthy is despicable to him, though all the world should approve it.

MODEL.—"The sky was clear, and the immense vault of the heavens appeared in awful majesty and grandeur." *Brydone.*

Analyze by the proper models, and parse *the, clear,* and *immense.*

The is a definite article, and belongs to "sky," according to Rule V., or Rule V., 1, *d.*

Clear is a qualifying adjective, and is used as the *attribute* of the proposition, and belongs to the subject "sky," according to Rule V., 1, *a.*

Immense is a qualifying adjective, and is used to *modify* "vault," to which it belongs, according to Rule V., 1, *b.*

2. *Construct examples of your own to illustrate the various uses of the adjective.*

183. The Noun or the Pronoun in Apposition.

1. **Rule VI.**—A noun or a pronoun used to **explain** or **identify** another noun or pronoun is put by apposition in the same case.

Ex.—William the *Conqueror* defeated Harold, the Saxon *king*.

2. The explanatory noun or pronoun must denote the *same* person or thing as that which it identifies.

It usually explains by showing the *office, rank, capacity, occupation,* or *character* of the principal term; as "Peter the *Hermit;*" "John the *Evangelist.*"

3. This construction may be regarded as derived from an adjective clause by abridging it.

Ex.—Paul, *who was the apostle to the Gentiles,* = Paul, *the apostle to the Gentiles.*

Hence, like the full clause, it may be *restrictive,* in which case it points out the individual; as, "William the *Conqueror;*" or it may be *explanatory* (**177,** 12); that is, it resumes the idea expressed by the principal noun, for the purpose of *amplification, rhetorical effect,* or even *argument;* as, "Moses, *the servant of the Lord,* died there in the land of Moab." Here "servant" is not used to distinguish this Moses from some other, but to show the writer's idea of his exalted character as the servant of the Lord. Mark, also, the following examples:—"The Lord, *the most high God,* the possessor of heaven and earth;" "You have ruined him, *your protector, your best friend,*"—that is, notwithstanding he is *your protector* and *your best friend.*

REMARK.—It is an error to suppose that a noun or a pronoun is in apposition with another noun or pronoun because the construction requires them to be put in the same case. The predicate noun is not in apposition with the subject noun, though it is required to be in the same case: in one case we *affirm* what in the other we *assume.* The second, or attributive object, after the active voice of copulative verbs, is not in apposition with the first, though in the same case. (See **187,** 9.)

4. Three cases of apposition may be distinguished:—

(*a.*) The noun in apposition, though subordinate to the principal, is made *prominent*, and receives the emphasis; as, "Peter the Hermit." In this case it is always placed last.

(*b.*) The noun, when put in apposition with a personal pronoun, though placed last, is so nearly equal in value with the latter as to render it sometimes doubtful which should be regarded as principal; as, "*Ye men* of Athens."

(*c.*) When used as a title, or part of a name, the noun in apposition loses the emphasis, is placed first, and may be taken with the principal noun as one complex name (**44**, 5); as, "*General Scott;*" "*Washington Irving.*" Some have supposed the leading noun here to be used adjectively. But when a noun is used wholly as an adjective, it denotes a *different* thing from that which it limits; as, "A *silver* cup."

5. When, for the sake of emphasis, the *same* name is repeated, it is in apposition with the former.

Ex.—A *horse!* a *horse!* my kingdom for a horse.

REMARK.—Any resumed construction, whether it be that of a noun, a pronoun, or any other part of speech, may be said to be in apposition; as, "To die,—to sleep; *to sleep*, perchance to dream." "He has *falsely* accused me of conspiring against my country :—*falsely*, or why has he not made his charges good?"

6. When the limiting noun denotes a person, it generally, though not always, agrees with the limited in *number, gender,* and *case.*

Ex.—Milton, the *poet.* The *Franks,* a *people* of Germany.

7. The noun in apposition is rendered more emphatic when joined by such connectives as *namely, as, to wit, that is.*

Ex.—Two *men, namely,* George and James. So that *he, as God,* sitteth in the temple of God.

8. A noun or a pronoun in the plural may be represented by two or more nouns which together are equivalent to it.

Ex.—The victims, a *brother* and a *sister.*

The reverse of this rule is equally true.

Ex.—Intemperance, oppression, and fraud, *vices* of the age.

9. In the case of the expressions *each other* and *one another,* the first words, *each* and *one,* are in apposition with a preceding plural noun or pronoun, or with two or more singular nouns taken conjointly.

Ex.—The boys struck one another, = The boys struck—*one* struck another. John and David love each other, = John and David love —*each* loves the other.

Each and *one* are in the nominative case, and *other* is in the objective case. It is better, in some cases, to consider the combination as an inseparable term; as, "He did not recommend the washing of *one another's* feet."

10. The proper name of a *place,* instead of being put in appo-

sition with the common name, is usually governed by the preposition *of*.

Ex.—The city of *Rome*.

11. A noun is sometimes in apposition with a sentence, and sometimes a sentence with a noun.

Ex.—They devoted their whole time to the promotion of our happiness,—*attentions* which we shall not soon forget. The *maxim, Enough is as good as a feast*, has silenced many a vain wish.

12. When possessives are in apposition, the sign of possession ('s) is commonly used with only one of them, and with that one which immediately precedes the limited noun.

Ex.—*John* the *Baptist's* head. His *majesty King Henry's* crown. For *Herodias'* sake, his *brother Philip's wife*. At *Smith's* the *bookseller*.

13. Sometimes a noun preceded by "as," without the sign and evidently without the signification of the possessive, refers logically to a noun or a pronoun in the possessive.

Ex.—What do you think of my *brother's* success as a *teacher?* As an *author*, his "Adventurer" is *his* capital work.

Rather than to consider *teacher* and *author* in the possessive case, here, it is better to suppose *teacher* to refer in sense to *brother's*, but to take its case from *success;* and *author* to refer logically to *his*, but grammatically to *work*.

184. Exercise.

1. *Analyze the following examples, and parse the nouns or the pronouns in apposition:*—

The patriarch Abraham was accounted faithful. The Emperor Nero was a cruel tyrant. James, the royal Scottish poet, was imprisoned in Windsor Castle. In the fifth century the Franks, a people of Germany, invaded France. Frederic William III., King of Prussia, son of Frederic William II. and Louisa, Princess of Hesse-Darmstadt, was born August 3, 1770.

MODEL.—"Daniel Boone, the pioneer of Kentucky, was born in Bucks county, Pennsylvania, in the month of February, 1735."—*Sparks*.

Analyze this sentence, and parse the subject, predicate, and all the connectives.

Pioneer is a common noun, of the third person, singular number, masculine gender, nominative case, and is used to identify "Daniel Boone," with which it is put in apposition, by Rule VI. (Repeat it.)

2. *Construct similar examples of your own to illustrate apposition.*

185. Noun or Pronoun in the Possessive.

1. **Rule VII.**—A noun or a pronoun used to limit the application of another noun, by denoting **possession**, is put in the possessive case.

Ex:—*Stephen's* courage failed. *Their* fortune was ample. *Whose* work is this?

2. The principal idea expressed by this relation is that of *possession:* yet this term should not be understood to mean simply *property.* The possessive case is employed to denote,—

(*a.*) **Property**; as, "The *farmer's* house."

(*b.*) **Source** or **origin**; as, "*Heaven's* command;" "the *sun's* rays."

(*c.*) **Agency**; as, "*Solomon's* temple," *i.e.* the temple built by Solomon.

(*d.*) **Adaptation** or **fitness**; as, "*Men's* hats."

(*e.*) **Kindred**; as "*Brother's* son."

(*f.*) **Time, weight,** and **measure**; as, "The ten *years'* war;" "a *pound's* weight;" "a *mile's* length."

REMARK.—The possessive case is used to limit the noun when we wish to express some agency emanating usually from a person or from some object treated as a person. It performs the office of the adjective, and is hence reckoned an adjective element.

3. The relation of the possessive is one of dependence. There must, therefore, be some noun for it to limit. This noun, however, may be understood.

Ex.—He worships at *St. Paul's* [*church*].

4. The present active participle, the present passive (with *being*), and the perfect participles (but never the past, or the simple passive), when used as nouns, may be limited by the possessive, and at the same time may have the limitation which they have when they are complete predicates.

Ex.—I heard of *your studying* Latin. I am in favor of *their bringing* the dispute to a speedy close.

SYNTAX—THE POSSESSIVE.

5. Instead of the possessive form, the preposition *of*, with the objective, is often used.

Ex.—The court *of the king,* = The *king's court.*

6. The possessive case may be either assumed or predicated.

Ex.—*David's* book. This book is *David's.*

7. An adjective sometimes, though seldom, intervenes between the possessive and the noun on which it depends.

Ex.—Of man's *first* disobedience.

When, in such case, the noun is understood, the possessive sign is annexed to the adjective used as a noun; as, " This is the *wretched's* only plea."

8. All possessive constructions may be divided into *simple, complex,* and *compound.* The construction of *simple* possessives is sufficiently explained by Rule VII.

9. A possessive is *complex* when a group of words, consisting of a principal and a subordinate term, is put in the possessive. Of this there are two cases:—

(*a.*) The subordinate noun may be in the objective after a preposition.

Ex.—The Duke of Wellington's sword.

Here the possessive sign is applied to an inseparable group. Although "duke" alone is in the possessive, it would not be improper to regard the whole group as a noun in the possessive, limiting "sword." When possession in a similar case is predicated (6, above), the sign is applied to the simple possessive noun; as, " There shall nothing die of all that is the *children's* of Israel."—*Exodus* ix. 4.

(*b.*) The subordinate noun may be put in apposition with the principal noun.

Here are two cases. (1.) When the subordinate noun unites with the other, forming a complex name (183, 4, *c*). In this case the sign of possession is applied to the last only, or that nearest the limited noun; as, *"General George Washington's* farewell address." (2.) When the subordinate noun is properly in apposition with a possessive noun; as, " For thy *servant David's* sake;" "At *Smith's* the *bookseller.*" Here the rule is to give the possessive sign to the one immediately preceding the governing noun, whether it be the first possessive, as in the second example, or the second, as in the first example.

10. A possessive is *compound* when the terms composing it are coördinate; and here also are two cases:—

(*a.*) The coördinate terms may individually limit a noun denoting *one* common object.

Ex.—*Gould, Kendall,* and *Lincoln's* store.

(*b.*) They may limit the same noun applied to different objects.

Ex.—"*Richardson's, Worcester's,* and *Webster's* Dictionary;" that is, *three* dictionaries.

In this case each noun has the sign, because "dictionary" is understood immediately after it. But in the other case the group has the sign, which is, by a general rule, applied to the noun nearest to the governing word.

REMARK.—There are two other constructions which are thought by some to come under the case of complex possessives: the one is the case of the predicate noun in an abridged proposition whose subject has been changed to the possessive; the other is that mentioned in **183**, 13. For these cases see **175**, *b,* and **183**, 13.

11. Sometimes a possessive and the limited noun unite and form a compound, which may be taken,—

(*a.*) **Literally**, and should be written without the possessive sign.

Ex.—*Tradesman, craftsman, ratsbane, doomsday.*

(*b.*) **Metaphorically**, in which case it should be written with the sign.

Ex.—*Job's-tears, Jew's-ear, bear's-foot, hound's-tongue, bear's-breech, lion's-tail, wolf's-bane, wolf's-peach,*—names of plants.

12. When a combination, consisting of a possessive and its governing noun, is used as an adjective, the sign should not be omitted.

Ex.—A *bird's-eye* view. A *camel's-hair* shawl. *Taylor's Kühner's Greek* Grammar. *Eden's garden* bird.

CAUTION I.—*In writing nouns in the possessive, never omit the possessive termination.* Write "*man's,*"—not "*mans.*"

CAUTION II.—*In using pronouns in the possessive, never insert the apostrophe in writing, nor add the letter* n *in speaking.* Write "*theirs,*"—not "*their's.*" Say, "*his, hers, ours, yours, theirs,*"—not "*hisn, hern, ourn, yourn, theirn.*"

CAUTION III.—*Never make the limited noun plural because the possessive is plural.* Say, "Their *decision*"—not, "Their *decisions;*" one only being meant.

186. Exercise.

1. *Analyze the following examples, and parse the possessives:*—

Charles's resignation filled all Europe with astonishment. The joy of his youth was great. Rotha's bay received the ship. Her ways are ways of pleasantness, and all her paths are peace. A mother's tenderness, and a father's care, are nature's gifts for man's advantage. A chieftain's daughter seemed the maid. Yet my last thought is England's. She stooped her by the runnel's side. Hushed were his Gertrude's lips. Our harps we left by Babel's streams.

MODEL.—"What, I say, was Cæsar's object?"—*Knowles.*

This is a complex sentence, consisting of a principal clause, "I say," and a subordinate interrogative clause, "What was Cæsar's object?" It is quoted directly (**163,** 1), and hence the interrogation point is used at the close (**163,** 6).

I is the subject of the principal clause, and **say** the grammatical predicate; it is limited by the quoted clause, which is subordinate in construction, and is an objective element of the third class. It has no connective (**163,** 4); its simple subject is "object," and is limited by the adjective element "Cæsar's;" the predicate is "was what," of which "was" is the copula and "what" the attribute.

Cæsar's is a proper noun, of the third person, singular number, masculine gender, possessive case, and is used to limit "object," by denoting possession. Rule VII. (Repeat it.)

2. *Construct similar examples of your own.*

187. The Object.

1. **Rule VIII.**—A noun or a pronoun used as the **object** of a transitive verb, or of its participles, must be in the objective case.

Ex.—He found the *object which* he desired.

(*a.*) **Copulative** verbs (9, below) in the active voice take a **direct** object, and predicate of it an **attributive** object, both of which form a double object.

Ex.—They called *him John.*

REMARK.—In the passive voice, the direct object becomes the subject, and the attributive becomes the attribute; as, "*He* was called *John.*"

(*b.*) Certain verbs, as **give, ask, teach,** and others (11, below), in the active voice, take two objects, one *direct*, and the other *indirect*.

Ex.—He gave *me* a *book*.

REMARK.—In the passive, the direct object should become the subject, and the indirect should remain in the predicate; as, "A *book* was given to *me*."

2. When a noun or a pronoun is used to complete the meaning of a transitive verb, without the aid of a preposition expressed or understood, it is called the *direct object;* but when it is added to a verb, either transitive or intransitive, to show that *to* or *for* which any thing is, or is done, or that *from* or *out of* which any thing proceeds, it is called the *indirect object*.

Ex.—Ellen gave an *apple* to her *brother*. They spoke *of his troubles*.

3. When an indirect object precedes the direct, the preposition should be omitted; when it follows, it should be expressed.

Ex.—I lent *him* a *book*, = I lent a book *to* him.

4. The indirect object is sometimes used alone with intransitive verbs, sometimes with an adjective, and in a few instances with a noun.

Ex.—He spoke of his *trials*. To *me* this rule is obvious. To the *hero* that was a proud day.

5. The object of a transitive verb may be an infinitive, or a substantive clause.

Ex.—I love *to write*. I have heard *that he was sick*.

6. Some intransitive verbs are followed by an object of kindred signification (82, 10).

Ex.—He ran a *race*. She dreamed a *dream*.

7. The object of the active verb becomes the subject of the passive.

Ex.—Romulus founded *Rome*, = *Rome* was founded by Romulus.

8. To avoid ambiguity, the object should be placed after the verb, especially when the subject and the object are both nouns.

Ex.—"Alexander conquered *Darius*,"—not "Alexander *Darius* conquered."

When the subject or the object is a pronoun, the form usually determines the relation; as, "*Him* followed his next mate."

9. The following copulative verbs, *make*, *appoint*, *elect*, *create*,

constitute, render, name, style, call, esteem, think, consider, regard, reckon, and some others, not only take after them a direct object, but predicate of it another object, which may, therefore, be called its *attribute.* The attributive object may be either a *noun,* an *adjective,* or a *verb.*

Ex.—They made *him* an *officer.* They made *him sick.* They made *him labor.*

Though it is evident that the attributive object, when a noun, denotes the same person or thing as the first, it is by no means in apposition with it. In the case of apposition, the principal noun completes the meaning of the verb, and the second limits the first; as, "They called *Miles,* the *carpenter.*" But in the case of two objects (the object and its attribute) both are necessary to complete the meaning of the verb; as, "They called *Miles a carpenter.*" In one case, the second noun has no grammatical relation to the verb; in the other, it is directly related both to the verb and to the first noun. In the first example, "*carpenter*" should be parsed as a noun in the objective, put in apposition with the first, by Rule VI. In the second example, "*carpenter*" should be parsed as a noun in the objective, forming, in connection with "*Miles,*" the object of "*called,*" being also an *attribute* to the first object. In a similar way parse "*sick,*" and "*labor,*" in the above examples; or, one may be called the *first* or *principal,* and the other the *attributive,* object of the verb.

REMARK.—This construction, in many instances, may be traced to an abridged proposition, in which the infinitive has been dropped; as, "They considered *him a poet,*" that is, *to be a poet.* In fact, the infinitive of the copula is often expressed, the first object representing, in the objective, what was the subject nominative, the second, in like manner, what was the predicate nominative, before the proposition was abridged; as, " I knew that *he* was a *scholar;*" " I knew *him* to be a *scholar.*" In such cases the infinitive and the second noun form the attributive object of the verb, the second noun being in the objective after "*to be.*" Some verbs, as *say, announce, hope,* and others, take only the full form of the proposition; others, as *believe, know, think,* and many others, admit either the full or the abridged form; while others, as *compel, constrain,* and others, take only the abridged form; as, " I *say* that he did it,"—never, *him to do it;* "I *believe* that he is honest," = him to be honest; " They compelled *him to go,*"—never, *that he should go.*

10. An *infinitive* may be the second or attributive object; the first object being its subject, and the two together forming a kind of abridged proposition.

Ex.—They ordered *the soldiers to march.* They ordered *that the soldiers should march* (**167,** Mod. 16).

11. The following verbs, *buy, sell, play, sing, get, lend, draw, send, make, pass, write, pour, give, teach, leave, bring, tell, do, present, throw, carry, ask, show, order, promise, refuse, deny, provide,* and some

others, take after them, besides a *direct* object, an *indirect* object, showing *to* or *from* what the action tends.

Ex.—Give *me* a book.

12. The indirect object sometimes, though with doubtful propriety, becomes the subject of the passive verb.

Ex.—He was asked his *opinion.* I was taught *grammar.*

Opinion and *grammar* are in the objective case after a passive verb, properly governed by some preposition understood.

13. Instead of a single word, or an infinitive, a substantive clause may become one of the objects.

Ex.—He informed *me that the boat had sailed.*

188. Exercise.

1. *In the following examples, analyze the sentences, and parse the nouns and the pronouns in the objective:*—

Ambition makes the same mistake concerning power that avarice makes concerning wealth. If you have performed an act of great and disinterested virtue, conceal it. (Imperial Rome governed the bodies of men, but did not extend her empire farther) In former times, patriots prided themselves on their own poverty and the riches of the state. He endeavored to inculcate right principles. He sought to follow the example of the good. They say that they have bought it. The truly great consider, first, how they may gain the approbation of God. He inquired, "Who comes there?"

MODEL I.—"Thou hast delivered me from the strivings of the people; and thou hast made me the head of the heathen."—*Psalm* xviii. 43.

This is a compound sentence, consisting of two coördinate parts, connected by "and." The first is a simple sentence, having "thou" for its subject, and "hast delivered" for its simple and "hast delivered me from the strivings of the people" for its complex predicate. (Point out all the modifications of the simple predicate.)

The second component part is also a simple sentence, having "thou" for its subject, "hast made" for its simple and "hast made me the head of the heathen" for its complex predicate. The simple predicate "hast made" is modified by "me the head of the heathen," an objective element, consisting of "me," the *direct*, and "the head of the heathen," the *attributive* object, both together forming a double object, used to complete the meaning of "hast made."

Me is a personal pronoun, of the first person, singular number, masculine gender, and in the objective case, and in the first clause is the object of "hast delivered," according to Rule VIII.; and in the second, the leading or direct object of "hast made."

Head is a common noun, third person, &c., and is the *attributive* object of "hast made," "me head," combined, being the double object, according to Rule VIII. a.

In the same manner parse **him,** and **to write,** in the sentence, "I commanded *him to write.*"

MODEL II.—"He gave me a promise."

"He" is the subject, and "gave" the simple and "gave me a promise" the complex predicate; "gave" is limited by "me" and "promise,"—the latter a direct and the former an indirect object of "gave." Let the learner parse each, and give Rule VIII. b, and Rule VIII.

2. *Construct examples of your own to illustrate the object after transitive verbs.*

189. Adverbs as Modifiers.

1. **Rule IX.**—**Adverbs** are used to limit verbs, participles, adjectives, and other adverbs.

Ex.—Lightning moves *swiftly.* He advanced, walking *slowly.* The night was *very* dark. The sound was heard *very* distinctly.

2. Some adverbs, instead of modifying any particular word, are either independent, or are used to modify an entire proposition: these are *yes, no, nay, amen, likewise, truly,* &c.

Ex.—Will you go? *Yes. Truly,* God is good to Israel.

3. An adverb or adverbial expression should be placed so near the word which it limits, as to make its relation obvious: yet no element of the sentence can be so easily transposed without causing ambiguity, as the adverbial. It may be placed at the beginning, in the middle, or at the end of the sentence.

Ex.—He *carefully* examined the document, = *Carefully* did he examine the document. He examined the document *carefully.*

4. Adverbs are used sometimes to limit the meaning of a preposition, sometimes of a phrase.

Ex.—He held his hand *exactly over* the place. We were absent *almost* a year.

5. Adverbs are themselves sometimes modified by *phrases* or *clauses.*

Ex.—He left *four years afterwards.* He came *some time ago.* He ran *faster* than his brother.

6. *What,* equivalent to *partly,* is sometimes used as an adverb (**75,** 7). *Once* = one time, is often used as a noun.

Ex.—Excuse me for this *once.*

So, also, *when, now,* and *then* are used as nouns; as, " Until *now ;*" "Since *then;*" " Since *when.*"

7. Conjunctive adverbs are complex words usually modifying two words, and at the same time joining an adverbial clause to the word on which it depends.

Ex.—We shall be present *when* the boat arrives (**135,** 2).

CAUTION I.—*Two negatives should never be employed to express a negation;* as, " I have *no* book,"—not " I *haven't no* book."

CAUTION II.—*Avoid the use of an adverb when the quality of an object, and not the manner of an action, is to be expressed;* as, " The apple tastes *sweet*,"—not " tastes *sweetly.*"

CAUTION III.—*Avoid the use of* NO, *to express negation, with a verb or a participle;* as, " I shall not change my course of action, whether you do or *not*,"—not "whether you do or *no.*"

CAUTION IV.—*Never use* HOW *before* THAT, *or instead of it; as,* " He said *that* he should come,"—not " *how* he should come," nor " *how that* he should come."

190. Exercise.

1. *Analyze the sentences, and parse the adverbs, in the following examples:*—

You both are truly welcome. Speak softly, for a breath might wake her. Yet we may strongly trust his skill. How heavily her fate must weigh her down! Freely to give reproof, and thankfully to receive it, is an indispensable condition of true friendship. How happy they who wake no more! How soon man's earthly enjoyments pass away! How easily are men diverted from a good cause!

MODEL I.—"Burke was deeply hurt."—*Macaulay.*

Analyze the sentence, and parse *deeply* thus:—

Deeply is an adverb,—comp. *deeply, more deeply, most deeply,*—and is used to limit "was hurt," by Rule IX. (Repeat it.)

2. *Construct examples of your own to illustrate the uses of the adverb.*

191. Case Independent and Interjection.

1. **Rule X.**—The nominative case **independent,** and the **interjection,** have no grammatical relation to the other parts of the sentence.

A noun or a pronoun may be independent,—

(*a.*) By **direct address.**

Ex.—*Plato,* thou reasonest well.

(*b.*) By mere **exclamation.**

Ex.—O wretched *man* that I am!

(*c.*) By **pleonasm,** or when the attention is drawn to an object before any thing is said of it.

Ex.—Harry's *flesh,* it fell away. *Gad,* a troop shall overcome him.

(*d.*) As **subject of an abridged proposition,** when, in connection with a *participle,* it is equivalent to a proposition of which it was the subject before the former was abridged.

Ex.—*He having arrived,* we returned.

(*e.*) As **predicate in an abridged proposition,** when it follows the *infinitive* or the *participle* of the copula and is uncontrolled by a preceding noun.

Ex.—I was not aware of his being a *scholar.* To be a *scholar* requires industry and perseverance.

In the last two cases the *noun* is said to be **absolute,** and the group of words to which it belongs, including the participle or the infinitive, has some connection with the rest of the sentence.

2. In the case of the *nominative absolute*,—that is, the nominative preceding a participle,—sometimes the *noun* or the *pronoun* is understood, and sometimes the participle.

Ex.—" Properly *speaking*, there is no such thing as cold;" that is, "*we*, or *one*, speaking properly." "This *done*, and all is safe;" that is, *being done.* " This matter at an end, we will proceed;" *being at an end.*

Both of the last two cases result from abridging a dependent clause. The abridged construction may usually be restored to a complete proposition.

192. Exercise.

1. *Analyze the following sentences, and parse the interjections and the cases independent:—*

Fair daffodils! we weep to see you haste away so soon. O day most calm, most bright! With thee, sweet Hope, resides the heavenly light. A horse! a horse! my kingdom for a horse! The pilgrim fathers! where are they? He having given us the direction, we departed. I was not aware of his being the preacher. O the times! O the manners! Ah, father! these are wondrous words. The savage rocks have drunk thy blood, my brother!

MODEL I.—"Alack! alack! Edmund, I like not this unnatural dealing."

This is a simple sentence, preceded by the interjections "Alack! Alack!" and the compellative, or the name of the person addressed. These have no part in the grammatical construction of the sentence.

"I" is the subject, and "like" the simple and "like not this unnatural dealing" the complex predicate. (Point out the limitations of the simple predicate.)

Alack is an interjection, expressive of grief, and has no dependence upon any part of the sentence, by Rule X. *a.* (Repeat it.)

Edmund is a proper noun, second person, singular number, and nominative case independent by direct address. Rule X. See *a.*

MODEL II.—" But, O vain boast!
       Who can control his fate?"—*Shakspeare.*

Boast is a common noun, third person, singular number, neuter gender, and nominative case independent by exclamation. Rule X. See *b*.

Model III.—"Gad,—a troop shall overcome him."—*Bible*.

Gad is a proper noun, third, sing., masc., nom. independent by pleonasm. Rule X. See *c*.

Model IV.—"The war having ended, the army was disbanded."

For the analysis of this case, see **174**, 1, Model III.

War is a common noun, third, sing., neut., nominative absolute with the participle "having ended." Rule X. See *d*.

Model V.—"He was displeased on account of my being a friend to his enemy."

For analysis, see **176**, 1, Model III.

Friend is a common noun, &c., and is in the nominative absolute by Rule X. See *e*.

2. *Construct examples to illustrate the use of the interjections and cases independent.*

193. Coördinate Conjunctions.

1. **Rule XI.**—**Coördinate** conjunctions are used to connect similar elements.

Ex.—*Abraham, Isaac,* AND *Jacob* were Jewish patriarchs.

2. These conjunctions are used only when the parts connected are of the same *rank* (**153**, 2, 3), and not even then unless there is some *similarity* or *contrast* in the thoughts or ideas expressed by the united parts.

Thus, when two thoughts are uttered, as, "The king sat upon his throne," "The south wind is blowing gently," they may hold the same rank as independent sentences, but, being wholly unlike in meaning, they cannot blend into one sentence. So, again, the adjective elements "old," and "brown," in the expression "That *old brown* house," are of the same rank, but do not express kindred ideas. Compare with these, "We have much to do, AND our time is short;" "A *wise* AND *patriotic* sovereign."

3. When the connection between two similar coördinate thoughts or ideas is to be made close, or one is to be made more emphatic

than the other, two conjunctions are used,—the one corresponding with the other, and both combining to form the connection.

Ex.—The prince is *both* virtuous *and* wise. He *not only* reads Shakspeare's plays, *but* he appreciates them.

4. Sometimes a thought or an idea sustains a double relation to another, the one simply *coördinate*, the other *causal, illative, concessive, augmentative, ordinative, partitive*, &c. The former is represented by the simple coördinate conjunction (sometimes understood) placed between the coördinate parts, and the latter by a connective (sometimes adverbial in its nature) associated with it.

Ex.—The south wind blows, [*and*] *therefore* there must be rain. She sings; [and,] *besides*, she plays beautifully.

5. When the coördinate thought or idea is purely causal, the causal or illative conjunction expresses the whole connection.

Ex.—The tree is falling, *therefore* run, = Run, *for* the tree is falling.

6. When correlatives are employed, the principal conjunction is usually placed at the beginning of the second or added clause, and its correlative is placed in the first, to give the reader or hearer an intimation of what is to follow.

Ex.—Whether the truth of the matter will ever be discovered *or* not is very doubtful.

Sometimes (inelegantly, however) *either* or *neither* is placed at the end of the sentence.

Ex.—I can not go, *nor* you *neither*, = *Neither* you *nor* I can go.

CAUTION I.—*In a series of coördinate terms, unless great emphasis is required, insert the conjunction between the last two only.* Say, "*Peter, James, and John,*"—not "*Peter, and James, and John.*"

CAUTION II.—*In using correlatives, be careful to place both conjunctions so as to mark correctly the prominent or contrasted terms.* Say, "He was *not only* poor, *but* idle,"—instead of "*Not only* was he poor, *but* idle."

CAUTION III —*Avoid dissimilar and disproportionate coördinate constructions.* Say, "I saw him *enter* the gate and *ring* the bell,"— not "I saw him *entering* the gate, and *ring* the bell."

194. Exercise.

1. *Analyze the following sentences, and parse the conjunctions:—*

Clouds and darkness are round about him; righteousness and judgment are the habitation of his throne. They were united both by ties of friendship and of kindred. I am debtor both to the Greeks and to the barbarians. The country was wasted,—partly by war, partly by famine, and partly by pestilence. The relations of the teacher will be treated as threefold: first, to his pupils, secondly, to his school officers, and thirdly, to the parents. A hero on the day of battle has sacrificed a meal, and shall we therefore pity him? The situation is not suited to his tastes; the compensation, moreover, is meagre. They have indeed honored them with their praise, but they have disgraced them with their pity. Not only can he gain no lofty improvement without labor, but without it he can gain no tolerable happiness.

MODEL I.—"Talent has many a compliment from the bench, but tact touches fees from attorneys and clients."— *London Atlas.*

This is a compound sentence, consisting of two coördinate principal clauses. They are related by contrast (193, 2), and hence readily unite to form one sentence. Let the learner analyze each separately.

But is an adversative coördinate conjunction, and used to join the second clause to the first, by Rule XI.

Here *but* is coördinate to join clauses of equal rank. It is adversative, since the clauses are not in harmony with each other, but the second restricts the thought expressed by the first, by shutting off or opposing any such inference as that the mere preëminence of talent with the *bench* implies universal preëminence. It also shows that the writer intended, by the contrast, to bring the second thought into greater prominence than the first.

And, in the second clause, is a copulative coördinate conjunction, and is used to unite the two elements "from attorneys and [from] clients," by Rule XI.

These two phrases are similar in form, similar in the ideas expressed, equal in rank, equal in emphasis, and in perfect harmony with each other. Hence they require not only a coördinate but a copulative conjunction.

MODEL II.—"The wolves have been exterminated, and therefore the flocks and herds are unmolested."

This is a compound sentence, containing two coördinate clauses, —the second being a partial compound. Let the learner analyze both clauses.

And, in the first case, is a copulative coördinate conjunction, joining the two clauses, as grammatically equal and in harmony with each other, by Rule XI.

Therefore is a causal coördinate conjunction, and is used to show that the second clause is a logical deduction from the first. It combines with "and" to join the two clauses,—the one grammatically, the other logically, but both coördinately, by Rule XI.

And, in the second clause, is a copulative coördinate conjunction, and is used to join the two subjects "flocks" and "herds," by Rule XI.

2. *Construct or select other sentences containing coördinate conjunctions, and explain their use.*

195. Coördinate Constructions.

1. **Rule XII.**—When a verb or a pronoun relates to two or more nouns connected by a coördinate conjunction,—

(*a.*) If it agrees with them taken **conjointly**, it must be in the *plural number*.

(*b.*) But if it agrees with them taken **separately**, it must be of the same number as the noun which stands next to it.

(*c.*) If it agrees with *one*, and *not* the other, it must take the number of that one.

Ex.—Charles and his sister *were* absent, but *they* were sent for. Charles or his sister *was* absent. Charles or his sisters *were* absent. Charles, and not his sister, *was* absent.

2. In the following cases, nouns in the singular *seem* to be taken conjointly, and yet the verb and the pronoun should be singular:—

(*a.*) When the coördinate nouns denote the *same* person in *different* capacities.

Ex.—This great *statesman* and *orator* died lamented by all *his* friends.

(*b.*) When the coördinate nouns are considered *separately*, by means of such limiting words as *each, every,* or *no*.

Ex.—*Each* day and *each* hour *brings its* own duties and trials. *Every* book and *every* paper *was* taken from *its* place. *No* book and *no* paper should be left out of *its* place.

(*c.*) When the coördinate nouns are distinguished with emphasis by means of *not, only, too, as well as,* or when there is an emphatic enumeration of individuals.

Ex.—George, and *not* James, *is* at *his* task. Truth, and truth *only*, *is* worth seeking for *its* own sake. The man, and his servant *too*, *was* re warded. The father, *as well as* his son, *was* in fault. Thine *is* the kingdom, and the power, and the glory.

(*d*.) When the coördinate nouns are regarded by the mind as representing *one thing*.

Ex.—Bread and milk *is* excellent food for children. The horse and chaise *is* in *its* place.

3. When the coördinate parts are of *different persons*, the verb or the pronoun agrees with the first rather than the second, and with the second rather than the third.

Ex.—*Thou* and *thy* sons with thee (that is, *ye*) shall bear the iniquity of *your* priesthood. *John, thou,* and *I* (that is, *we*) are attached to *our* country.

4. When the coördinate parts are each *singular*, and of *different genders*,—

(1.) The *verb* may relate to them *conjointly*, while the *pronoun* may relate to but one.

Ex.—*James* and his *sister were* destroying *her* bonnet. *James* and his *sister were* destroying *his* cap.

(2.) The *pronoun* may relate to them taken *conjointly*, while the *verb* relates to them taken separately.

Ex.—"*James* or his *sister has* destroyed *their* dictionary,"—the dictionary being theirs by a joint ownership.

(3.) If the *pronoun* has a common reference to both coördinate nouns taken *conjointly*, the gender cannot be distinguished by the pronoun, since the latter is plural, and consequently has, in English, the same form for all genders.

(4.) If the *pronoun* refers to two or more coördinate nouns taken *separately*, there is no personal pronoun, in English, applicable to each, and there is an inherent difficulty in constructing the expression properly.

Ex.—John or Ellen has lost *his* or *her* pencil.

To use *his* alone, or *her* alone, would reveal the ownership, which is supposed to be unknown. Hence it does not avail to say that the *masculine* is preferred to the *feminine*, and the *feminine* to the *neuter;* for either would become explicit, as in case 4, (1), above. To avoid this difficulty, it is best to recast the sentence, or so construct it as to escape such a dilemma. Yet, contrary to the general rule (**177**, 5), frequent instances occur in which the pronoun, in such cases, is put in the *plural*, and thus the gender is concealed; as, "Then shalt thou bring forth that *man* or that *woman* unto thy gates, and shalt stone *them* with stones, till *they* shall die."

5. When each of the coördinate parts is denoted by the *same* word, and that a singular noun referring to different objects, and each, except the last, is understood,—being represented by some modifying word,—the agreement of the verb or the pronoun follows the general rule.

Ex.—" A Webster's, a Worcester's, and a Richardson's *dictionary were* consulted;" that is, three dictionaries. A literary, a scientific, a wealthy, and a poor man *were* assembled in one room.

6. Coördinate terms are taken separately when one is affirmative and the other negative, or when one is opposed to, or contrasted with, the others: in such cases, if both or all the terms are plural, the pronoun or the verb must, of course, be plural. When a verb or a pronoun relates to two coördinate terms, connected by *as well as, save, but, but not,* or *and not,* it should agree with the former, and be understood with the latter, whatever be its number.

Ex.—The minutest insect, *as well as* the largest quadruped, derives its life from the same omnipotent source. None *but* he can heal the malady of the soul. There was no stranger with us in the house, *save* we two.

7. Two terms may be coördinate logically but not grammatically.

Ex.—*Godliness* with *contentment* is great gain, = *Godliness* and *contentment*, &c.

In such cases the verb or the pronoun should agree with the term to which it refers grammatically.

196. Exercise.

1. *Analyze the following sentences, and point out and parse the verbs and the pronouns which illustrate the rule:—*

Where was it when winds and clouds were his only visitors, and when the sun and blue heavens by day, and the moon and stars by night, alone looked down and beheld it; the same as they behold it now? One day the poor woman and her idiot boy were missed from the market-place. Neither his vote, his influence, nor his purse was ever withheld from the cause in which he had engaged. Neither the captain nor the sailors were saved. Whether one person or more were concerned in the business, does not appear. Every insect, and every bird, was hushed to silence.

Note.—For models, see **178**, 1, and **180**, 1, Models II. and III.

2. *Construct or select other examples to illustrate this rule.*

197. Prepositions.

1. **Rule XIII.**—A **preposition** is used to show the relation of its object to the word on which the object depends.

Ex.—George *went* INTO the *garden*. A life *of* virtue is a life *of* happiness.

2. The noun or the pronoun following the preposition is always dependent on some term,—usually a *preceding* one,—and the preposition is used to *show* that dependence.

Properly speaking, the objective is not the object of the preposition, but of the preceding term. In the case of the transitive verb, there are two terms,—the verb itself, and the objective,—and the relation between them is closer than between those in which the preposition is used; the objective is not called the *object* of that relation, but rather of the antecedent term, the verb. Yet custom makes the noun the *object* of the preposition.

3. Sometimes the antecedent term is omitted, and sometimes the subsequent.

Ex.—*In a word*, he is ruined, = To express all *in a word*, &c. "He looked *around*" (supply *him*).

When the object is understood, the preposition is usually parsed as an adverb.

4. *For*, used before an infinitive and its objective subject, when the group is taken as the subject of a proposition, has no antecedent term.

Ex.—*For* him to lie is base.

The *to* of the infinitive, when both together constitute the subject, represents no relation to an antecedent term; as, "*To* lie is base."

5. *Between* and *betwixt* refer to two objects; *among* and *amongst*, to more than two.

Ex.—He walked *between* the trees (two trees). He walked *among* the trees (many trees).

6. Sometimes the preposition is involved in the antecedent term, or at least is suggested by it.

Ex.—*Near* [*to*]; *like* [*to*]. *Near* the lake where drooped the willow.

REMARK.—When the preposition is placed at the beginning of a sentence, or when, with its object, it precedes the antecedent term of the relation which it shows, the relation may be easily discovered by rearranging the sentence. Thus, *"Of all the topics involved in this theme, it will be impossible for me to speak,"* = It will be impossible for me to *speak of* all the *topics,* &c.

CAUTION.—*In expressing the relations between words, be careful to employ appropriate prepositions.* Say, "That is different *from* what I expected,"—not "different *to* what I expected."

These relations may be found in any good dictionary.

198. Exercise.

1. *Analyze the following sentences, and parse the prepositions:—*

I call to you with all my voice. From end to end, from cliff to lake, 'twas free. Her tears were now flowing without control. She is like some tender tree, the pride and beauty of the grove,—graceful in its form, bright in its foliage, but with the worm preying at its heart.

MODEL.—" Of all his errors, the most serious was, perhaps, the choice of a champion," = " The most serious [error] of all his errors was, perhaps, the choice of a champion."

Analyze and parse *of*.

"*Of*" is a preposition, and in the first instance shows the relation of "errors" to "error" understood; in the second instance it shows the relation of "champion" to "choice." Rule XIII. (Repeat it.)

2. *Construct examples of your own to illustrate the use of the preposition when the antecedent term is a* NOUN, *an* ADJECTIVE, *a* VERB, *an* ADVERB.

199. The Object of the Preposition.

1. **Rule XIV.**—A noun or a pronoun used as the **object** of a preposition must be in the objective case.

Ex.—The ruins of the *Parthenon* stand upon the *Acropolis* in the *city* of *Athens.*

(*a.*) Before nouns in the objective, denoting *time, measure, distance, quantity, value,* or *direction,* and before such as follow *near, nigh, like,* and *worth,* the preposition is usually omitted.

Ex.—The wall is six *feet* high. We walked twenty *miles* that *day*. He helped a worthy man, and is not a *penny* poorer. My friend has gone *West*. He is like his *father*. They live near the *city*. The book is worth a *dollar*.

2. The preposition is omitted as in **187, 3**; and in dates there is usually an omission of several prepositions.

Ex.—[At] Boston, [on] Monday, [on] the 10th [of] February, [in the year] 1860.

REMARK.—The word *worth* is by some called a preposition; but it can be predicated of a noun like an adjective, and may be qualified by an adverb; and, what is more, it expresses an *idea* of quality, rather than a *relation* between words; as, "The lesson is *well worth* learning;" "It is *richly worth* the money." *Worth* is sometimes a noun, and sometimes a verb; as, "The *worth* of a dollar;" "A person of great *worth;*" "Woe *worth* the day!" In this last example, *worth* is a verb in the imperative, equivalent to *be to*, and day is the indirect object of it.

3. *But* and *save*, in the sense of "except," are generally used as prepositions.

Ex.—Whence all *but him* had fled.

Yet they are not unfrequently used as conjunctions; as, "Neither knoweth any man the Father, *save* the Son, and *he* to whomsoever the Son will reveal him."

4. Prepositions are sometimes followed by *adjectives*, or *adverbs* used substantively, with which they form adverbial phrases; as, *in vain, on high, for this once, till now, from thence, from above.*

5. *Than* before *whom* has been erroneously supposed by some to be a preposition.

Ex.—*Than whom* none higher sat.

Than is no more a preposition here than in case of any other proper use of the word. It denotes comparison, and the construction requires that it should be followed by the nominative, instead of the objective *whom*. Though used by some good writers, it should be avoided as anomalous. In this case it should be disposed of by saying that it is the objective by the figure enallage (**216, 7**).

CAUTION.—*Never use the nominative as the object of a preposition.* Say, "Between you and *me*,"—not "between you and *I*."

200. Exercise.

1. *Analyze the following examples, and parse the prepositions and their objects:—*

A similar improvement may be made of the memory of our good deeds. What ground of hope is there so sure to his spirit, next to the mercy of his God and the intercession of Christ his Saviour? It was not long before he returned with his man, whom he introduced to me as a person of exceeding honesty; and we went into the yard all together.

MODEL.—"*We live in an age of sifting.*"—*Neander.*
Let the learner analyze this sentence.

Age is a common noun, third, sing., neut., obj., and is the object of the preposition "in." (Rule XIV.)

Sifting is a participial noun, in the objective case, and is used as the object of the preposition "of." (Rule XIV.)

2. *Construct examples in which any of the prepositions* (140) *shall join adjective or adverbial phrases.*

3. *Change the phrases consisting of a preposition and its object, into equivalent* ADJECTIVES *or* ADVERBS:—

The dew *of the morning* has passed away. The temple *of Solomon* was destroyed by the Chaldean monarch. The messenger was sent *in haste.* The laborer entered upon his task *with eagerness.* The waves dash upon the rocks *with fury.*

201. Subordinate Connectives.

1. **Rule XV.**—**Subordinate** connectives are used to join dissimilar elements.

Ex.—He *that* hath pity on the poor lendeth to the Lord.

2. Subordinate connectives, unlike coördinate, show a relation of dependence, and are used to join, not clauses of equal rank, but dependent clauses to an antecedent term, which they serve to modify, except as below (3).

3. *That, whether,* or the various interrogatives, *when, where,* &c., when used to introduce a substantive clause employed as the subject of a proposition, do not connect the clause to an antecedent

term, since the subject can be subordinate to no other part of the proposition.

The connectives thus used serve to convert a principal proposition into a subordinate substantive proposition, which, like any noun, may be used as the subject.

4. In many cases the subordinate connective has a corresponding word in the principal clause, called the correlative.

Ex.—*Then*—*when, there*—*where, if*—*then, though*—*yet, so*—*that, so*—*as, as*—*as, the, this, that, these, those*—*who, that,* or *which.*

5. Though a subordinate conjunction appropriately joins a *clause* to some preceding term, yet *than* and *as* sometimes appear to connect *words* only.

Ex.—Less *judgment* than *wit*, is more *sail* than *ballast.* The *moon* as *satellite* attends.

Though this connection seems to resemble coördinate, the terms joined are not of the same rank. *As* has a peculiar use when thus employed to connect an attribute, either predicated or assumed, to the noun to which it belongs: it not only gives emphasis, but expresses the idea of *capacity* or *office;* as, "He was employed *as* clerk." "The fruit was considered *as* good." "He offered himself *as* printer." "I do not respect your rules *as such.*" "What is a pronoun *as* distinguished from a noun?"

6. *Than* or *as*, when used to show comparison, instead of connecting words only, generally introduces an elliptical clause, which becomes so on account of the similarity of its construction to that of the principal clause.

Ex.—"He is more nice *than* wise;" that is, "than *he is* wise." "He is *as* old *as* his cousin;" that is, "as his cousin *is old.*"

Sometimes the subsequent term is not only elliptical, but abridged; as, "The patient is *so* well *as* to sit up;" that is, "so well *as that he can* sit up." The boy knows better *than* to disobey (**167**, Mod. 16, Ex.).

7. *As*, following an adjective, and sometimes a noun, and without a correlative, gives an adversative signification to the subordinate clause.

Ex.—*Defenceless as* we were, we still maintained our ground, = Though we were defenceless, &c.

8. *That* or *as*, after a noun, has a similar construction to denote *concession.*

Ex.—*Fool* that [or *as*] I was, I entered the army.

REMARK.—Subordinate connectives are a kind of *preposition* placed before a sentence which is to be converted into a *noun*, an *adjective*, or an *adverb*. Hence their position is almost invariably at the head of the clause (*pre*-position).

CAUTION.—*In using a noun or a pronoun in an elliptical clause following* THAN *or* AS, *avoid both ambiguity and an incorrect construction.* Say, "My brother is older than *I*,"—not "*than me.*"

There is danger of ambiguity only when two *different* cases occur in the principal clause; as, "Lovest *thou me* more than *these?*" that is, "more than these love me," or, "more than thou lovest these."

202. Exercise.

1. *Analyze the following examples, and parse the connectives:*—

While there is life there is hope. However friendly he might appear, his heart was full of anger. Whether the moon has an atmosphere, has not been ascertained. He that plants trees loves others beside himself. What comes from the heart goes to the heart. Time will bring to light whatever is hidden. The more we serve God, the better we serve ourselves. As far as the eye could see, all was ruin and desolation. Work as long as you can. The more one has, the more he requires. Revenge always costs more than it is worth. That you may be loved, be deserving of love.

MODEL I.—"If we draw within the circle of our contemplation the mothers of a civilized nation, what do we see?"—*Webster.*

This is a complex interrogative sentence, consisting of a principal and a subordinate clause.

We is the subject of the principal clause, and **do see** is the simple predicate. "*Do see*" is limited by the interrogative "*what*," and by the conditional clause "*If we draw,*" &c.

If is a subordinate connective, and joins the subordinate clause, which it introduces, to the predicate of the principal clause. These elements are dissimilar in *rank*, in *meaning*, and in *form;* they are connected by Rule XV. (Repeat it.)

MODEL II.—"As ye have therefore received Christ Jesus the Lord, so walk ye in him."

Therefore, in this complex sentence, is a coördinate conjunction, joining the whole sentence, as an inference, to a preceding sentence.

SYNTAX—THE INFINITIVE. 255

As is a subordinate connective, having as its correlative the adverb **so** in the principal clause. It joins the subordinate clause, "As ye have therefore received," &c., to "walk." Rule XV.

2. *Construct examples in which any of the* RELATIVE PRONOUNS *shall join adjective clauses* (**143**, 17),—*others in which* THAT, THAT NOT, *or any of the interrogatives, shall join substantive clauses* (**143**, 16),—*and still others in which any of the connectives* (**143**, 18) *shall join adverbial clauses.*

203. The Infinitive.

1. **Rule XVI.**—The **infinitive** has the construction of the *noun*, with the signification and limitations of the verb, and, when dependent, is governed by the word which it limits.

Ex.—*To err* is human. They desire *to travel in a foreign country*. He wishes *to obtain a treatise on the deposition of dew.*

(*a.*) After the active voice of *bid, dare, let, need, make, see, behold, hear,* and *feel,* and some others, the **to** of the infinitive is omitted.

Ex.—I saw him *do* it. They let him *go*.

REMARK 1.—The infinitive is properly the simple *name* of the verb, and, as such, was originally used without a preposition, as subject or object, in a proposition. Of these uses, we have the *form* of one only remaining, namely, that of object after the auxiliaries (**111**, 4); as, "shall *write*," "will *read*," "do *love*," &c. But here the principal verb has lost its original character,—has become an auxiliary, a mere index of *time* and *mode*,—and the infinitive is changed from object to attribute.

REMARK 2.—The infinitive, as now recognized in the language, is the dative case of the ancient infinitive; or the simple infinitive with the preposition *to* prefixed. The two words are so united as to be regarded as an inseparable phrase; as, "*To live* is Christ, and *to die* is gain."

2. The infinitive may be used with or without a subject (**167**, 3).

Ex.—We wish *you to stay*. We wish *to stay*.

3. The infinitive may have a **subject** in the **objective**, when its subject has not already been expressed in the sentence.

Ex.—They ordered *him to leave.*

(*a.*) The infinitive of the copula or of any copulative verb may also have a **predicate objective.**

Ex.—I knew *him* to be a *preacher.* Let *him* be called *Nathan.*

(*b.*) The infinitive, and its subject, may be the **subject** of a proposition; the phrase must then be introduced by *for.*

Ex.—*For you to deceive* is criminal. For *him* to be a *scholar* is impossible.

(*c.*) The infinitive and its subject may be made the **object** of a transitive verb, or of the preposition *for.*

Ex.—He ordered *the horse to be harnessed.* They considered *him* [to be] a *traitor.* They appointed *him* [to be] *chairman.* They ordered some water *for the boy to drink.*

4. When the subject has already been expressed or is not required, the infinitive is used without a subject, and may be,—

(*a.*) The **subject** of a proposition.

Ex.—*To retaliate* is censurable.

(*b.*) The **attribute** of a proposition without the sign **to** (III, 4).

Ex.—I do *love.* They may *learn.*

(*c.*) The **attribute** of a proposition with **to** prefixed.

Ex.—To obey is *to enjoy.*

When the infinitive is thus used, it denotes,—(1.) An *equivalent* term; as, "To pray is *to supplicate.*" (2.) What is *possible* or *obligatory;* as, "The passage *is to be found;*" "Our duty *is to be done.*" (3.) What is settled or determined upon; as, "The work *is to commence to-morrow.*"

(*d.*) The **object** of a transitive verb, a preposition, or it may be used to complete the meaning of some intransitive verbs.

Ex.—He wishes *to remain.* They are about *to go.* She went *to weep.*

(*e.*) An **adjective element** or **noun in apposition,** limiting another noun.

Ex.—Time *to come.* A desire *to go.* A hope *to recover.* A wish *to stay.*

(*f.*) An **adverbial** element used to denote **purpose** or **motive.**

Ex.—What went ye out *to see?*

In this use the infinitive is sometimes said (though perhaps not properly) to be absolute; as, "*To confess the truth,* I was in fault," = *That I may confess the truth,* I was in fault.

(g.) To denote a **result**, after **too, than, so — as.**

Ex.—He is *too* proud *to beg.* He is wiser *than to attempt* such an enterprise. Be *so* good *as to hear* me.

5. The infinitive is often understood.

Ex.—They considered him [to be] upright.

CAUTION I.—*The preposition* **for** *should never be used before the infinitive employed to express* **motive** or **purpose**; *also, the sign* **to** *should not be used at the close of a sentence.* Say, "He went *to see*,"—not "*for* to see." "He spoke, or intended to speak,"—not "He spoke, or intended to."

CAUTION II.—*Do not use the perfect for the present infinitive.* Say, "It was your duty to *warn him*,"—not "*to have warned him.*"

204. Exercise.

1. *Analyze the following sentences, and parse the infinitives:—*

I have brought a book for you to read. Johnson declared wit to consist in finding out resemblances. These passages prove that materialists will sometimes find Hume to be a very dangerous ally. For him to assert and deny the same sentiment on different pages is proof of the instability of his opinions. It was well for him to die at his post, with his armor on. I heard him repeat whole pages of poetry. Few things are more destructive to the best interests of society than the prevalent but mistaken notion that it requires a vast deal of talent to be a successful knave. It is a disgrace to be the author of such a report. To take away the benevolent affections from the moral world would be like extinguishing the sun from the natural. I love to roam over the green fields. He seems to think the rule inapplicable to his case. They appear to rest upon the solid earth. A desire to see his face once more induced us to attempt the journey. The work is to be commenced to-morrow. To be good is to be happy. They remained to see what was to be done. He was too feeble to write a letter. Will you be so good as to pass me that book?

MODEL I.—"To see the sun is pleasant."

Analyze the sentence, and parse *to see* thus:—

To see is an irregular transitive verb: it is the present tense of the infinitive, and is used as a noun of the third pers., sing., neut., nom., and is made the subject of the proposition. Rule XV.

Model II.—"I have heard say of thee, that thou canst understand a dream to interpret it."—*Bible.*

This complex sentence has an infinitive in each clause.

Say is an irregular transitive verb, having "of thee" for an indirect, and the subordinate clause for a direct, object; infinitive, present tense, and, with its objective subject (*men* understood), forms the object of "have heard." Rule XV. See also 5, *c*. It is put in the infinitive without the sign *to*, by Rule XVI. *a*.

To interpret is a regular transitive verb, infinitive, present, and is used to limit "canst understand" as its object, by Rule XVI. By an ancient idiom, its proper object is made the object of the principal verb, and is then pleonastically represented by "it." In modern style it would be, "understand *how to interpret a dream*," or "understand a dream *so as to interpret it.*"

2. *Construct examples of your own to illustrate the uses of the infinitive.*

205. Participles.

1. **Rule XVII.—Participles** have the construction of *adjectives* and *nouns*, and are limited like *verbs*.

Ex.—He, *stooping* down, and *looking* in, saw the linen clothes *lying;* yet went he not in. A habit of sincerity in *acknowledging* faults is a guard against *committing* them.

2. The participle used as an adjective assumes of its subject what the verb asserts.

Ex.—Hyacinths *blooming.* Hyacinths *bloom.*

(*a.*) When the participle is used wholly as an adjective (93, 2, *b*), it is called a *participial adjective*, and is placed before the noun.

Ex.—The *rising* sun. The *roaring* billows.

(*b.*) When the participle is used like an adjective, having the same signification and limitations as the verb, the participle, with the words which limit it, is then called the *participial construction.*

Ex.—*Encouraged by this magnificent invitation*, the inhabitants of the globe considered labor as their only friend.

(*c.*) The participle of the copulative verbs may be followed by the predicate nominative,—(1.) When the noun or the pronoun to which it belongs is nominative. (2.) When the noun or the pronoun to which it logically belongs is changed to the possessive.

Ex.—*He* being an accomplished *writer*. I have heard of *his* being an accomplished *writer*.

(*d.*) The participle of copulative verbs may be followed by a predicate objective when the noun or the pronoun to which it belongs is in the objective.

Ex.—We regarded *him* as being a good *writer*. He intrusted his son to a *gentleman* named *Edric*.

(*e.*) The participle, like the adjective, may be used with the copula, to form the predicate; but in this construction it is regarded as a form of the verb.

Ex.—They were *riding*. He was *deceived*.

(*f.*) Participles, such as *admitting*, *speaking*, *granting*, and others, are used, as some say, independently; more properly they belong to some noun or pronoun understood.

Ex.—Properly *speaking*, there is no such thing as chance, = *We* speaking properly, &c.

3. The participle may be used either wholly as a noun, or as a noun having the meaning and limitations of the verb.

Ex.—It is pleasant to walk at the *rising* of the sun. We should avoid *giving* pain to others.

(*a.*) The participle used wholly as a noun is preceded by an article or an adjective, and followed by *of*.

Ex.—The *sighing* of the poor. The *crying* of the needy.

In this case the participle cannot be limited, like the verb.

(*b.*) The participle having the construction of the noun, with the meaning and limitations of the verb, may be the *subject* or *predicate nominative*, or the *object* of a transitive verb or a preposition.

Ex.—*Loving* our neighbor as ourselves is *fulfilling* the law. *Stealing* is *taking* without liberty. We should avoid *breaking* a promise. On *approaching* the house, the sound of a bell was faintly heard.

(*c.*) In this construction the participle is called the *participial noun*, and, as such, may be limited by a noun or a pronoun in the possessive.

Ex.—What do you think of *his writing* a letter, — *his being* a writer?

4. The participle, like the Latin gerund, may limit the

predicate by **expressing** a *concomitant action*, yet may belong grammatically to the subject.

Ex.—They remain *standing*. He stood *amazed*. He fell at his master's feet, *weeping*.

5. The participle is often equivalent to the infinitive.

Ex.—We saw them *approaching* the shore, = *approach* the shore.

206. Exercise.

Analyze the following examples, and parse the participles:—

We expect the dancing-master to teach our children "manners," as well as the art of cutting awkward capers to music. Why is the experiment of an extended republic to be rejected? He came near being devoured by a panther. The case is well worth considering. They came upon him without his being apprized of their approach. The urchin's becoming so respectable a man surprised every one. The gentleman's reputation as a scholar was the cause of his being appointed professor of rhetoric. They narrowly escaped being taken prisoners. Being convinced of his guilt, we resolved to punish him. We descried a vessel stripped of its masts. Having declined the proposal, I determined on a course suited to my own taste. They have said, Come, and let us cut them off from being a nation. There is no doubt of his being a great statesman. The young maiden was seen standing on the shore, exposed to the merciless winds, and extending her hands towards heaven. Whom having not seen, ye love; in whom, though now ye see him not, yet, believing, ye rejoice. In avoiding one error, do not fall into another. By consulting the best authors, he became learned. Stretching from horizon to horizon, losing itself, like a limitless wall, in the clouds above, it came pouring its green and massive waters onward, while the continual and rapid crash of falling forests, and crushed cities, and uptorn mountains, thus prostrated, one after another, under its awful power, and the successive shrieks that pierced the heavens, rising even above the roar of the on-rushing ocean, as city after city, kingdom after kingdom, disappeared, produced terror and horror inconceivable, indescribable.

MODEL I.—"Immured in cypress shades a sorcerer dwells."—*Milton.*

Let the learner analyze the sentence. It is a simple sentence, or may be regarded as a contracted complex.

Immured is a passive participle, or past participle with a passive meaning (*immure, immured, immured*), and, like an adjective, belongs to "sorcerer," by Rule XVII., or Rule V.

MODEL II.—" The admiral was too desirous of presenting himself before the sovereigns to protract his stay long at Palos."—*Prescott.*

This is a simple declarative sentence. The subject is "the admiral;" the simple predicate is "was desirous," of which "was" is the copula and "desirous" the attribute. The attribute is limited by "of presenting himself before the sovereigns," an indirect objective element, complex, of which "of presenting" is the basis, "of" is the connective, and "presenting" is the object. "Presenting" is limited, first, by the objective element "himself," and second, by the complex adverbial element "before the sovereigns." "Desirous" is further limited by "too," which intimates the degree or intensity of his desire, and points, as a kind of correlative, to the phrase "to protract his stay long at Palos," used to express the result of the desire. It expresses a kind of comparison, and is equivalent to another construction with *so — as not,* thus :—so desirous *as not* to protract, &c.

Presenting is a present participle, from the verb *present* (*present, presented, presented*), used as a noun, and is the object of the preposition *of*, by Rule XIV., and is limited according to Rule XVII., like the verb "present," from which it is derived.

Construct examples of your own illustrating the various uses of the participle.

II. INCORRECT USE.

207. Incorrect Use defined.

1. The **incorrect use** of words is any violation of the laws of good usage. It is commonly called *false syntax.*

REMARK.—It must be apparent to every one that the mere rules of Syntax do not guard against some of the most glaring defects in the use of spoken or written language. To provide for some of the most obvious of these, special cautions will be given.

2. Besides a faulty construction, there may be errors in *spelling, pronunciation,* or *the use of capitals,* errors in the *application* of

words, errors arising from an improper *omission* or a *repetition* of words, from an *insertion* of unnecessary words, an improper arrangement of the parts, and errors from a neglect of any of the distinguishing marks which good usage requires.

208. Errors in Construction.—False Syntax.

1. Examples under Rule I.

You and me will go together.

Model.—"You and me will go together" is incorrect, because the objective pronoun *me* is made the subject of the verb *will go;* but, by Caution I., the objective should never be used as the subject of a finite verb. Correct, "You and I will go together."

Him that is studious will improve. She found the place sooner than us. Them that seek wisdom will be wise. They are people whom one would think might be trusted. Who told you the story? Him and her. I know it as well as him or her. Who saw the eclipse? Us. Them are the ones. My brother is a much better singer than him. We are not so much to be blamed as him that upset the boat. Who came in at the door? Me. Scotland and thee did each in other live. Avoid whomsoever is in a passion. There were present only him and me. You are in fault, and not me. I know not whom are expected.

Us boys are forming a base-ball club. Him and me are going to town this afternoon. Mary can walk faster than me. I will promote him who I think most deserving. Whom do you think called on me this morning? Not always does the world applaud him who is most deserving of praise; but him who is most successful receives the homage of men. Thee must not forget my advice. She is a lady whom I know will interest you.

2. Examples under Rule II.

It is **her**.
I took it to be **he**.
You is the second **person**.

Models.—"It is her" is incorrect, because the attribute "her" is in the objective case; but, by Caution I., the attribute of a finite verb should never be in the objective case. It should be, "It is *she*."

"I took it to be he" is incorrect, because the nominative "he" follows the infinitive "to be," preceded by its objective subject "it." By Caution I., it should be, "I took it to be *him*."

"*You* is the second person" is incorrect, because "you," being a pronoun, is not a person, and hence is falsely identified by "person." By Caution II., we should avoid such constructions. It should be, "You is *of* the second person," that is, a pronoun of the second person.

Correct, by the Cautions, not only the following examples, but any similar ones heard in conversation:—

Is it me? No; but it is him. I never thought of its being him; I took it to be she. Whom do you think it is? It may have been her, but I always supposed it to be he. Whom do people say it is? They say they do not know whom it is. Who do you think it is? I think it is them. I cannot believe it to be he. If I were him, I would know whom it is. If I had been sure of its being her, I should have been present.

The noun is the agent, and the verb is the action. What part of speech is each boy in this room? The first person is the speaker. The animal horse is a noun. To be convicted of bribery, was then a crime altogether unpardonable. *I* is the first person. "Have written" is the present perfect tense.

It was me who told you. It is not us who are in fault. If I were her, I would talk less. Whom do men say that I am? It was George that answered you, not me. They had no suspicion of its being me. They were a long time in doubt whom he might prove to be. It is us who suffer by your carelessness. It is not I, but him, you ought to blame.

3. Examples under Rule III.

Correct by **177**, 1, *a*, *b*, *and the several Cautions, the following examples, and avoid all similar errors yourself:—*

The committee were unanimous in its action. The army was badly cut up, but made good their retreat. Let every chair, every book, and every slate be put in their places. Peace and happiness are by no means granted to the rich alone; yet it is supposed by many to depend upon wealth. The president or secretary will favor us with their presence. Many words they darken speech. That girl she is very ignorant. The king he is very angry. The teacher approving the plan, he immediately adopted it. Whom when they had washed, they laid her in an upper chamber. What he said, he is now sorry for it. Let each scholar who thinks so raise their hands. A person can content themselves on small means. Let every one answer for themselves. Rebecca took goodly raiment, and put them upon Jacob. Can any one be sure that they are not deceived? Thou hast no right to be a judge, who art a party concerned. A hawk caught a hen, and eat her in her own nest. A purse was lost in the street, which contained a large sum of money. There are millions of people in the empire of China whose support is derived almost entirely from rice. I and you may go, if I and he can agree. I and you and Harriet are going. Father said that I and Henry should stay at home. Horace and I and you are invited. There was a certain householder which planted a vineyard. He has a soul who cannot be influenced by such motives. This is the dog whom my father bought. The lady which we saw was highly educated. He has some friends which I am acquainted with. The judge which pronounced the sentence was an upright man. Those which desire to be happy should be careful to do that which is right. Though thou art wise, you sometimes misjudge. Do thyself no harm, and no one will harm you. This is the man who discovered our distress, and that brought us relief. I know you whom thou art, that annoyest me at thy gate. O thou who art all-wise, and that rulest over all! I labored long to make thee happy, and now you reward me by ingratitude. Let no boy or girl drop her pencil. James and you must attend to his studies.

If any of you have aught to say against this man, let them now speak. I paid for the molasses, and the grocer said he would send them immediately. What one of you can sit silent when they hear their friend abused? Each of you may choose for yourself. If any one calls, tell them I am not at home. England expects every man to do their duty. Please examine my watch, and see what ails her. Now you have heard the news, what do you think of them? Wealth and poverty have its temptations. Neither the Greek nor the Roman had cooking-stoves in their houses. Every drafted man or his substitute reported themselves on the day appointed. When a rat is driven into a corner, they will often turn and fight furiously. It is impossible to fix the exact number of known languages, but its number can hardly be less than nine hundred. Horace as well as Juvenal satirized the follies of their age. Milo began to lift the ox when he was a calf. He is the same person whom I took him to be.

4. Examples under Rule IV.

Correct by **179,** 1, *a, b, and the Cautions, the following examples, and be careful to avoid all similar errors:—*

Where was you this morning when I called? He dare you to do it. They was unwilling to go. Relatives agrees with their antecedents. There's ten of us going. Was you certain of it? We was allowed the privilege. Circumstances alters cases. Has those books been sent home? The committee has accepted their appointment. The majority was disposed to adopt the measure which they at first opposed. Blessed is the people that know the joyful sound. The fleet were seen sailing up the channel, where afterwards it anchored. The peasantry goes barefoot without endangering their health. The public is requested to attend for their own benefit. The church have no power to adopt the measure which it advocates. Thinks I to myself, I'll do it. Yes, says I, we'll go together. Oh, dear me, says I, (as vulgarly contracted, "Oh, dear me, *suz.*") The derivation of these words are uncertain. The story, with all its additions, were believed. The increase of his resources render the change necessary. The number of applicants increase. The general, with all his soldiers, were taken. The sale of the goods take place to-morrow. The hope of retrieving his losses increase his diligence. I seen him when he done it. Some one has broke my pencil. Tell them to set still. She laid down by the fire. He soon begun to be weary of the employment. I am going to lay down. Mary has wrote a letter. I see him when he went. Ain't it true? We ain't going this evening. He has drank too much. The tree has fell. You have not did as I told you. John has stole the knife. They are going to our house next week. He give me a great many books. He knowed his lesson better than Henry. They had sang very well. I have lain your book on the shelf. Will you sit the pitcher on the table, and let it set there? The ship lays in the harbor. I done my sums first.

There is six cents to pay you for your trouble, my little man. Why did you say you was coming? There was four of us went a fishing. "Spare Hours" were written by Dr. John Brown. This fashion is one of the most foolish that ever was imposed on us. A band of robbers were captured by means of a little negro boy. Forest after forest fall before the axe of the white man. Not a feature, not a muscle, were seen to move. The night was dark:

neither moon nor star were visible. There was no data given. The ladder was forty foot long. There have been quite an increase in the receipt of butter. Nearly six thousand head of cattle was brought to New York market last week. A number of distinguished people was present. The mob were composed of the worst characters in the city. There seems to be no good reasons for refusing. Three months' probation are enough to decide it. He dare not touch a hair of Catiline.

5. EXAMPLES UNDER RULE V.

Correct the following examples by the principles and Cautions under Rule V.:—

He found a acorn in the woods. He was a honorable man. It is an wonderful invention. He is an younger man than we thought. She showed an uniform adherence to truth. This is an hard saying.

I do not like remarks of these kind. Those sort of people are very disagreeable. Will you buy six pair of boots? I have bought eight foot of wood. It cost a thousand pound. The lot is fifty foot in width. The water is six fathom deep. We walked three mile in a short time. He ordered ten ton of coal.

I found them books on the table. Which of them scholars recites the best? Go and tell them boys to come here. Ask them children to bring them apples here.

She dresses neat. The time passed very quick. The ship glides smooth over the water. The stream flows silent on. It is not such a great distance as I thought it was. He behaved much wiser than the others. Mary speaks French very fluent. I am exceeding sorry to hear such tidings.

He was the larger of them all. He was the oldest of the two brothers. He preferred the latter of the three. Which is the oldest of the two? John is the wisest of the two.

After the most straitest sect of our religion I lived a Pharisee. This was the most unkindest cut of all. The rose is most fairest of all flowers. The chief of the Arabian tribes is styled the sheik. The chief magistrate is called the emperor. He was an abler financier than a negotiator.

You cannot mix the oil and the water. The imagination is necessary to the poet. The fire is a useful servant, but a hard master, to a man. A pen is mightier than a sword. A lion is sometimes called a king of beasts. The time and the tide wait for no man. He examined every phenomena with the eye of a philosopher. He was much pleased with these good news. Bring me a thimble and scissors. The grizzly bear, as well as buffalo, are natives of North America. The ship displayed a red and white signal, and we distinctly saw them both. The elephant has a powerful and a flexible trunk, which he always carries with him on a journey. I cannot buy, for I have a little money. I could buy it if I chose; for I have little money yet. The carpenter forgot to bring his ten-feet pole. I counted thirteen sails of vessels lying at anchor in the stream. The apple tastes sweetly. Industry and Frugality are Fortune's servants: this acquires wealth, that saves it. Just taste of those molasses.

I bought an Andrew's and a Stoddard's Latin Grammar, and left it in the book-store. What sort of an animal is a mink? It is a kind of a quadruped. We were charmed with Everett, the orator, the statesman, and the diplomatist. One would think him a better pupil than a teacher. At the North and South Poles the latitude is 90°, and longitude from 0° to 180°. Let us honor our flag,—the red, the white, and the blue. The administration of Washington and establishment of the government formed an important era in our history. He did not demand the principal, but interest. He delivered the address clear and distinct. How do you do? I am some better; my health is tolerable good. He rode past so quick I scarce saw him. You do not treat me polite. The bear had not been fed for two days, and he began to growl savage. How did Walter perform his part? Very good.

6. Examples under Rule VI.

Correct, by the rule, the following examples:—

I am going to see my friends in the country, they that we visited last summer. Washington will be remembered by our posterity as him who was the father of his country. The Echo Song was sung by Jenny Lind, she who delighted the whole country.

He is writing the life of Cromwell,—not the Protector, but he who was the friend and pupil of Wolsey, and afterwards minister of Henry VIII. He treats me ill,—I, who would so gladly serve him.

7. Examples under Rule VII.

Correct the following examples by the Cautions:—

On Lindens hills of blood-stained snow. It was the grand sultans palace. The nations hopes were blasted. Next Mars, Piazzis orb, is seen. It is against the laws of Plutos empire. His brothers offence is not his. Midst glorys glance and victorys thunder-shout. The mans story was false. If of Drydens fire the blaze is brighter, of Popes the heat is more regular and constant.

This book is your's. I listened to it's song. The slate is hisn. This map is theirn. This knife is mine, and not yourn. That handkerchief is hern. These sheep are ourn. Will you drive yourn out of the pasture? Our's is a pleasant task.

I will do it for your sakes. We intend, for our parts, to follow his advice. Their healths have improved. We will submit to our lots. It was not worth their whiles to remain so long in port.

After a pleasant two hours sail, we went ashore to lunch. Please call at Little's and Brown's book-store and get me the last Galaxy. His friends opposed him going into the army. Which is the neatest boot, your boot or my boot? This is a book of my friend. The elephant and beaver's instinct approaches closely to reason. James sister thinks too much of dress. I would like to see that saucy servant of your's. That is a robin, thrush, or sparrow's nest.

8. Examples under Rule VIII.

Correct the following examples by the rule:—

Who did you see yesterday? Who did he marry? They that help us we should reward. He who committed the offence thou shouldst punish, not I, who am innocent. Who should I find but my cousin? Will you let him and I sit together? I did not know who to send.

Let him and I row the boat back. I can't tell who you mean. Let the able-bodied men fight, and they that are feeble do guard duty at home. Ye have ever been my friends, and ye only will I trust. Both candidates are popular men, and it is quite doubtful who the people will choose. He that made the last speech the audience cheered.

9. Examples under Rule IX.

Correct, by the Cautions, the following examples:—

I will not take that course by no means. I did not like neither his principles nor his practice. I cannot write no more. Nothing never can justify such conduct. He will never be no better. Neither he nor no one else believes the story. I never go nowheres. I am resolved not to trust him, neither now, nor any other time. No one knows neither the causes nor the effects of such influences.

His expressions sounded harshly. Satin feels very smoothly. Give him a soon and decisive answer. Such incidents are of seldom occurrence. The then emperor issued a decree. Did he arrive safely and sound? She seemed beautifully.

Know now whether this be thy son's coat, or no? Tell me whether I shall do it, or no. I will ascertain if it is true, or no.

He said how he believed it. She told me how that she would come if she could. He remarked how time was valuable.

I will send thee far from hence to the Gentiles. George wrote a description of our picnic where he mentions all of us under assumed names. I never got no favors in the army. It isn't good for peartrees nor apple-trees to trim them often. He delivered the address clear and distinct.

10. Examples under Rule X.

Oh, unfortunate me! why did I not heed your counsel? Me excepted, they were all members of the club. Him guiding, we took the forest-path in confidence. They refused to begin the contest, us absent. Them assisting, the performance will be successful.

11. Examples under Rule XI.

Correct the following examples by the Cautions:—

They confess the power and wisdom and love and goodness of their Creator. John and James and Henry and Charles will return this evening. His conduct was unkind and unjust and unmerciful.

He neither came nor was sent for. We pervert the noble faculty of speech when we use it to the defaming, or to disquiet our neighbors. We hope that we shall hear from him, and that he has returned. I always have and I always shall be of this opinion. The work was executed with rapidity and promptly. It is a region distinguished by many charming varieties of rural scenery, and which may be termed the Arcadia of Scotland. He retired voluntarily, and a conqueror.

Are we not lazy in our duties, or make a Christ of them? In many pursuits we embark with pleasure and land sorrowfully.

It is a good which neither depends on the will of others nor on the affluence of external fortune. Either sentences are simple or compound. His fortune has not only suffered by his folly, but his health. This is not merely a question of interest, but of right also.

He was not a rich man, and he is good to the poor. A man may smile and smile, and he is a villain. Charles V. retired to a convent, and chess is a fascinating game. Back to thy punishment, false fugitive! and to thy speed you may add wings. Genius hews out its figure from the block, and with the sleepless chisel he gives it life. Neither Whigs or Tories foresaw the bad effects of the passage of the bill. No one gave his opinion as modestly as he.

12. Examples under Rules XIII. and XIV.

Correct, by the Cautions, the following examples:—

I am engaged with my work. Mesopotamia lies among two rivers. I left my book to home. Come in my house. They insist on it that you are wrong. My friend has a strong prejudice to the candidate. That mother is too indulgent with her child. With what are you so intent? We should profit from the experience of others. That boy is not careful with his books. With what does he excel?

Who you spend your evenings with is well known. Go, little insect: the world is wide enough for you and I. Mankind's antipathy for snakes is derived, some say, from Adam. Do you know who you are speaking to? Gibbon was engaged with his great work about twenty years. Where shall we turn, and in whom can we rely? Though a young man, he presided upon the assembly with much dignity.

So you must ride
On horseback after we.

But it were vain for you and I
In single fight our strength to try.

13. Examples under Rule XV.

Correct, by the Caution, the following examples:—

Who can write better than him? Whom does he honor more than I? I know James better than him. The lion can devour a sheep as well as a wolf. He is no better speller as I.

14. Examples under Rule XVI.

Unless rain comes, we shall be sure for to go. I expected to have seen you yesterday. Govern your own temper, and thus teach others to. As we marched through the streets, half the town, I should think, came out for to see us. With a few simple words he proved the previous speaker to have been mistaken. Buy the best in the market, or, at least, try to. While standing by the door, I saw the procession to pass round the corner. The colonel bade me to deliver this message. I should have preferred to have taken an outside seat.

209. Errors to be corrected by Special Cautions.

1. Caution I.—*Avoid* **vulgarisms.**

These are low expressions which the uneducated are sure to adopt.

Ex.—You can't *come that game.* That is *tip-top.* *Go it,* boys. Keep your *eye peeled.* I'll break *your top timbers;* and others without number.

2. Caution II.—*Avoid all* **perversions.**

These come sometimes from a corruption of the true word, sometimes from a mistake in the sound of a word.

Ex.—Where is the place for the *refuge* matter? He was *necessiated* to stay *to hum.* We all got into a *voilent prespiration.* The *foilage* of the trees in autumn is beautiful. The *causalities* of that battle were fearful. *Them cowcumbers* are not fit to eat. I *disremember* what you told me. That depends upon your *ipse dixie.*

3. Caution III.—*Avoid* **provincialisms.**

These are expressions confined to certain localities in the same country.

Ex.—My father is a *heap better.* I *reckon I will* never succeed. You will have a *right smart chance.* *Directly* we started, it *commenced* to rain. *Well (wal),* I *guess* that will do.

4. Caution IV.—*Avoid* **misapplications.**

These consist in using words either with a wrong *meaning* or in a wrong *connection.*

Ex.—I have brought the *balance* of the books. This is a *likely* youth. Fruit in a damp cellar is *incident* to decay. It didn't hurt me *any.* Which of these six pencils will you take? I will take *either.* We had seven pear-trees, but *neither* of them lived. The two boys were so angry, they would not speak to *one another.* The farmer had *fewer* hay than he expected. He had *less* fruit-trees than his neighbor. If you will not *go* to me, I shall *come* to you. We *rode* down the river in a flat-boat. The teacher *learned* the boys arithmetic. The woodsman will *fall* the trees. The council *was setting* all night. The sun is *sitting in* a cloud. Do you *love* maple sugar? I *expect* some of the boys broke that sled. I *carried* my brother to school *in a horse and sleigh*. The river *has overflown* its banks. The medicine *has affected* a cure. Where was he *raised?* The ship *laid* in the harbor a whole month. I feel as *though* I could do it. Let him do *like* I do. He gave a demonstration *where* he proved two sides equal. He was averse *from* the undertaking. I differed *with* him. He is independent *on* his father. I shall confide *on* your advice.

5. CAUTION V.—*Avoid improper* **ellipses.**

For ellipses, see **216,** 3.

Ex.—It is a long road has no turning. He alienated the affection of his acquaintance as well as his best friends. Solon was banished his country. It is an offence which does not admit an apology. We pledge our lives, fortunes, and our sacred honor. Your friends never blame you for making short credits and calls. It is not so easy to get money as spend it. I would rather live with honest boors than false gentlemen. He never has succeeded, and never will. She placed me near the desk, and James the farther end of the room. I do not know whether he has been engaged by the defendant or plaintiff. I was surprised at the manner he received it. His stories are as hard to swallow as Baron Munchausen.

6. CAUTION VI.—*Avoid* **unnecessary repetitions.**

Repetitions are not *always* censurable. The caution is intended to guard against a needless repetition (1) of the same *word* or any of its *derivatives;* (2) of the same *idea*, or one nearly allied to it.

Ex.—In the *formation* of the different *forms* of the verb, we should be careful to use the present participle in *forming* the progressive *form*, and the passive participle in *forming* the passive *form*. Her *faithfulness* and *fidelity* deserved much praise.

7. CAUTION VII.—*Avoid* **unnecessary words.**

Ex.—Have you sold your house? No; but Mr. Jones talks of buying *of* it. He never denied *but* that he was opposed to the law. This line of railroad opens *up* a fine prospect for this section of the State. The Board offer their grateful acknowledgments for the support hitherto so liberally extended, *and* which has so greatly contributed to this satisfactory result. I meant to be present at the meeting, but *which* I was unable.

Have you *got* any good tea? (a common abuse, which should be avoided.) He has *got* no good land for raising strawberries.

We have no ague in this *here* place. Stop that *there* noise. (*This 'ere* and *that 'ere* are sometimes heard.)

I felt the chills *to* run all over me.

If I would keep it a secret, he said *how* that he would tell me.

He *had* ought to work.

They have more friends among us than you think *for*.

And there are several *other* such ways of evading the law.

Bartholomew Gosnold *first* discovered Martha's Vineyard in 1602.

I could not for a moment admit *of* such a plea.

The committee carefully investigated *into* all the circumstances.

I *kinder* like him after all. It is a pretty smart *sort of a* town.

They presented the superintendent *with* a gold hunting-watch.

The old cat, having lost all but one of her kittens, *she* carried that one away and hid it.

The Indians, before they declare war, *they* hold a solemn council.

After his defeat he was the *most* unhappiest man I ever saw.

More sharper than a serpent's tooth is vile ingratitude.

The diet cures more than the doctor.

One vote would decide who should be *a* captain.

The oxygen gas is the vital part of the atmosphere.

I can't consent by any *manner of* means.

A pair of pincers will do equally *as* well. It is equally *as* good.

The days, *the* hours, and *the* minutes dragged *slowly* along.

That wise and *that* benevolent man has gone to his rest.

By *the* listening to his conversation I avoided talking myself.

You have been wandering about long enough: you ought to marry and settle *down* somewhere.

Common laborers are now *being* paid two dollars a day.

Complaints are now *being* made of the course of the commissioner.

San Francisco is the largest *of any* city west of the Rocky Mountains.

8. CAUTION VIII.—*Avoid an improper* **arrangement.**

Errors in syntax sometimes arise from an improper arrangement of the words of a sentence. This often renders the thought obscure, ambiguous, or even equivocal.

Mr. Brown needs a physician who is sick. These delicious oranges came in a large wicker basket which we eat. Found, a gold watch by a gentleman with steel hands.

The preposition should be placed as near to its object as possible.

S

To let, a well-built two-story house, containing eleven rooms, a large, dry cellar, and a new furnace, with a French roof. A man brought home my Newfoundland dog in his shirt-sleeves.

I feel obliged to *reluctantly* remind you of your promise. He ought to be *without doubt* regarded as the real inventor. After the firing ceased, he was seen to *slowly and cautiously* retreat.

9. Caution IX.—Avoid **unbecoming** expressions.

Language is *unbecoming* when, in style, it is not suited to the thought to be expressed. In common discourse, the *ancient, poetic,* or *sacred* style should be avoided. In *apostrophe,* in *addresses to the Deity,* in poetic and elevated composition, the familiar style is in the highest degree offensive.

Ex.—*Art thou* feeding the cows? *Camest thou* to school late? He *hath* caught a trout. Mr. Jones *liveth* at No. —— Washington Street. *Adieu to you,* fair Rhine! O *you* Parnassus! whom I now survey.

210. Miscellaneous Examples.

A new hotel is being built.—(*is building.*) Large supplies of these goods are *being thrown* upon the market. How old are you? I am *going on for* twelve.—(*in my twelfth year.*)

He *used to was, used to could* (vulgarisms).

Turn your toes out when you walk, *like* I do.—(*as.*)

They were not fortunate in choosing a day, *like* we were.

James is not *as* tall as George.—(*so* tall.)

He brought home gloves and laces, and all *those* sort of things.

The ascent was not *as* difficult as they feared.

You will find *these* kind of apples excellent for winter use.

I *had* rather stay at home.—(*would* rather.)

We *ain't* going to have any drones in this hive.

It *ain't* any use for a fellow like me to try.

There is a *good* deal of idle capital in the country.—(*great* deal.)

He sent a great *deal* of fat cattle to Brighton.—(great *number.*)

Our minister is just recovering from a severe *attackt* of the gout.

They *attackted* us in the night; and we Yanks were busy enough till morning, I tell you.

You mustn't go near the water, for I'm afraid you will be *drownded.*

Have you milked the cows, John? I *didn't* yet, sir.—(I *haven't.*)

It was impossible to say *who* it was fired by.

The pleasure of your evening's party depends very much upon *who* you have for company.

Haven't you *no* idea who it was?

I don't think *no* worse of him for that.

SYNTAX—IMPROPER USE.

You could *not* do it justice by no description you could give.
I *reckon* we shall have a dry *spell* now, after so much rain.

The word *reckon* is generally used in the Southern States, as *guess* is in New England, for *think*.

How old is your father? I *guess* he is about eighty.
The number of the convicts *of* the State Prison is two hundred.—(*in*.)
I meant *to have told* you the meeting was postponed.
He sent us word he would have liked to *have* come.
They *come* with us into the city yesterday.—(*went*.)
I shall certainly *come* to Philadelphia this week, if I can.
I am *jealous* that the cat catches my chickens.—(*suspicious*.)
How came all these weeds among my parsnips? I *expect* they grew.—(*suppose*.)
The general will arrive *in* Boston about four o'clock P. M.—(*at*.)
He has both talent and capacity *in* business.—(*for* business.)
And the beggars and *wretcheder* poor keep themselves warm by sundry recollections of summer.
Overcome with fatigue, I *laid* down under the first tree I came to.
He is an uneasy child; he cannot *lay* still or *set* still a moment.
After a hen has *lain* a certain number of eggs, she generally wants to *set*.

Lay is a transitive, *lie* an intransitive verb. *Set* is sometimes intransitive, but usually transitive; *sit* is always intransitive.

My brother has promised to *learn* me to skate.—(to *teach*.)
How do you do, Mr. Brown? Oh, I'm *tolerable* well.
I have lost the knife father *give* me last Christmas.
The robin finally *alit* on the branch just above me.
What time did you say it *was?*
Who told you the Governor *was* to be present?
I never knew before that Russian America *had* such a mild climate.—(*has*.)
After a good night's sleep, he *woke* much refreshed.
About midnight we were suddenly *awoke* by the ringing of the bells.
All talking ceased when he *begun* to speak.
On trying to get up, he found his leg was *broke*.
I waited till noon; but no one *come*.
He only *done* his duty. Who *done* it? I *done* as you told me.
I *drunk* no tea or coffee for two years. They *fit* like tigers.
I *forgit* his name. It is time to *git* up.
He *meaned* well. I have *rode* so long, I would like to walk a while.
They have jumped over the fence and *ran* away.
His vessel was *spoke* off the coast of Chili.

Byron, while in Venice, is said to have *swam* three miles.
Ask all to come: we *will* then see who are your friends.
Deceiving is much the same as *to lie*.
It is the same book *what* I told you about.
The company *which* she had taken so much trouble to select were evidently not well pleased with each other.
The result of his waste and extravagance *were* plainly foreseen.
The influence of wealth and friends, in such cases, *carry* the day.
Brown and Jones both did well, but neither of them *were* equal to the last speaker.
The wisdom and justice of his decision *is* now apparent.
Your letter, with the proof-sheets of the new arithmetic, *were* received last night.
Each day, each hour, *bring their* temptations.
His manly principles, and not his fear of the world, *restrains* him.
The audience *wears its* hats in the pit.*
And far into the night the soft dip of the oar, and the gurgling progress of the boats, *was* company and gentlest lullaby.
And I think the perfume, as it steals mitigated to your nostrils out of an open church door, is the *reverendest* smell in the world.
It was commended, I assure you, by the very *selectest* circle in our village.

These violations, by good writers, of the rule for comparison are not uncommon nowadays: they will eventually be recognized, no doubt, as lawful usage.

The resort to begging, in such cases, is *more universal* in the south of Italy than in the north.
And nature, from *its* seat sighing, through all *its* works gave signs of woe.—(*her.*)
Ex.-Gov. Curtin, of Pennsylvania, delivered *an* eulogy.
I have seen him do it *an* hundred times.
I cannot give you the *why's* and *wherefore's:* but these are the facts.
The *Mussulmen* believe in fate, and yet wear *talismen* round their necks.
Mix two *spoonsful* of cayenne pepper with three or four *handsful* of oat-meal, and give it just before sunset.
It is the girl *what* lives near the depot.
I never *have* and I think I never shall see another sight like that.
Call about noon: I shall be *to* home at that time.
Which is the *largest* city, Baltimore or New Orleans?
I think James is the *handsomest* of the two.

III. PECULIAR USE.
211. Definitions.

1. A word has a **peculiar** use when it varies from its usual *classification, meaning,* or *relation* in construction.

2. A *word* or an *expression* has an **idiomatic** use when, with the sanction of good authority,—

(1.) In the *same language,* as in the English, for example, it departs from its general analogies.

Ex.—"We *were told* an exciting story," instead of "An exciting story was told us."

(2.) In *different languages,* the same thought is expressed with a marked and uniform difference.

Ex.—*How do you do?—English.* = *How goes it with you?—German.* = *How carry you yourself?—French.*

(3.) In *any language,* it deviates from the principles of general grammar.

Ex.—In addressing a single person, we say, "How *are you?*" The principles of general grammar require us to say, "How *art thou?*"

REMARK.—All languages have their idioms, but the English abounds in them. This is chiefly owing to the character of the language itself, as a mixture of many others. Says Professor De Vere, "In English, all the existing nationalities of Europe—the Sclavonic alone excepted—meet and mingle together." With the words of these nations came more or less of their peculiar modes of expression; and these, after having been moulded and adapted, have become a part of our mother-tongue. The grammarian cannot change these if he would. The growth of language, its new formations, and its decay, are above and beyond his control. "Try to alter the smallest rule of English, and you will find it is physically impossible."—*Max Müller.* And he would not change them if he could: he must not attempt to adjust the words of an idiom to his grammatical rules, and thus rob the language of some of its choicest elements of life and strength. In the following section the peculiarities that often perplex the learner are arranged under appropriate heads, and should be consulted in cases of difficulty.

212. Special Examples.

1. The same word may belong to different classes.

(**1.**) **Idea-words,** or those which form the *substance* of the language.

(*a.*) From the **same root,** *without change.*

Own.—I *own* a horse (verb). The horse is my *own* (adj.).

The idea of peculiar ownership is its prevailing meaning. It is used with possessives to render that idea emphatic. *My* house, *my own* house; *my* composition, *my own* composition.

Summer.—In the *summer* (noun); a *summer* shower (adj.); to *summer* any one or any thing (verb).

Nearly all the common or household words of the language are thus used, *without change, as nouns, verbs,* and often as *adjectives.* Thus, we have "good *iron;* he will *iron* the thief; an *iron* bar; an *eye;* they *eye* him; a cool *spring;* I *spring;* a *spring* morning." In many cases, when the word does not become a distinct adjective by usage, it becomes such in effect by being prefixed to a noun with an intervening hyphen, as a part of a compound noun. Thus, we have "*eye*-glass, *eye*-witness; *dog*-tooth, plural *dog*-teeth; *dog's*-tongue (**185,** 11), *dog's-tail* grass; *bear*-skin, *bear's*-foot;" and others almost without limit.

(*b.*) From the **same root,** *with some modification.*

Gold.—The *gold* of California (noun); a *gold* watch (adj.); to *gild* (verb); a *golden* opportunity (deriv. adj.); *gold*-cloth, *gold*-dust (adj. in effect).

(*c.*) From **different roots.**

Well.—From Anglo-Saxon **weallan,** *to boil.*—A *well* twenty feet deep (noun); the water began to *well* up (verb). From Anglo-Saxon **wel.**—A *well* man (adj.); he does *well* (adv.). Thus, we have **bear** (from A.-S. beran), *to carry,* **bear** (from A.-S. bera), *a quadruped,* and **bear** (from A.-S. bere), *a kind of barley.* We have **bay,** *brown;* **bay,** a *body of water;* **bay,** a *berry;* **bay,** *a barking, to bark:*—really four different words.

Besides these, there are many words which are the same in orthography but different in pronunciation, or are the same in pronunciation but different in orthography; as, **bow** (bŏw), **bow** (bō), **beau** (bō); **an'gust, august';** **lye, lie; dye, die.** These may belong to the same or to different classes, according to their use.

Remark.—A very profitable exercise may be introduced here by requiring the pupil to take any word, as *form, feed, silver, fair, close,* and determine into what classes it falls from its various uses, either in its unchanged form or by any form of derivation. Let him be required to write or give orally a sentence containing each of its uses.

(**2.**) **Complex words,** or those which express *ideas,* and at the same time *connect* or *limit.*

SYNTAX—PECULIAR USE. 279

REMARK.—It should be observed that their *general* use is to express *ideas* and *connections*. In some cases they are mere *limiting* words or mere *connectives*.

(*A.*) **Subordinate connectives,** having also a *substantive* use.

Who, Which. (1.) *Pronouns* and *subordinate connectives* at the same time.

Who, Which, (2.) also, *When, Where, Why, How,* and all other interrogative words. *Interrogative pronouns,* or *interrogative adverbs,* when used to ask a question.

Who, Which. (3.) *Indefinite interrogative pronouns* and *subordinate connectives,* and the others *conjunctive adverbs,* when the interrogative sentence is incorporated into another sentence. (See **78,** 4, 5.)

What. Besides the uses mentioned on page 78, it is,—
(1.) An *indefinite interrogative pronoun:* "He asked *what* happened."
(2.) An *adverb:* "The enemy, having his country wasted, *what* (partly) by himself and *what* (partly) by the soldiers, findeth succor in no place."

For **whoever, whosoever, whatever, whatsoever,** see **177,** 14, 15.
For the uses of **that,** see page 78.

(*B.*) **Subordinate connectives,** having also an *adverbial* use.

As. (1.) A part of a **compound preposition.** "*As to* that matter, he was silent." "*As for* me and my house."
(2.) **A subordinate connective.**
    (*a.*) Conjunctive adverb of *manner:* "Speak *as* you think."
    of *comparison:* "He is *as* tall *as* his brother."
    of *time:* "I arrived *as* (when) he was taking his leave."
    of *cause* or *reason:* "*As* (since) you take the responsibility, I will proceed."
    of *correspondence:* "As the door turneth on its hinges, so doth the slothful man on his bed."
    of **an adversative meaning:** "Fatigued *as* I was, I walked four hours."

(*b.*) A *relative pronoun* (not strictly, but by an ellipsis): "Such *as* I have give I unto thee."

(*c.*) An *index of apposition:* "The moon *as* satellite attends." "They regard him *as* innocent."

In this last use the connective serves to join only a *term* (not a proposition) to a superior term, and so far resembles the preposition. It must not, however, on this account be so called. The preposition is used to show a relation between terms representing *different* things; whereas the term after *as* denotes the *capacity, rank,* or *character* in which the *same* thing is to be regarded. This use of *as* is often troublesome to the learner, especially when the reference to the antecedent term is in *sense* rather than in *construction* (see **183,** 13) Sometimes it is used to limit the antecedent term to some particular *view* or *attribute* of itself. "Vice considered *as* vice." "We shall consider man *as* man." "Whatsoever ye do, do it heartily, *as* unto the Lord." The subsequent term is often an adjective or a participle, and therefore cannot follow a preposition. "They regarded him *as having attained* the highest rank."

(3.) An **adverb:** "*As yet* (until now) I have made no new discovery." It is an adverb when used as the first part of a correlative: *as — as.*

REMARK.—When *as* is used to introduce *illustrative examples,* it is a conjunctive adverb: "A noun is the name of an object; *as* [is] *John, Boston,* [or] *house.*" Sometimes we must supply *it:* "The rule is *as* follows,"—*it* follows, or *as that which* follows.

After, and many other words, such as *before, since, till, until, ere, except, save, for, notwithstanding,* &c. (see **143,** 18), are *conjunctive adverbs* when they connect subordinate clauses; when they are followed by a noun or a pronoun as object, they are *prepositions.* Several of them are used as mere *adverbs.* Thus, we have, "He came *after* me. *After* I left he wrote his friend. We left soon *after.* He has been at home *since* noon. I have not seen him *since. Since* I returned, I have been ill." Most of the prepositions are in some uses adverbs: thus, "*over* head; the rain is *over;* he went *under;* it is *under* the house."

(3.) **Defining** or **connecting words,** or words used chiefly to *limit, unite,* or show *transitions.*

A and **The** are articles, or a division of limiting adjectives, when they belong to nouns. **A** is a preposition when placed before a participle; as, *a hunting;* and in composition; as, *aground, aloft.* **The** is an *adverb* when prefixed to an adverb or an adjective; as, "*The* more I see him, *the* better I like him."

SYNTAX—PECULIAR USE. 281

All, Any. (1.) (Noun.) Deprived of his *all*. *Any* not used as a noun.
    (2.) (Adj.) *All* men are mortal. *Any* house better than none.
    (3.) (Adv.) And cheeks *all* pale. *All* the better. *Any* better.

Also, Besides, Likewise, Even, Else, are used sometimes as coördinate conjunctions. Sometimes they are found in connection with such conjunctions, and modify the general effect of the whole added clause. They have the force of *adverbs*.

Again. (1.) (Adv.) I saw him *again*.
    (2.) (Conj.) *Again*, this assumption is not sustained by the facts in the case.

Alone, Only. (1.) (Adj.) I found him *alone*. The *only* lesson taught.
    (2.) (Adv.) To sit *alone*. I wrote *only* to amuse myself.

Ay, Yea, Nay. (1.) (Adverb.) He answered *nay* or *yea*, = no or yes.
    (2.) (Noun.) The *nays* will rise, and the *ays* will remain seated.
    (3.) (Coör. conj.) He did all that, *yea*, more. And now do they thrust us out privily? *nay*, verily; but let them come themselves and fetch us out.

But, Save. (1.) (Coör. conj.) He is not sick, *but* faint. And that no man might buy or sell, *save* he that had the mark.
    (2.) (Prep.) They gave him all *but* one. Whence all *but* him had fled.
    (3.) (Adv.) We saw him *but* twice.

Save and *but* are obviously followed by the objective in many constructions, as the pronoun shows. Thus, Wordsworth says,—

    "God save you all, *save* this cursed friar.
    And all desisted,—all *save him* alone."

Yet many cases may be cited in which the pronoun is in the nominative. Thus, Shakspeare says, "All the conspirators, *save only he*, did that they did, in envy of great Cæsar." "There was no stranger with us in the house, *save we two* [were]."—*Bible*. The question is, In what case is the *noun* after these words? Its form does not decide. Most recent grammarians, and both Webster and Worcester, call *save* and *but* prepositions, and regard the noun as in the *objective*. Such is the present tendency; and it may well be regarded as the settled usage.

Both. (1.) (Adj.) *Both* methods are good.
    (2.) (Correl. conj.) He is *both* virtuous and wise.

24*

For, To. (1.) (For, subor.-conj.) See *After*.
(2.) (Prep.) I will call *for* you. He will send *to* me.

Either may be supplied before the indirect object: "He bought [for] *me* a knife." They lack the antecedent term when used before a phrase as subject. "*For* him to deceive me is inexcusable." "*To write* the same things is not profitable."

Much. (1.) (Noun.) Where *much* is given, *much* is required.
(2.) (Adj.) *Much* ado is made.
(3.) (Adv.) I was *much* pleased with the visit.

No. (1.) (Limiting adjective.) He had *no* funds.
(2.) (*a.*) (Adverb,—a modifier.) *No* longer.
(*b.*) (Adverb, independent.) "*No*, I never will do it." To this add, as independent adverbs, *yes, will, why.* "Are you going? *Yes*," = I am going. "*Well*, what shall we do? *Why*, I do not know."

Now. (1.) (Noun.) *Now* is your time.
(2.) (Adverb.) Come *now*.
(3.) (Coördinate causal conjunction.) *Now* the serpent was more subtle than any beast of the field.
(4.) (Correlative connective.) *Now* high, *now* low, *now* master up, *now* miss.—*Pope*.

Rather (adv.), also *lief, better, best*, are used with *had* to express equal willingness or preference. Probably they were originally mistaken interpretations of the abbreviation *I'd*,—i.e. *I would;* not *I had*. They are idiomatic expressions, and are in good use. "I *had rather* speak five words with my understanding." "I *had as lief* go as not." "You *had better* stay."

So. (1.) (Adverb of manner or degree, = *thus*.) Do it *so*. The air is *so* clear.
(2.) (Subordinate connective.) *So* he can gain his point, he is unscrupulous as to the means.
(3.) (A *substitute*, used to avoid the repetition of an expression.) I am *in earnest*, but he is more *so*, = *in earnest*.

There. (Adv.) It is opposed to *here*. "Darkness *there* might well seem twilight *here*."—*Milton*.
(Adv. expletive.) It has no special value in this use. "*There* is a pleasure in the pathless woods."—*Byron*.

Then. (1.) (Adv.) *Of time* merely. "Till *then* who knew the force of those dire arms?"

Of succession. "First cast out the beam out of thine own eye, and *then* shalt thou see clearly," &c.

(2.) (Conj.) If this be so, *then* man has a natural freedom.

Then is used sometimes with *so* or *now* to indicate an advance in an argument, the speaker assuming that a previous point is established. "*So, then,* faith cometh by hearing." "*Now, then,* be all thy weighty cares away."

Thereby (1.) (Adv.), also *therewith, whereby, wherewith, therein, wherein, hereby, herein,* &c. "You will gain *thereby.*" "*Hereby* shall I know that you are true men." "*Herein* thou hast done foolishly."

(2.) (Conj. adv.) "Acquaint thyself with him, and be at peace; *thereby* good shall come unto thee."—*Bible.*

It is to be regretted that these relative words, so expressive, and so common in the language a century ago, are passing out of use, and with them such words as *thither, hither, thenceforth,* &c. It is difficult to supply the place of *whither* or *thither*, for example. These denote *direction*, whereas *where* and *there* denote, rather, *place.*

Worth. (1.) (Noun.) "It has a real *worth.*"

(2.) (Adj.) "A ring he hath of mine *worth* forty ducats," = *of the value of.* The idea of a preposition is involved in the word, as in *like* or *near.*

(3.) (Verb.) "Woe *worth* the man," = Woe *be to* the man, imper. mode, or infin. after *let* understood.—"Let woe be to the man."

Yet. (Adv.) *Yet* more. The deed was made *yet* darker by the profession of friendship.

(Coör. conj.) *Yet* I say unto you, That even Solomon in all his glory was not arrayed like one of these.—*Bible.*

2. Certain **phrases** or **combinations** become idiomatic, and practically inseparable, when their meaning and force are lost by analysis.

REMARK.—To study these, as authorized forms of expression, is far more useful to the student than to follow them with the tenacity of the grammarian till *every word* is adjusted to its proper class and rule of construction.

A noun with a noun.—We have the following combinations:—

(1.) **Coördinate;**—as, *brother and sister; man and wife; joy and sorrow; vice and misery; horse and chaise; bread and milk.*

(*a.*) These may be connected with a term—as a predicate, for example—which is compatible with *each* separately: as, "The brother and the sister are at home," = The brother is at home and the sister is at home.

(*b.*) They may be united to a term which can only belong to the combination as such, and yet be looked upon separately; as, "Vice and misery are inseparable."

(*c.*) By a common and idiomatic use, they may come to be regarded as *one* thing, and unite with a term accordingly; as, "The horse and chaise *is* at the door." "Bread and milk *is* the best food for children."

(2.) **Subordinate;**—as, *David's* harp; the Apostle *John;* an *oyster*-saloon.

(*a.*) The *possessive* noun unites subordinately with the principal, primarily to show that the object named by the latter is owned by the person named by the former; as, *John's* coat.

Most of the peculiar uses of the possessives are mentioned under Rule VII. (**185**). Observe that the two nouns denote *different* objects.

(*b.*) The noun in *Apposition;*—Arnold the *traitor;* King Henry; George Washington; *Ye men* of Athens.

For the idiomatic uses of this combination, see Rule VI. (**183**, 2, 3, &c.) Here the nouns denote the *same* object.

(*c.*) As an *adjective;*—as, A *variety* store; a *stone* wall; a *brick* house.

The principles of general grammar require that when a noun becomes an adjective it shall undergo some change of termination; as, "A gold-*en* harvest; a leather-*n* girdle." But in English almost any noun, without change, may be used as an adjective. This use is idiomatic, and leads to a variety of consequences.

First.—The adjective-noun must be placed before the other; as, "An *iron* gate."

Secondly.—Unlike the case of apposition, it means a *different* thing from the limited noun; as, "A *berry* pie."

Thirdly.—It becomes only *partially* an adjective, still retaining some of the characteristics of the noun. It is *limited* like the noun; as, "A high-*pressure engine*,"—not "a *high* engine," nor "a *highly pressure* engine."

Fourthly.—To avoid ambiguity, the hyphen is often used to unite the two into a compound word. This is often the case when no such result would follow; as, "A *white-oak* pail, a white *oak-pail*." See in the Dictionary the compounds of *dog, bear, fire*, or almost any common word.

Fifthly.—The noun thus used must be in the *singular number*, even when limited by an adjective signifying plurality: as, "A *foot* pole;" "a *ten-foot* pole;" "*forty horse* power,"—not *horses'* power. This must be so even when the noun otherwise is used *only in the plural;* as, "A *bowel*-complaint, a *spectacle*-maker,"—not "a *bowels*-complaint, a *spectacles*-maker."

A noun with a verb,—

(*a.*) As **subject.**—The *steak eats* well. That *sentence reads* well.

Here the *verb* is used passively, to denote the capacity of the subject to receive the act. In a similar way we have the progressive form; as, "Flour *is selling* high;" "The house *is building;*" "Efforts *are making*," &c.

(*b.*) As **object.**—They *laid siege* to the city. They *found fault* with him. They *lost sight* of the object.

In such cases the objective noun has become so closely allied to the verb as to form apparently a part of it. In using the passive the grammarian's rule gives a feeble construction. Compare *"Sight* was lost of the object" with "The object was lost sight of." "He was found fault with." Here *sight* and *fault* remain by idiomatic use in the objective. The language abounds with similar constructions. It is deserving of notice that these rich and vigorous expressions are formed from the most familiar Anglo-Saxon elements.

(*c.*) A **double object,**—a *noun* and *an adjective;* as, to lay the *head low,* to drink the *cup dry,* to plough the *furrow deep,* to bake the *bread brown.*

Here the adjective expresses an attribute which is imparted to the object by means of the action of the verb: hence it helps to complete the meaning of the verb, inasmuch as it gives a new attribute to the noun,—*attributive object.* See **187,** 1 (*a*).

An adjective with a verb; as, to *walk lame,* to *come late,* to *get rid* of (*rid,* pas. part., to get one's self *rid* of).

Here the adjectives or participles belong to the subject, but modify the action.

A preposition with a verb; as, to *act up to;* to *buy in, off, out;* to *come to* (accent on *to,* to recover from a swoon), to *bring to,* to *come by,* to *go by,* to *go over with,* to *do on* = don, to *do off* = doff, to *do up,* to *do for,* to *lay up,* &c

Examples of this kind, in which one or two prepositions are so closely united to the verb as to form a part of it, are almost innumerable. They go with the verb into the passive voice, and whenever taken from the verb the expression not only becomes weakened, but is often entirely changed in meaning. These must be called *adverbs,* if taken alone. If joined to the verb as an inseparable part of it, they are not to be parsed by themselves.

A preposition with a preposition (coördinately); as, *over and over, by and by, through and through,* &c.

These should be taken together as inseparable adverbial phrases.

A preposition with an adjective (some noun being understood); as, *in vain, at first, at large, at most, at least, on high.*

These are to be taken as inseparable adverbial phrases.

A noun, preposition, and noun; as, *hand to hand, hand to mouth, end for end, cheek by jowl, face to face, year by year, day by day,* &c.

All such expressions are *adverbial*, and lose their force by analysis. If they are to be separated, the first may be regarded as nominative absolute with a participle understood, or, perhaps better, governed by a preposition understood. "They fought hand [being] to hand," or "[with] hand to hand." The second is governed by the preposition expressed.

Two or more prepositions, without a conjunction,—

(1.) *The first used as an adverb:* as, "He came *out into* the open field. He went *up to within* ten feet of the enemy's works" (up, *adverb*, to, *prep.* governing the expression *within ten feet*, = *space*, within, *prep.* governing *feet*).

(2.) *Both used as adverbs.* "The rule must be lived *up to*." "The whole subject was gone *over with*."

Two or more conjunctions; as, "*Now when* these things were thus ordained, the priests went always into the first tabernacle." "*Nor yet that* he should offer himself often."

REMARK.—Each connective has its use, and should always be explained.

3. The same *word* in the **same connection** may perform several functions at once.

It may stand as different parts of speech at the same time.

(*a.*) The adjective used as a noun may be a noun in its regimen, but an adjective in its limitations; as, "We honor *the brave*." "The *most degenerate* were abandoned." When an adjective becomes wholly a noun, it is limited as a noun.

(*b.*) The *participle* or the *infinitive* may have the construction of the noun, but the tense and limitations of the verb, at the same time; as, "*His* not having written *the letter* was the occasion of much inconvenience." "To see *the sun* is pleasant."

(*c.*) All relative pronouns have both a *substantive* and a *connective* value at the same time. *What*, in the example, "He received *what* instructions were required," is at once *adjective, substantive*, and *connective; i.e.* it has *case*, it *limits*, and it *connects*. (See **77**, 5.)

213. Exercise—Idiomatic and Peculiar Constructions.

1. *Analyze and parse the following examples:—*

The learned pagans ridiculed the Jews for being a credulous

people. That the barons and freeholders derived their authority from kings is wholly a mistake. It is certainly as easy to be a scholar as a gamester. I am not sure of there ever having been such a man as Casper Hauser. The boy has more excuses than can be considered in the allotted hour. Six times six are thirty six. He received sixty-two and a half cents for every three pounds he furnished. The thought of being good ought to arouse us to action. The higher one is, the farther he can see. Cursed is he that setteth light by his father or his mother. The distance fell a little short of twenty miles. The wind blows cold. For Jacob my servant's sake, and Israel mine elect, I have even called thee by thy name. To be good is to be happy. I rejoice in your success as an instructor. He introduced me to the president,—an honor which I shall not soon forget. They struck one another. The rain and the sunshine have each its appropriate work to do. It is man's to err. I am my beloved's, and my beloved is mine. There shall nothing die of all that is the children's of Israel. Were you at Beecher's last evening's lecture? In Henry the Eighth's reign England and Wales were completely united. This book was purchased at Little and Brown's. Whom have they elected chairman? What do you call it? By the world, I would not care a pin if the other three were in. For one to steal is base. To confess the truth, I was in fault. Then shalt thou bring forth that man or that woman unto thy gates, and shalt stone them with stones till they shall die. He was so much affected as to weep.

2. *Parse and explain the words in italics:—*

To affect to be a *lord* in one's closet would be romantic madness. I am not aware of his ever having been a *teacher*. Was this owing to there *being* twelve primary *deities* among the Gothic nations? Wheat is worth a *dollar* a *bushel*. The whole affair is of no account *whatever*. (All things *whatsoever* ye would that men should do to you, do ye even so to them.)

Whoever thinks a faultless piece to see,
Thinks *what* ne'er was, nor is, nor e'er shall be.

Whoever may oppose, we shall press the measure vigorously. Excuse me this *once*.

And all the air a solemn stillness holds,
Save where the beetle wheels his droning flight.

A messenger came *rushing* from the crowd. The fire turned the cup *black*. The knife was ground *sharp*. *The* more I read it, *the* better I like it. "*Who are you?*" was his greeting to this strange intruder. "*I will not hurt you,*" was the answer. *Let* there be *light.* Every thing depends *upon* who compose the committee. We found four persons: *namely,* two *men* and two *women.* He is *both* witty *and* wise. Parrots will talk *like persons.* The boy is *like* his *father.* He gave some *apostles,* and some *prophets,* and some *evangelists,* and some *pastors* and *teachers.* He bids *whoever* thirst to come. *Though* he was rejected, he had the boldness *even* to renew his application. They *talked* the *night away.* They *ran* the *train* at the rate of fifty miles per hour. This is—*what do you call it?* I *know* not *whom* to send.

They rose *but as* your fathers rose. Let your communication be *yea, yea, and nay, nay.* If they kill us, we shall *but* die. Give thanks unto the Lord, *for* he is good; *for* his mercy endureth forever. The cloth is five *dollars a yard.* They go *a* begging to a bankrupt's door. They are beautiful in themselves, and *much* more *so* in the noble language peculiar to the great poet. Though all the winds of doctrine were let *loose* to play upon the earth, *so* truth be in the field, we do injuriously to misdoubt her strength. Discourse oft wants an animated *no.* Go, and sin *no more.* *Not* this man, *but* Barabbas. *Now* Barabbas was a robber. I live *as* I *did;* I think *as* I *did;* I love you *as* I *did.* There I brought her, *as* pitying her hard usage. *As* poverty is not a crime, let us not try to hide it. He enlisted *as* a substitute. We cannot regard results *as* separated from causes. Such *as* were sick received furloughs. I have no more such *as* this. Sunday *as* it was, we were compelled to labor. The terms of the agreement are *as* follows. Rich *as* he was, he had no power. *As* far *as* the east is from the west, *so* far hath he removed our transgressions from us. *As* for your threats, I pay no heed to them. *As yet,* nothing has been heard. The government sent out a stone fleet, *as* it was called. *As* an artist, his success was all that could be wished. *All at once,* the noise of the interior ceases, and the whole of the bees about the doors re-enter.

> Her voice was *all* the blind man knew;
> But that was *all in all* to him.

Will you go, or stay? It is *all* one to me. "For *all* that," resumed the pendulum, "it is very dark here." There is no reason *at all* for refusing him. He counted us to see if we were *all* present. He then dismissed us *all.*

I tell thee *what,* corporal, I could tear her.—*Shak.* *What* time

SYNTAX—FIGURES. 289

I am afraid, I will trust in thee. We found broken glass, old chairs, tattered clothing, and *what* not. What! could ye not watch with me one hour? I should be sorry if it entered into the imagination of any person *whatsoever that* I was preferred to all other patrons. *The* more he exercises, *the* stronger he is. There is nothing *at all besides* this manner. I will bring him word *again*. But *even* then the morning cock crew *loud*. He was not *even* aware of it. It is he, *even* he. It must be repeated *again and again*. What *else* shall I give? Let the *boy alone*. Man shall not live by bread *alone*. His *only* child was left *alone*. I will give it to him and *him only*. *Both* the sons were present: I saw them *both*. How can a thing be *both* bitter and sweet at the same time? Wherever *there* is sense or perception, *there* some idea is actually produced. *Now and then* we saw a distant sail. *Now* is your time.

> *Till then, who* knew
> The force of those dire arms?
> They wandered *here and there.—Milton.*

Take that and make *much* of it. How *much* can he give? I had *rather* be a dog and bay the moon, *than such* a Roman. Is the peach mellow? *Rather so.* Yes, the *ays* prevailed. What is your watch *worth?* It is *worth a hundred dollars.* Woe *worth* the day! *As yet no* results are apparent. He was admonished *again and again, yet* he would persist. Or did a sable cloud turn forth its *silver* lining on the night? He wears a *wide-awake hat.* Where is the *scissor* (*s?*) grinder? How smooth Cowper's lines *read!* The beacon was lost *sight of.* The boy was *laughed at.* That nuisance must be *got rid of.* Can you pump *the cistern dry?* How *lame* he walks! He struck *the stone such a blow that* it was crushed into a thousand pieces. I will *sell out* my interest if you will *act up to* your agreement. The fainting child did not *come to* for *nearly* an hour. What rule shall we *go by?* He paced the ground *over and over.* At *first*, I thought my labor was *all in vain.* We met the enemy *face to face.* Let the beam be turned *end for end.*

FIGURES.

214. Definition.

1. A **figure** is any deviation from the grammatical or ordinary form, construction, and application of a word.

25

Figures are divided into three classes,—figures of Etymology, of Syntax, and of Rhetoric.

215. Figures of Etymology.

1. A **figure of Etymology** is a deviation from the ordinary *form* of a word.

2. Figures of Etymology consist either in a *defect*, an *excess*, or a *change* in some of the elements of a word.

3. **Aphæresis** cuts off a letter or syllable from the *beginning* of a word; as, *'gainst, 'gan,* for *against, began.*

   Ex.—Around *'gan* Marmion wildly stare.

4. **Syncope** removes a letter or syllable from the *middle* of a word; as *o'er, e'er, lov'd,* for *over, ever, loved.*

   Ex.—Kind nature's bounties *o'er* the globe *diffus'd.*

5. **Apocope** cuts off a letter or syllable from the *end* of a word; as, *th', tho',* for *the, though.*

   Ex.—The merrier fool *o' th'* two, yet quite as mad.

6. **Prosthesis** adds a letter or syllable to the *beginning* of a word; as, *a*down, *en*chain, for *down, chain.*

   Ex.—And tears *adown* that dusky cheek have rolled.

7. **Paragoge** adds a letter or syllable to the *end* of a word; as, without*en*, bound*en*, for *without, bound.*

   Ex.—And taught *withouten* pain and strife to yield the breath.

8. **Synæresis** contracts two syllables into one; as, *thou'rt, 'tis,* for *thou art, it is.*

   Ex.—Others *you'll* see, when all the *town's* afloat.

9. **Diæresis** separates two vowels which otherwise might form a diphthong; as, *coördinate, zoölogy.*

   Ex.—We ask your *coöperation* in this noble enterprise.

10. **Tmesis** separates a compound word by inserting a word between its parts; as, *to us ward,* for *toward us.*

    Ex.—On *which* side *soever* we turn.

216. Figures of Syntax.

1. A **figure of Syntax** is a deviation from the ordinary *construction* of a word.

2. Figures of Syntax consist in a *defect*, an *excess*, or a *change* in some of the elements of a sentence.

3. **Ellipsis** is the omission of a word, phrase, or clause which is necessary to complete the construction.

Ex.—We were absent [during] one day.

REMARK.—It should be understood that the words omitted by this figure as truly belong to the sentence, grammatically considered, as those which are expressed. They are omitted for rhetorical effect,—that is, to render the sentence more agreeable and forcible.

4. Ellipsis generally takes place,—

(*a.*) In *coördinate* constructions, to avoid the repetition of some common part.

Ex.—There are some who write, [and who] talk, [and who] think so much about vice and [about] virtue, that they have no time to practise either the one or the other.

(*b.*) In certain *subordinate* constructions, especially those which denote comparison, for the same reason.

Ex.—Revenge is a stronger feeling than gratitude [is]. Our minds are as different as our faces [are].

(*c.*) In certain *idiomatic* constructions,—

(1.) *In elements of the first class,*—the *subject* of imperative sentences; as, "Go [thou]." "Awake [ye]." The noun after adjectives or after the possessive case; as, "The *violent* [persons] take it by force." "This book *is mine;*" *i.e.* my book.

(2.) *In elements of the second class.* The *connective* may be omitted. Examples.—The *to* before the indirect object; as, "He gave [to] me a book." The *to* of the infinitive after *bid, dare, let, make, hear, need, feel, see. To* or *unto* after *like, near;* as, "Like [to] his father." "Near [to] the house." *During, over, for, in,* or *on,* before nouns denoting *time,* the *measure* of *distance, magnitude,* or *excess;* as, "They left [on] Monday." "They travelled [through] twenty miles."

The *object* may be omitted; as, "The leaves were scattered around [us]." In such cases, the preposition is usually called an adverb.

(3.) *In elements of the third class.* The *connective* may be omitted in substantive clauses in the objective; as, "My heart whispers, [that] God is nigh." In adjective clauses when the relative is in the objective; as, "The paper [which] we purchased is damaged." "The house [which] we went to stands on a hill."

The *subject* and *copula* in expressions like "If [it is] possible, if necessary, if convenient, when agreeable, while absent," &c.

The *whole clause* between *as* and *if*, *as* and *though.*

Ex.—He seemed as [he would seem] if [he were] deranged.

(d.) In *exclamatory* sentences, in *responsives*, in *inscriptions*, and *titles.*

Ex.—[It is] strange! Whom did you see? [I saw] George. [This is] the New Testament.

5. **Pleonasm** is the use of superfluous words.

Ex.—I know *thee who thou art.*

Note.—Pleonasm is the opposite of ellipsis, and may be said, in general, to take place where ellipsis should, but does not, take place.

6. Pleonasm takes place,—

(a.) When the same idea is repeated in the same or in different words.

Ex.—*Verily, verily,* I say unto you. All ye *inhabitants* of the world, *and dwellers on the earth.*

(b.) When a noun is introduced into a sentence, and then immediately represented in the same relation by a pronoun.

Ex.—Now *Harry he* had long suspected.

(c.) When a noun or any other word is repeated in the same relation, for the purpose of modifying it.

Ex.—*That great God* whom you see me daily worship; — * — * — *that God* who created the heavens and the earth; — — * — * — *this God* who has done all these great things — * — * — *this great God*, the Creator of worlds, of angels, and men, is your Father and Friend.

7. **Enallage** is a change of one part of speech for another, or some modification of a word for another.

Ex.—They fall *successive* [ly], and *successive* [ly] rise. *We*, Alexander, Emperor of Russia.

Here the plural number is used for the singular.

SYNTAX—FIGURES OF RHETORIC. 293

8. **Hyperbaton** is the transposition of words.

Ex.—While its song rolls the *woods along*.

217. Figures of Rhetoric.

1. A **figure of Rhetoric** is a deviation from the ordinary *application* of a word; it is commonly called a *trope*.

2. **Metaphor** gives to an object the appropriate name of another object, on account of a resemblance between them.

Ex.—Man! thou *pendulum* betwixt a smile and tear.

3. **Simile** is a formal comparison introduced by *like, as,* or *so*.

Ex.—He shall be *like a tree* planted by the rivers of water.

4. An **Allegory** is a continued metaphor, forming a kind of parable or fable.

For examples, see Pilgrim's Progress. See, also, the Eightieth Psalm.

5. **Personification** attributes to inanimate objects some of the qualities of living beings.

Ex.—The sky *saddens* with the gathered storm.

6. **Metonymy** is a change of name.

Ex.—"You will address the *chair*;" *i.e.* the *president*.

7. **Vision** represents imaginary objects as real and present to the senses.

Ex.—See lofty Lebanon his head advance;
See nodding forests on the mountains dance.

8. **Synecdoche** is the use of a part for the whole, or the whole for a part, as a *sail* for a *ship*, a *roof* for a *house*, the *head* for the *person*.

Ex.—"I was ordered to call *all hands*" (hands for *crew*).

9. **Irony** is the use of a word for its opposite.

Ex.—"He was as *virtuous* as Nero;" *i.e.* as *vile* as Nero.

10. **Antithesis** is the placing of contrary or opposite objects in contrast.

Ex.—*Immortal,* though *no more,* though *fallen, great.*

11. **Hyperbole** magnifies or diminishes an object beyond the truth.

Ex.—*Rivers* of water run down mine eyes, because they keep not thy law.

12. **Exclamation** is used to express some strong emotion of the mind.

Ex.—Oh the depth of the riches both of the wisdom and the knowledge of God!

13. **Interrogation** is used to express a strong affirmation under the form of a question.

Ex.—Hath he said it, and will he not do it?

14. **Apostrophe** is a turning off from the subject to address some other person or thing.

Ex.—Death is swallowed up in victory. O death, where is thy sting? O grave, where is thy victory?

15. **Climax** is a series of members in a sentence each rising in importance above the preceding.

Ex.—What hope is there remaining of liberty, if whatever is their pleasure it is lawful for them to do, if whatever it is lawful for them to do they are able to do; if what they are able to do they dare to do; if what they dare to do they really execute; and if what they execute is noway offensive to you?

PUNCTUATION.

218. Definitions and Distinctions.

1. **Punctuation** is the art of dividing written composition by means of points.

2. Points are used to separate either *entire* sentences, or the *elements* of sentences.

REMARK.—Let it be understood that an element may be either a *word,* a *phrase,* or a *clause.*

3. A point should not be used,—
(*a.*) To separate the parts of a *simple* element.
(*b.*) To separate two *united* elements when arranged grammatically and closely joined.
(*c.*) To separate two united elements simply because, in the *utterance*, a *pause* should be made.

Points are used to mark the *sense*, rather than the *pauses*. It is true that a pause should generally be made where there is a point; but it is not equally true that a point should be placed wherever there is a pause.

4. A point is required,—
(1.) Always at the end of a full *sentence*.
(2.) Always between the *members* of a loose sentence.
(3.) Generally between two *elements* of a sentence,—
    (*a.*) When several *similar* elements come together.
    (*b.*) When an element is *loosely* connected.
    (*c.*) When more closely connected, but *transposed*.
    (*d.*) When closely connected, but greatly *extended* in length.
    (*e.*) When some important word is *omitted*.
    (*f.*) When, in any case, the meaning would be *obscure* or *ambiguous* without a point.

As an example of the effect of pointing, see the change of meaning in the following words:—

James Johnson says he has written beautifully. James, Johnson says he has written beautifully. "James Johnson," says he, "has written beautifully." James Johnson says he has written "beautifully."

5. The principal punctuation marks are the *comma* (,), the *semicolon* (;), the *colon* (:), the *dash* (—), the *parenthesis* ( ), the *period* (.), the *interrogation* point (?), and the *exclamation* point (!).

POINTS USED WITHIN A SENTENCE.

219. General Uses of the Comma.

1. The **comma** is used principally in separating the *elements* of simple or complex sentences.

2. As the comma interrupts, in some measure, the union of two elements, it should never be employed to break the connection when one necessarily restricts the meaning of the other.

3. When an element to be pointed off stands at the beginning or the end of a sentence, **one** comma only is used; but when it stands within the sentence, **two** commas are usually employed.

Ex.—In fact, the people are the dupes of demagogues. The people, in fact, are the dupes of demagogues.

4. The comma is often used to mark the omission of a word, especially that of the verb in closely connected clauses.

Ex.—Semiramis built Babylon; Dido, Carthage; and Romulus, Rome.

5. The comma may be used to separate,—

(*a.*) *Coördinate elements.*

(*b.*) A *principal* from a *subordinate element.*

(*c.*) Two *principal elements.*

(*d.*) An *independent* or a *parenthetic element* from the rest of the sentence.

220. Coördinate Elements.

1. All coördinate elements may be divided into,—

(*a.*) **Coördinate pairs,** or *couplets*, consisting of two coördinate terms.

(*b.*) **Coördinate series,** consisting of three or more coördinate terms.

Thus, "*Nouns and pronouns*" is a couplet; "*Nouns, adjectives, pronouns, and participles*" is a coördinate series. In the following example we have a series of couplets, or compound terms:—" But, whether *ingenious* or *dull, learned* or *ignorant, clownish* or *polite,* every innocent man, without exception, has as good a right to liberty as to life."—*Beattie.*

2. The pointing of couplets depends chiefly upon the closeness of the connection.

As a general rule, two elements are most closely connected when correlatives are used, except when used for *contrast* or *emphasis;* less closely connected when a single conjunction is employed; and least of all when none is used; as, " He was both *virtuous* and *wise;*" " He was *virtuous* and *wise;*" " He was *virtuous, wise.*"

3. The terms of a coördinate couplet, as a general rule, should not be separated.

Ex.—*Hope* and *fear, pleasure* and *pain,* diversify our lives. *Virtue* or *vice* predominates in every *man* and *woman.*

PUNCTUATION—COÖRDINATE ELEMENTS. 297

4. The terms of a **coördinate couplet** should be separated,—

(*a.*) When the conjunction is **omitted**.
(*b.*) When the terms are **identical** or **equivalent**.
(*c.*) When the terms are **contrasted** or **emphatically distinguished**.
(*d.*) When either term is **limited** by an element not **applicable** to the other, or is more **extended** than the other.
(*e.*) When both are limited, and thus considerably extended.

Ex.—(*a.*) The *sweetest, wildest* land on earth. (*b.*) *Rise, rise,* ye wild tempests. *Verily, verily,* I say unto you. We sailed into an *inlet,* or *bay.* (*c.*) 'Tis certain he could *write,* and *cipher* too. The fellow was *wicked,* not *weak.* (*d.*) Undue susceptibility, and the preponderance of mere feeling over thoughtfulness, may mislead us. (*e.*) *Integrity* of understanding, and *nicety* of discernment, were not allotted in a less proportion to Dryden than to Pope.

Contrasted *words*, having a common dependence, and not emphatically distinguished, should not be separated; as, "He led an *easy* but *useless* life." Not so with contrasted *phrases;* as, "It was not the result *of a hasty,* but *of a deliberate,* judgment."

5. The terms of a **coördinate series**, whether simple, complex, or compound, should be separated by the comma.

Ex.—In pronouncing the words *lilies, roses, tulips, pinks, jonquils,* we see the things themselves, and seem to taste their beauty and sweetness. The good man is alive *to all the sympathies, the sanctions,* and the *loves of social existence. Sink* or *swim, live* or *die,* I give my hand and my heart to this vote.

Castles and villas, titles, vassals, land,
Coaches and curricles, and fours-in-hand.

6. The **final term** of a couplet or a series is generally not separated from the term grammatically dependent upon it, except,—

(*a.*) When the conjunction is omitted.
(*b.*) When the terms are considerably complex.
(*c.*) When the meaning is made clearer by the point. (See **222**, 2, *b.*)

Ex.—*Capture, demolish,* and *burn* their cities. (*a.*) *Capture, demolish, burn,* their cities. (*b.*) Ingratitude for favors, undue regard for self, and forgetfulness of others, are marks of a weak and sordid mind.

By some, yet erroneously, the last noun of a compound subject is separated from the verb, even when the conjunction is used; as, "*Homer, Virgil, and Horace*, were the most renowned of the ancient poets."

7. When the terms of a couplet or a series consist of **coördinate clauses**, whether the propositions themselves are principal or subordinate, a comma should separate them, except as in **227**, 1, *a, b,* 7.

Ex.—That their poetry is almost uniformly mournful, and that their views of nature were dark and dreary, will be allowed by all who admit the authenticity of Ossian. I was hungry, and ye gave me no meat.

221. Exercise.

1. *Explain* (**220**, 3) *why the following couplets are not separated:*—

Peter and John went up together into the temple at the hour of prayer. His bitter and scoffing speech had inflicted keener wounds than his ambition. The powers of their mind seem to be parched up and withered by the public gaze. In his letters and conversation he alluded to the greatest potentates. He acted neither wisely nor prudently. Either you or I must go.

2. *Explain the punctuation of the following syllables* (**220**, 4, *a, b, c,* &c.):—

Liberal, not lavish, is nature's hand. We often commend, as well as censure, imprudently. He can eat, and sleep too. None, but thou, can aid us. For Christ sent me not to baptize, but to preach the gospel. Public charities, and benevolent associations, for the gratuitous relief of every species of distress, are peculiar to Christianity. Powerful friends, and first-rate connections, often assist a man's rise, and contribute to his promotion. Illustrious men have often lived unrewarded, and died unlamented. Blow, blow, thou winter wind. Freeze, freeze, thou bitter sky. A comma is a point, or mark. Dear, gentle, patient, noble Nell was dead. The deaf, the blind, the lame, and the palsied were there. Decrepit age, and vigorous life, and blooming youth, and helpless infancy poured forth to gather round her tomb. She plans, provides, expatiates, triumphs there. The rich and the poor, the high and the low, the learned and the unlearned, have access alike to this fountain of peace. The air, the earth, the water, teem with delighted existence. Children climb the green mound of the rampart, and ivy holds together the half-demolished buttress.

When riseth Lacedæmon's hardihood,
When Thebes Epaminondas rears again,
When Athens' children are with arts endued,
When Grecian mothers shall give birth to *men*,
Then thou may'st be restored;—but not till then.

Blessing, honor, glory, might,
Are the Conqueror's native right;
Thrones and powers before him fall,—
Lamb of God, and Lord of all!

222. Principal and Subordinate Elements.

1. A subordinate element generally is not separated from the principal element to which it belongs when used restrictively, or when the connection is close.

Ex.—He *that hath no rule over his own spirit* is like a city *that is broken down*. The kings *of the earth* set themselves. The precise period *when the discovery was made* is not known.

2. The **adjective** element should be pointed off in the following cases:—

(*a*.) When an adjective clause, either *full*, or in its equivalent *abridged* form, is *explanatory* (**177**, 12, *b;* **183**, 3, Rem.).

Ex.—We venerate the name of Washington, *who was styled the father of his country*. Passion is like a whirlwind, *prostrating indiscriminately whatever comes in its way*.

In this case, *two* commas (**219**, 3) are used when the clause comes within the sentence before the predicate.

(*b*) When the antecedent is a coördinate series (**220**, 1), even a restrictive clause is pointed off, to show that the relative belongs equally to each of its terms.

Ex.—The oxygen, nitrogen, and carbonic acid, *which unite to form the atmosphere*, are mingled in unequal proportions.

(*c*.) The noun in *apposition* may be considered as derived from an adjective clause containing a predicate noun, and is always to be pointed off when it is *explanatory* (**183**, 3).

Ex.—Moses, *the servant of the Lord*, died there in the land of Moab. I have killed the king, *my husband*.

(*d*.) A noun in apposition, when used restrictively, or when with a personal pronoun or another noun it forms a close combination, is not pointed off.

Ex.—*King John. General Gates. Ye winds. Gladding brothers.*

Yet, when two closely combined names are inverted, the comma is used, as, "Lincoln, Levi;" "Harrison, William Henry."

(*e.*) A noun in apposition, if modified by phrases or clauses, is usually pointed off.

Ex.—Theodore, *the hermit of Teneriffe.*

(*f.*) A noun in apposition, or an adjective or participial phrase equivalent to a subordinate clause, when employed to introduce a sentence, is pointed off.

Ex.—A professed *Catholic*, he imprisoned the Pope. *Cradled* in the camp, Napoleon was the darling of his army.

3. The **objective** element, being closely connected to the verb on which it depends, unless transposed, should not be pointed off.

Ex.—The ox knoweth *his owner*. They long *to see that day*. I know not *what we can do*. *The impending storm which threatened us*, we all escaped.

(*a.*) Though, as a general rule, inverted and loosely connected phrases or clauses should not intervene between the object and its governing verb, when such cases do occur, commas should separate them from the verb and its object.

Ex.—He wishes, *in fine*, to join his companions. He has bought, *as I am told*, a large tract of uncultivated land.

(*b.*) When an objective clause is a direct quotation, and is separated by the principal clause, the latter should be pointed off by two commas; otherwise, by one.

Ex.—"For all that," said the pendulum, "it is very dark here." I say unto all, Watch.

(*c.*) The double object of a copulative verb should not be separated when the first has the emphasis, or when they are equally emphatic.

Ex.—They called *him John*. They called *Miles a carpenter*.

But when the emphasis falls strongly on the second, it should be pointed off; as, "And they called *Barnabas, Jupiter;* and *Paul, Mercurius.*"

4. The **adverbial** element is often more loosely connected than either the adjective or the objective, and is, consequently, more fre-

quently pointed off on account of its transposition; yet, when arranged in its natural order, or when closely connected, it should not be pointed off.

Ex.—Rejoice not *when thine enemy falleth;* and let not thine heart be glad *when he stumbleth.* *On the summit of the mountain* the air is cool and refreshing. The child was treated *kindly.*

(*a.*) All loosely connected adverbial expressions, whether words, phrases, or clauses, and especially such adverbial and conjunctive words and phrases as *again, now, then, however, therefore, too, besides, further, once more, in fine, in general, on the contrary, without doubt, as it seems to me,* and the like, should be pointed off (**227**, and **220**, 3).

Ex.—*On the contrary,* the truth lies here.

(*b.*) Phrases and clauses which in the natural order would be so closely connected as to need no point, are usually pointed off when inverted, and always when the meaning would be doubtful without a point.

Ex.—*But to Ossian,* thou lookest in vain. *When thou goest,* thy steps shall not be straitened.

In the case of inverted *phrases* which commence a sentence, the point is often omitted; as, " *On the third day* Burke rose."—*Macaulay.*

(*c.*) Adverbial clauses, especially when long, and always if loosely connected, are pointed off, wherever placed.

These are generally such as denote *condition, purpose, concession, cause, time,* or *place.*

Ex.—Kiss the Son, *lest he be angry, and ye perish.*

(*d.*) When a subordinate element is connected by means of correlatives, it is closely united, and, therefore, not generally pointed off, especially when *than* or *as, so — that,* or *such — that,* are used; but is used more or less by way of contrast in all other cases, and, hence, pointed off.

Ex.—Never take *more* food *than* is conducive to health. *Though* thou be sought for, *yet* shalt thou never be found again. Though *deep,* yet *clear.*

223. Exercise.

In the following examples, point out the principal and the subordinate elements; and show why the comma is or is not used, according to **222,** 1, 2, 3, 4.

He that covereth his sins shall not prosper; but whoso confesseth and forsaketh them shall have mercy. The wicked flee when no man pursueth. Some have wondered how it happens that those who have shone conspicuously at the bar should have been eclipsed in the senate. He had faults unknown to all but his most intimate friends (2, *a*, *b*, *c*). Men of strong minds, who think for themselves, should not be discouraged on finding occasionally that some of their best ideas have been anticipated by former writers. There are many good-natured fellows who have paid the forfeit of their lives to their love of bantering and raillery. The oranges, lemons, and figs which grow in the northern range of the Southern States are of an inferior quality. No thought can be just, of which good sense is not the groundwork. I, therefore, the prisoner of the Lord, beseech you. Thus saith the Lord, your Redeemer, the Holy One of Israel, I am the Lord your God. General Howe commanded the British forces. Otis, James A. O ye laurels! He called the name of that place Bethel. Daniel Webster, the great American statesman, died at Marshfield. I at first believed that all these objects existed within me. And cried, "I've caught you then at last." "My dear Edward," said he, "this is truly kind." Fortunately for him, a little below this place was an island. The beginning of strife is as when one letteth out water. If one burden can be borne, so can another and another. I am willing, for the general satisfaction, to assign my reasons.

224. The Principal Elements.

1. Except when the complex subject is very long, no comma is required between it and the predicate.

Ex.—He who masters his passions conquers his greatest enemy.

2. It can scarcely be called an exception to this rule that a point should be placed before the predicate when preceded by a phrase pointed off by **222, 4,** *a*.

Ex.—The most delicious fruits, *generally speaking*, are found in tropical climates.

So, by **220, 6,** *a*, a comma should be placed before the predicate; as, "*Patience, meekness, humility,* are among the noblest Christian virtues."

When the logical subject ends with a verb, or when without a comma the meaning might be doubtful, a comma should be placed before the predicate as, "Whatever is, is right."

3. When the attribute is a clause, a comma should be placed between it and the copula.

Ex.—The reason is, that the proposition itself is preposterous.

225. Exercise.

Show by **221,** *1, 2, 3, 4, why the comma is used or omitted in the following examples:—*

The fate of a brave people was to be decided. Each of the negotiators had what the other wanted. Some, from a diseased fancy, cannot confine themselves to a single spot. All these mistaken pursuers of good, sooner or later, are the prey of excessive ennui. Industry, frugality, economy, are essential to thrift. The want of fuel, of water, and of forage, compelled the party to retreat. He who has learned to obey, may hope to govern. He that seeketh, findeth. The truth is, that the whole of the surface of these beautiful plains is clad throughout the season of verdure with every imaginable variety of color. The question is, "Where shall we go?"

226. Independent and Parenthetic Expressions.

1. **Independent expressions** should be separated from the rest of the sentence by a comma.

Ex.—Yet once more, O ye *laurels!* Gad, a troop shall overcome him. *This said,* he formed thee, *Adam,* thee, O *man!* *To confess the truth,* I was in error. *Generally speaking,* little can be done after the first month. Saying, *Lord, Lord,* open unto us.

(*a.*) When a direct address is expressive of strong feeling, the exclamation point is used.

Ex.—O *Desdemona! Desdemona!* dead!

(*b.*) Interjections in many cases require no pause, but, when pointed off at all, are separated by the comma, if not emphatic; otherwise, by the exclamation point.

Ex.—*Oh,* sing to me of heaven! *Lo,* here is Christ! *Oh,* what a situation I am placed in!

(*c.*) Expressions used *parenthetically* should be pointed off by the comma.

Ex.—Thou knowest, *come what may,* that the light of truth cannot be put out.

227. The Semicolon and Colon.

1. The semicolon is used to separate the parts of a sentence which are loosely connected.

Ex.—Make a proper use of your time; for the loss of it can never be regained.

(*a.*) **Coördinate principal clauses** are separated by the semicolon when the conjunction is omitted, or when the connection is not close.

Ex.—Life is short; art is long. A clownish air is but a small defect; yet it is enough to make a man disagreeable.

(*b.*) **Subordinate parts,** when extended, if they form a coördinate series either at the beginning or end of a sentence, are separated by the semicolon, when not so closely connected as to require a comma.

Ex.—Philosophers assert that Nature is unlimited in her operations; that she has inexhaustible treasures in reserve; that knowledge will always be progressive; and that all future generations will continue to make discoveries of which we have not the slightest idea.

(*c.*) The semicolon should be placed before *as*, used to introduce an example. See the use of *as*, in (*f*), below.

(*d.*) The semicolon is used before *namely, viz., to wit,* when the subdivisions of a preceding term are introduced in a formal way; otherwise, the comma or comma and dash are used.

Ex.—Pronouns are divided into three classes; *namely, Personal, Relative,* and *Interrogative.*

Less formally, thus:—"Into three classes,—*Personal, Relative,* and *Interrogative.*"

(*e.*) The colon is now but little used, except before examples following the expressions *as follows, the following examples, in these words,* &c.

Ex.—Perform the following exercises: He used these words: Mr. President: &c.

(*f.*) It is also used to separate the terms of a proportion.

Ex.—A : B :: C : D.

228. Exercise.

Insert the comma, the semicolon, and the colon, where they are required in the following examples:—

Never value yourself upon your fortune for this is the sign of a weak mind. Pope had perhaps the judgment of Dryden but Dryden certainly wanted the diligence of Pope. The great tendency and purpose of poetry is to carry the mind above and beyond the beaten dusty weary walks of ordinary life to lift it into a purer element and to breathe into it more profound and generous emotion. Write on your slates the following example Mary and John will go Endeavor to excel much may be accomplished by perseverance. He has two coats namely a black one and a gray one. The noun is the name of an object as *Boston paper*.

229. The Dash and Parenthesis.

1. The **dash** is used where there is a significant pause, an unexpected transition in the sentence, or where a sentence is left unfinished.

Ex.—He sometimes counsel takes, and sometimes—snuff. But I must first——.

2. The dash is now frequently used instead of the parenthesis.

Ex.—The colonists—such is human nature—desired to burn the town in which they had been so wretched.

3. The dash, or comma and dash, may be placed before the parts which resume a whole, or before a construction which is resumed.

Ex.—There are three persons,—the *first*, the *second*, and the *third*. You speak like a boy,—like a boy who thinks the old gnarled oak can be twisted as easily as the young sapling.

4. The **parenthesis** is used to enclose a part of a sentence not necessary to the construction, but in some way explanatory of the meaning of the sentence.

Ex.—Consider (and may the consideration sink deep into your hearts!) the fatal consequences of a wicked life.

5. The parenthesis should be,—

Used when an incidental clause or expression is so disconnected as to admit of its being dropped without affecting the construction or the sense of the main sentence.

Ex.—Mathematics (see Davies's Bourdon) is the science of quantity.

Followed by whatever punctuation mark the interrupted parts would require if the parenthesis were removed.

Ex.—To others do (the law is not severe)
What to thyself thou wishest to be done..

If we exercise right principles (and we cannot have them unless we exercise them), they must be perpetually on the increase.

In the first example no point would be required; in the second, a comma would be inserted. This seems better than to place the required point before each curve, as some do, especially as the expression in parentheses often requires at the end a different point of its own. (See 6, below, and example.)

REMARK.—Many parenthetical expressions occur which are to be pointed off by commas. They are usually connected with the construction or the sense so as, in some measure, to be a part of the sentence. Expressions like *said he, in my opinion*, were formerly included in parentheses, but now are pointed off by commas.

6. The part within the parentheses should be punctuated as if it were an independent expression.

Ex.—An axiom (who denies it?) is a self-evident proposition.

230. Exercise.

Insert the dash and the parenthesis where they are required in the following examples:—

Horror burst the bands of sleep; but my feelings words are too weak, too powerless to express them. The Egyptian style of architecture see Dr. Pocock, not his discourses but his prints was apparently the mother of the Greek. While they wished to please, and why should they not wish it, they disdained honorable means. If thou art he, so much respected once but, oh, how fallen! how degraded! The atmosphere is composed of three parts oxygen, nitrogen, and carbonic acid gas. Greece, Carthage, Rome, where are they?

POINTS USED AT THE CLOSE OF A SENTENCE.

231. The Period.

1. The **period** is used at the close of a declarative or an imperative sentence.

Ex.—Knowledge is not only pleasant, but useful and honorable. Know thyself.

2. The period is used after abbreviations.

Ex.—The age of MSS. is, in some instances, known by dates inserted in them. I was invited to meet Mr. and Mrs. Clifford.

3. The period is placed after any *word, heading, title,* or other expression used independently and alone.

Ex.—*Exercise. The Period. H. Cowperthwait and Company.*

4. The period is used after letters or figures used in enumerating the parts of discourse.

Ex.—V. XII.; 1. 2.

In arithmetic it is used as a decimal point, or to mark periods in the roots: thus, 5.375; 87642.

232. Exercise.

Insert the period where it is required in the following examples:—

Truth is the basis of every virtue It is the voice of reason Let its precepts be religiously obeyed Never transgress its limits Abhor a falsehood I would say to the people, You cannot, without guilt and disgrace, stop where you are The oration was delivered by J L Thompson, Esq The event occurred B C 1001 To R H Dana Jun Esq the well-known author of "Two Years before the Mast," the community are greatly indebted But the seasons are not alike in all countries of the same region, for the reasons already given See Chap VI ¿ 2 ¶ 4 p 330 See **257**, 4 Little and Brown's store A new thing under the sun Ripe apples for sale Chapter XX Sec X Part I

233. Interrogation and Exclamation Points.

1. An **interrogation point** is used at the close of an interrogative, and an **exclamation point** at the close of an exclamatory sentence.

Ex.—Who comes there? How unsearchable are his ways!

2. When an interrogative sentence is used as a subordinate clause,—

(1.) The interrogation point is employed when the clause is quoted directly.

Ex.—He said, "Why do you weep?"

(2.) The interrogation point is not employed when the clause is quoted indirectly.

Ex.—He asked me why I wept.

3. An exclamation point is often used within a sentence, after an exclamatory expression or an interjection.

Ex.—O Jove supreme! whom men and gods revere! Oh! let soft pity touch the mind!

234. Exercises.

Insert interrogation and exclamation points where they are required in the following examples:—

Daughter of Faith awake arise illume the dread unknown the chaos of the tomb Whither shall I turn Wretch that I am To what place shall I betake myself O Pascal thou wert pure in heart in this world, and now thou art in full sight of God Apostles of liberty what millions attest the authenticity of your mission Did she fall like Lucifer never to hope again To purchase heaven has gold the power Who shall separate us from the love of Christ What kill thy friend who lent thee money, for asking thee for it The secret I implore: out with it speak discover utter

Punctuate correctly in all respects the following examples:—

What a piece of work is man How noble in reason how infinite in faculties in form and moving how express and admirable in action how like an angel in apprehension how like a God The air was mild as summer all snow was off the ground and the skylarks were singing aloud by the way I saw not one at Keswick perhaps because the place abounds in birds of prey. Dr H Marsh F R S &c Bishop of Peterborough b 1757 d 1839 As the pupil is often obliged to bend all his faculties to the task before him and tears sometimes fall on the page he is studying so it is in the school of God's providence there are hard lessons in it

235. Other Marks used in Writing.

1. *Brackets* ([ ]) are used when a word or a phrase is introduced into the language of another for explanation or correction.

<small>Ex.—He [the teacher] thus explained the difficulty. Neither of the boys were [was] in attendance.</small>

2. The *Apostrophe* (') is used to denote either the possessive case, or the omission of a letter.

<small>Ex.—John's. O'er.</small>

3. The *Quotation Marks* (" ") are used to include a passage taken verbatim from some other author.

<small>Ex.—He said, "I relinquish my claim."</small>

4. The *Asterisk* (*), the *Obelisk* (†), the *Double Dagger* (‡), and the *Parallels* (||) are used to refer to notes in the margin or at the bottom of the page. Sometimes the *Section* (§) and the *Paragraph* (¶) are thus used. Also, small letters or figures which refer to notes at the foot of the page.

5. The *Caret* (∧) is used in writing to show that some letter, word, or phrase has been omitted.

<small>Ex.—The pencil lies ⟨on⟩ the table.</small>

6. The *Hyphen* (-) is used to separate the parts of a compound word.

<small>Ex.—Book-binder.</small>

When placed at the end of a line, it shows that the word is divided, the remaining part being carried to the next line.

7. The *Ellipsis* (***), (———) is used to denote the omission of certain letters or words.

<small>Ex.—C***ll. K——g.</small>

8. The *Brace* (⌒) connects a number of words with one common term.

9. The *Index* (☞) points to some remarkable passage.

10. The *Section* (§) also denotes the divisions of a treatise.

11. A *Paragraph* (¶) also denotes the beginning of a new subject.

12. The vowel-marks are the *Diæresis* (··), placed over the second of two vowels which are separated; the *Long* sound (−), placed over a long vowel; the *Breve* or *Short* sound (⌣), placed over a short vowel; and accents, *Grave* (`), *Acute* (´), and *Circumflex* (∧).

The best practical exercises on all these marks and points will be given by the teacher. Let the pupil be required to construct sentences requiring the use of them; or, let the teacher read from some book any passage which demands their use, and let the class be required to insert them in their proper places.

236. Exercise.

Punctuate properly the following examples, and insert the capitals:—

what was cæsar that stood upon the bank of the rubicon a traitor bringing war and pestilence into the heart of that country no wonder that he paused no wonder if his imagination wrought upon by his conscience he had beheld blood instead of water and heard groans instead of murmurs no wonder if some gorgon horror had turned him into stone upon the spot but no he cried the die is cast he plunged he crossed and rome was free no more *knowles.*

what sort of eyes can you have got said he
why very good ones friend as you may see
yes i perceive the clearness of the ball
pray let me ask you can you read at all

QUESTIONS FOR REVIEW.

What is Syntax? What does the word mean? What is a sentence? What is the subject? The predicate? When does a sentence express an indefinite thought? A definite thought? What is a modifier? What are the elements of a sentence? What is Synthesis? Analysis? Into what three parts is Syntax naturally divided? What is a declarative sentence? An interrogative? An imperative? An exclamatory? A mixed? What is a simple sentence? A complex? A compound? What is a proposition? When is a proposition a sentence? An element of a sentence? What is the principal proposition? The subordinate? How are entire sentences united into paragraphs?

What are the principal elements of a sentence? The subordinate? When are elements coördinate? Explain *governs* and *limits* when applied to the elements? How are coördinate elements connected? What joins a subordinate to a principal element?

When is an element substantive, adjective, or adverbial?

Define an element of the first class. Of the second class. Of the third class. Define a simple element. A complex. A compound. The grammatical subject.

How many elements must the simplest sentence have? In what three ways may the logical subject be formed by using elements of the first class? Illustrate each. In what three ways may the logical predicate be formed? Illustrate each.

What is discourse? Direct? Indirect? How are substantive clauses divided?

What are the elements of a compound sentence? How may a compound sentence be contracted? Illustrate by examples. How may a complex sentence be contracted? A subordinate clause? When is the subject dropped? Name the two classes of abridged propositions.

When is a sentence transformed? What are equivalents? In what three ways may the form of a sentence be changed?

What three uses of a word are recognized? Define a rule of syntax. Repeat the rules for the regular use of words.

What is the rule for the subject? When is a noun in the nominative absolute? In the objective absolute? Repeat Rule II. What is the rule for the attribute in abridged propositions? Repeat the rules for the pronoun and antecedent. What is said of the use of *it?* Of the erroneous use of *they?* Of things personified? Of the position of the pronouns? Of their construction? When is the relative restrictive? When explanatory?

What are the rules for the agreement of the verb with its subject? Repeat the observations and cautions under this rule.

Give the rules for the adjective as modifier and predicate. When should the article be omitted? inserted? repeated? not be repeated?

Give the rule for the noun in apposition. Distinguish the three cases of apposition.

What is the rule for the noun in the possessive? What is the possessive used to denote?

Give the rules for the object.

What is Rule IX.? Repeat the observations and cautions under the rule. Repeat Rule X. Mention the five cases in which the noun is independent. What is Rule XI.? Repeat the observations and cautions under the rule. Repeat the three rules for coördinate constructions.

What is the rule for the preposition? Give Rule XIV. When is the preposition omitted?

What is the rule for subordinate connectives? Give the observations and cautions under the rule.

Give the rules for the infinitive. What is Rule XVII.? Repeat the observations under this rule.

Repeat the Special Cautions.

When has a word a peculiar use? An idiomatic use?

PROSODY.

237. Definitions.

1. **Prosody** treats of quantity, of accent, and of the laws of versification.

By *quantity*, in Prosody, is meant the time taken in pronouncing a syllable; and by *accent*, the stress of voice laid upon it.

2. **Versification** is the art of composing poetic verse.

3. **Verse** is a succession of accented and unaccented syllables, constituting a line of poetry.

The nature of the difference between verse and prose will be seen at once by comparing the two.

If any mán love the wórld, the love of the Fáther is not in him.
    Then shóok the hills with thúnder ríven!
    Then rúshed the steéds to báttle dríven!

In the last example, it will be noticed, the accent occurs regularly on every other syllable; while in the first there is no such regularity of recurrence. This regular recurrence of accented syllables is called *metre*.

4. **Poetry** is imaginative composition in metrical or rhythmical language.

5. Poetry is expressed either in *Rhyme* or *Blank Verse*.

6. **Rhyme** is the correspondence of sound in the last syllables of two or more lines.

7. A true and perfect rhyme requires that *the syllables be accented;* that the sound of the vowel and of the letters following the vowel be the same; and that the sound of the letters preceding the vowel be different.

Thus, *bold* rhymes with *cold, sold, fold; weary,* with *dreary; view,* with *you;* but *I* does not form a true rhyme with *high* or *eye,* because the sound of the syllables is identical; *own* and *none* are imperfect rhyme, because the vowel-sound is different; so, also, *beneath* and *breath, cease* and *ease, angel* and *tell, merrily* and *silly,* are faulty rhymes.

8. An accented syllable standing alone at the end of a

line forms a *single rhyme;* an accented syllable followed by an unaccented one forms a *double rhyme;* an accented syllable followed by two unaccented ones forms a *triple rhyme.*

Ex.—*Man, began; burning, turning; dependency, ascendency.*

9. Syllables in the middle of a line sometimes rhyme with those at the end.

Ex.—Once upon a midnight dreary, while I pondered, weak and weary.

10. **Blank Verse** is verse without rhyme.

Ex.—There is a nobler glory, which survives
Until our being fades, and, solacing
All human care, accompanies its change.—*Shelley.*

Greek and Latin poetry is in blank verse. It was, however, but little employed in European languages, except in dramatic composition, until "Paradise Lost" appeared.

238. Different Kinds of Poetry.

1. The different kinds of Poetry are *Epic, Dramatic, Lyric, Elegiac, Didactic, Pastoral, Satirical, The Ballad, The Sonnet, The Epigram, The Epitaph.*

2. An **Epic** poem is a narration of national or mythological events of momentous interest, and usually celebrates the actions of distinguished men, or heroes.

Ex.—The "Iliad" and "Odyssey" of Homer. The "Paradise Lost" of Milton. The "Æneid" of Virgil. The "Jerusalem Delivered" of Tasso.

3. A **Dramatic** poem is a picture of human life adapted to representation on the stage. It is divided into Tragedy and Comedy.

Ex.—Shakspeare's Plays.

4. A **Lyric** poem is an ode or song set to music, and, in modern times, an expression of the individual emotions of the poet.

Ex.—Anacreon, Pindar, Sappho, and Horace were ancient lyric poets. Collins's "Ode to the Passions," and "Alexander's Feast" of Dryden, are well-known examples in English poetry.

5. An **Elegy** is a poem on some mournful theme, expressive of sorrow.

Ex.—Gray's "Elegy written in a Country Church-Yard" is the best instance in our language.

6. **Didactic** poetry inculcates truths in science or morals.

Ex.—Lucretius, among the Latin poets; Pope's "Essay on Man."

7. A **Pastoral** poem has for its subject nature, agricultural pursuits, or rural life.

Ex.—The Idyls of Theocritus; the Eclogues and Bucolics of Virgil.

8. A **Satire** is a poem in which vice and folly are exposed with severity.

Ex.—The Satires of Juvenal and Horace, and of Dryden, Pope, and Byron.

9. A **Ballad** is a short relation, in simple but forcible rhyme, of some brave exploit, national event, pathetic love-tale, or rustic adventure.

Ex.—The literature of Spain, England, and Scotland abounds in ballads.

10. A **Sonnet** is a short poem usually complete in fourteen lines.

Ex.—The Sonnets of Petrarch, Tasso, Spenser, Shakspeare, Milton, and Wordsworth, are the best known.

11. An **Epigram** is a brief poem of a witty or humorous character.

12. An **Epitaph** is a short poem in praise of the virtues of a departed friend.

Ex.—Underneath this stone doth lie
As much virtue as could die;
Which when alive did vigor give
To as much beauty as could live.—*Ben Jonson.*

239. Poetic Feet.

1. The lines of poetry are divided by accent into small parts, called *poetic feet*.

2. A **Foot** is a certain number of syllables—usually two or three—forming a part of a line in poetry.

3. In English, an accented syllable is considered *long;* and an unaccented, *short*.

4. A straight line (-) over a syllable shows that it is long, or accented; a curved line (⌣), that it is short, or unaccented.

5. The principal feet in English are the *iambus*, the *trochee*, the *anapæst*, and the *dactyl*.

6. The **Iambus** consists of a short and a long syllable.

Ex.—*Ĭnvīte, dĕvōte, bĕnīgn*.

7. The **Trochee** consists of a long and a short syllable.

Ex.—*Grātefŭl, griēvoŭs*.

8. The **Anapæst** consists of two short syllables and one long one.

Ex.—*Ĭncŏmplēte, cŏndĕscēnd*.

9. The **Dactyl** consists of one long syllable and two short ones.

Ex.—*Pōsĭtĭve, lōnelĭnĕss*.

10. Besides the kinds of feet mentioned above, four others sometimes occur,—the *pyrrhic* and the *spondee*, the *amphibrach* and the *tribrach*. The *pyrrhic* consists of two short, and the *spondee* of two long syllables; as, "*ĭn thĕ (vale);*" "*vāin mān.*" The *amphibrach* has three syllables, of which the first and third are short, the second is long; as, "*cŏntēntmĕnt.*" The *tribrach* consists of three short syllables; as, "*(innu)mĕrăblĕ.*"

11. These last four feet are seldom found in English poetry. They sometimes mingle with other feet, and give thereby a pleasing variety.

Ex.—Frŏm pēak | tŏ pēak | thĕ rāt-|tlĭng crāgs | ămŏng,
    Lēaps thĕ | līve thŭn-|dĕr! nŏt | frŏm ōne | lŏne clōud.

REMARK.—Here, in the second line, the first foot is a *trochee*, and the second is a *spondee*. They occur in a single verse of an Iambic poem.

12. The character of the different kinds of feet is seen at a glance in the table which follows:—

Feet of two syllables are the

Iambus	first short, second long	‿ —
Trochee	first long, second short	— ‿
Spondee	both long	— —
Pyrrhic	both short	‿ ‿

Feet of three syllables are the

Dactyl	one long and two short	— ‿ ‿
Anapæst	two short and one long	‿ ‿ —
Amphibrach . . .	first short, second long, third short .	‿ — ‿
Tribrach	three short	‿ ‿ ‿

240. Different Kinds of Verse.

1. The different *kinds* of verse receive their names from the kind of feet of which they are formed. Thus, there are the *iambic,* the *trochaic,* the *anapæstic,* and the *dactylic* verse.

2. Verse is also named according to the *number* of feet in each line. *Monometer* is a line of one foot; *dimeter,* of two feet; *trimeter,* of three feet; *tetrameter,* of four feet; *pentameter,* of five feet; *hexameter,* of six feet; *heptameter,* of seven feet; *octometer,* of eight feet.

3. When a syllable is wanting, the line is said to be **catalectic;** when the measure is full, the line is **acatalectic;** when there is a redundant syllable, it is called **hypermeter,** or **hypercatalectic.**

4. **Scanning** is the dividing of a verse into the feet which compose it.

5. A **Couplet** is the combination of two lines which usually rhyme together. A **Triplet** consists of three such lines.

6. A **Stanza** is the combination of several lines forming a division of a poem or song.

241. Iambic Verse.

1. *Iambic of one foot,—monometer:—*
    Thĕy gō
    To sow.

2. *Iambic of two feet,—dimeter:—*
    Tŏ mē | thĕ rōse
    No longer glows.

3. *Iambic of three feet,—trimeter:—*
    Nŏ rōy-|ăl pōmp | ădōrns
    This King of righteousness.

4. *Iambic of four feet,—tetrameter:—*
    Ănd cōld-|ĕr stīll | thĕ wīnds | dĭd blōw,
    And darker hours of night came on.

5. *Iambic of five feet,—pentameter:—*
    Ŏn rīft-|ĕd rōcks, | thĕ drāg-|ŏn's lāte | ăbōdes,
    The green reed trembles, and the bulrush nods.

6. *Iambic of six feet,—hexameter:—*
    Hĭs heārt | ĭs sād, | hĭs hōpe | ĭs gōne, | hĭs līght | ĭs pāssed;
    He sits and mourns in silent grief the lingering day.

7. *Iambic of seven feet,—heptameter:—*
    Thĕ lōf-|ty hīll, | thĕ hūm-|blĕ lāwn, | wĭth cōunt-|'lĕss beaū- | tĭes shīne;
    The silent grove, the solemn shade, proclaim thy power divine.

8. *Iambic of eight feet,—octometer:—*
    In the spring a fuller crimson comes upon the robin's breast;
    In the spring the wanton lapwing gets himself another nest.

9. Iambic of five feet is called **Heroic** verse; that of six feet is called **Alexandrine.**

10. In the **Long Metre** stanza each line has four iambic feet.
    Through every age, eternal God,
    Thou art our rest, our safe abode;
    High was thy throne ere heaven was made,
    Or earth, thy humble footstool, laid.

In the **Short Metre** stanza the first, second, and fourth lines contain three iambic feet, the third four.

> Sweet is the time of spring,
>   When nature's charms appear;
> The birds with ceaseless pleasure sing,
>   And hail the opening year.

An iambic of seven feet is commonly divided into two lines,—the first containing four feet, the second three. This is called the **Common Metre** stanza.

> The lofty hill, the humble lawn,
>   With countless beauties shine;
> The silent grove, the solemn shade,
>   Proclaim thy power divine.

11. Each species of iambic verse may have one additional short syllable, thus:—

(*a.*) Rĕlēnt-|ĭng.
(*b.*) Upōn | ă mōun-|taĭn.
(*c.*) Whĕn ōn | hĕr Mā-|kĕr's bō-|sŏm.
(*d.*) Fīrst thĭs | lārge pār-|cĕl brīngs | yŏu tī-|dĭngs.
(*e.*) Ēach sŭb-|stănce ōf | ă grĭef | hăth twēn-|ty shād-|ŏws.
(*f.*) Thīne eye | Jōve's līght-|nĭng sēems, | thy voīce | hĭs drēad-|fŭl thŭn-|dĕr.
(*g.*) Hŏw gāy-|ly ō-|vĕr fĕll | ănd fēn | yŏn spōrts-|măn līght | ĭs dāsh-|ĭng!

242. Trochaic Verse.

1. *Trochaic of one foot:—*
    Chānging,
    Ranging.

2. *Trochaic of two feet:—*
    Fāncy | viēwĭng,
    Joys ensuing.

3. *Trochaic of three feet:—*
    Gō whĕre | glōry | wāits thĕe,
    But when fame elates thee.

4. *Trochaic of four feet:—*
   'Twăs thĕ | hōur whĕn | rītes ŭn-|hŏly
   Called each Paynim voice to prayer.

5. *Trochaic of five feet:*
   Ăll thăt | wălk ŏn | fōot ŏr | rīde ĭn | chărĭŏts,
   All that dwell in palaces or garrets.

6. *Trochaic of six feet:—*
   Ŏn ă | mōuntăin, | strētched bĕ-|nēath ă | hōary | wĭllŏw,
   Lay a shepherd swain, and viewed the rolling billow.

7. In trochaic verse, the accent is placed upon the odd syllables; in iambic, on the even.

8. Trochaic verse may take an additional long syllable; as,—
   (*a.*) Whēre wĕ | māy
       Think and pray.
   (*b.*) Ănd ăt | mōrn thĕy | plāy,
       In the foaming spray.
   (*c.*) Heaving | upward | to the | light.
   (*d.*) Wherefore | thus my | weary | spirit | woo?
   (*e.*) Reared 'mid | fauns and | fairies, | knew he | no com-|peers.
   (*f.*) Casting | down their | golden | crowns a-|round the | glassy | sea.

243. Anapæstic Verse.

1. *Anapæstic of one foot:—*
   Bŭt ĭn vāin
   They complain.

2. *Anapæstic of two feet:—*
   Whĕre thĕ sūn | lŏves tŏ paūse
   With so fond a delay.

3. *Anapæstic of three feet:—*
   Frŏm thĕ cēn-|trĕ ăll rōund | tŏ thĕ sēa,
   I am lord of the fowl and the brute.

4. *Anapæstic of four feet:—*
   O, yŏung | Lŏchĭnvār | ĭs cŭme oŭt | ŏf thĕ wēst!
   Through all | the wide bor-|der his steed | was the best.

5. In anapæstic verse, the accent falls on every third syllable. The first foot of an anapæstic verse may be an iambus; as,—

    Ănd mŏr-|tăls thĕ swēets | ŏf fŏrgēt-|fŭlnĕss prŏve.

244. Dactylic Verse.

1. *Dactylic of one foot :—*
    Chēerfŭlly,
    Fearfully.

2. *Dactylic of two feet:—*
    Făthĕr ăll | glŏrĭŏŭs,
    O'er all victorious.

3. *Dactylic of three feet:—*
    Weārĭng ă-|wāy ĭn hĭs | yoŭthfŭlnĕss,
    Loveliness, beauty, and truthfulness.

4. *Dactylic of four feet:—*
    Shăme ănd dĭs-|hŏnŏr sĭt | by hĭs grăve | ēvĕr,
    Blessings shall hallow it never, oh, never!

5. Few poems are perfectly regular in their feet. Dactylic verse is very irregular; the final short syllables are often omitted, as in the last example. The different kinds of feet are often mingled in the same verse, thus:—

    Ĭ cōme, | Ĭ cōme; | yĕ hăve cālled | mĕ lōng;
    I cōme | ŏ'er thĕ mōun-|tăins wĭth lĭght | ănd sōng.

245. Poetic Pauses.

1. Besides the pauses required by the sense or grammatical construction of verse, two pauses—the *final* and the *cæsural*—may also occur.

2. The **final** pause occurs at the end of each line, whether the sense requires it or not.

The **cæsural** pause is a natural suspension of the voice, which occurs in the line itself, and is readily perceived when the verse is well read. It is found in long lines, and generally, but not always, about the middle of the line.

Ex.—The earth grew silent | when thy voice departed;
The home too lonely | whence thy step had fled:
What was there left for her, | the faithful-hearted?

REMARK.—The skill of the poet is shown in making these pauses occur where the thought requires them.

246. Poetic License.

1. **Poetic License** is the indulgence in a peculiar use of language granted to poets by common consent.

This freedom from a strict compliance with the usage of prose writers is rendered necessary by the requirements of quantity, accent, rhythm, and harmony.

2. Many of the deviations from the ordinary use and construction of words have been already considered in the articles on Figures of Etymology, Syntax, and Rhetoric. (See **215, 216, 217.**)

3. Besides these, the poets make use of—

(1.) **Antiquated words** and **phrases**; as, *yclep'd, mote, sooth, trow, welkin, yon, whilom, ope, fount, erst, eke, ween, wight, hight.*

Ex.—For well I ween
He saved the realm, who saved the queen.

(2.) **Compound epithets**; as, *new-spangled, gray-hooded, flowery-kirtled, violet-embroider'd, silver-shafted.*

Ex.—Had ta'en their supper on the savory herb
Of knot-grass *dew-besprent.*

(3.) **Foreign idioms.**

Ex.—He knew *to sing* and *build* the lofty rhyme.
Long were to tell what I have seen.

(4.) Of an **unusual** and **inverted arrangement** of words.

(*a.*) The subject follows the verb.

Ex.—Come I to speak in Cæsar's funeral.

V

(*b.*) The object is put before the verb.
Ex.—These *delights* if thou canst give.
(*c.*) The adjective is placed after the noun.
Ex.—   And Twilight *gray*
    Had in her sober livery all things clad.

247. Exercise.

1. *Scan the following, and tell what kind of verse it is:—*

Art is long, and time is fleeting,
   And our hearts, though stout and brave,
Still, like muffled drums, are beating
   Funeral marches to the grave.—*Longfellow.*

From Greenland's icy mountains,
   From India's coral strand;
Where Afric's sunny fountains
   Roll down their golden sand;
From many an ancient river,
   From many a palmy plain,
They call us to deliver
   Their land from error's chain.—*Heber.*

Hail, holy Light, offspring of Heaven first-born,
Or of the Eternal co-eternal beam!
May I express thee unblamed? since God is light,
And never but in unapproachéd light
Dwelt from eternity, dwelt then in thee,
Bright effluence of bright essence increate!
Or hear'st thou rather, pure ethereal stream,
Whose fountain who shall tell?—*Milton.*

Ye nymphs of Solyma? begin the song;
To heavenly themes sublimer strains belong.
The mossy fountains and the sylvan shades,
The dreams of Pindus and th' Aonian maids,
Delight no more!—O thou my voice inspire,
Who touched Isaiah's hallowed lips with fire!—*Pōpe.*

Ruin seize thee, ruthless king!
   Confusion on thy banners wait!
Though fanned by conquest's crimson wing,
   They mock the air with idle state.—*Gray.*

Earth may hide—waves engulf—fire consume us,
But they shall not to slavery doom us.
If they rule, it shall be o'er our ashes and graves,
But we've smote them already with fire on the waves;
And new triumphs on land are before us.
To the charge!—Heaven's banner is o'er us!—*Campbell.*

Hail to the chief who in triumph advances!
  Honored and blest be the ever-green pine!
Long may the tree in his banner that glances
  Flourish, the shelter and grace of our line!
    Heaven send it happy dew,
    Earth lend it sap anew,
Gayly to bourgeon, and broadly to grow,
    While every highland glen
    Sends our shout back again,
Roderigh Vich Alpine Dhu, ho! ieroe!—*Scott.*

The night-winds come and go, mother, upon the meadow grass,
And the happy stars above them seem to brighten as they pass;
There will not be a drop of rain the whole of the livelong day,
And I'm to be Queen o' the May, mother, I'm to be Queen o' the May.—*Tennyson.*

  Then read from the treasured volume
    The poem of thy choice,
  And lend to the rhyme of the poet
    The beauty of thy voice.

  And the night shall be filled with music,
    And the cares that infest the day
  Shall fold their tents, like the Arabs,
    And as silently steal away.—*Longfellow.*

Know ye the land where the cypress and myrtle
  Are emblems of deeds that are done in their clime,—
Where the rage of the vulture, the love of the turtle,
  Now melt into softness, now madden to crime?
'Tis the land of the East!—'tis the clime of the Sun!—
Can he smile on such deeds as his children have done?
                                         Byron.

THE END.

www.ingramcontent.com/pod-product-compliance
Lightning Source LLC
Chambersburg PA
CBHW022017240426
43667CB00042B/839